THE AMERICAN ENTERPRISE PARTY

Volume II

American Enterprise Manifesto

JERRY RHOADS
Founder and CEO

Copyright © 2024 by Jerry Rhoads

All rights reserved. This book or any portion thereof may not be reproduced or transmitted in any form or manner, electronic or mechanical, including photocopying, recording, or by any information storage or retrieval system, without the express written permission of the copyright owner except for the use of brief quotations in a book review or other noncommercial uses permitted by copyright law.

Printed in the United States of America
ISBN:
        Softcover   979-8-9910186-1-6
        eBook

Published by: Rhoads Publishing
Publication Date: 06/25/2024

THE AMERICAN ENTERPRISE PARTY

Volume II

American Enterprise Manifesto

JERRY RHOADS
Founder and CEO

"This book is a must-read for anyone regardless of political preference or perspective. who might be contemplating political and economic change for the nation."

— Batya Weinbaum, The US Review of Books

"One other unspoken message coming through these pages loud and clear, is Jerry Rhoads' deep love of America. He obviously cares enough about his country to think deeply about its sad state and come up with some potential solutions."

— Dan MacIntosh, Pacific Book Review

PREFACE

AMERICANISM MISSION STATEMENT

In America we now have two tribes fighting each other and losing the American Dream. The Left and the Right forgo the middle American voter, for one party control. A THIRD-PARTY SWING VOTE that breaks ties, does cost benefit analysis for accountability, and keeps the money-tics and partisan politics honest in operating the Great America Enterprise profitably. Using generally accepted accounting principles GAAP for reporting the financial condition of the Republic. By being the referee for consensus cost via benefit decisions making to avoid one-party control and bankruptcy. In God we trust, when Monetary Capitalists share and Human Socialists care, and where free market enterprise is truly laissez-faire.

THAT'S WHAT MAKES AMERICA ENTERPRISE GREAT,

WITH THE CHALLENGE OF GLOBAL TRADE.

WE NEED PEACEFUL COEXISTENCE DETENE TO,

KEEP AMERICAN ENTERPRISE RETURN ON OUR INVESTMENT COLLATERAL GREAT.

PEACE THROUGH STRENGTH IS A STRONG ECONOMIC BASE (COST OF SALES AND OVERHEAD), ROI, CASH FLOW, AND NON-PROLIFERATION OF NUCLEAR WEAPONS OF MASS DESTRUCTION.

"We the people expect all American citizens to ask not, what you can do for your party. Ask what you can do for your own American Dream."

WHAT THE STATUTE OF LIBERTY REPRESENTS

(Not Blinded by the Light of the Benjamin Might)

Americanism the process of American monetary capitalism merged with American Socialism produces laissez-faire market enterprise, profits, capital, ROI, and cash flow. Financed by our system of laissez-faire competitive, color-blind economics. Human capital, the skills, knowledge, and experience invested in laissez-faire enterprise drives collective wealth.

$E=mc^2$ ... Enterprise = monetary capital times human capital squared = profit, cash flow, ROI in GDP, and GNP. Economics = cost of sales and budgetary spending and deficits = +/- spendable surplus for research and development that drives national growth and prosperity.

What do the scales of Lady Justice represent?

The balance (scales) represents weighing facts, and evidence to decide a verdict. It also shows her duty to restore balance to society. Although many people think of Lady Justice as wearing a blindfold, she can also be shown without one. Both versions highlight her impartiality. The rule of law prevents the rule of rulers and regulators.

BLINDED BY THE BENJIMAN'S MIGHT. Ask not what you can do for your party. Ask what you can do for your country.   THE AMERICAN ENTERPRISE PARTY TRILOGY

AMERICANISM AND HUMANISM ARE THE AMERICAN DREAM

VOLUME ONE: THE MISSION OF AMERICANISM

VOLUME TWO: THE QUASI-REORGANIZATION OF DEBT AND DEFICITS

VOLUME THREE: RESTORE AMERICAN WORK ETHIC WITH HUMANISM

The America Dream's American Enterprise Rhoads theorem E=mc2

Laissez-faire enterprise equals American Monetary capital times Human capital squared.
AMERICANISM = American Capitalism gestated by American Socialism multiplies prosperity to be shared by the shareholders, human capital, and stakeholders.
The Ten Tenets of Laissez-fair enterprise.
This formula works daily in all American businesses, small, medium, and large international enterprises.

Tenets of American Laissez-Faire Enterprise:

It's a world of competitive global forces attacking our values and internally woke reasons for changing our way of life. It's a war of doubt and fear won with faith and leadership standing up for the 10 tenets of American laissez-faire. Then the American Dream tenets of the Many are one result of each American striving for a quality of life.

1) Reward received is determined by the amount of risk taken. Protected by US bankruptcy laws and the rule of law.

2) The law of supply and demand for measuring markets.

3) Sharing is based on the skill to bill and the risk taken to produce goods and services creating GDP and GNP.

4) Earning is based on risk taken by learning a skill to bill for goods and services. Profits, shared squared is the $E=MC^2$ generating new capital, growth of GDP and GNP and cash flow for serving debt, by eliminating deficits. .

5) Competition creates optimal quality, innovation, and cash flow from GDP/GNP creating retained earnings for capital growth and reinvestment.

6) Quality creates cost savings and profits. Profits create growth. And capital for R&D and market expansion.

7) GAAP reports actual financial and operational results. Stock and bond markets report derivatives.

8) USA Debt clock and financial analytics are based on GAAP, a guideline for collective prosperity based on the cost of sales, profits, and cash flow.

9) USA balance sheet, sustainability is a current ratio of two times current assets and current debt, including accruals for future obligations, less than 85% of GDP and GNP.

10) Accountability for the above 9 tenets is the bottom line for measuring leadership. It's cashflow rewarding shareholders, funding workers for profit sharing, stakeholders for benevolent, and capital growth. Where shareholders share and stakeholders receive donations, not profits.

American Enterprise is not Woke capitalism or socialism. It's a free-market enterprise Capitalism (money) managed by Socialism (workers) for the prosperity of its investors practicing the above 10 tenets. Nor is there a need for a FREE-MARKET enterprise to practice or use the ESG index (environmental – social – governance) for evaluating Governance. That is done by www.usdebtclock.org, www.nationaldebtclock.org GDP, GNP,

GAAP, and the WORLD global marketplace.

Supported by keeping the dollar as the reference currency as asset based in global trade exchange rates based on the power of the USA collateral reported by the www.usdebtclock.org

Precious metal reserves	$ 1,221,800,000,000
Mineral reserves	$ 5,701,800,000,000
Real Estate	$75,344,400,000,000
Land	$24,502,000,000,000
Stock Market	$50,908,000,000,000
Recaptured assets	$ 7,537,000,000,000
New energy	$ 3,970,000,000,000
Total USA collateral	$169,187,000,000,000
Per citizen	$503,700

Increasing at a trillion per month based on $E=mc^2$.

This dwarfs the old gold standard for debt and deficit backing. The problem is liquidity, and the American Enterprise Party proposes additional capital, not using taxation but Trade War Bonds to support the Volume Two of the Trilogy proposal for a quasi-reorganization of the debt and deficits using GAAP accounting principles and financial statements utilized to move Federal Reserve banking into the US Treasury department and using central banking and crypto our dollar currency for global trade exchange rates.

Finally, the underlying is rebranding America as Americanism based on humanism, replacing all the other isms. Americrats, Meritocracy, Ameritics as the branding for the voters to have a voice in what makes America Great, nothing else. The rest is how to Keep America Great. Ask not what you can do for your party. Ask what you can do for your country to Keep it Great. This is the capital and society working together as a laissez-faire enterprise, to protect a three-party debatable point of view for the constitutional and judicial secure vote to protect our financial and social standing as the United States of America leading peaceful coexistence in a volatile world.

THE AMERICAN ENTERPRISE PARTY

(How to do it)

The Trilogy Volume II

American Enterprise Manifesto

Mission Statement

In America, we now have two tribes fighting each other and losing the American Dream. Pe Left and the Right forgo the middle American, for one party control. A third-party swing vote breaks ties and keeps money-tics and partisan politics honest. By being the referee for bipartisan decision making to avoid one-party control. Where Monetary Capitalists share and Human Socialists care, so free market enterprise is truly lasses-faire. A marriage made real by the American Dream founded on Humanism and American Enterprise practicing Laissez-faire.

JERRY RHOADS Founder and CEO OF **THE AMERICAN ENTERPRISE PARTY**

THE HOLOCAUST OF 2024

.. THE WWW.USDEBTCLOCK.ORG DEPICTING THE HOLOCAUST OF USA'S DEBT AND DEFICISTS CREATED BY A TWO-PARTY POLITIICAL SYSTEM. CLICK ON THE QR CODE TO ACCESS THE WEBSITE FOR THE REALITY OF AMERICA'S MONITIZED FAILURE IN LEADERSHIP OF THE DEMOCRATS AND REPUBLICANS. JUSTIFYING THE ENTERY OF A SWING VOTE PARTY ... BRANDED AS THE AMERICAN ENTEPRISE PARTY THAT REPRESENTS GOVERNMENT OF THE PEOPLE, BY THE PEROPLE, FOR THE PEOPLE TO KEEP AMERICA GREAT AND PROSPEROUS UNTIL DEFICITS AND DEBT DO US PART.

THE HOLOCAUST OF 9/11

America's Trade Centers the symbol of American Enterprise
Became the holocaust of 9/11
Lives lost and strength gained
A marriage made in heaven

Ground zero of the 21st century's worth
Marks the reason America will rise
As the Beacon of Light for the earth
And the center of human enterprise

Yes, our holocaust loss of 3,300 lives
Holds our attention
But more so that justice never dies
Committed to prevention

Prevent the terrorist high
By being more than fear can breed
With the new symbol in the sky
Built as a model for the American creed

America's strength is its values
Not extreme Jihadist religious dogma
It's from sea to shining seas
Much more than hate and drama

The rest of the world is in awe
When they come to New York's skyline
Taking back with them what they saw
The Statute of Liberty still saluting hate's decline

Replacing the devastation with our character
By again leading the world to peace and trade
With a dedication to not allow that fear to reoccur
By being the tower of what freedom has made

To those that built and rebuilt
This holocaust of 9/11 has willed
The symbolic beauty of America the free
We toast this day in their honor and those killed
That USA isn't the Planet of Terrorist Apes
It still stands as the Statue's beacon shapes
To make its breadth from sea to shining sea
"Give us liberty or give us death"

The cost of being free

In honor of those holocaust victims in the world who have died for liberty

Our nation awakes for cleansing the earth of tyranny

Being the land of the free led by the Few adjudged and earned by the Many

Overcoming the tyranny of Russia, Nazis, Jihadists and Marxists that impose ill will and use holocausts on millions of their followers to control 8 billion lives for the Axis of Evil 's demented will to destroy free market democracy.

THE AMERICAN ENTERRPRISE PARTY
THE TRILOGY VOLUME TWO
AMERICAN ENTERPISE MANIFESTO

Swing vote solutions (Drain the Swamp by Reigning in Big Brother and the Brotherhood) How to Do It!

Table of Contents

American Enterprise Manifesto
It's the best of times and the worst of times. A Tale of two parties............... 1
Our Statue of liberty (Not Blinded by a Benjamin's Might)............. 20
My America... What America Means to Me 22
My America the bountiful 24
Is Washington Burning? 57
Executive Orders Swamp the Swamp... 74

Articles of Quasi-Reorganization ... America's Recovery Plan
Articles of Quasi-Reorganization ... America's Recovery Plan Articles of Quasi-Reorganization to be filed under and subject to the terms and conditions of this Business Plan, canceling all issued and outstanding shares, authorizing the new shares of capital, changing name to The American Enterprise Party, Org. and appointing persons designated by the Creditors' Meeting to be the board of directors and otherwise substantially in the form annexed as Article Thirteen to this Plan of Quasi-Reorganization.

Article One... USA War on Debt, Crime and
                    China's Cold Warfare... 113
Article Two ... Marxism, Avoid 1984... 202
Article Three ... Capitalism Embraces Socialism 223
Article Four ... Value of the dollar, Fiat Money, World Order 248
Article Five ... Health Care for All, Save Medicare 259

Article Six ...... USA Enterprise is Laissez-- Faire 313
Article Seven ...Humanism and Peaceful Coexistence 340
Article Eight ... Honor the Flag and Our Leaders........................ 362
Article Nine .... Leadership, American Creed and Patriotism 383
Article Ten ...... American Enterprise Economics 413
Article Eleven ...Quasi Reorganization of the Institutions 434
Article Twelve ... American Enterprise Politics............................. 443
Article Thirteen ... American Enterprise Party Platform 461

EXHIBITS

Exhibit A: Big Brother Biden Swamps The Swamp 500
Exhibit B: The Ongoing Demise of American Liquidity 517
Exhibit C: Downsizing of
      Federal Government Enterprise Model 527
Exhibit D: Government Commits Fraud and Abuse 530
Exhibit E: Definitions for Health Care ACRONYMS................... 535
Exhibit F: What is a Problem Versus an Issue 542
Author's Bio 559
List of Sources 563

Manifesto: "A public declaration of policy and aims, especially one issued before an election by a political party or candidate". Where wealth blinds our liberty by the power of privilege and influence, we have lost our democracy. When money is the fuel that drives the great American Enterprise System ... it is also the pendant of power, that is the celebration of success, or the crucifixion of our society's values as our mores and ethics become secondary to its use. Not to say, wealth isn't the pendant of success from the American Dream but not for the destruction of our values. What are our country's priorities? Wealth for self-indulgent material excesses or for sharing with those that make it happen. Sharing meaning our nation's soul in contemplation of change to "Keep America Great".

The soul of our country,

    has been sold,

    by the rulers of the gold ...

    by taxing the floor,

    to conceal the ceiling,

    then closing the door ...

    Keeping them down and poor,

    an unnoticed death toll,

    to our enterprising soul,

    since America's peace,

    is believing equality with equity can't cease,

    for opportunity to pursue a skill to bill,

    And the wisdom to learn to earn ...

    from work, with time to spare,

defending our freedom to share,

So, in God and our country,

we trust but with risk,

for its reward we dare,

Laissez-faire.

Dr. Martin Luther King "I Have an America Dream"

"Now is the time to make real the promises of democracy. Now is the time to rise from the dark and desolate valley of segregation to the sunlit path of racial justice. Now is the time to lift our nation from the quick sands of racial injustice to the solid rock of brotherhood. Now is the time to make justice a reality for all of God's children.

So even though we face the difficulties of today and tomorrow, I still have a dream. It is a dream deeply rooted in the American dream. I have a dream that one day this nation will rise up and live out the true meaning of its creed: We hold these truths to be self-evident, that all men are created equal.

I have a dream that one day on the red hills of Georgia, the sons of former slaves and the sons of former slave owners will be able to sit down together at the table of brotherhood.

I have a dream that one day even the state of Mississippi, a state sweltering with the heat of injustice, sweltering with the heat of oppression will be transformed into an oasis of freedom and justice.

I have a dream that my four little children will one day live in a nation where they will not be judged by the color of their skin but by the content of their character. I have a dream today.

I have a dream that one day down in Alabama with its vicious racists, with its governor having his lips dripping with the words of interposition and nullification, one day right down in Alabama little Black boys and Black girls will be able to join hands with little white boys and white girls as sisters and brothers. I have a dream today.

I have a dream that one day every valley shall be exalted, every hill and mountain shall be made low, the rough places will be made plain, and the crooked places will be made straight, and the glory of the Lord shall be revealed, and all flesh shall see it together."

A quote of Martin Luther King ... a true American and a great leader inspiring all of us to practice humanism.

As founder and CEO, I propose in this manifesto, that American Enterprise is built on this foundation of no color line to fulfill the American Dream ... not white, black, brown, yellow or red ... all humans having the right to the proclamation of humanism. Jerry Rhoads Founder and CEO of the American Enterprise Party.

It's the best of times and the worst of times.
A Tale of two political parties.
(In Contemplation of Change... et tu Brute')

Creaser's/Trump's last words ... You too Brutus ... VP. Pence)
The best of times ... Donald J. Trump, a GOAT businessman, is an upset winner; elected the 46th POTUS. The American Dream is saved, making America great again. Attracting the downtrodden from competing third world economies to compete with low paid workers not taking on 8 million American unfilled jobs. An enabler for bringing manufacturing and supply lines back to America. Honoring Martin Luther King's diversity plea, "I still have a dream. It is a dream deeply rooted in the American dream". The stock market is above 35,000 up from 20,000 after the 2007 depression that was turned around using free market enterprise and global trade. Under former President Trump's leadership, the Pandemic was turned into a "Warp Speed" development of a vaccine saving the economy and millions of worldwide lives.

Energy independence was attained as well as no significant conflicts in the Mid- East, North Korea, Russian, Ukraine, or with China. The borders came under control with the building of the wall and DEA deportations. Drug and human trafficking were reduced compared to past administrations. Crime in the cities was stabilized until the George Floyd riots. Proving President Trump's leadership of peace through strength will bring peaceful coexistence and prosperity. Peace agreements were being pursued in the Middle East and talks with Canada, Mexico, Russia, North Korea and China regarding trade partnerships insuring America's efficient and profitable supply lines.

Thereby reducing the imbalance of trade deficits and USA dependence on foreign energy and supply line products. With the strategy to make America solvent by reducing national debt and increasing GDP. Repair balance of trade deficits by bringing back production lines replacing Eurasia supply lines, so we don't buy from everyone else they buy from us increasing GDP and cash flow, that reduces shipping costs, debt and negative net worth. All of this stopped January 6, 2020 as elections have consequences. Some positive most negative because of the following uni-party Congress result.

The worst of times ... Post 9/11 holocaust, et tu Brute'; the bully was unseated, in a landslide mail-in vote, from his pulpit. By progressive Joseph R. Biden, an attorney, 47-year tenured Senator and bureaucrat elected s as CEO of the largest enterprise in the world. With no business enterprise experience. The victory was inconceivable with an election that had negative consequences and destroyed a booming economy in the first 1,000 days of his leftist administration. Proven by his reversing of Trump policies of the free-market enterprise solutions.

Resulting in a long four years with the closing of the Keystone Pipeline, opening the southern borders to 2.5+ million illegal immigrants, the disastrous exit from Afghanistan, perpetrating Putin's Third World War on the Ukraine. It's clear that the World Economic Reset is real. As China's yuan is being proposed by the International Monetary Fund, the World Bank and the World Trade Import Export Banking system, as the reference fiat currency. When this happens, the dollar will crash. Under this administration the debt limit will be raised to $31+ trillion, to avoid a shutdown of the US government.

For the first time since World War Two the $31 trillion debt exceeds the national GDP of $24 trillion. Making America insolvent and inflating the derivative bubble to bankruptcy levels. This is only based on booked debt not GAAP accrued obligations, that are increasing at the rate of $250 billion per week totaling $158 trillion per the debt clock. www.usdebtclock.org. An economic and societal disaster as USA is faced with a cold global trade war.

The 9/11 holocaust and Osama Mohammed bin Awad bin Laden haunts our foreign policies when it comes to a threat of World War III much like Pearl Harbor changed America's involvement in World War II. All this as newly elected President Biden signed 54 executive orders, 23 memorandums, 98 proclamations, 21 notices = 196 edicts implementing policies reversing Trumps policies. Essentially, closing down energy independence, opening the borders letting in 250,000 illegals per month, causing crime increases due to defund the police movement pursuing the 2019 George Floyd BLM revolution, allowing China fentanyl from Columbian and Mexican drug cartels to come through open borders and increase overdose deaths by 50%. Then President Biden, calling 10% to 15% inflation transitory not due to spiking energy costs caused by Green New Deal policies and loss of supply lines to Southeast Asia. Causing the Federal Reserve planned increases in discount rate to their member banks of at least 5 to 10% over the next three years. (See Exhibit B for the ripple effect of such monetary mismanagement). While dumping 300 years of currency into the world marketplace during the Pandemic.

On top of these negative consequences, the January 6th Trump protests resulted in et tu Brute'. When former President Trump (Caesar) was cancelled from his bully pulpit Twitter account. Preventing him from expressing his views on why he lost a questionable mail-in vote and was impeached twice for a Clinton conspired Russian collusion. Making him a fire brand leading America toward a better world. Unfortunately, he was ineffective when challenged for his bullying and poor planning methods, leading to his inconsolable, resounding defeat to an underdog, weak leader... in the person of Big Brother Joseph Robinette Biden. Bringing with him, inept VP Kamala Harris, and the Wizard of Oz crew of Pelosi, Schumer, AOC squad, a teleprompter leadership and a gridlocked Congress. Topped off by Hunter Biden, President Biden's iterant son selling his father's name for peddling privilege that creates a conflict of interest with China, Russia and Ukraine while he and his father profit from treasonous activities. Proving emphatically that elections really do have negative economic and social consequences.

All of which is depicting how a divided America can lose its democracy ... AKA, "Washington and MAGA Burns January 6, 2020" ... the modern- day "ides of March" resulting in Caesar's assassination. Et tu Brute in 45 BC and et tu Robinette with Trump's 2019 demise to the fake news Brotherhood in 2020. Triggered by VP Pence assignment of Task Force Leader Anthony Fauci, who caused the synthetic virus to be released during gain of function experiments with bats.

MAGA, President Trump's mantra is replaced by Biden's BBBBG Build Back Better Bigger government. Proven when President Biden's

(Pompey) signed 54 executive orders totaling 196 edicts reversing President Trump's policies that were working, for a transformation to the Progressive Socialist Democrat party, in the image of Carl Marx and Big Brother Obama. Using a diabolical Big Brother government deficit spending spree of a trillion here and a trillion there is $1.9 trillion stimulus payout, $1.2 trillion infrastructure bill and $3.1 trillion Save America jobs bill totaling $6.2 trillion. "Stating it is paid for and won't cost American's one penny". With Biden defending this lunacy with the statement that "this spending will reduce debt" and inflation is temporary and creates jobs. Proving why he flunked third grade economics.

With his Treasury Secretary Yellen, former Fed Chairman, proposing a 100- year treasury note to fund the deficit spending. This is after the Fed put 300 hundred years of currency into circulation during the Pandemic. Only Obama's idea of a trillion-dollar bit coin mined by the USA, that could be deposited at the Fed to cover the debt limit shortfall. Proving former Senator Dirksen's quote "a trillion (thousand billion) dollars here and a trillion (thousand billion) dollars there is still a lot of funny money". Or my quote "a trillion dollars saved here and a trillion dollars not spent there is less debt and zero deficit spending".

Sounds familiar, when former President Obama said the same thing about free health care. "It won't cost Americans one dime". That elicited a response from Addison Graves "Joe" Wilson the Republican's assistant whip for the House of Representative from South Carolina. Who retorted "you lie," who was reprimanded then kicked out of Congress for telling the truth? It was and is in fact costing $40.5 trillion dimes per year for our bloated health care program. That proves Biden's promised tax increases to the wealthy will pay for everything, but the interest on $30 trillion in cash basis debt. Leaving $158 trillion in unrecorded obligations to later generations in the next century to pay.

How can this happen in such a short period of time with a changeover that is supposed to be seamless. History has it that these symptoms result in not only a new world economic reset but a return to nationalism and fascism in Putin's Russia and Biden/Sanders' America. Quotes from Epoch Times, "But it doesn't have to stay that way if we educate ourselves about our rights and responsibilities. Each right represent a portion of our freedoms ... for example the right to freely worship, speak and congregate, along with the right to a fair trial in a court of the Rule of Law, to name just a few. (AKA ... January 6th included). When even one of the God-given rights is not maintained in our country, that portion of our freedom disappears". Depicted by Dictator Putin saying that the war on Ukraine "is a cleansing of society" of Nazi's, as the entire country is destroyed. Reminiscent of Adolph Hitler's Nazi holocaust on the Jewish society as the inferior race. Making this more real is to consider the impact of the petrodollar and nuclear weapons as the driving force for peaceful coexistence and humanism worldwide. American style free market enterprise fulfills the intent of the New World Order to preserve the race and our natural habitat in a better but not bigger world economic order.

Each of 8 billion individuals make up a world of values most likely seeking the same opportunities of family before country and freedom before communes that can thwart initiative for survival as a race, only really threatened by greed and influence driven by wealth. That corrupts even those who profess sanity and honest concern for the Many and still take preference in peddling privilege and violence.

The comparation of January 6th 2020, "Washington is Burning" to "The Ides of March 15th 45 BC as **Rome is Burning**" et tu brute', is meant to be prophetic. The writings of Sr. Alexander Frasser Tytler in the 1700's wrote about "The Decline and Fall of the Athenian (Roman) Republic." As a history professor at University of Edinburgh, he is known to have listed the "Cycles of Nations". David Myer points out in the Epoch Times (January 5,2022). "Considering America's history this seems too also be prophetic. You'll notice the progressions and regressions of American history in this sequence. You also may recognize that the average age of the world's greatest civilizations is 200 years, (AKA ... America 1776 to 2020 = 224 years) and they have all passed through the following sequence":

    Notice the Progressions:
    "From bondage to spiritual faith.
    From spiritual faith to a great courage.
    From great courage to liberty.
    From liberty to abundance".
    Now notice the transgressions:

From abundance to selfishness.
From selfishness to complacency.
From complacency to apathy.
From apathy to dependency.
From dependency back to bondage".

Problem: "Our great nation is one step from bondage as our dependency is shifting to government from God and Self-reliance. How have we found ourselves in this condition? The answer is between what we found in what happened between abundance and selfishness. We began to take our blessings for granted and were no longer thankful ... and when we aren't thankful, we stop being responsible. The lack of remembrance of how our nation progressed from bondage to abundance can only be found in our true and accurate history. Without a thankful heart and a responsible attitude, neither America nor any other nation has the ability to remain great. And without knowledge of its history, no nation has the ability io be thankful and responsible". Newt Gingerich feels, and I quote, "America's survival depends on moving away from the narrowly political and toward the historic in our national policies".

As an Obama protégé, Big Brother Biden, is dividing Americans into apathy towards woke values and dreams of building back a bigger, better government with the big business Brotherhood (AKA Orwell's 1984). In his first 365 days he built the derivative, speculative bubble bigger than ever filling it with inflation, deficit spending and debt generation approaching the unknown condition of insolvency. With the have nots demanding a share of abundance and the wealthy protecting their rights by supporting more protection from BLM by the police letting the criminals drift into downtown retailers and suburbia.

"From abundance to selfishness.
(Stock market inflating and Debt exceeding GDP).
From selfishness to complacency. (Wealth of the haves astounding).
From complacency to apathy. (Racism triggering riots by the have nots).

From apathy to dependency. (Socialist woke values for culture change). From dependency back to bondage". (Freedoms taken by lawmakers).

This is how a divided America is in the process of being destroyed (et to' Brut'e.. "Washington is Burning" with Senate Majority Leader Schumer "calling for a transformation of America" and Speaker Pelosi bivouacking 25,000 troops "protecting her and our people's Capitol" from another January 6th clownish protest resulting in the death of one protestor, turned riot. Then ignoring the use of the same 25,000 national guard to prevent two million illegals from crossing the "Biden" open borders. Also, not even close to the George Floyd nationwide riots of 2020 that for 120 days looted, burned, attacked court houses and police precincts, caused more than 30 deaths, injured 2,000 policemen, and destroyed $8 billion in property damage, under the banner of peaceful protests and a BLM revolution for reparation. Then et tu Brute' President Trump's dumped by an unexplainable plurality. Is this democracy or bondage?

BONDAGE

I'm bound for the city of destruction
I'm bound for the outskirts of myself
I'm bound for the country of affliction
I'm bound for the bounty of wealth

And more

My bondage is with my own arms
My bondage is with my own doubt
My bondage is simple indecision
My bondage is floundering about

The score

Is my mind tied in a knot?
And my courage held hostage
Bonded to a have or to have not
The bondage of myself at this stage

Or I will break free

To be the new unbounded me
The new me will be stronger
For crucial decisions
I will take longer

For me

The new me will be smarter
To hell with being a self-starter
Sure, I can exchange bondage
For a peaceful old age

But there is an encore

I can rearrange the stage
By turning my next page
To an unbound tale of freedom
An Enterprising American in good health

Having thrown off the bondage for abundance
"Learning and earning" for my own income
"From a skill to bill" competing for my own wealth
Surprise there's no color line in enterprise

In the Great Enterprise called America the Bountiful

By bonding American Capitalism and American Socialism

Solution: As an idea that has arisen to fend off the age of revolution, a third party endowed The American Enterprise Party is for reconciliation and reorganization to stop the burning. We cannot allow America to Self-destruct with a partisan uni-two-party gridlock. Washington is burning much like the rise and fall of the Roman Empire in 63-45 BC, from its historic cultural revolution over a monarchy and established a new order that included a Senate of Nobles, elected Assemblies, dispersion of central power, term limits, a constitution, due process of law, habeas corpus, and individual liberties.

This was two thousand years before the American Declaration of Independence, its Constitution, the Gettysburg address and the Civil War. It was Rome's redistribution of wealth that collapsed the empire ... broke and forever broken. Ironically, Caesar (Trump) et tu brute, the pontiff maximus of the rise of Rome was assassinated by members of the Senate, electing Pompey (Biden) pontiff, who managed the decline and fall of the empire. AKA known as the open border policy to save the immigrants from tyranny here or there. Economically, Biden just added two million more vagrants to our 200 sanctuary cities and towns' welfare programs while in his mind he has emboldened thankful voters for Democratic candidates. (Example 800,000 noncitizens to be allowed to vote in the New York elections).

Unless this is stopped in Washington, a divided America will fall. Our insurance is our values of freedom to believe in and live the American Dream, with opportunity for all and family units governed by decentralized State controls. A great example is our failure to elect leadership that focuses on root problems not issues, for financing and measuring results with logical and common-sense solutions to serious problems. I call this an American ideology, where our enterprises need a skill to bill and ethical workers who must learn to earn. There lies the idea of the American Dream. Americanism, with these color neutral objectives for positive results, embodies these goals and outcomes of "how to do it". Where Peace is from Strength and our Military is the first responders to any crisis started by those who only seek power thru wealth, might and bondage.

Where we need to apply this, first and foremost is in the elimination of ghetto living and welfare spending. Not contrived white supremacy and government intervention for climate change issues. Our biggest problems are inner city poverty (70 million in poverty), homelessness (533,000 living on the streets, with one million criminals in 30,000 gangs terrorizing their hoods and breaking into railyards for container theft and into city boutiques for reparation payments). And 2.5 million new immigrants uncontested, during 2021 and 2022, flooding our open borders and communities with only welfare checks for sustenance. How can we stop this regression that is now a transgression from liberty to selfishness? From selfishness to riots and riots to bondage. We enterprising Americans must challenge the Few who are leading the Many, with promises never kept and a government that is a monster eating the prosperity meant for the have nots.

Fast forward to 2020, in my opinion, we now have leadership of our two parties more concerned with control by identity politics, climate change and bridges than they are about the squaller and crime in our inner-city slums and disadvantaged small rural communities. I Quote. "They (the leadership) erected residential boundaries, through violence and law ... thereby penning the minorities and migrants into black only districts that proved to be embryonic ghettos". Per Dr. Flamming's 2006 study of redlining black ghetto housing in Los Angeles and Chicago. Even now, with progressives, Biden, Harris, Pelosi, Fauci and Schumer opening the borders and condoning Democrat sanctuary cities and States that are courting illegal immigrants to come, one come all to our ghettos or homeless shelters. Who then are vagrants on our streets, with welfare and other means to survive. Such as begging, prostitution or drug dealing for the cartels. But wait a minute, NY offers voting rights to 800,000 undocumented Dreamers and LA is putting up drug users in apartments making sure they have sanitary drug paraphernalia. All of which, will most certainly vote Democrat. And be the first to march for equality and equity in our former America the Beautiful. Then be available to march in protest with BLM then use riots to take it themselves.

More Solutions: My party's campaign is to eradicate social poverty and red lining, before we do anything else. Then the residents have to learn how to work ethnically, by developing a skill to truly build back better and sustain it for their children. I call this the learn to earn and skill to bill ideal. This ideology will replace criminals teaching gang members complacency, with teaching and financing reconstruction, with patriotic work ethics and small business ownership. Turn problem makers into problem solvers by offering gang members, who are entrepreneurial, the right to work and build it back better. This takes away their justification for theft, drug dealing, prostitution and killings.

Why will this work? Because it brings with it pride of ownership and a great place to live. Because currently we waste more than it will take to fix it. With more effective policing ... i.e. Mayor Giuliani style of stopping crime, where it starts, and institute fair prosecution with bonding and imprisonment. Currently, apathy means we aren't investing any money to make our inner cities livable. Instead, what we are financing is more rhetoric about the Green New Deal, while ignoring our inner cities which will kill the golden goose that the have nots want a share of. At the same time eradicate the BLM call to defund police with a purge on crime with swat teams cleaning out the crack houses and gang hangouts, confiscating drugs, guns and habitual criminals for cash bonding and aggressive prosecution. Because crime is first a moral problem and policing to stop it at its root ... is reenforcing morality.

How can this be done without building high rise low rent housing such as Chicago's Cabrini Green and free housing for vagrants and addicts in LA and San Francisco, breeding crime and raising more criminals? Wasting billions on a false positive that looks like we care. That is the true dysfunctional socialism. Replace the government sponsored welfare programs and American jobs act with the Enterprise Model of social rehabilitation ... using the enterprise private business platform, employ those with a skill to bill and who want to learn to earn a piece of the American Dream pie. Turn the inner-city gangs from problem makers into problem solvers using education and career planning at "warp speed." Dedicate the transformation to the heritage of the black and brown man being a hard productive worker not a slave to the ghettos. A member of the enterprising American class that rules the ruling class with change.

When the soul of America lives within all its people to eliminate woke rewrite of history and embraces American work ethics with patriotism, we have Americanism. I call this American Humanism. The new monetary Capitalism that marries human Socialism for a stronger society and unbeatable nation. To accomplish this before the revolutionaries take over our cities, we must act accordingly to solve the root causes (see below) of criminal behavior in those neighborhoods and replace with the Great American Enterprise Model values (see below) to act in collective might to make America Greater than the Romans, the Chinese, the Russians and any other ideologies that threaten Americanism and the American Dream. Using Humanism as its creed.

Principal causes of escalating crime in the cities:
- Squalled houses and environment,
- Low quality education facilities and teachers,
- Drug dealing,
- Prostitution and gambling,
- Gun dealers trafficking,
- Drive by crime, carjacking, smash and run robbery,
- Child abuse and teen pregnancies,
- Human trafficking of immigrants,
- Corrupt enforcement and imprisonment,
- Shortage of police and detectives,
- Lack of job opportunities for unskilled workers and felons.
- Not profiling suspected criminals using analytics and DNA to incarcerate known offenders,
- Not stopping and frisking for known criminals and influx of immigrants,
- Not using cash bail for all certain crimes including misdemeanors,
- Not establishing punitive charges to match the crime,
- Not confiscating guns and weapons, using warrants and snitches.

Preventive criminal reduction approaches:
- Appoint Crime Czar Ruddy Giuliani for consultation with major city Mayors regarding prevention and reduction of inner-city crime,
- Find criminals where they live, and break the pledge of silence in families and neighbors,
- Incarcerate habitual criminals, set standards for severity of offenses,
- Rehabilitate through education and jobs,
- Profiling suspected criminals using analytics and DNA to incarcerate known offenders,
- Stop and frisk for known criminals and influx of immigrants,
- Cash bail for all crimes including misdemeanors,
- Confiscate guns and weapons, using warrants and snitches,
- Better schools in the hoods,
- Better living conditions,
- Teach skill to bill and learn to earn values,
- Restore a strong family's unit to replace gangs as the pseud family unit,
- Create opportunity to replace drug dealing and care jacking,
- More diversity in police, more teaching than preaching, less enforcement and more reinforcement with financial incentives versus just moral incentives,
- Adequately fund police and first responders.

Objective: Designate Enterprise and Opportunity Zones for private enterprise investment and form the Enterprise Corps of Engineers and Swat Teams for cleaning up the inner-city ghettos, homeless shelters, street vagrancy, homeless migrants, users and addicts living on the streets across America. Ignoring the problem, with apathy, by calling it a political issue or imprisoning the problem is dehumanizing our American Dream by using government programs to magnify the problems by making the victims dependent upon welfare. This is dehumanizing the rest of us as well, when we turn to incarceration of problems thereby making it worse (prisons and ghettos as concentration camps creating another holocaust) or ignore it until it turns to protests then into riots (Ferguson, East St. Louis, Baltimore, Philadelphia, Chicago, Minneapolis, Milwaukee,

Waukesha, Kenosha, LA, NY, DC January 6th, etc.). This is being highlighted by record increases in crime in our cities and at the southern border. The open border policy has allowed cartels to commercialize immigration with drugs and human trafficking. With woke prosecutors in our cities practicing bail reform and allowing misdemeanors out without bail. Resulting in 20 to 50% increase in crime and murders. This is called the bleeding-heart diversion from solving the problem calling it an issue.

Goals: The solution is to form the Enterprise Corps to stop dehumanizing the have nots by teaching them the American Dream with work projects to clean up the streets, tear down the slum landlord squalor to rebuild our American cities and under privileged communities for pride of ownership and aspired equity. In America enterprise should be free and capitalists must learn to share, and the socialists need to learn how to work ethically and patriotically for a skill to bill. On the other hand, we need the capitalists to be trustworthy and comply with government rules and regulations but we don't need government officials running our businesses. American enterprise, government and enterprising workers must cohabitate in concert by competing with other isms with humanism.

Motto of the Enterprise Corps and Peace Corps: Work for pride of ownership by learning to earn the American dream with a skill to bill for humanism values. Financing of this should be line one of a balanced budget plan replacing the other inflationary infrastructure Build Back Better bills and the climate change initiatives in the Green New Deal that don't fix America for all Americans. As a second thought the current administration is assisting and financing the Taliban's takeover of Afghanistan, appeasing Russia's behavior in the Ukraine, ignoring North Korea's firing missiles over South Korea and Japan, Iran's missile tests and down playing China's wolf warfare using threats of Hypersonic missiles, to destroy American democracy. And counter these actions using "peace with strength" by resurrecting the Peace Corp for, a worldwide campaign teaching the American Enterprise methods and politics while protecting the rights of the working class and the have nots. The solution is a third-party action activating the Peace Corps. by using foreign aid being wasted on regime change, with the endgame being, funding to convert communism to Americanism promoting peaceful coexistence around the world.

A SONG OF PEACE

I've heard of the wars of evil
I've seen the ravages of man
I've read of the primeval
I have followed the Ten Command

I have marched to the music of others
I have saluted our flag's flare
I've respected my brothers
I have bowed my head in prayer

I have shed a tear for all who decease
I have thanked God that love was there
And now I write a song of peace
To veterans a call a voice to care

Singing we shall overcome
Under one sun
One flag
One God
Wars be done

That we can only live as one
If we can touch each other's hand
Reach out touch the tips that heals
For it is the brotherhood to band
Around beliefs and ideals

By touching each other and being one
We are united together we stand
We are the same under the sun
We live in freedom of this land

We worship the same God
We love for the same reasons
We cultivate the same sod
We live through the same seasons

And having read the poet's lines
We are the same in the Maker's eyes
Yes, I've seen the signs
As all come upon the earth with the same mirth

About our energy source and how we must not cease
And we must live together in happiness
Imploring the credence of my song of peace
And attempting to climb out of the abyss

To have lived in God's eyes at all
Then and only then will the family of man
Standing for peace or together we fall
Be at Peace and make a stand

Against wars
Against power and closed doors
Against unfettered Government
Against control of resources and where they went

Against the song for war that promotes decent

For in peace, we stand
In the grace of what's right
Sharing the prosperity from the land
With no guns to fight

Singing we shall overcome
Under one sun
One flag
One God
For we can only live as one

Wars be done
Peace has won

Procedures: The idea is simple, bring together the capitalist (monetary) and the socialist (Human capital) as we have in every business in America, to tear down the slum landlord businesses and rebuild it in the image of a modern city with quality single family-dwelling town home units, modern schools, small businesses, that the families can be proud to own and call their home. Now the inner city or small-town American nightmare. From this grows respect and teams of people planning, setting objectives and goals for living the American Dream. The enterprise is USA, Inc. the team is the Enterprise Corps, restoring America's roots and fixing animosities of the past. During transition and the rehabilitation period the Enterprise Corps would be housed in motels managed by private enterprise. Funded by the Human New Deal. A trillion dollars spent here and a trillion dollars not spent there, is ultimately how we fix America with a recovery plan. Then we can use our enterprise methods to teach our offspring the principles of work and faith in America and avoid the Marxist woke principles of supremacy and racism.

Conclusion: The reconciliation from a gridlocked Congress that is perpetuating the art of the filibuster ... by avoiding problem-solving calling everything an issue with no positive outcomes. Or creating problems by misusing the filibuster to avoid solutions. Effectively, they cause the problems not solve them. This justifies a third party with the skills I used in turning around despicable nursing homes. I know this can be done. In managing and owning skilled nursing homes, we found in the same conditions that Mayor Daley caused by flattening the Cabrini Green type prisons into racist based rowhouse ghettos ... the owners of nursing homes were dehumanizing the workers and families with a lack of pride of restoring the patients' health and dignity so they could return home. This was fixed by the Enterprise method, in a matter of months, using my "skill to bill and learn to earn" program, humanizing long term care with education and the resurrection of the obligation to sustain the family unit.

Results: By making government accountable we have then wiped the despicable slate clean and implemented the American Enterprise Dream. Turning wasted unaccountable government spending of taxable incomes and debt financing into positive outcomes. Once this is accomplished the problem makers become the problem solvers by sustaining the victory over apathy to maintain dignity and quality of life ... this is what happened at Fox Valley (AKA Death Valley) and 140 other skilled nursing facilities that All-American Care restored to the American Dream and will Save America from extinction.

By: JERRY RHOADS Founder and CEO of the American Enterprise Party.

Example: History has it that, reminiscent of the Roman Republic two millennia ago, September 3, 301A.D, was the declaration of independence by the" freak of freedom" known as San Moreno, the world's oldest and surviving Republic until the American Declaration of Independence in 1776. Though, as a country, San Moreno only comprises 38 square miles currently with 33,000 inhabitants. Landlocked and surrounded by Italy. It's their secret of peace and prosperity that resides there. They have the original Statute of Liberty with a stone cross inscribed with the word liberty proclaiming "All (M)en belong to themselves because they pay no homage to anyone amongst themselves, but only to the master of all". AKA...their Christian God. For most of their 17 centuries of existence, it's been one of the freer and more tolerant of the world's countries. Having survived the pagan Roman authorities after Rome's collapse and their Great Persecution of Christianity during the Crusades and the Hundred Years' War (1337 to 1453. (Paraphrased from the Epoch Times article by Lawrence Reed).

(In my opinion The Epoch Times is the only source of consistent and reliable news and human-interest content. For years I read the Chicago Tribune for its national and international news. No more. It has fallen into the issues trap of tabloid shock jocks, not reliable reporting of problems searching for solutions. And common sensical reporting of the uncovered facts. Jerry L. Rhoads, Founder and CEO of The American Enterprise Party standing for Americanism and Humanism. Author of the Trilogy "The American Enterprise Party, Founder and CEO of a third party that supports Americanism and Humanism as the swing vote solution to our broken two party gridlocked system).

The second endowment of a Statue of Liberty, by The French government, signifies freedom and opportunity as an ideology in America since 1886. For my purpose, San Moreno is the model for The American Enterprise marriage of capitalism and socialism that coexist in American businesses. By using work ethic, patriotism and peaceful coexistence as a renewed Republic we should declare September 3rd as American Enterprise Day ... to be celebrated as the renewal of our love for our country, its flag, her heritage and thy neighbors who embrace Americanism by pursuing Humanism. Envision this: American Capitalism and American Socialism working together, like our American small businesses, to run our Great American Enterprise kicking the ass of Chinese-Russian Capitalism/Communism in the Global Trade War. With the swing vote third party American Enterprise Party to pull the left and right, the liberal and conservative tribes towards the middle for common sense policies and politics. Having San Moreno as the model of how humanism and peaceful coexistence works.

OUR STATUE OF LIBERTY

I LOVE HER LIGHT
(Not Blinded by a Benjamin's Might)
Published by Jerry Rhoads in
"The Tenth Wonder of the World"

The Statue of Liberty and
The Lady Scales of Justice
Emanate the light
Not blinded by the injustice
Of money and might
To enforce our right
To her laser beam of opportunity
That focuses on life liberty and the
Pursuit of happiness
Illuminates the paths by common sense

(She holds her light for me as well as immigrants
Without prejudice of mind or race)

To signify freedom that will never die
In my heart to honor our country's start
Embrace the principles of democracy
The philosophy of equal opportunity
And you receive her embrace
For the warmth of love
For the warmth of enterprise
For the warmth of family
We salute our constitution, tis of thee

I love her light
Whether dull or bright
She stands for my life
Through past trials and strife

To show my appreciation
All I have is my affection
Towards our great enduring country
Which makes me free
From sea to shining sea
Yes, her light is love
Emanating from our creator above
In that God we trust
For the pursuit of happiness
Is just

The Statue of Liberty
The Lady Scales of Justice
Not blinded by the injustice
Of money and might
Emanates the light
To enforce our right
For the rule of law
For the law of rule
The rule for rulers without fear
The constitutional judge of all our peer
Our country our honor our sphere
For legal immigrants who become citizens
She's your Statue of Liberty
Standing for secure borders that shall never cease
Surprise there's no color line in free enterprise

Then
Love her or leave her in peace…

WHAT THIS COUNTRY MEANS TO ME
By Jerry Rhoads

Looking across the countryside
I must do so with great pride
America is the spirit applied
And the heart that always tried
For the sake of those alive then died

For all I can see is the work of man
Though there are things
I don't understand
I'm amazed at making concrete from the sand
Growing food from the land
Creating technology from the mind of man
Woman's ability to convert seedlings to birth
Of abundance of an earth without girth
Granaries stand as shadows in the sky
A salute to humanities' mortal cry
Get me work or let me die

This is what this country means to me
It means so much to say I'm free
To stand up each day after I pray
And know that I have a chance
To create reality from circumstance
For there aren't many in this world
With themselves unfurled
Before the Almighty spirit
Embodied in humans that we touch
Before a God we respect so much yet fear it
Holiness and happiness is the caress
That our country can certainly bless
Individuals creating their individuality
In a land where it's we not just me

So, the country is collective in totality
The country is above and beyond passing time
By not condoning ordinary crime
And washing away the inner-city dirt, grit, and grime
It is the here and now divine
For those who are so inclined
It stands there as a symbol of verve
Saluting those who have enough nerve
To risk, sacrifice and serve
To remake themselves out of nonsense
And mark our historical prominence
As a nation of patriotic and ethical common sense

Yes, that's what this country means to me
It means together we are free and
Divided we are alone in our uncertainty
*United we become a **bountiful history***
That's our Statue of Liberty not blinded by money and tyranny ...

That will divide America and make our shared values disappear, never to wake up to living the American dream that becomes the nightmare being "woke" up in the pursuit of abject equality and equity as our contrived salvation.

MY AMERICA THE BOUNTIFUL

By Jerry Rhoads published in "The Eighth Wonder of the World"

My America is the feeling of freedom. It's the feeling good when you get up in the morning and can decide what you're going to do that day, who you're going to see, and what you're going to say.

It's the feeling that you can make a difference in pursuit of good health, happiness and prosperity.

It's the feeling you can produce your product, you can sell your produce, and you can benefit from your hard work, ethically unhindered.

It's the feeling when you help your children with their homework so they will be able to use their knowledge for growth, for maturity, for their pursuit of opportunity in a great country.

It's the feeling when you send them off to school, knowing they will receive a concerned teacher's attention, sensitivity, and guidance. And knowing as they grow up, they will thrive on their freedom to communicate, to express themselves, to direct their own destiny.

It's the feeling when they graduate from grade school, junior high, and high school that they are taking the steps toward a better life. And when you give their hand away in matrimony, that happiness shall be theirs. For together as husband and wife, they can create the same and even more opportunities for their offspring.

It's that feeling when you can unchain your dog and watch her run free for at least a little while, to watch the expression on her face when she's released from the shackles and the sadness that reappears when she must be chained.

It's the feeling of being in good health, happy with my spouse, with a family as my wealth; as My America is the opportunity to pursue such prosperity unbridled and unfettered.

My America is the freedom of choice to buy the bread I want to buy, to acquire the goods I can afford to acquire, to invest the capital I have saved in ventures I want to take for the love of my family and my country.

My America is being able to communicate in writing, speaking, and in whatever form, language takes, my opinions, my thoughts, my prayers, my visions, and my dreams to those who want to listen and protect my family from those enemies of the American way who in themselves have not discovered America.

My America is the blooming rose that has the freedom to grow toward a clear sky and a warm sun, being able to complete its cycle from bloom to plumage to autumn to a dormant grave, only to rise again to a fertile earth.

My America is the personal commitment to grab opportunities that will better the country and to set an example for those who follow; that what you give must be proportionate to what you take, or the erosion shall remove the sky, the sun, the earth from our grasp.

For in our America and the world resources are limited; the energy, though absolute, is redistributed by our wills. The more astute, the freer we are to create, the better the use of the resources. And left in God's hands, through our America, we create good will, good products, good people, and peace of mind.

My America the bountiful, oh yes, my America Dream, the vision of the poet, the words of the orator, and the minds of the leaders be kind, be patient, be wise, but above all be humble to the reasons and the heritage of our freedom for all.

Lead us not into temptation, but deliver us from evil ventures and purposes, for thine is mine America, the Kingdom, the power, and the glory, forever.

Amen.

"The Catch 23rd RIP psalm of the devil" ... those of you who believe that our happiness is Big Brother's responsibility, that our health is Big Brother's responsibility, that our prosperity is Big Brother's responsibility will inherit the scourge of the earth. Those who believe that freedoms can be parceled out to the elite Few for the sacrifice of the Many shall die an unhappy, unhealthy and impoverished life. Along with billions in Communist countries".

Signed: Jerry Rhoads Founder and CEO of The American Enterprise Party.

In Volume One of the American Enterprise Party Trilogy, I covered the reasons why we must have a swing vote **to break ties, prevent a partisan gridlock of the two-party system** and save the great American enterprise, where the American constitution is what holds the democracy and republic together. To separate the ideology of personal freedoms, from the throes of collective dictates governing human behavior, I offer the ideology of Humanism, virtues of an enterprising human being, are to be the platform for political and economic recovery.

Any attack on its principles of conduct will reduce our people to a mass of individuals without hope and slowly dying from loneliness. Humanism and the constitution are the roots to love, family, peace, work, belief in a higher authority are the foundation of individual freedom and free market enterprise. Any other cultural ism ideology shall make our lives dependent on conformity to control by the elite Few and kill individual initiative. While humanism holds our people together as one against the other isms focused on destroying our collective strength of our will, patriotic work ethic and honor.

Definitions to help decide your political party philosophy:

Tenets of American Laissez-Faire

It's a world of competitive forces attacking our values and internally woke reasons for changing our way of life. It's a war of doubt and fear won with faith and leadership standing up for the 10 tenets of American lasses-faire. Then the American Dream tenets of the Many is one result for each American striving for a quality of life.

1) Reward received determined by the amount of risk taken.
2) The law of supply and demand for measuring markets.
3) Sharing is based on skill to bill produce and services.
4) Earning is based on learning a skill to bill for goods and services.
5) Competition is creating optimal quality, innovation and cash flow from GDP/GNP.
6) Quality creates cost savings, taxable profits and ROI ca. Profits create growth and capital.
7) GAAP reports actual results. Stock market reports derivatives.
8) USA Debt clock and financial analytics are a guideline for collective prosperity.
9) Sustainability is debt less than 50% of GDP and GNP.
10) Accountability for above 9 tenets is the bottom line for measuring leadership. It's money funding workers for profit sharing and growth.

American Enterprise is not Woke capitalism or socialism. It's free market enterprise Capitalism (money) managed by Socialism (workers) for the prosperity of its investors practicing the above 10 tenets. Nor is there a need for an enterprise to practice or use the ESG index (environmental – social – governance) for evaluating Governance. That is done by the debt clock, GDP and the marketplace.

Wait a Minute What is WEF and ESG? The 2022 W.E.F. World Economic Forum in Lyon, France, sponsored the Davos presentation of the Great Economic Reset by Klaus Schwab and Thierry Malleret authors of the new World Economic Order in their book Covid-19: The Great Reset. AKA, worldwide Zeitgeist Socialism with a stakeholder socialism reset of shareholder capitalism, is supporting an ESG Monopsony government, owning all property and enforcing dictates to limit rights and rules of behavior for the Many.

In other words, "you will own nothing and you will be happy" ... or else. The model is Chinese capitalism and the China Social Dream. Governance by the Few ruling class for the equality and equity of the Many, using rules dictating behavior that require conformity for the Many and don't apply to the intellectual Few. Interpreted and paraphrased by Jerry Rhoads, author of The American Enterprise Party Trilogy.

Agenda of W.E.F. and E.S.G. Index: rating system to test existing corporations, by bigger woke stakeholder corporations, bigger institutions, for woke suppression of freedoms, using snitching, discouraging individualism, artificial intelligence, facial recognition and surveillance, government sanctioned discrimination against unvaccinated, and the allocation of an equitable social income. Isn't that the dystopia described in Orwell's 1984 and Animal Farm?

Yes and AKA, BLM's cancel culture demand for reparations, take down of statues, renaming offensive labels and defunding the police. While ANTIFA's revolutionary demand for equity; black revolutionaries destroying small businesses and professing destruction of white supremacy. And the public education teacher's unions defending the change in curriculum to embrace C.R.T. history and 1619 theories of slaves being the first Americans whose heirs are now demanding equality and equity for all races, genders, and sexes. The USA's Great Social and Economic Reset being pursued in 2020 – 2022 infamita.

The KPMG (public accounting firm) E.S.G. (environmental, social and government) index is used as a scorecard to isolate offenders of identity politics and races to facilitate the conversion of shareholder corporations to woke stakeholder institutions as the advent of the new economic order reset. For example, Greentech stands for implementation of the American Green New Deal, as the first step to the Great American Economic Reset to comply with the new world order reset. Paraphrased from, The Great Reset Book, by Richard Florida.

The American Enterprise Party is opposing this W.E.F. and E.S.G. index as Marxism with highlighting the marriage of American capitalism with American Socialism. AKA, free American Enterprise. Using the foundation of free market enterprise underpinning of constitutional freedoms, guaranteeing property ownership and choice of employment opportunities in shareholder capitalism. The American Dream is built on American Capitalism funding shareholder enterprises for American Socialism. Then enterprising Americans who are, risk taking, and competing in pursuit of the American Dream also comply with "the learn to earn, skill to bill" 10 tenets of lasses-faire.

Populist embodies the will of the people rather than the establishment government. A popular idea of reversing government control of the risk-taking nature of the haves and enticing the following of the have-nots for the greater good. Populist is a derivative of population not human behavior. Conventionally, known as Libertarian.

Humanist beliefs stress the potential value of goodness of individual human beings that emphasize common human needs, and seek solely rational ways of solving human problems leaving issues to common sense. America is a country of 330 million individual human beings having human problems. Why wouldn't Americans want a political party that represents the majority so the minority extremes are pulled to a middle for rational resolution of problems. It's like having a referee arbitrator for moving towards peaceful coexistence with our opponents and enemies. Conventionally, known as Humanism.

Marxist founder Karl Marx, in creating the Communist Manifesto, designed the 10 planks AS A TEST to determine whether a society is becoming socialist then communist or not. The 10 PLANKS stated in the Communist Manifesto and some of their American counterparts progressive or populist. Marxist theory that races rather than class to justify the Black Revolution with the socialist platform called the Black Lives Matter movement due to social and economic inequality will become a third party standing for race not caste or class using identity over substance. This will include defund police, promote the 1619 project, use critical race theory in their campaign, open borders, sanctuary states and cities, massive spending on infrastructure, climate change, Green New Deal, Ear Marks, Welfare reform, limit military spending, counting on 18 to 20 million more voters to become the swing vote. Funding to be generated through the Big Box companies, Big Media, Hollywood fund raisers, Big Brotherhood Business. Conventionally, known as 1984 Big Brother Communism.

Progressive ideas ... the progressives (politicians) of the twenty-first century who seem to believe in the SOCIALISTIC and NEO-COMMUNIST concepts, especially those who pass more and more laws, rules and regulations implementing those ideas, are contradicting their oath of office and to the Constitution of the United States of America that sets out the way the majority have agreed to be governed. "Johann Wolfgang Von Goethe" — 'None are more hopelessly enslaved than those who falsely believe they are free".

USA constitution was compromised by a progressive Supreme Court from 1937 to 1944 ... by Rob Natelson in the Epoch Tines 3/15/2022. Progressives rewrote the constitution when the court stopped protecting the constitution's limits on the Federal Government. The first through sixth amendments related to how the justices tried to balance the demands of Franklin D. Roosevelt's New Deal with constitutional rules (AKA now the Green New Deal progressives are bypassing the constitution with disregard to fiscal responsibility and priorities).

In 1937 FDR began replacing sitting justices with progressive New Deal enthusiasts who had no prior judicial credentials. The remodeled bench discarded limits on Federal spending, Federal property ownership rights and Federal economic regulations. Abandoned in one case Habeas Corpus, and right to a jury trial.

This record from 1937 to 1944 continues to affect USA today. Then FDR was pushing for packing the court with 12 jurisprudence candidates for term limits to keep progressives in the majority. Now we have the progressive democrats spending doing the same thing for passing the Green New Deal and other progressive trillion-dollar agenda transformational items ... such as get rid of the debt limit and avoid GAAP accounting.

To avoid becoming the next Rome, Russia, China, Venezuela, Cuba, Great Britain or Nazi Germany as another example of how a great empire (the United States of America) became a canceled culture. A new third party (the American Enterprise Party) will emerge and become the swing vote in the gridlocked no consensus Congress to implement problem solving and bring the left and right extremes towards the middle using peaceful coexistence for the greater good of its enterprising people; practicing humanism as a restored, rational, common-sense, patriotic culture. Thus, saving the Great American Enterprise for the benefit of its enterprising, competitive American citizens and its constituencies, while not limiting the spread of the wealth to qualified legal immigrants. Who will speak our language, pay taxes, become citizens of the Great American Enterprise in pursuit of the American Dream so they don't later "turn coat" and lead the Asian revolution to unseat America as the world leader in commerce, technology and military strength.

Enterprising Americans are workers who defend our country, believe in a greater power, freedom of speech and choice of work, feelings of security in our homes and communities, patriotic to the history and work ethics of the past. Willing to compete and take a risk to better their life and country. Respect our flag, history and icons of the past. Responsible for quality behavior values passed to their children. Expect a government that will be accountable for its fiscal affairs and is a believer in American democracy, the Republic, our constitution and foreign policies. To this end, those enterprising Americans who individually contribute to our America's prosperity, shall share in that end following the ideology of sharing by "learning to earn by having a skill to bill" in the lasses-faire market place. As a member of the American Enterprise Party, they are dedicated to a fiscally balanced budget, with a constitutional government of the people, by the people, for the people, and a duly elected Congress, Presidency and Supreme Court according to the Rule of Law.

Pure progressive-regressive, socialist, communist and totalitarian characteristics: Activists and revolutionaries, in cultural denial, heavy taxation, bloated welfare, excessive government payroll, self-serving bureaucracies, political correctness, atheistic philosophy resulting in leniency towards crime, adulterous sexual lifestyles, undermined family values, curbing rights of the many, over consumption, vulgarity and divorces, unsustainable economics, heavy regulation, replaced gold standard with floating currency (bit coins and crypto currency), and an eroding national sovereignty. Examples: is it BLM, ANTIFA, CCP, USSR, the Republic of North Korea or the blessing of the Taliban and its terrorists' cohorts, resulting in the loss of Afghanistan to tyranny.

Foreign Policies: Per the Epoch Times series on "How the Specter of Communism is Ruling our World by Infiltrating the West". "There are four reasons young intellectuals become fond of communism":

1) Disenchantment with capitalism and wealth distribution.
2) Belief in a materialistic philosophy of life. A simpler lifestyle.
3) Intellectual pride and superiority.
4) Unfulfilled religious belief.

"They, who seem to be ruled by radical ideologies and ego centric idealism, altruism and self-sacrifice, fall in love with communism. This segment of the Epoch Times series envisions the high ground by being righteous with faith and moral elevation to have humanity guard itself from communism. That may not work out with tyrannical leaders".

Now it's playing out in the war crimes and genocide being imposed upon Ukraine by Russia. Using a war on Ukraine as a prelude to expanding Russian holdings to the old USSR. Threatening with the nuclear hole card, and targeting, Poland, Scandinavia, Balkans, Romania, Belarus, Georgia, Crimea, Netherlands under the Sycle flag of communism. Including a war pact and chest provided by China, Iran, North Korea, Venezuela and other Asian and African socialist/communist countries.

Much like Hitler's war pact in 1938 with Mussolini and Tajo to finance the purge on Europe, Asia and Africa. Regardless, these are the reasons that Ukraine must not be the sacrificial lamb for the new world order economic reset of Russian/China/Iran/North Korea Axis of Evil regime.

While 70% of the earths people are governed by communists' doctrines it is imperative that the NATO, EU, UN, BRI, North and South American countries take an aggressive approach to defending democracy with a counter strategy of offense not defense. With a counter strategy of offense does not defense contingent on Article5 of the NATO pact, (Offensive movers like when President Trump told Putin, who was threatening to push the button in Syria releasing the chemical and nuclear weapons. President Trump supposedly countered by saying go ahead but remember I have a bigger button. He then dropped a dirty bomb at the military airport to emphasize the point). With counter threats of having nuclear arsenals, and the latest military and hypersonic strategic weapons including a space force but offering up peaceful coexistence with American Free Market Enterprise as the model.

America has to lead from the front not the behind the scenes acquiescing by allowing Hunter Biden and the "big guy" to use influence and identity politics to enrich themselves. While USA pension funds, stock market, politicians, chamber of commerce members are invested in Chinese corporations controlling the American supply lines and the Russian energy capitalism.

Ironically, the CCP, Inc's. belt road investments are teaming up with the communists, using capitalism and socialism politburo that goes way beyond Marxism or Lenin's communism. While Russia is struggling with capitalism and a dictatorial leader, China, India, Philippines, Taiwan, Great Britain, Germany, France, Italy, Canada, Mexico, South and Central America are pursuing trade and enterprise as their monetary weapon to replace America's preeminence in the world.

This is the new world order offense to protect free enterprise independence from the shackles of poverty, cartels and oligarchs. That exists with totalitarian dictators or war lords using the Marxist and Communist philosophy and aggression in competitive trade using theft of technological secrets and cyber hacking to finance their war on America democracy.

Therefore, the members of NATO, UN, EU must attack them with the trade war dominance based on the collective wealth of the free world competing with the other high population and low aspiring poverty isms. Our leaders must have an immediate third choice at the ballot box based on the American Enterprise Party principles and platform.

Functioning as the swing vote to implement the quasi-reorganization plan proposed by the American Enterprise Party Manifesto. Keep America Great and leading the world of competitive trade policies under the flag of humanism and peaceful coexistence.

Unfortunately, this is the current state of affairs, in the USA where we have conflicting divisions tearing us apart in the grasp of impure capitalist and socialist democratic characteristics:

Government gridlock due to contrary objectives for profitability, benefits, sharing of the profits, private ownership of property, deemed individual rights. Can these two conflicting philosophies be unified into a pluralistic political philosophy and party of synthesis for parity in intent based on individual effort in a free market society? The answer is yes with a third party representing those values ... AKA as the Great American Enterprise Party. This is in contrast to the compromising communist theory of contrition for the greater good decided by a government of the Few making laws for the Many and enforcing them with surveillance and fear. One party representing all lives ... for strength is fear and control is conformity.

Uni-party, binary "winner take all," American partisan politics:

Where the current partisan uni-one party Congress (gridlocked) is a transition to Marxist Communism with no objective debate or resolution for its enormous debt and irresponsible legislation.

Marxism states that Democracy, especially multi-party democracy, is just too unruly ... too 18th century, too enlightenment, for the modern tech era. Tocqueville wrote "Democracy in America, is the independent self-starting citizens, who formed so many nongovernmental patriotic organizations for the betterment of all". Communism promises replacing the rights of the individual with sharing of the risk and return equally for the greater good of the society ... with a Few having the authority to distribute the fruits of the Many workers equally and equitably for the greater good. The leaders having the authority to resolve any disagreements or curtail all debate for the collective benefit of the proletariat.

In conflict is a money driven uni-party government where objective debate doesn't exist. It is the (CCP, Inc.) Chinese Communist Party's approach to control. China, Russia, communist philosophy with their politburo has a uni-party government. One mind, one controlling system that doesn't allow for risk-taking, independent thought, investment of time and effort for profit of the individual, failure isn't rewarded, while family is for procreation only, future is what Big Brother says it is and the Brotherhood polices dictated for behavior of the proletariat. It is a temporary aura of equality and equity that disappears with the loss of personal initiative when the Many realize they have lost their freedom of thought and action. When the revolution results in a compromise of these values and the evolution of personal development stops, the perceived wealth disappears and the Many falls into apathy and hopeless intoxication (AKA, "I would rather drink then think"). Look at the fall of Russia, East Germany, Venezuela, Viet Nam, Cuba and ultimately China.

So, what is capitalism and socialism American style? Risk taking is the driving force of our enterprises. The profit motive is pursued. The business enterprise is expanded. The quality of family life is aspired. The work ethic is practiced. Advancement is inspirational. Ownership is investment of time, effort and work. Happiness is a fruitful lifestyle. The very components of capitalism and socialism in a democracy that is the American Dream society. Why then are these aspirations pitted against our humanity when it takes all to produce a successful enterprise. The truth is that the capitalist needs to share in the wealth based on the contribution of the human capital (socialism) that forms a peaceful coexistence culture. America has evolved into the very thing that stops communism in its tracks. The freedom to fail and start over again, is the very connection that allows for a peaceful environment envisioned in our constitution. The more the debate of the balance of capitalism and socialism is the very strength of dialogue for political problem solving. The very underpinning of a democracy and constitutional government. The equation is reason minus religion and racism equals resolution. Reason meaning individual happiness, health and prosperity and resolution is democracy for the collective transformation culture of Humanism. How then do we know it will work ... well work is the solution as I found out in turning around bankrupt businesses ... the boss capitalist needs to share in the wealth based on the socialist workers learning to earn their share by having a skill to bill and compete for jobs in a laissez-faire society.

Symptoms of Money Driven Uni-party Government:

- A gridlocked partisan Congress and State legislatures with no meaningful debate or resolution for the insolvency.

- Unaffordable legislation and inaccurate forecasts on cost and benefit.
- A financially challenged budget.
- Deficits and excessive debt collapsing the USA economy.
- Rulemaking without consensus.
- Dilation of or dilution of the Rule of Law.
- Money-tics over democratic politics and money-talks over common cents.
- Loss of freedoms ... speech, security, civil rights, right to work law, Rule of Law, liberty for all, health and welfare.
- Cooking of the cash-based budget and books hiding deficits and debt at all levels of government.

  For example: The Social Security/ Medicare Trust Funds have been drained of cash by the General Fund borrowing for funding wars and deficit spending.
- By not using generally accepted accounting principles.
- Authoritarian rule with Oligarchy in charge. In economic terms a Monopsony (government is purchaser of last resort).

Blue States 23 with 80 million voters in 2020 election for President system renders us to gridlock. Generally, it is the west and east coast for Biden ... the polarization of our political big states and large cities that vote for the Democrats. Remarkably this is the money driven uni-party strategy for liberal progressive Democrats.

Red States 27 with 70 million voters in 2020 election for President Trump... on the other hand the mid-America and smaller states and community's vote for republicans. Remarkably this is the money driven uni-party strategy for alt right conservative Republicans.

This renders the USA to no swing vote to break up differences of philosophy or ideology that keep both parties focused on following the constitution that sets out the way the majority have agreed to be governed and protecting its enterprising American citizens from anarchy and economic ruin. "Freedom is never more than a generation away from extinction. We don't pass it on to our children in their bloodstream." President Regan (or main stream money-tics... Jerry Rhoads)

It results in ineffective, inefficient, unaccountable Government gridlock due to contrary objectives for profitability, benefits, sharing of the profits, private ownership of property, deemed individual rights. Can these two conflicting philosophies be unified into a pluralistic political philosophy and party of synthesis for parity in intent based on individual effort in a free market society? The answer is yes with a third party representing those values ... AKA as the Great American Enterprise where it takes society to make capitalism work for all. This is in contrast to the compromising communist theory of contrition for the greater good decided by a big government of the Few making laws for the Many and enforcing them with surveillance, censorship and fear by big media and business. Thus, one party representing all lives ... for strength is fear and control is conformity (1984 George Orwell prediction of dehumanizing society).

So, I have developed the platform with a campaign strategy of becoming the "swing vote party" **to break ties and prevent partisan gridlock of the two-party system** at every level by eliciting legalized voting support from all Enterprising Americans from the left, right and the middle to solve the problem that Big Brother Government and Big Business Brotherhood cannot solve without us. By being the following backbone of the Great American Enterprise.

1. The seventy-seven million baby boomers and 13 million voters of color.
2. The 100 million middle- to low-income enterprising American families to vote for doing away with the control of our country by the elite Few for the Many.
3. See Article 12 for strategy where we must sell our party to the forces that control the media, the internet to educate and

involve the patriots that still dwell in every community and business.

This will unlock the gridlocked uni-party "winner take all "system where the fusing of the republican and democrat parties with 19 republican senator turncoats votes for a two-step $6.5 trillion infrastructure (green new deal) ten-year spending bill and a $6 trillion budget package that commits the USA to $100 trillion deficit spending forever. Effectively, our uni-party "winner take all" has evolved into taking us down the path of financial destruction promising to save the planet, provide free health care for all, free public education for all, free welfare checks, free college for all, free voting systems, guaranteed annual income for all, open borders to all who want to get a piece of the American pie and a one-party "winner take all" government for the greater good of all. "A 1,000 billion here, a 1,000 billion there, and pretty soon you're talking real money." Senator Everett Dirksen's quote converted to 2021 trillion dollars not billions.

IN CONTEMPLATION OF CHANGE

Life liberty and the pursuit of happiness that's America

Will that give us peace
Is it a life free to choose or the happiness of its pursuit
For it's the quest which is fulfilling
It's being on the edge which is thrilling
It's not knowing which is blowing in the wind
Catch it catch it if you can
But only the venturesome understand

That happiness is not a time
It's not a place

It's not a destination
But an opportunity
And though it isn't tangible
And it cannot be anything but a fleeting moment
It's the pursuit which is the fulfillment
Not the capture

That is why the fisherman throws back the largest catch
That is why the lover wants a friend not a slave
That's why the businessman wants a fortune only to gamble again
That's why dynasties are gambled and lost
That's why the world must turn to change
That's why the latest will always become obsolete
That's why common knowledge is already passé
That's why the revenant keep seeking the truth
Rather than accepting the word of Big Brother

And the future is always now
And no crystal ball or bible can bless us with happiness
Tis the pursuit of a dream
Rather than the capture of a vision
That gives us the thrill
Which gives us an illusion
That will not come from a pill

Then making concessions to
Reality and submit
Personal sacrifices unto
Unhappiness hoping for happiness
When it is merely not being unhappy
Wishing with bleeding hearts that capturing
Life liberty and the pursuit of happiness
Is for the greater good

That never could be happy
In contemplation of change

Then during the worst Pandemic since 1918 allow a state of fear to dictate that we must save everyone for the greater good regardless of how it started, how we can protect our individual immunity, who is at fault, when will it end, what are the risk driven alternatives to mass shutdowns of our schools. More importantly, according to Dr. Fauci and Governor Cuomo to not triage, for survival of the un-fittest, first to save those at highest risk. ***(With 17,000 dying in NY nursing homes and 70,000 nationally, because of these quack science and political policies)***. Plus choosing nonessential businesses that exclude big business, big tech, big unions, big media, big government who continued to thrive on mass hysteria and were able to et tu Brute' Trump and elect Biden.

Even now, the American Hospital association, the American Medical Association and the American Nursing Home Association are silent on early treatment and acceptable medications to slow the infection rate based on age, comorbidities, location, race, social and mental illnesses. Without, justifying why government and big business are essential and small businesses and school's nonessential for shut downs. And have medical professionals decide on in-home quarantines, the effectiveness of testing, contact tracing, in-home schooling, social distancing and masks for all ages. Using risk analysis by actuarial projections based on triaging before creating wholesale panic. Without politicians and unions allowed to choose essential businesses. That included big tech, big unions, big media, big government who continued to get their pay checks plus the stimulus checks, thereby thriving on mass hysteria and were able collectively, to dump Trump and elect Biden using mail-in Pandemic voting.

With hindsight President Trump's leadership triage instincts, if allowed to prevail, would have saved hundreds of thousands of lives in nursing homes and over the age of 60 who had diabetes, pulmonary and lung problems. Even so he was instrumental in getting the vaccine produced in "warp speed," ... demonstrating that free enterprise is already working to solve social problems. To support my premise that America Capitalism and American socialism are already working together; as they do every day in our 140,000 small businesses, 15,0000 big business for the benefit of each enterprising American and 22 million first responders, teachers and patronage government bureaucrats.

All it takes to stop this disastrous knee (fear) on the neck of society and let Americans breathe freedom is to choose and sacrifice ourselves for the good of our families. This means there will be a third alternative swing vote **to break ties and prevent gridlock of the two-party system** at every level of the federal and state legislative branch races, school board races, gubernatorial races, local mayoral races, city councils' races, to break the strangle hold of the gridlocked uni-party Oligarch we now have.

After reading Volume One and starting to read Volume Two

I am asking you if you're philosophically a Socialist or a Capitalist? Or neither or both? The choice holds our future in its answer as you will learn in Volume Two.

Before you answer, ask yourself ... do I believe that top-down answers to society's issues are superior to bottom-up problem solving created by the free market? This will determine whether it is the good of the community that takes priority over that of the individual. Then ask will I give up my freedoms to get that. If you say neither meets you needs, maybe you're looking for a more acceptable definition for your vote. In free market enterprise can you have both, problem solving for the individual for the good of the country?

The common-sense answer is yes. As an individual you are a team member in a capitalistic endeavor called free market enterprise. The pursuit of profit is for you as well as the investors of capital. You are free to pick and choose the enterprise for employment or it picks you as an individual. Your share is what you earn as an individual that results from your choice for a career and/or job. It's for the good of yourself, the company and your family. The very essence of socialism.

In America this marriage of individual to a company, is the best of both worlds with profit sharing, otherwise you're asked to pledge allegiance to profit over your family. If you choose profit from investment, you're a capitalist and if you choose profit for the sake of your family, you're by choice a socialist. If you serve both masters, you're an entrepreneur or risk taker ... in the marketplace called America and you're living the American Dream. On the other hand, in my opinion, if you choose to sacrifice your freedoms for the better good of the community regardless of your freedom to choose, you're a pure socialist, a steppingstone to communism and totalitarian top-down dictation.

If you choose to serve and secure your family, you're a capitalist first and a socialist second. In an American enterprise you are both in pursuing what makes American Great for attaining the American Dream. This is a marriage of profit sharing with the good of the family supporting your choice in an American enterprise. My point here is to marry the concept of serving the individual with the pursuit of profit to serve and secure your family is a democratic society. Without free enterprise there will be no Democracy. So, why would you sacrifice your family's future for the greater good of a controlling pure socialist or communist government? And allow a Uni-party "winner take all" Democrat and Republican ad hoc Congress to destroy consumerism in the greatest economy in the world.

It's this consumerism that stocks our shelves. American Enterprise used to produce, with products and technology USA created, that are now provided by foreign producers and manufacturers creating the biggest American trade deficit ever ... for this there should be a market share charge for the shelf space to be paid just like Coca-Cola pays for its shelf space in our Big Box stores and neighborhood grocery stores. I call this a market share fee for all foreign trade products sold in our country to reduce the current trade imbalance and reverse the shipping costs for foreign products being shipped to our shores and stores.

Side Bar: Between 2000 and 2014 USA lost over 31% of our manufacturing jobs and created a built-in supply shortage if China and other Asian manufacturers decide to control our economy. For example, China's GDP grew from $383 billion in 1991 to $14.7 trillion in 2020. Along with a $300 billion dollar shift of wealth to China and Asian countries for technologies developed by America and manufactured Which created capital from "the retirement savings and 401.k plans of millions of Americans that currently finance Beijing's military modernization. Also, that capital also supported Chinese businesses enabling a massive Chinese military buildup and takeover of our supply lines. Resulting in $1.9 trillion shipping costs (fixed overhead) absorbed by American companies. America's financial position is obviously in jeopardy due to the shift from being the manufacturing hegemon to distributor and consumer which removes substantial cash flow from our coffers. And creates debt to our competitors and uncontrolled shipping costs for getting the goods to our retailers. With no competition, quality controls and competitive pricing. This is the first place we will have inflation from a worldwide recession. The US is at the qualms of the communist takeover of our economy. We become more like China, then China becomes us. This is a non-shooting and nonnuclear cold trade war.

Why did American enterprise shift the manufacturing supply lines to China and Eur-Asia countries in the first place, when it's counterproductive to our economy. Underlying this shift in policy, was America's high labor costs in the 60's and 70's. The cause was the powerful labor unions demanding higher wages for the supply line workers, plus better pensions and more time off for personal reasons. Basically, a socialist move to equalize the profits the manufacturers were supposedly making and not sharing with its employees. Plus, the stock market demands on the manufacturers, for better price to earnings ratios. The shift started with manufacturing nontechnological products, such as clothing, food supplies and toys. Then it became patented technological products of computer chips, TV's, computers, cell phones, solar panels, automobiles, weapons, pharmaceuticals; then steel, aluminum and fabrics. Now, everything imaginable. This supply line insanity is being mismanaged by a Biden administration that is accused of peddling influence to other countries by the likes of Hunter Biden. Isn't that the worst of insider trading?

This allowed China and others to reverse engineer our trade secrets and improve them. Then sell them back to our consumers at lower prices, competing with our domestic suppliers, thus stealing from our wholesalers and retailers. Plus, the foreign suppliers didn't ship FOB destination, nor did they unload the goods, nor transport the goods to the resellers, nor did they rent space at the ports for backed up supply lines, even during the Pandemic. Thus, inflating our consumer's cost of goods and services. Great, effectively USA manufacturers reduced their labor costs by paying China, etc. way more in increased burden for cost of goods sold then displayed them free on our retailers' shelves at higher prices. A fool's trade is a fool made.

In fact, they had their own humungous, container cargo ships, charging $3,000 shipping per container, that was increased to $30,000 per container during the Pandemic. All those masks, PPE, and prescription drugs to treat the virus, were on these container ships. On top of that China was making the containers and cargo ships to keep up with the demand. Now having 4,500 ships servicing the world market.

President Trump and a Republican Congress were making policies to reverse this horrendous mistake. Renegotiating the Obama administration's Pacific Rim Tran-Pacific partnership (TTP) agreements. Without a replacement 11 of the 12 countries proceeded to form their own alliance with China, leaving America out until changes could be negotiated by the Trump Administration. With new President Biden's administration's appeasement policies, it's likely to lock USA into an unprofitable position as has TTP. It was designed to bring manufacturing back to the US and lower the $1 trillion dollar cost to our economy each year due to the imbalance of trade ... USA consumers buy $1 trillion dollars more from its competitors than our wholesalers and retailers sell to foreign consumers. Primarily, China, Japan, India, Mexico, Russia, South Korea and Canada. President Trump had negotiated a new USMACA trade agreement with Canada and Mexico, effective July 1, 2020 to replace the 25-year-old trillion-dollar loss leader, NAFTA agreement.

The American Wealth and Economic Reset over the last 40 years from manufacturing of, clothing, soft goods, pharmaceuticals, weapons, refining our own oil and gas and selling our Agra products ... becoming the servicing distributors, wholesalers, retailers and humongous government overhead. With a government payroll of 22 million workers. A $1.9 trillion payroll including pensions is a 40% burden on American businesses' cost of goods sold. So, these trade agreements are saving no money on labor costs as was the reason for shifting supply lines in the first place. First to Japan, then China, Viet Nam, South Korea, Russia, Indonesia for supplies, etc. and OPEC, Russia and Iran for fossil fuel energy. These countries have received a shift of our wealth as well when they reengineer our technology and sell if back to us with a markup and shipping costs.

Who are the current wealthy? They are distributors, wholesalers, retailers, transporters, technology, media and servicing companies. The top 1% of wealth $60.8 trillion controlled by the Fortune 500 companies and wealthy individual American. The bottom 50% wealth $1.8 trillion is controlled by the rest of us. Currently, the Oligarch of 545 federal government officials control the entire $118 trillion National net worth through lawmaking and political connections. The question is, does money-tics continue to use the golden rule ... those with the gold shall rule? Or will our constitutional government prevail with government of the people, by the people for the people. Following are the wealthiest American companies and their wealthy owners:

Amazon World Services $1.6 trillion, Jeff Bezos net worth $200 billion
Microsoft net worth of $1.7 trillion, Bill Gates net worth of $66 billion,

Berkshire $500.6 billion, Warren Buffet $50 billion
Face book $732 billion, Mark Zuckerberg $103 billion
Twitter $40.8 billion, Jack Dorsey $11.2 billion
Zoom Video Technologies, $12 billion, Eric Yuan $35 billion
Google (Alphabet) $1.24 trillion, Larry Page $78.1 billion
Tesla Motors net worth, $770 billion, Elon Musk $185 billion
Exxon Oil net worth of $486 billion, Walmart $447 billion,
Walton family $86 billion
Apple Technology net worth of $2.2 trillion, Steve Jobs estate $10.6 billion
Home Depot $295 billion, Bernie Marcus $5.9 billion
Target $90.8 billion, Brian Cornell $116 million CVS Pharmaceuticals $152 billion,
Walgreens $43.7 billion
General Motors $50.7 billion,
Fiat Chrysler $30.9 billion,
V.W. $108.2 billion,
Ford Motor Company $42.1 billion

And the GDP's of those leading trade competitors with an imbalance of trade deficit for 2021 with America:

China GDP $17 trillion, Japan GDP $5 trillion, India GDP $3 trillion, South Korea GDP $1.7 trillion, Germany GDP $3 trillion, Canada GDP $1.8 trillion, Mexico GDP $1 trillion, Russia GDP $1.6 trillion, EU GDP $16 GDP, OPEC GDP $2 trillion collective, Spain GDP $1.4 trillion,
Totaling negative imbalance of trade $1 trillion per annum

As shown above the wealth of the Nation has shifted to non-supply line businesses while supply lines were sent overseas. And the wealth of individuals has shifted to the new billionaires of media giants and service companies from the traditional American manufacturers and landowners. As depicted above, are the statistics that bear out this diabolical mistake. We only compete in the world market with gas driven automobiles, while Tesla is a Green New Deal darling. The ruling class has become our wealthy politicians, peddling privilege (AKA, Joe and Hunter Biden) and the Brotherhood of Big Tech, Big Media, Big Unions, Big Box, Big Pharma who elected Joe Biden to convert the country to progressive ideas. Well, that is the devil in the deep blue sea, drowning us in more debt and deficit spending. Just waiting for America to default on its interest payments so they can call for collateral for the taking. I.e. gold, silver, uranium, plutonium, diamonds or our natural resource water, grain, food, labor.

With the "Wizard of Oz" Biden Administration taking over the 2021 through 2024 economy, US businesses are facing higher taxes, increasing entitlements (minimum wage, government pensions, unemployment, workers' comp, rates), increased energy costs, all of which are causing inflation in consumer's cost of goods and services. This will increase the imbalance of trade and continue to lose more manufacturers who are seeking profits over seas. As the imbalance increases, along with America being insolvent, with its debt and deficit spending, our economy is destined to lose its currency's preeminence around the world. To date this is the primary reason for the Federal debt being $30 trillion and its unrecorded obligations being $158 trillion dollars. In other words, we have been losing money every year since World War Two by shifting wealth overseas because of foolish trade policies, high corporate taxation and uncontrolled imbalance of trade.

This affects the American stock market that will shift from a bull market to a bear market while the Federal Reserve increases the discount rates to its banks to fight off inflation. Certainly, this will sink the ship faster. The only fix is an administration that understands it's a worldwide trade war and changes its foreign policy with procedures for managing the American Enterprise economy before it's too late ... in 2022, 2024 and the future. In the process, Congress needs to reduce the socialist unions power and the public education unions woke policies by electing American Enterprise Party swing vote candidates at all levels of government. During 2021 and 2022, much of the country, as a result of virtual in-home education due to the Corona Virus, had mothers and father begin to question the curriculum being taught to their children, via virtual zoom connection. Presumably, approved by local school boards for use in public schools. Suddenly, the problem was, the apparent grooming and preparing students at an early age to accept transgenderism, early sex education, promiscuity and insinuating that Christian teachings were bigoted, not diverse, with equity and inclusion for minorities.

During 2021 under the new Biden Administration the curriculum of the public schools garnered this progressive approach and supportive of such teachings. As a result, many of the parents were turning to private schools or home schooling themselves to take charge of curriculum.

There is an increase in the support for Charter Schools and school choice. It got so combative in the school board meetings, with parents expressing concerns, there were outright challenges, demanding that this orientation to progressive thinking was not what the schools should be teaching. But should guide the students through the 3 R's and STEM subjects not doing the parents job of dealing with real life. School choice and Charter Schools are becoming more popular with better results in math, reading and science.

Chinese Communist Party (CCP, Inc. a low overhead very efficient competitor in the USA's economic, globalization war)

CCP, Inc. is the largest enterprise in the world. It has 98 subservient companies with 12 on the Fortune 500 list. It has 775 million proletariat workers with no say. It has a politburo board of directors with one President. It has no unions, no Articles of Incorporation. It has no by-laws or rule of law for accountability. It has no restraint of trade limitations or anti-trust law. It has no HR human relations department. Its only investor is a communist party politburo. It has only one stockholder with total veto power. It has no contract with its employees. It has no complaint department. It has no work ethics standards. It doesn't need efficiency experts. It has no required quality control. CCP, Inc. has a more efficient labor force without interference of human rights, unions and strikes. Yet in the background are the 350 million believers in Falun Gong who have opted out of the CCP and support human rights and free market capitalism. The next twenty years will decide if the USA will lead the world out of war and poverty by establishing Humanism and peaceful coexistence as a United Nations' standard.

CCP, Inc's research and development is hacking and stealing secrets of others for its technology. It embeds its citizens in its competitors Universities and communities for stealing ideas and technical applications. It has no 50 Republic States to control or satisfy. It has investors from its competitors ... American union pension funds, foundations and group mutual funds are investing in stocks and bonds of CCP's subsidiary companies in a single economy (unwittingly American investors are investing in a communist regime to the tune of $400 billion dollars per year, one-third is from the USA government Treasuries, that will grow to $1 trillion in market value by the end of 2021). This creates a dichotomy with current international politics with the USA using sanctions, tariffs, that are anomalies when it comes to winning the globalization cold war ... the reverse of CCP investing in USA companies is closely controlled by the CCP, a monopsony and a monopoly (a one buyer and seller market that controls all trade agreements and enforcement of competitive influences). All this converts to low quality with little to no overhead for its subsidiary companies. Also, no strikes, no work stoppages, media attacks, no protests other than religious groups, compared to 40% fixed government overhead to run USA enterprises.

CCP, Inc. taxes small to large companies 2.5% to 15% Individuals 3% to 45%, on worldwide income. Therefore, CCP, Inc. is low overhead and high return on investment. On the other hand, 59% of the CCP workers are over 50 years old with a mandated social security program. 90 million drop out of the work force per year. Of the 775 million workers 10% are over 70 with a 54 average retirement age. Chinese national health care covers 90% of its vast 1.4 billion population as a private and public partnership with a variety of options. It is not a free cover all policy.

CCP, Inc. follows a single standard time offset even though it spans five time zones and borders 14 countries in Asia. China is the fourth largest with 2.6 million square miles behind Russia's 6.6 million, Canada's 2.8 million and the USA 2.7 million square miles. With the USA and Canada leading with natural resources. China trails the USA in GDP with $14 trillion to the USA of $21 trillion. Japan is third with $5 trillion, Germany fourth with $4 trillion, India fifth with $3 trillion. From these recent analytical figures, the USA is leading in GDP from a work force of 170 to 200 million enterprising Americans with the highest overhead costs and lowest return on investment compared to China ... that is catching up by controlling the supply lines with low labor costs and high technological theft.

In summary, the stated Chinese Dream is to use Chinese Capitalism to defeat the American Dream that's chasing American Socialism. Using the façade of global warming and climate change as the catalyst, China plans a takeover of global institutions. Example: China states it will phase down fossil fuels, while America's Green New Deal socialist position is to phase out CO_2 fossil fuels by a date certain. The race isn't racism or globalism, but communism versus Americanism for world supremacy of American democracy. In President Xi's eyes, China is a democracy ... Chinese style. Thus CCP, Inc. (Chinese Communist Party) envisions China democracy to be the new world order for bringing all socialist and communist countries together to compete with American Capitalism and American Socialism (monetary capital and human capital) practicing peaceful coexistence with Humanism as its constitutional foundation.

This is the focus that the American Enterprise Party and its version of Americanism, brings to the partisan two-party (red and blue) gridlock. A pathway of equity for both the Haves and the Have nots using a bipartisan swing vote in the houses of Congress and the Republic for which it stands under God and the constitution of the United States of America.

Americanism and The Great American Enterprise
IDEA OR AN IDEOLOGY

Marxism is an idea that involves one person rule and a Few who decide the rules for the Many that exempts the Few from the rule, a snake whose head needs to be removed to stop its poisoned rights,

Americanism is an ideology that involves millions of patriotic, enterprising Americans who are dedicated to a work ethic of competitive "risk-reward humanism" and the American flag.

What makes America Great. Is it an idea or an ideology? Think about it ... you can kill an idea with rejection but not an ideology. It's my premise that Americanism economic ideology, marries capitalism and socialism in its very basic democratic values, established by our founders, in the constitution. Using freedom and opportunity to override the idea of Marxism to control subservient behavior.

As pointed out in an op ed in the Epoch Times, Cheng Xia Nonong established that Karl Marx made two mistakes. First, he believed there are only two completely opposite roads in the world. Socialism and capitalism. In fact, the CCP's (Chinese Communist Party) history proves that it has grafted the two systems to make Chinese capitalism. Marx's second mistake he believed the communist party will bury capitalism and be replaced by socialism.

However, the CCP completely subverted his theory with CCP communist capitalism. In fact, the CCP favors USA capitalism over China's socialism. As demonstrated by President Xi's takeover of a corrupt communist state by digging a grave for corrupt capitalism but unwearyingly digging a trap that will ruin the communist's regime. It is still the corruption of wealth for the few, that is destroying China's capitalism. Liken the process to my interpretive ideology that the American Enterprise movement is to marry American capitalism and Democratic socialism to produce a powerful economic formula, for taking American democracy worldwide. Kill the Marxist Chinese communist capitalism idea and replace it with American ideology of free market, with a "risk-reward work ethic," and patriotic allegiance to the American Flag (Laissez Faire Enterprise American Style).

In other words, for lasting prosperity, of the enterprising American worker, is the ideal formulation (marriage) of capitalism and socialism as an enterprise founded on democratic principles of Humanism ... those with the capital shall share with those with the patriotic work ethic for the good of the individual's wealth and the success of the capital funded team (a sports analogy and an economic ideology) for winning the worldwide trade and political war with communism.

Such are every small, medium and large business enterprises in America, that each day produces wealth for themselves and the rest of the world with the economic democracy (ideology) of consumption and fulfillment of the Wealth of a Nation, envisioned by Adam Smith in his book The Wealth of a Nations. With our current two-party system, the USA isn't building on our founder's formulation of the ingenious method of sharing and employing the gold, for expanding our success around the world. Instead, we have unwittingly fallen into the Marxist "idea" that the many will overthrow the few for the good of the individual's share. But with the few still controlling the wealth.

In the process, as in any revolution, the wealth of a nation is destroyed ... such is the imbalance of trade deficits that have transferred trillions of dollars to CCP to build their communist version of capitalism, to destroy America's Great democracy ... made up of individual risk takers with the competitive, enterprising and patriotic work ethic, being woked down by those idealistic Marxists, to destroy the ideology of Americanism.

The question is ... will America fall for the false promises of the left and right (Red and Blue) for the greater good that we, as individuals, should allow wealth, power politics and revolutionaries to dictate our future. As the founder and CEO of the American Enterprise Party I pledge my support to the ideology of American Enterprising American workers practicing Humanism, above all promised ideas.

In summary, Americanism requires the capitalist to share in the wealth of the nation and the workers need to deliver a patriotic and ethical product every time on time.

AMERICANISM AN IDEA OR AN IDEOLOGY

An idea involves one person
An ideology involves billions of faith

You can kill an idea
But you can never kill an ideology
An idea is a fleeting thought of the future
While an ideology is the culture from the past
For the future good of the individual

We in America have democracy as an ideology
That is why we say we are the land of the free
Though we have the criminal element that aren't
Thus some must earn their freedom

Which ideology is right or wrong?
That is the worldwide question
That is threatening us all
To be destroyed by an idea

Evolving from the past idea
That we only are here because of creation
Or some atomic infusion and conclusion
Deciding our fate and life's state

Ironically, we come from the same place
And will return to the same destination
Though we cannot agree to how or why
It is certain we all will die

That idea for some will distort
Into a Koran or a Bible that builds faith
On being right or wrong
Not why we are one and the same

Leaving no one to resurrect or blame

Except those that are here for an ideology
Not some courted idea of Marxism
For justifying the dropping of an A-bomb

So, the idealists can swallow their last prayer
To the Gods and Satan's that were never there

And God Bless Americanism the ideology of Laissez-faire

Is Washington Burning?

The resemblance to Rome is astounding.

Wake up America, et tu Brute ', Washington is burning much like the rise and fall of the Roman Empire from its historic cultural revolution over a monarchy and established a new order that included a Senate of Nobles, elected Assemblies, dispersion of central power, term limits, a constitution, due process of law, habeas corpus, and individual liberties was two thousand years before the American Declaration of Independence, its Constitution, Gettysburg and the Civil War. It was Rome's redistribution of wealth that collapsed the empire ... broke and forever broken.

Will America be the modern-day Rome? That is the question and the answer is in the American Enterprise Party Trilogy.

Even as Rome was under attack from outside forces, it was also crumbling from within thanks to a severe financial crisis. Constant wars and overspending had significantly lightened imperial coffers, and oppressive taxation and inflation had widened the gap between rich and poor. (Isn't America emulating Rome by losing to a woke cultural revolution, reverse racism and progressive forces that support collectivism for the sake of the greater good).

"Rome is burning during the Ides of March" that had won democracy then lost it five centuries later to a rise and fall of Emperor Julius Caesar and the Republic due to a culture of violence, vulgarity and excesses. (Such be, the rise and fall of America these days of BLM, ANTIFA anarchy, woke cancel culture, escalating crime, disrespect of the constitution, the American flag, the national anthem, the Presidency and ignorant disregard for fiscal accountability).

Since the advent of the Roosevelt post war Great Society Programs, we have evolved into a similar culture of violence, vulgarity and disproportionate excesses of prosperity divided by partisan politics, big business and big tech media. I believe this is due to the failure of the leadership of our two parties, blinded by money-tics, that will forego freedom and liberty of American enterprise values for government control.

Of course, this requires each person must decide, at their own level of risk taking, when it comes to pursuing personal health, education and their welfare, otherwise we live in a vacuum for behavior and our pursuit of happiness. This justifies that government should not pick winners and losers while dictating behavior to reduce the greater goods risk to zero. Otherwise, we have more and more rules and regulations for dictating behavior governing risk taking. Risk taking is a cultural behavior encouraged by the constitution of the USA, that sets out the way the majority have agreed to be governed.

For example, et tu Brute', Vice President Pence's hand-picked government task force of bureaucrats headed up by the Institute of Health head, Tony Fauci, who possibly financed with government grants, the very virus that started the Pandemic. He then supposedly absolved himself by enforcing the same strategy and tactics as used in 1918 for the Spanish Flu, having all Americans comply with bending an undefined curve, with 6' social distancing, nonessential business lockdowns, 14-day quarantining, contact tracing, single or double masks (108 billion masks, worldwide, presumably manufactured by China, discarded every month contaminating our environment). Then he and the CDC predicting more lockdowns, mandated masks usage to stop unlimited variants of the Corona virus to keep control of the state of fear to make taking vaccines a law. All of this failed to stop the 1918 Spanish flu let alone the 2019 China Pandemic worldwide. Conspiracy theories that China released the virus worldwide were cancelled by the social media, twitter, Instagram and national media outlets. But have been resurrected when the Wuhan Lab was questioned about three of the lab technicians being hospitalized in September 2019. Why haven't the American Medical Association (physicians' trade union) or the American Hospital Association (hospital trade union) been an active participant in the management of the

Pandemic? Because there was no representation on the Corona Virus task force nor advisors to et tu Brute' President Trump.

For instance, why no early treatment at home or physician office? To reduce hospitalizations and deaths. Or use of proven therapies to avoid hospitalizations and ICU deaths. Well, it's because of the CARES (corona virus aid relief and economic security) Act a $1.7 trillion dollar bill signed into law, that instituted provider incentives for only using treatments dictated by the National Institute of Health (Dr. Fauci). These bounties must be paid back if not recorded as a Cortona Virus primary diagnosis. Earned by making Covid-19 the primary diagnosis and following Covid protocols to include:

1) Free PCR tests for every patient with a fee to hospital or test site by the Federal government.
2) Bonus for each physician or hospital Covid-19 diagnosis.
3) Bonus for Covid-19 admission regardless of underlying conditions as primary.
4) 20% bonus from Medicate on total bill for use of Remdesivir instead of ivermectin.
5) Larger bonus if using admission to ICU on a ventilator.
6) More money for Covid-19 deaths recorded as primary diagnosis.
7) Extra payment for Corona virus death certificate by coroners.

No conspiracy here, just contrived bribes for exaggerating the number of cases and deaths resulting from Corona Virus. Also, hospitals, coroners and physicians make more money on Covid if they follow the protocols of the NHI (Dr. Fauci) and FDA (Dr. Mayne) and CDC (Dr. Redfield then Dr. Wilensky for Biden. Since when do public health officials (bureaucrats) run medical practices and hospital admission protocols?

Of course, it's graft, using value payments for compliance with mandates such as mandated PPE, vents and vaccines. We have yet to get legitimate analytics on cases, hospitalizations and deaths by age group, location, comorbidities, length of illness, length of hospitalization and number of doctors' visits. A good actuary could have started with this analysis, not after the virus has done its damage. With the likelihood the virus was synthetic and allowed to get out of the Wuhan Chinese lab, we've been Fauci'd by quack science for bending a suspicious curve without analytics, mandated masking, 14 day quarantines and national lockdowns imposed by Dr. Fauci Director of the National Institute of Health ... who's fingerprints are all over the "gain of function testing from bats to humans", that occurred using NIH funding, under Dr. Fauci's direction ... unless China cooperates, we may never know who to blame for 6 million deaths, to date, as it mutates. A result of the China Virus Pandemic, the first since the 1918 Spanish Corona Virus killed 50 million worldwide.

President Biden's administration continues to have Dr. Fauci and Dr. Wilensky handle the public relations for the latest Omicron variant. It's more contagious but less deadly. Regardless the scientists are still leading the State of Fear campaign into the 2022 political midterms. Keeping the voters doubting who should run the country for winding down the panic, during an inflationary economy, with the shrinking dollar value and increased cost of living. While keeping our so-called enemies appeased. A long way from where we were a year ago, before the borders were opened and two million illegal immigrants flooded our sanctuary cities and small communities, our fossil fuel energy resources closed down causing us billions of dollars saved by energy independence under Trump. And $6.9 to $10 trillion funded by tax increases and more debt, for the commitment to a Green New Deal and jobs bill called infrastructure program. To put us through deprivation for the sake of building back bigger better government for controlling mother nature and her trade winds and unproven climate changes.

Yes, it took an entrepreneur President Donald Trump and risk-taking free market enterprises to supply ventilators, oxygen respirators and hospital beds; then develop a vaccine in warp speed that will potentially eradicate and prevent wholesale fear of taking a risk for the individual good. When President Trump offered that the presumed cure is worse than the fear, thus inducing the conformity that is driving the virus and the fear of taking the vaccine, he was blamed for being cavalier about saving everyone from themselves. Then being dumped as President for being right.

Example of OMG, such is the thinking of the total zero deaths (TZD) Green New Deal strategists toward zero deaths in traffic accidents who claim that as long as Americans' risk acceptance exists there is no way to reach the vision of TZD, for zero traffic deaths. In other words, until social imperatives necessary to eradicate risky behaviors, are instituted, so individuals engage in protective behaviors, to embrace traffic safety policies, TZD cannot happen. Then of course why not eradicate the same risk-taking tendencies of our capitalists and entrepreneurs who are hurting the chance of TZD Social Utopia for the greater good or our military that marches into harm's way for liberty. While us enterprising Americans say let Americans decide their own fate when they drive our own car and not TZD driverless cars. Therefore, individual risk-taking freedoms take over woke rules dictating behaviors.

Example: Here is why we Americans should never relinquish our right to take risks for our own individual benefit. This is the tacit foundation of American enterprise. Myles Peteron, age 18 and an entrepreneur in Canada is advising others to take risks for their dreams. He says pick a goal and believe you can to achieve your goal. He is an industrious Canadian teen who has put his investment money where his mouth is when it comes to plastic waste (the world's #1 environmental waste problem) by utilizing it as a component to his patented particle board … enterprise wins again… save the planet with conservation not deprivation … recycled plastics, batteries, tires, etc. not windmills, not cap and trade, not kill the cattle not the Green New Deal nightmare with its fear demands to conformity by the Many not the Few.

Example: Save the Planet, are you crazy, Mother Nature and Father time can save themselves? The world is 4.5 billion years old. We are 92,958,412 miles from our sun. There are 200 billion galaxies in the universe. There are two trillion galaxies in the Cosmos. How big is the

Cosmos ... known as deep space it stretches 13 billion light years between the white holes and the black holes? Mankind is roughly 200,000 years old. Population of earth 7,830,458,560 as of now. Net zero emissions in a world of diverse populations using energy to live and pursue prosperity. Does any of this hit you as a minute speck in the big picture of climate that we cannot and will not control with mortal rules for our speck in the Universe. Mother nature, Father time and their Sun are on their own schedule. How old is our sun? It is 4.5 billion years old. It will last 7 to 8 billion years. Stephen Hawking speculates that the cosmos had no beginning nor will it end.

According to the scientists our so-called greenhouse effect is dissipating faster as the carbon dioxide is consumed by earth's green house plants as remaining gasses are protecting earth from overheating as does the greenhouse protect its plants. Those scientists who calculate the accumulation of gases have yet to calculate the amount that our plant base absorbs. Do you really think that Joe Biden, AOC, the Green New Deal and the Paris Accord can change how El Nino and La Nina affect the jet stream and trade winds, net carbon greenhouse affecting weather on the worldwide farmed ground, or the Pacific and Caribbean Hurricanes, the Atlantic Nor'easters, the typhoons in the South China Sea, heat and winds of the Mediterranean, the extreme cold of the North and South Poles, the heat and rainless Sharia Desert, India and China's smog and smoke stacks, Mexico's blight and poverty, Puerto Rico, Haiti, Virgin Islands, East and West Indies hurricanes and poverty, USA's forest fires, Canada's Nor' westerns and blizzards, Russia's Siberian winters, without fossil fuels and carbon burning factories that produce electricity for making solar panels, electric cars and wind mills and so-called wind farms. AOC you can trick American once not twice.

Excerpt from an op ed from the Epoch Times ... according to Dr. Elmer Deitch a science teacher on climate every action has a reaction. Yesterday's winds are today's sunlight. The lower winds are ball bearings that support the upper winds. The Chicago effect was finding that high rise buildings impact the weather the next day 50 miles away by deflecting the lower winds. The jet stream and trade winds absorb sunlight and effect the convection of heat on the surface of the earth. Natural winds decide the next day's temperature. Any new patterns affect plants, draughts, forest fires, storms and weather. Humans must preserve Mother Nature's ways of evolving climate change using natural coals, gases and use conservation to manage the carbon dioxide impact on weather by unplugging solar panels, electric windmills and unnatural technologies that mismanage nature and punish the earth's surface, for decades.

Green New Deal DOA this century ... Mark Mills Epoch Times 3/22/2022 makes the case that materials needed to make the transition from fossil fuels to renewable energy underestimates population growth, innovation, entrepreneurs who are far better at inventing new ways to use energy than produce it. Also, current air travel uses 2 billion barrels of oil per year and 80% of the world population don't fly and USA has 80 cars per 100 people. The rest of the world has 5 cars per 100 people. Electric airplanes are a stretch any way you want to look at it. Hospitals use 250% more energy than high rise buildings.

Moreover, drug manufacturing is intensive users of energy that exceeds cars and aircraft. Aside from ignoring these physical and economic and fiscal realities of materials, the aspirants of a transition, underestimates how much more 8+ billion people around the globe will need. Also, we're talking about building hardware for transition aspirations (wind, electric, solar) that will require an unprecedented increase in global mining at scales unachievable this century. That will come from technology (cloud and robotics) mining for rare earth minerals, nickel, copper, cobalt, for semiconductors used in computers, cell phones, lithium for batteries and AI bloc chain software for businesses, etc. This is on top of fossil fuel intensive infrastructure energy expenditures for the manufacture of concrete, steel and glass.

There has to be an estimate of attainable transition for the population growth, not optimistic roadmaps saying we can do it by 2050. Even 2200 may be a stretch and then not approach zero emissions ever. And when we calculate the pulldown of CO_2 to the earth with more people breathing it and more cultivational ground absorbing it ... we may find that there is a good reason that GND was dead on arrival. Proving that global warming and the greenhouse effect is as much a hoax as masks, social distancing and shutdowns were in 2020-2022 for the Fauci Virus. Paraphrased by Jerry Rhoads of Mr. Mills' excellent Epoch Times article and expert opinion.

The bottom line is what are we doing chasing something that the environmentalists can't justify by creating a fear agenda that the seas are rising, and the storms are coming and the forests are burning because of human beings creating the emissions of carbon at a death-defying rate. The science and numbers don't bear out spending upwards to $100 trillion dollars over the next decades on a pipedream. What are we ignoring while progressives chase a speck on our earth's windshield?

1) USA urban squalor, crime sites and home of gang warfare. 20 to 30% of our country's poverty and 8% of USA population and .1% of land mass is in the 100 largest inner cities. How many Urban street gangs in our inner cities that are spreading to the suburbs and smaller communities? It is estimated we have 20,000 to 30,000 with over a million members. Their source of income is crime ... drug dealing, trafficking sex and breaking and entry to urban and citywide auto theft. It's estimated that a single gang member can earn $1,000 per week dealing drugs or prostitution. Or a total of $300 to $500 million in illegal activities. Small businesses are street corner vendors of drugs and prostitution and sin trading enterprises for distribution of alcohol, gambling and fast foods. The estimated GDP generated in the inner cities is $0!

2) How many policemen and women do we have on the streets, protecting us from our self-imposed problem. 696,644 making an average of $67,600 per year with fully paid pensions of $30,000 per year. All are Federal and State employees total $5 billion per year salaries and $2.5 billion per year pension costs.

3) How many people live in the inner-city ghettos? 1 in 15 people live in ghettos in America or a total of 22 million. Ghettos may be a way for new migrants to adjust to a different cultural environment. Some 200,000 per month will enter the country during 2021 or 2.4 million migrating into our largest inner cities without jobs and source of income and turn to crime to feed themselves and family members. This will result in a rise in crime as those coming through MS-13 gangs and cartels will turn to that source of income and those from the mid-east through terror States will embed themselves to commit jihad on our homeland. That is another $100 million in criminal activities per year.

SOBRIETY of SOCIETY

(Are our ghettos a reflection of a sober society? I say no!
They have lost hope with the demise of the family unit
and the opportunity that some sense of security provided
by belief in education and attainable
prosperity solving their deprivation)

To prove we aren't a racist society
With the virtues of Humanism
Our leaders must return with piety
And deliver sobriety to our society

Then fathers are necessary
Mothers aren't contrary
With children of good stock
Yes, America is suffering from family shock

The family of man and woman
Doesn't seem to understand
As a part of the family of God
We need a b-attitude towards the staff and rod

As discipline by example
With faith more ample
Praying for strength and power
Soaked by the positive shower

To wash away negative dirt of poverty
With the positive cleanliness of the home
And learning a skill
Those employers can bill

So, we can avert
The destruction of the family
And build an arch of sincerity
To weather the storm
And mend indifference that will form

From unsettled differences we've unfurled
By Priests and Preachers who worship the pseudo world
In words and feelings that make no sense
While we must pledge allegiance

To the loving flag of motherhood
And the strong arm of fatherhood

Life is hard as it is, hard as a rock
It's got to deal with family shock
A bridge built by never not loving
Or committing to separation without shoving

While our nation is in divorce mode
Domestic abuse
Chemical use
Sexual abuse
Family's excuse
Results in making it harder for the family abode

Are we not in love anymore?
Is it the demise of amour?
Will it require that our society
Get a lobotomy for brain sobriety

Restoring simple loyalty for security
With families taking stock
Not accepting family shock
Breaking up that hard rock of poverty

Assisted by government subsistence
With an entrepreneurial private investment perk
Solving a societal problem's resistance
We can proudly put enterprising Americans to work

As an intervention for a sober society

4) How much infrastructure money to be invested in inner city clean up and business investment as enterprise zone markets. $0. Anyone that has been to a third world city would think our ghettos are worse than theirs, because of the gangs, black on black crime, drive by shootings, carjacking, random shooting of children who are cut down by crossfire for initiation into the gang activities. Dilapidated buildings, squalled living conditions and collapse of the nuclear family unit. Drug dealing and prostitution are the main ways to make money for buying guns and hot cars. This is an attitude of the have nots to steal it if you can't earn it.

The police (65% who are black or brown) hands are tied by liberal prosecutors and mayors who let them go so they don't end up in adult prisons that teach them ways to step into bank and casino robberies. And worst of all are the public schools that are breeding grounds for dropouts. Where 90% don't graduate and those that do are reading at a second-grade level. Even the black and brown politicians, who are typically Democrats, ignore the squalled living conditions. They keep their base at bay by promising they will fight off the Republicans who are the bad guy capitalists as slum landlords. Uni-party money-tics weds the ghettos to a failing woke culture calling it racism. The American Enterprise Party will be the swing vote in Congress and Legislatures that force these problems out of the issues column into proposed solutions called the Human New Deal by deferring the Green New Deal to the political junk bond file. This is Americanism at its best by focusing on Humanism for all.

In summary we need the Green Human Deal that directs savings from conservation of our farmlands and oceans into pursuit of better Green Human Deal that replaces the wasteful Green New Deal and directs savings from conservation of our farmlands and oceans to include our cleanup of inner cities, for the pursuit of better healthcare and lifestyles of the aging, unhealthy ghetto Americans.

Example: Biden announces the new Climate Change Office (his top priority). "The price of Panic" per Jay Richards in his article says he would expect this new Climate Change office to start promoting restrictions on ordinary activities that invoke the use of hydroelectric energy and eliminate hydrocarbons. In fact, that seems to be the reason for the Office in the first place." While 750,000 Americans face eviction due to the Supreme court decision to block the Biden administration Covid-19 foreclosure moratorium with another 3.5 million behind on their rent? How will funding the new $6.2 trillion Climate Change Agency and the Green New deal handle the fear of American citizens losing jobs, housing and livelihood due to closed small businesses? And the 2 to 3 million low paid immigrant workers needing jobs?

Answer: By controlling the risk-taking habits of the majority of hard-working enterprising Americans with fear of future Pandemics, allows the new Climate Change Office to control enterprising American's behavior.

Also, there is a proposal in the Climate Office and the Green New Deal (GND) of having Personal Carbon Allowances (PCA's) for each American using a computer app to track carbon producing habits similar to the apps used by insurance companies to track individual driving habits with the promise of reduced insurance rates. The strategy of the GND and the transformational Biden administration is to remove the risk-taking culture of our Americans by taking away freedoms using fear and tax credits. The GND theory is, for the greater good, we can have accident-free electric autos and clean air to breathe, regardless of science, by controlling the risk-taking habits of the majority of hard-working enterprising Americans using fear of further Pandemics and self-driving accidents. This kind of tyrannical thinking is coming from the control freaks who are running China and other communist countries.

Listen up: Have you heard of RGGI (regional greenhouse gas initiative) using cap and trade strategies in member states (all blue ... NY, NH, MA, RI, VT, NJ, CT, MN, VA (until new governor retracted membership). Theorizing that the cap-and-trade coupons will be the enticement for compliance. RGGI the brain child of AOC and the squad, to ramp down fossil fuel exploration and usage that will cost energy companies $1 billion to $1.5 billion to comply. Results, no evidence to support this will reduce net CO_2 gases going to the greenhouse effect. But it does prove there will be Job losses due to ineffective management of CO_2 capture by our farmlands and forests. This creates a net zero in changing Mother Nature's climate change or global warming. Also, the allegation that RGGI will reduce the emissions, including human and animal waste thru excrement and our lungs exhaling CO_2 gasses, represents the hair brained nature of this folly. It only increases the cost of fossil fuel energy needed to run our country until we wake up and change our bad lifestyle habits and. Marxist leadership.

I also write about" how to do it", after being told an effective third party will never happen, because money-tics blinds the voters to the loss of freedom and liberty with the golden rule ... those with the gold will prevail ... well, that is exactly why we need to find solutions not fighting issues wasting time and money on speculation, but like socialism everything is wonderful until we run out of the other people's money.

For example: The George Soras influence at the national and community levels is tainting our justice system where there has to be consequences for committing crimes at the misdemeanor entry level to control the "soft on crime escalation and defund the police with cashless bail" insanity, at the felon level, through a return of selective "stop and frisk and profiling" of known criminals using analytical data in the police surveillance vehicles. Prosecutors must use the same data for applying cash bail bonds and/or incarceration for habitual felons or first timer misdemeanors. Hard on crime isn't standing down for riots forming as peaceful protest. Our most valuable first responders are the policeman and women risking their lives when crime isn't just gun controls it's finding and imprisoning the users of the guns against society, that's socialism at its best. While BLM, ATIFA, a gridlocked two-party system and social media use the constitution as toilet paper. And the two-party system has taken us down the worm hole of voter's rights when it comes to woke rewrites of our history books. Resulting in the impossible American dream and negative outcomes.

So, leadership and timing are everything and the time has come to balance the books and the power. With President Biden leading the progressives taking over building back Bigger government Big Brother will finally regulate the Great American Enterprise to its everlasting death. Unless the binary, uni-party "winner take all" system of government is turned upside down. The proposed how to make sure a third party is viable there are thirteen ways (articles) to make it happen and why it will work.

We need leaders who are problem solving in the public and private sectors not debating issues in a gridlocked and binary establishment Congress. The synthesis of capitalism and socialism is Humanism which makes this happen. This means changing our antiquated budgetary system of accounting to an accrual generally accepted accounting principles (GAAP) basis in order to report our true financial condition to keep up with China's warfare plans, that's doing the same thing.

The bottom line for Volume Two is how American enterprise wins the war on debt by draining the swamp, reducing crime and dealing with China's warfare tactics and other threats by focusing on taking back our supply lines, fix our public service and inner-city infrastructure based on current priorities, defend the flag, honor our police, protect our artifacts and the American Dream risk taking culture. That provides freedom and opportunity for all its citizens in a healthy, safe and financially secure environment. I call this humanism … the remedy for the other isms that create controversy and don't promote peaceful coexistence … as the problem solver by not using a bullet and a revolver.

Definition of Humanism … an outlook or system of thought attaching prime importance to human rather than divine or supernatural matters. Humanist beliefs stress the potential value and goodness of human beings, emphasize common human needs, and seek solely rational ways of solving human problems. It is based on the axiom from an ancient wisdom of mankind that tells us: "one righteous thought conquers one hundred evils", i.e., when a person's pursuit of the American Dream by the many to one flag, destroys pure dehumanizing communism saluting the Chinese flag.

Socialism as the introduction to communism and (in Marxist and Lenin's Communist Manifesto) a transformational dehumanizing social state (termed progressive) between the overthrow of capitalism and the realization of Communism. "Then the comrades can have a new totalitarian regime and a new maxim: "According to the seven commandments all comrades are created equal. But some comrades are more equal than others". George Orwell in Animal Farm.

Communism a political theory derived from Karl Marx and Vladimir Ilyich Ulyanov alias Vladimir Lenin, advocating class war and leading to a society in which all property is publicly owned and each person works and isn't paid according to their abilities and needs. Such as China, Russia, North Korea, Cuba, Venezuela and Viet Nam.

Monarchies: the political theory of blood line is supreme. Such as Britain, France, Japan, Scandinavia, South Africa, etc. are primarily derivative monarchies.

Tyrannies: The political theory that power is supreme. North Korea, Iran, Iraq, Afghanistan, African warlords, Fascism in Nazi Germany, Mussolini Italy, primarily socialist or Venezuelan nationalists.

Democracy: The political theory that free market enterprise is supreme. The great American Enterprise is objective pursuit of subjective values for its survival. The only rational and moral solution to totalitarianism, a monarchy or communism.

Capitalism is based on individual initiative and favors market mechanisms over government intervention, while socialism is based on government planning and limitations on private control of resources.

Enterprise in the USA is the only pure democracy since Rome and the American Enterprise Party marries a new version of capitalism and a new type of socialism (a public and private partnership) into an enterprising society of humanism protecting and sharing of the wealth based on effort, talent and intelligence. And producing better jobs, better wages, better lives and better government. Where tribes are converted into productive teams with goals to earn income from outcome. We all have been given life for free but love of life has to be earned and shared in good faith for a higher purpose.

So, wake up America, where woke followers are following the followers into the ghetto ... a political holocaust and crematory. Our concentration camps are our complacency in and apathy believing that Bigger is Better, equality is freedom, equity is prosperity, safety is more laws and regulations, security is Big Brother and the Brotherhood media, peace and equality is Big Government control. That's the problem in our inner cities, ghettos, small under privileged communities, schools, churches, politics, foreign affairs, voting scams, that are founded on a false positive called democracy funded by money-tics.

We are no longer free to voice our opinion when our friendly Face Book cancels our opinion on the internet because they are Big enough to fund a political party that will support their right to cancel us. In my books I warn of this happening in 2084 not 2022 and 2024. I guess we need to wake up now. It didn't happen in 1984 as predicted by George Orwell when Big Brother had a surveillance system of cameras and a system of finger pointing like Face Book or Instagram or Tic Toc or You tube to cancel certain dissidents and lovers of freedom. They then were victims of the system of brain drain and a swamp of woke haters.

Biden/Sanders Executive Orders Swamp the Swamp

Is America the land of laissez faire for profit?

Yes, where the Ayn Rand objective Monetary Capital marries the subjective Peter Drucker Human capital gestates into the great American Enterprise to create patriotic humanism ... as effective subjects manage themselves within the team objectives. Thus, management by objectives becomes the science of managing human behavior for the good of the American enterprise profits.

"Government is the best which governs the least ... because it's people who discipline themselves".. .. Thomas Jefferson.

BIG BROTHER BIDEN SWAMPS THE SWAMP: SOURCE BALLOTPEDIA (Cross reference to the documents)

As of June 9, 2021, President Joe Biden (D) had signed 54 executive orders, 21 presidential memoranda, 87 proclamations, and 15 notices. (The first step to socialism is total government control and appeasing our enemies. After the ideology of bigger government transitions to a gridlocked Congress, Supreme Court, and President these 545 elitists become the politburo transitioning America to Bernie Sander's version of Democrat Socialism.

The Sanders/Biden Manifesto is behind the scenes with a speechwriter guiding the President. Examples: shut down the Keystone Pipeline, open our borders, appease our enemies, control the voting system, the media and big business.

Each of these presidential transformational documents is different in authority and implementation. Executive orders are directives written by the president to officials within the executive branch requiring them to take or stop some action related to policy or management. They are numbered, published in the *Federal Register*, and cite the authority by which the president is making the order.[1][2]

Presidential memoranda also include instructions directed at executive officials, but they are neither numbered nor have the same publication requirements. The Office of Management and Budget is also not required to issue a budgetary impact statement on the subject of the memoranda.[3]

In his 2014 book, *By Order of the President: The Use and Abuse of Executive Direct Action*, Phillip J. Cooper, a professor of public administration at Portland State University, wrote, "As a practical matter, the memorandum is now being used as the equivalent of an executive order, but without meeting the legal requirements for an executive order."[4]

Proclamations are a third type of executive directive that typically relate to private individuals or ceremonial events, such as holidays and commemorations.[3][5]

See Exhibit A for specific orders, memoranda and proclamations.

- **Executive orders**
- **Presidential memoranda**
- **Proclamations and Notices**

PROCLAMATION AND DECLARATION OF DEPENDENCE BY BIG BROTHER AND THE BROTHERHOOD IN THE USA

"Most bad government has grown out of too much government" … Thomas Jefferson.

The progressive socialist Executive orders, Presidential memoranda and Proclamations are the edicts of a Marxist culture regime transforming America away from a Democracy to a binary two- party "winner take all "Politburo run by Big Brother, the Brotherhood and the swamp woke alligators (Pelosi, Schumer, Sanders, Warren and the Squad). They began swamping the swamp with open borders, implementing the Green New Deal that Biden says is America's biggest problem, reversing all of President Trump's capitalist policies and offering up $9 trillion in debt for bailing out the Pandemic when he claims credit for saved lives.

Without a Republican led counter America the Bountiful will be a socialist state similar to what Castro promised Cuba or Stalin Russia or Mao China or Kim Jong-un North Korea. The Biden/Sanders Manifesto using a woke rewrite of history is at work to promise equality and equity to identities not individual freedoms. Alexandria Ocasio Cortez known as AOC, with parents from Puerto Rico, is a former bartender, student and freshman Congresswoman representing the Bronx of Queens New York, and the squad have been one upped by this imperialist coup.

If you are left or right of center or conservative or liberal, how can we stand by and let Orwellian 1984 arrive with the 2020 elections, with these 173 culture changing dictates by a President that called himself a moderate, hid during a no-show campaign, then proffered them by a flagrant voting system of uncontrolled drop boxes, mail in votes and harvesting inner city voters. The estimated "swamp the swamp" cost of implementing these Biden-Sanders Manifesto Big Brother 173 policy money wasting edicts, by the Biden Administration are … Presidential executive orders, proclamations, memoranda and notices totaling an estimated $16.6 trillion over the next decade to bring American schools, businesses, churches, immigration, energy, foreign relations and aid, health care, justice by policing, security by military, NATO, WHO, WTO, World Banking, Federal Reserve and stock market under the control of the White House, Senate and House and 50 Brotherhood Governors.

America will be transformed into a one-party "winner take all" oligarch in a power grab pitted against China's autocracy ignoring human rights, constitution, historical culture and declaration of independence. As Aristotle's rule of one, a monarchy, rule of two aristocracy and rule of three polity degenerates into dysfunctional versions of tyranny, oligarchy and democracy with socialism then communism as the Trojan Horse promising equality and equity that becomes the monarchy's throne of the few and the confinement of the many.

"Our most pressing problem is climate change and white supremacy" … Joseph Robinhood Biden with 173 transformational executive orders and actions in his first 100 days of 2021, opening the borders and creating inflationary moves based on deficit spending with tax increases to pay for **Bigger not better** government. As of 1,000 days into the Biden administration: we have:
1. Open borders with 250,000 illegal immigrants crossing the border in one month and two million predicted for 2021 and 800,000 more, by the 2022 mid-terms where, with Biden's approval rating below 30%, the Republicans are favored to take back the Senate and House in a landslide.
2. Spending bills passed or proposed for $6.5 trillion for stimulus and infrastructure (earmarks and Green New Deal) and a $6 trillion operating budget. The Fed's printing press is in full production, reducing the value of the dollar and increasing demand and inflation.

3. A desertion of Afghanistan leaving thousands at the mercy of the Taliban, ISIS and al-Qaida Islamic Jihadists leaving an $800 million dollar embassy paid for by USA and $85 billion of military equipment and technology.
4. More and more taxes to support a Socialist one-party regime.
5. Government of a elite Few (Biden, Sanders, Pelosi, Schumer and the Squad) dictating behaviors for the Many using a state of fear triggered by the China virus and climate change.
6. Our energy program was put into a Green New Deal manic mode by closing the Keystone Pipeline and allowing Russia's pipeline to Germany be blessed by Biden's appeasing inaction. The worst inflationary decision in 40 years.
7. At the same time by appeasing President Biden, Russia and China are supporting Iran in restoring the nonproliferation agreement with the USA. To make things worse the for quid pro, the Ayatollah Ruhollah Khomeini is calling for removal of the sanctions that are the USA's only leverage.

8. As I'm finishing this book on why America is losing the trade war and leadership in the world for peace and prosperity for all. Russia's President Putin, testing an appeasing President Biden, invades the Ukraine eastern states Tuesday, February 22, 2022. While the Wizard of Oz Biden contemplates sanctions the tanks and missile launchers take over a portion of Ukraine, the former USSR holding. Without any resistance by Biden, Putin has continued his reconstruction of the former communist party's property holdings. Along with Georgia, Crimea and now Ukraine he is testing the NATO waters for his next takeover moves for consolidating the Balkans, into the new USSR.

Putin intentions are, reminiscent of British Prime Minister Neville Chamberlain signing the Munich Agreement, annexation of Sudetenland, as a peace treaty with Adolph Hitler and Benito Mussolini, fascist leader of Italy. Unbeknownst to Chamberland, that Hitler planned a Nazi invasion of Czechoslovakia, shortly thereafter. On their way to taking over Europe and making an air attack on London. England. Putin intentions and Biden's appeasing sanctions delivered too late to stop him, may produce the same affect ...

(If I were the NATO Secretary the voting members should take Ukraine into membership immediately. Then NATO, based on Article five, must defend them with NATO members, including American forces, against Russia. Then demand a no fly zone and cease fire or else. Then move your troops out of Ukraine. If he doesn't the entire UN security council and occupation by NATO, needs to come down on him).

The world must enforce peace with strength then diplomacy.

Why? BECAUSE THIS IS THE DOMINO THEORY ALL OVER AGAIN? If we ignore history, it will repeat itself. Reminiscent of Hitler, with the backing of Mussolini took Europe, the Balkans, Scandinavia, Africa, etc. and was only stopped by the Russian winters. As history also shows, if Ukraine is the first domino to fall, Russia won't stop there. Like Hitler, Putin will be emboldened to take back all of the past USSR territory. President Biden thought he had outflanked Putin, but even with SWIFT banking rights being withheld, increased sanctions for Putin personally, and funding of an arsenal of weapons, didn't deter his invasion on Kyiv, the capitol of Ukraine. But this attack on Kyiv is pressuring President Zelensky to consider peace talks with Putin in Belarus. Even with the backing of NATO members weapons support and Germany killing the Nord Stream 2 pipeline deal with Putin, he may be on his way to becoming the USSR supper power, with CCP China and Iran's backing to bring communism to the Continents of Europe, Asia and Africa.

The combined population of those continents is 7.0 billion people of which 1.3 billion live in deprivation, hunger, fear and poverty. The biggest reason for the advances of communism around the world, is the socialist promises of equal shares in the new prosperity ... that never arrives ... yet the masses are still controlled by the wealth of the Few leaders, called the Politburo. In other words, 1984 will arrive as USSR, CCP, Iran form. as Eur Asia, as predicted by George Orwell's book of that name. About his homeland Russia and Germany, and my book revisiting Orwell's 1984 Oceania, called 2084 Americania. Page Turner Press and Media 2022.

Wall Street Journal and NY Times postings.

Mr. Biden's dramatic political transformation has exposed what many have always suspected: Moderate Democrats aren't socialists unless they think they can adopt socialist policies and survive politically.

The Biden-Sanders "Unity" manifesto envisions the socialism of an all-encompassing welfare state, with virtually every need a right, and every right guaranteed by taxpayer funding. Housing becomes a right, and "no one should have to pay more than 30 percent of their income for housing." Public colleges will be "tuition-free" for "roughly 80 percent of the American people." Student loans are expunged, payments are capped and eventually forgiven. School lunches, along with breakfast and supper, will be universally free.

Here are key points from the Biden/Sanders Unity Manifesto:

- Health care: Expanding government-run plans, without 'Medicare for all,'
- Criminal justice: Broad agreement on many priorities, but not on marijuana,

- Climate change: New near-term targets, but no fracking ban,
- The economy: Closing racial gaps and creating jobs programs The American Enterprise Party Volume Two: American Enterprise Manifesto,
- Education: Rethinking Obama-era priorities,
- Immigration: A focus on undoing Trump policies.

The American Dream turned into a four-year nightmare using Biden/Sanders/Pelosi/Schumer) transformational policies and actions:

Is a Big Brother President Joseph Robinhood Biden the transformation to a progressive oligarch or a regressive failing America?

- Inflationary policies and executive orders.
- Debt ridden and deficit poor financial position.
- Declining dollar value causing inflationary economy and a stagnate foreign policy.
- A $600 trillion derivative bubble ready to explode (the stock market, economy, currency value and the Green New Deal).
- Declining approval ratings. (27% at last count)(12% for Congress).
- Bigger government is Better and conformity is required.
- Open borders letting two million illegal migrants into our communities in 2020 and 2121that will destroy American sovereignty by embedding cartel criminals, drug dealers and Jihad terrorists into our society.
- By leaving Afghanistan without proper preparation disserting 30,000 citizens and interpreters at risk and a $800 million dollar investment in the embassy in Kabul (looks bigger than

the White House), $85 billion in military equipment and technology as the result of this disastrous execution of a flawed foreign policy resulting in a rushed departure strategy.
- HR1 open voting and S1 endorsement of harvesting of votes.
- Higher taxes (a mileage tax on top of increases in the gas tax) to fund infrastructure, with earmarks for climate change, the Democrat welfare state and deficit spending.
- Closed freedom of speech through Big Tech and Post Office surveillance and denying usage. Twitter et tu Brute' shut down President Trump while allowing the Taliban free range propaganda rights.
- Closed fossil fuel Keystone pipeline while allowing the Russia to Germany pipeline to be completed.
- Closed fossil fuel exploration and land leases for fracking.
- Green New Deal promising zero emissions by 2035 or is it 2050?
- Per our leader and his cabinet, white supremacy, racism and climate change are America's biggest problems and national priorities.
- Anonymous complaints allowed on policing and civil penalties. Remake America into a banana republic.
- Police to no longer have immunity. Mass exodus from policing as we know it.
- Farmers of black, brown, American Indian, Asian, Pacific Islanders get loans balances forgiven (Injunction judged racist).
- Supporting CRT and 1619 Project subjects in public schools.
- Capitalizing on a crisis called the Pandemic of Covid-19 variants. Dr. Fauci still has free rein over American health care response to the Pandemics.

- Biden takes credit for solving the Pandemic and saving American lives with mandated masks and vaccine distribution on the horizon.
- Bottomline Cost of $1.9 trillion Pandemic stimulus, $1.2 bipartisan America Jobs Act invest in infrastructure bill, $2.3 American Green New Deal (GND) jobs plan $6.5 budget proposal… a trillion here and a trillion there turns out to be a sinking ship bigger than the Titanic … America Laissez--faire free market enterprise.
- Acquiescing on our responsibility to protect USA interests in Europe by mishandling of the Russian war crimes in Ukraine. The Biden Administration Should have insisted in April, as Russia was putting troops in Belarus, that NATO admit Ukraine to membership immediately. Then be prepared to join a military occupation to protect that Ukraine from Russia, that is inciting a World War III takeover of their former USSR holdings. As a result of leading from behind by putting acquiescing diplomacy in front of strength, Europe is reeling from the obvious takeover by Russia of sovereign nations. That's in violation of worldwide peaceful coexistence, that's penalized by expulsion from the UN and a proclamation of war on humanity that must be ceased for peace. That was wiped in one Putin threat of using weapons of mass destruction (chemical and nuclear). The world froze in fear that he would chance destroying his regime for a tactical error is preposterous. He is bluffing. The strength of USA, NATO, UN, EU are the deterrent to call his bluff by taking Ukraine into NATO and cut off his plan to reinvent the USSR. He has the most to lose if he uses any WOMD's. It happened in Syria when Trump

told Putin he has a bigger button and dropped a dirt bomb in his midst, stopping not only Putin but ISIS. Peace through strength is the only way to deal with a tyrant. Biden is a protégé of the Obama red line "lead from behind" strategy. Another worst of times tragedy caused by et tu Brute".

TAKE FROM THE RICH

I've never met a Robin Hood
Have you?
The story goes like this ...
Robin Hood stole from the rich
To give to the poor
Then the rich would kill the goose
So they could get more

Criminal minds at work
Take from their neighbors
Without a qualm or quirk
To feed a chemical habit as it occurs

White collar crime and deals
Have become the norm
Take from another before he steals
Your business and racing form

Politicians are known to cheat
By taking graft for a stash
Willing to deal then repeat
Preference and anything for cash

(Hunter Biden's stash to get smashed)

Businessmen have had their share
Since the beginning of time
Claiming it's just for a four square
When it's for their gain and dime

Preachers and teachers get it on
By getting the summer off to belong
Then going into business and con
Their way all winter long

Congress on the other hand
Taxes the small businesses
Then gives it as contraband
By entitlements for which they stand
Until Robin Hood turns in his grave
When the poor only get rich by the gamble
From the Lotto just to misbehave
Getting nothing from ideas and the scramble

As a result, our nation
Is no longer in the promise land game
Just a piece of land and a ration
Can get you 30 seconds of fame

Going viral in the passing lane
Give it away to get your way
And disabled parking for the lame
Takes from the poor who can't pay to play

Will there be a revolution
Looking for a solution
Or
Where will it all end
With human dignity being the last to defend

I for one and not for all
Think our government should take the fall
They created the ball game
For their own wealth and fame

So, evolution may not be enough
And a revolution hurts the poor
Then the solution is political stuff
Opposition parties to explore

Opening the rich man's door
And elect a brother from the Hood
Giving good jobs to the poor
A peaceful evolution doing as it should

Or Reelect a Joseph Robin Hood Biden
As the goose who is abidin'
And defends the golden egg ration
To save the nation

Where taxes and the Green New Deal are taking from the rich
Making everyone poor

My question of the Republicans is, where or where is the Republican party that allowed an effective president to be categorically impeached twice with no proof:

Accepted a mail in fruad of an election to put this incompetent administration and congress in charge of our future and all you can talk about is wait for the 2022 mid-terms and 2024 Presidency take over by the Republicans?

All I hear from you Republicans is the blame game without moving to put national gurard troops at the open borders to stop cartel drug dealers and embeded terrorists and not take back the Bagram airport in Kabul and evacuate our American citizens, Afghan supporters and interpreters.

How can Biden get away with blaming President Trump for a plan he should have followed. Who elected the Taliban to become the owner of Afghanistan anyway? Telling us what to do as they bring in their allies … al-Qaida and ISIS to conduct their worldwide jihad? Yeah, where is our two "winner take all" binary political party when we need them.

While America is transformed, in the first 800 days of the Biden Wizard of Oz administration into, a socialist oligarchy from a Trump monarchy, run by the gridlocked gang of 545 (100 Senators, 435 Congressmen, 9 Supreme Court Justices and 1 President). Orwellian in its intent and substance as Washington burns while Biden, Harris, Pelosi and Schumer fiddle with a transformational Marxist politburo government.

Now The Biden Administration is wanting a budget of $6.3 Billion for Afghan and Ukraine refugees on top of billions in the infrastructure bill for illegals streaming into our blue cities... But no money for restoring the squaller that exist in our inner cities. While proposing a $450,000 payment to illegals for Trump policies that separated families, who have broken the immigration laws and expecting Biden to appease them.

BECAUSE I CAN

The Lord's Prayer has 56 words
Lincoln's Gettysburg Address has 268 words
Bill of Rights has 652 words
The Declaration of Independence has 1,322 words
Constitution has 4,543 words
Bible has 73,137 words
Government regulations 1.1 million words

While faith has but two words
I can
or
I can't

In successful enterprise we are striving on these two words.

We are battling "I can't" negative problems with faith
Faith that a risk taken is an "I can" opportunity pursued
Inflation is quelled by ingenuity- economies of scale--
Productivity through better management
Recession is turned on opportunities

With conservation of resources and
Elimination of waste with investment in better management

Donald Trump did it with creative financing and negotiation
Bill Gates did it with the personal sale's touch
Steven Jobs did it with ingenious technology products
Warren Buffet did with investing in staples
Free Market Enterprise where risk makes the sunrise

Presidents generally aren't good businessmen
Good businessmen are usually good leaders
Are they good presidents? Rate them
On where they're going and where they've been
Good presidents in my opinion must be good salesmen
They are selling risky ideas and solutions to risky problems
Not compromising issues created by problem making lawmakers
Wedding our future to dependent risk averse takers

Reagan Kennedy Clinton Trump
Were salesmen of GDP with invention
Looking for problems to solve
With less government intervention

Johnson Carter Nixon Bush Obama Biden
Were attorney lawmakers making the problem
Looking for issues to table and defer solutions
By creating more laws and regulations
"Just to go along to get along"

We have to have an "I can" salesman
In the White House not an "I can't" as its spouse
To clean the House
And Senate
Of its money-tics
Drain the swamp
"To get along to go along"

> Reign in Big Brother government of money-tics
> And its Brotherhood who pay for play politics
>
> Read my lips it's a risk-taking Enterprise evolution
> Not a staid monolithic Institutional revolution
>
> Where the Stature of Liberty is blinded by Money-tics over democratic politics and money-talks over common cents,

This transformation will certainly give rise to the need for an effective "swing vote" third party based on those principles of the constitution of the USA, that sets out the way the majority have agreed to be governed applied to equality and equity earned by humanism to save the Great American Enterprise. Surprise there's no color line in free enterprise. Answering the question of "how can we all be better off if we are all the same". That's the American enterprise Party as documented in the three volumes on why, how and who will do it. Without it, America is doomed to lose to China in a trade and cold war followed by Russia and other communist countries. And to an illusionary climate crisis directed by fear, that is but a crisis of deniable truth:

TRUTH

Truth which needs justice
Is only a folly
Our courts do not decide
The truth
Truth which needs proof
Isn't true

Laws being the proof of
Rational man's need to conform
Justice is only an interpretation
Of a rational civil reform

Truth isn't the right from wrong
It's the fortune given by nature
It's the sensitivity of the soul
It's the peace of believing in freedom

It's God
It's belief
For only God is truth
Not the courts of justice
Not mortal proof

Who is right or wrong?
Is not truth
Until history tells us
With facts as proof

Like the judge of poetry is you
Not me in the confession booth
It's how it applies to your stew
That's truth

SCALES of JUSTICE

Weight is relative to the lift each plate

take or give

Of the one side is the Rule of Law

And on the other will be the Rule

of Rulers

Red then Blue

In the old days the fat lady
Was the queen in the tent
Her scales tipped for money
Now those scales aren't worth a cent

Who says lady justice is always just
Though blind folded and anointed
For the scales of the righteous
She should never be exploited
Tipped and tattered
Laws and morals scattered
To the far corners of what once mattered
She's banged and battered

Scales of snakes thus dampen
For their skins are bait
Truth can't just happen
Nor can it wait

For without this check to see it true
And for what has and should have been
Colors red could turn white lies to blue
The laws of nature must prevail again

Bash the Scales of Justice
For ignorance of both past and present
Though She has never crushed us
Against each other till we repent

And towards ourselves
Liars and
cheatersLine the
morgue's shelves
Society unrestrained
from wife beaters

And saddened when they go
For they never learn to tame
What most don't know
That truth and love are one and the same

For truth to yourself is where justice came
To balance the scales
And then it can be the claim
As one and all prevails

And for whom the scales toll
Though tipped it doesn't bust
Ensuring life's justice for all
For truth makes the Lady just

While the fat lady only sing for

us when the game bell rings

As Truth becomes Justice

In Volume Three of the American Enterprise Party Trilogy, I write about Humanism as the synthesis of capitalism and socialism and who will do it ... we must first restore worker patriotism and work ethic that has been destroyed by apathy and how to ... "Restore the American Work Ethic" ... "Where oh Where has it Gone." It focuses on improving our human output by revamping our input of monetary capital values that learns to share the wealth not just tax it. Work for the sake of patriotic pride and the quality of life not just for the sake of money and job security. But an enterprise that reinvests wealth in the Great American Enterprise for better leverage competitively in the worldwide marketplace.The American Enterprise Party Volume II: American Enterprise Manifesto

As for my work ethic I have owned small businesses for 37 years, that I have started from scratch, creating jobs, and envisioning better management systems and methods for principally health care facilities.

I have never been unemployed, never drew unemployment or worker's comp and have missed no time from my employment in 59 years. I have either been extremely lucky or an image of my father a Great common, every day, blue collar, enterprising American who worked in the Firestone Factory in Des Moines, Iowa for 32 years. And even today I remember accompanying my father to union meetings and being influenced as a factory worker myself when I was employed by Firestone one summer. Those images were and are the foundation of the work ethic we seem to have lost and the scenario I propose as the solution to the demise of the American work ethic victim of the new entitlements.

Because the infringement of Big Institutional Government (Big Brother) on individual creativity and freedom, for the sake of control by the Bigger Box stores, Bigger Technology, Bigger media and Bigger Universities and Bigger Unions (the Brotherhood) is economically called a "Monopsony". (Definition is the opposite of Monopoly ... Monopsony means market controlled by the buyer of last resort ... government and its service agencies). As a Monopsony, we are hampered by our own incompetence because of a lack of competition and quality as defined by humanism in a Laissez--Faire free market enterprise.

To alter this **"Rome is Burning"** mentality we have to have a balance of the Private Sector and Public Institutions using Laissez-Faire as our pendant or we will evolve into a world of continued declining initiative, poor health and more divorces of thought, marriages and families. Such as, Russia, North Korea, China, Viet Nam, Venezuela, Afghanistan, Iran, etc.

For example: The Social Security/Medicare Trust Funds have been drained of cash by the General Fund borrowing for funding wars and deficit spending. The trust funds don't have real money saved in it. It

What it is, when the Federal government has monetized trust fund money by giving them an IOU for paying lobbyist earnings, proxy wars, Ponzi schemes in regime change and developing more WOMD's for sale to the wolf warriors of the world. Also, Congress has monetized the security market and stock market by claiming that the economy is under control so long as it is stimulated by deficit spending and debt financing using The Feds Keynesians theory that interest is cost of capital that controls capital to stimulate the economy but kills the enterprise.

By governing illegally, the government fraudulently issued IOU's (Treasuries). Because $2.6 trillion has been borrowed from the Trust Funds. Social Security and Medicare are running cash deficits each year. Recipients can expect to see their benefits cut by as much as 23% by failing government taketh away tactics. Senior citizens faithfully paid into the Social Security system their entire working days based on the promise that their money would be there for them in their golden years. Do you believe Congress is obligated to fulfill their promise to senior citizens? If so, you need to vote for The American Enterprise Party as the swing vote for balancing the books and budget.

LAISSEZ-FAIRE

America the land of laissez-faire
defined

Abstention of government
Unrestraint of trade for profit
Free enterprise demand
Free trade supply
Free-market capitalism
Capitalists chasing profits
Humans chasing income
The profit motive

How can we be better off if we're all the same

What is the profit motive ... is it?
Economics American style or

Control by capitalists
Control by workers
Control by corporations
Control by unions
Control by government
Control by seller ... a monopoly

Control by the buyer ... a monopsony
Or free market control by supply and demand

Or is it?
Control by Congress
90% attorneys
Lawmakers
Regulators
Givers or Takers

Squeezing out the
Market makers
Business shakers
Sleazing in the
Criminal fakers
Immigrant slackers
Foreign hackers

The balance is in jeopardy
Being twisted by regulators
Being pounded by dissenters
Being grounded by speculators
Being questioned by Senators
Being challenged by legislators

Let's save the Great American Enterprise

Will it be the Blue party ... no
Will it be the Red party ... no
Will it be the independent party or the tea party ... no
Capitalism Socialism ism ism ... no
Who or what will it be????

Ask the 200 million enterprising workers
Who pay all the bills
46 different taxes and growing

Carrying 40% Government overhead from
Regulations heaped on small business costs

Or the Federal Reserve unfettered
Creating a debt driven economy
And a derivative bubble
Abating economical trouble

Minimum wage
Guaranteed annual income
Paid Leave
Free college
Free health care
Food stamps
Unemployment
Disability
Unfilled Job openings

All the new entitlements create
The demise of American patriotism
And work ethic
Of the risk-taking American Dream
With 8 million job openings
Due to the new income entitlements

With the real entitlements in jeopardy
Medicare and social security aren't to count
To be called so makes no sense it isn't free
It's our money in a personal savings account

To save the true entitlements
How about electing
Someone like a humble Donald Trump
And fifty governors who represent
The Great American Enterprise
And call it the American Enterprise Party

With a voting bloc of
200 million workers
77 million baby boomers
40 million independents
40 million AARP members

If you agree join today
The American Enterprise Party
A political party for Laissez-Faire
Where being the same isn't better
If I get my fair share

(Dedicated to the axiom "Lazy isn't Fair")

OPINION & PRIDE

If you can't see beyond
The end of your own opinion
Take my word for nothing
But look at my actions
Before you spout reactions
It may get more than your intentions

If you don't look beyond
The end of your own pride
Take my route if you doubt
But don't fake being on my side
It may take you on a long slide

If you aren't looking beyond
The end of your own need
Of course, it may be justified
But if you have not agreed
As the only one who has tried
Then didn't succeed

For the world is full of
The emotional breed
But no world will buy
Selfish intentions forever
Though they're sold by the day
And taken by night
Creates neurosis and fright

Such foibles transacted leave in divorce
So don't hide your eyes and sever
The end of your own opinion and pride
As the reward for being too clever
For even your survival instincts may have lied

Hearsay being founded on opinion
And pride being based on foul play
Leaving the rest of the onion
With passion and emotions
Pealing and repealing your devotions
Down to the core
Of what we are forever more

Then defending your opinion and pride
Caused by you is all this upheaval
When you called a spade a spade,
A goddamn shovel
That Trumped a Trump

Our 46th President Joseph Robinhood Biden
Possibly the worst President of all time

NO OTHER SALVATION

I have no other salvation
Then my own thoughts
When I think of God
I think of family and our nation

It's with this realization
That I prepare each day
With mental thoughts I pray
To sustain God's creation

The creation of jubilation
Through a state of mind
Which won't know doubt
By believing in positive elation

By those who shed guilt
Quell lies
Expose untruth
Expound on our youth
Reward faith and
Dispel thoughts
Of never believing
Of negative feelings
Of never conceiving
Such utterances
But achieving
Respect for our acts
Belief in the facts
Relief from immoral attacks

The savior of what my life lacks

(So, take my opinions as salt in the wounds
of tyranny with humanity's facts as its salvation)
Jerry Rhoads, author, founder and CEO of AEP

The Fall of the Great American Empire ... the tipping point, of dominos that fall, to reach the breaking point and burst the giant $600 trillion international derivative bubble.

The dominos that will fall to reach the breaking point of a uni-party government:

#1 the Biden administration of the Wizard of Oz leadership ignoring the debt ceiling resulting in spending deficits of $10 trillion to fund the Green New Deal, economic stimulus termed the infrastructure jobs bill to be funded by tax increases and treasury's printing press. All of this tied to the administration commitment to the Green New Deal to be emissions free by a date certain, destroying the USA's ability to economically compete with a world that doesn't comply with the Paris Accord requirements. Especially China, India, Mexico, Russia, Mid-East and Britain. The GND is dead on arrival with its 2050 deadline.

#2 the national debt if $158,000 billion 158,000,000,000,000,000 trillion using (GAAP) generally accepted accounting principles increasing at the rate of $300 billion per day. See the debt clock www.usdebtclock.org for true financial condition of America.

#3 the 2021 Federal and State deficit spending $15,000,000,000,000,000 trillion using cash basis budgeting and accounting.

#4 the stock and bond markets (stock 40,000 DOW, Treasuries $34,000 000,000,000,000 trillion in Federal debt).

#5 the Federal Reserve Banking System cash reserves $5 billion excluding member banks reaching insolvency to cover interest payments.

#6 the impact energy and supply line inflation have on the economy ... 1% means it takes $1.01 to buy a dollar' worth of goods, 100% means it costs $2 dollars, etc.

#7 the value of the dollar impact on the cost of goods sold ... a decrease in the value of a dollar means a dollar is now worth 50 cents ... this means it takes $4 to purchase a dollar's worth of goods. The exponential impact drives prices up and demand down. This means America's GNP costs 10% more to produce market ready products and demand drops 10% leaving a GDP stagnation of $4 trillion dollars or a drop to $17 trillion.

#8 the competition by China's control of costs and pricing of the supply lines. This enables China to dictate the cost, pricing and quality. This drives 15% of America's GDP down $3 trillion dollars per year since our inflation of market ready products costs depend on China's prices and container shipping costs for delivery and distribution rising to $30,000 per container from $3,000 pre-Pandemic. And delayed delivery to American shelves due to a lack of trucks and drivers who seem to want to stay home rather than keeping America in business.

#9 the competition by Russia, Saudi Arabia, Iran and Germany for the cost of energy supplies for driving the American grid, limited manufacturing and distribution services. This drives the cost of energy up with the negative impact on American GDP of $1 trillion per year while increasing the imbalance of trade and the debt that now exceeds the total annual GDP by 30%.

#10 The Biden Administration has mismanaged the processing of the supply chain imports because of the Pandemic by issuing stimulus, rent subsidies and child welfare checks mandating that workers stay home until they are vaccinated. This unanticipated consequence has a far-reaching impact on unemployment and new job forecasts that are affecting the American GDP, that depends on having the shelves and online ordering businesses fully stocked to have an adequate inventory supply for the holidays and everyday shopping demand. If not, stagnation follows with inflation of cost and prices close behind. At this point, stagnation sets in and the American GDP is no longer $21 trillion per year but $14 trillion compared to China's $17 trillion GDP (a 15% increase) and Russian $700 billion GDP (a 15% increase in GDP) based on American inflation, stagnation and deflation decreases in demand, productivity and inflates the cost of goods sold.

The breaking point is estimated to occur by 2024 when the stock market also declines 25% to 20,000 DOW, the Fed discount rate to member banks is increased from 2.5% to 5.0% increasing prime interest rate cost of capital to 10% and American inflation continues to spiral out of control to 25% resulting in small business failures and big business mergers. The $600 trillion derivative bubble bursts at that time creating worldwide panic as the dollar is replaced by the Chinese Yuan and Japanese Yen with the South Asian Sea consortium moving to control the world market for microchips, electric automobiles, lithium batteries, pharmaceuticals, production of copper, manganese and rare earth, Covid-19 variant's vaccine production, pharmaceuticals and PPE. At the same time moving to take over control of the World Health Organization, the World Trade Organization, the World Bank and the UN.

The only way to stop this crash of momentous proportions is to break the current Uni-party political gridlock by electing swing vote positions in the Senate of shards and House of cards and a President who understands worldwide enterprise, humanism and peaceful coexistence for establishing a government of the people, by the people for the people. This will win the battle over woke values and Marxist ideologies that are taking over our institutions. Then marry monetary capital and human capital into a third party. The American Enterprise Party.

The Marriage Vows
(In Contemplation of Change)

With these vows, we do officially, thee wed the American capitalist owners with American socialist workers. Owners who share the wealth and workers who "learn to earn for a skill to bill", ethically and patriotically their work for the collective good of the free market enterprise. I call this Americanism. Then our individual freedoms are based on our constitutional civil right to work. To deliver produce in time and on time, for our share of the profits or losses from our chosen American enterprise. A God given reward, to each enterprising American owner and worker, in relation to the competitive risks they willingly take and the quality of the products they make. For it takes an ethical, competitive and patriotic country, to succeed. Thereby, vowing to "Keep America Great", by pledging our collective wealth and enterprising work for practicing humanism. A better union of monetary capital with human capital in our competitive American enterprises with prosperity for all those, who honor our constitution, heritage and American Dream.

To further the American Enterprise Party mission, is to be the swing vote pulling the extremes toward the middle ground. A political party that vows to work for bipartisan agreement on policies to preserve the Great American Enterprise with fiscal and physical strength for winning the global trade war. With peaceful coexistence in our internal politics and around the world. The best of times winning over the worst of times. The tale of three parties forming bipartisan policies in the middle ground of, "building a bridge over troubled waters" ... then winning the global trade war over the new world order being contrived by China, Russia and Iran. China has alliances with India, Africa, Brazil, Argentenia, Cuba, Mexico, Candia, OPEC countries, Central America drug cartels, building their ports of call with robotic cranes, with spy cameras attached for gathering data on military development of weapons for mass destruction to hold China accountable for unfair labor tactics and having a shipping and distribution Monopoly that controls global trade worldwide. Check out my podcast where I tell you how it was done behind the scenes and without restraint from the UN. And now want to have land leases under the oceans using subs to drill for fossil fuels. While they and Russia are co-secretaries of the Security Council. While being the biggest violators of sovereignty of third world countries and champions of the World Health Organization, assuring the Paris Accord they will move toward compliance, as they drill for fossil fuels and rare earth and precious metals in Africa and South America. Jerry Rhoads, Founder and CEO, .Podcaster and producer of You Tube videos regarding the China Mart strategy of marketing.

Imagine

Let's imagine a sharing humanitarian world envisioned by liberal John Lennon in his 1971 song:

Imagine there's no heaven
It's easy if you try
No hell below us
Above us, only sky

Imagine all the people
Livin' for today
Ah

Imagine there's no countries
It isn't hard to do
Nothing to kill or die for
And no religion, too

Imagine all the people
Livin' life in peace
You

You may say I'm a dreamer
But I'm not the only one
I hope someday you'll join us
And the world will be as one

Imagine no possessions
I wonder if you can
No need for greed or hunger
A brotherhood of man

Imagine all the people
Sharing all the world
You

You may say I'm a dreamer
But I'm not the only one
I hope someday you'll join us
and the world will live as one

While Carl Marx sings the
melody and Lenin plays the harp

Yes, I can imagine a bountiful America Leading the World to Humanism with Peaceful coexistence following the Ten Tenets of American Laissez-Faire market enterprise:

Therefore, as a voter ask yourself, who would you pick a "better Red than dead pragmatic Republican" or a "Blue blood bleeding-heart phlegmatic Democrat" … or an "enterprising market driven American Enterprise Party Humanitarian" that wants every American citizen to be successful and healthy in pursuing their own American Utopian Dream of Humanism with peaceful coexistence.

BORN TO CHOOSE
The declaration that we are all born equal
Needs an amendment saying born to choose to be equal

Winners are born not made
Losers are made not born
What this says
And it says it well

Is that everyone's born a winner
Until they learn to be a loser
So, they're born with the potential
And everything essential

For being a winner
But along the way
During some stormy day
They learn to lose

Left to fate to choose to be sinners
Losers are made not born
From the soul of winners
To whit we mourn

They had their chances you say
If they're losers
They must want it that way
To whit we are all choosers

We winners cannot condone
With their failures at play
With their lack of guts and backbone
Or just doing it their way

Or we too shall be in the red zone
Winners are born to not lose
Left with the epitaph of theirs alone
Since you're what you choose

Starting with ingredients
Much like wines and marmalades
Add the good sense
And age it for a few decades

For aging will add a tasteful finish
And the sweet caress of the winner
But hanging on the vine will diminish
And let those losers be the sinner

And if they care to wilt thou explosion
Either in their mind by circumstance
The vine they have chosen
Or the lack of romance

Because if they care to become wine

Then let them seek the incline
To be divine
Above all including being the vine

But is this too cruel
Of our great American opportunity
Is this the curtailment of the fuel
Given to us by the redeemer of infidelity

Maybe if we would pry open the loser's eyes
Not for each to his own and his own to be
Making those decisions for being wise
May be better than misunderstood reality

Help him realize
Here under God's sun
That winning a prize
Is available to anyone

For to us he gave the power
To become a blooming rose
And not a wilted flower
In a dejected pose

So maybe you preachers should preach
And maybe the books can tell
So, you teachers can teach
That all is not well

Pick yourself up as beginners
So, losers can stay out of hell
Not just listen for the winners'
First round bell

Wipe yourself off
And if somebody calls you a replete
Scoff
While standing on your own feet

For the mind of the Almighty Design
Is winners are born not made
And losers are made not born or benign
And choosers make up their own lemonade

Hopefully not waiting too long
With pretentions
Losing may be just missing the gong
With purgatory only full of good intentions

Of those born to choose not lose

AN AMERICAN DREAM

Is it a façade or a fact?

Dreams are not idled by wrath
Nor are they the pastime of the narrow path
For to dream
Is the start of a higher esteem

The pursuit of life liberty and happiness
As the freedom we bless
Or the bondage we've broke
Ignored by those who pantomime a joke

But taken to heart in romance
Which is made by a dream
Rather than chance
Instead of listening to my inhibitions
That color my creations

With dreams of greatness
That warrants the same stress
For being ordinary is just as hard as being best
When you consider the pressure
Of just thriving on pleasure

Each time seeking a bigger thrill
Creates a habit for another synthetic pill
So to make a dream come true
Is to dedicate fantasize to radiate

And the expression
"He who dreams of higher things
shall be the leader of human beings"
Is to eradicate
That the human drive
Is a skill not a trait

But only to those dreamers
Who are making use of their visionary fate
Praise be to them for they are the state
Of a successful seed and flower
Which grows into intellectual power

Beyond what the mortal
Gene may seem
And belief will redeem
Called a success worthy scheme

Having personal goals
Praising God
Wanting better souls
Living on a stable sod

Called our Mother Earth
Mating Father time
Creating our birth
Of opportunity, luck is mine

Pursing the American Dream of self-worth
Where all humans have been given life for free but love of life
Has to be earned and shared in good faith for a higher purpose.
Jerry L. Rhoads, founder and CEO of the American enterprise Party

Article One

USA's War on Constitution, Debt, Crime and China's Cold Warfare

(Wake up, America—Save USA Constitutional Government from Uni-Party Gridlock, Debt, Crime and China's Cold Warfare)

With newly elected President Biden, the Delaware Wizard of Oz, saying climate change, and xenophobia are America's biggest problems, when Washington (aka Rome) is burning, and China is the incinerator with tyranny as the smoke stack. Now there is another answer when the borders are purged, and our foreign policy is dumped into the laps of our enemies. It's acquiescing to "Wolf Warrior China" in Alaska, as a peace gesture by our Secretary of State Tony the Statue of Liberty blind man, Blinken, made out to be a savior of American democracy.

Is the CCP, Inc. (Chinese Communist Party) currently residing in America as a Trojan Horse? For example, China's Fox Hunt program, an operation launched by CCP to repatriate Chinese fugitives (there are hundreds of Chinese on USA soil who are on CCP'S Fox Hunt list). Most are Green Card holders, naturalized US citizens, or folks with important Rights under the protection of USA laws, now allowed to profit by spying on American companies and stealing trade secrets. How about the imbalance of trade with China of $40 to $60 billion per month and $400 to $700 billion per year? How about the $1.3 trillion we owe China for this imbalance? How about China's capitalizing on economies of scale for low labor and overhead costs dictating the supply lines for major American companies and our consumption driven free market enterprise? How about technology theft from embedded students in major universities and tech companies? How about 100 million Americans using Chinese video games 12 hours per day and 80 million using Tik Tok videos as a surveillance robotic source? How about the influence on American habits China has by using brain drain hacking the algorhythms of data provided by Google, Facebook, Instagram for psychological warfare? How about China's ownership of 400,000 acres in Texas and other locations for constructing wind farms and buying out failing small businesses?

How about Chinese campaign funding of American politicians? How about the $40 billion contributed to American colleges and universities and infiltrating education with Confucius Institutes in the US? How about Chinese students first in STEM courses in their government-controlled education and the USA is 38th in Math out of 71 countries and 24th in science while the most expensive for less advancements in academic achievement? How about China's 77,000 PhD's produced per year compared to USA's 40,000? How about the 7.47 million immigration applications and 712 thousand green card applications with 20% being from Asia, submitted in 2020 with 56% approved? How about 90% of PPE, personal protective equipment, being produced in China to deal with the China Covid-19 virus released from the Chinese Wuhan lab?

Is this a conspiracy theory or facts that has "Washington Burning" Roman Style with the collapse of the American political system using a socialist manifesto devised by President Biden and his team of Harris, Pelosi, Schumer, Sanders, Warren and the AOC squad for fulfilling the Marxist philosophy of President Obama and his father?

Yes China, a monopsony (one buyer market), is taking away America's sovereignty in multiple ways under its "Wolf Warrior" campaign to destroy USA democracy and command the worldwide economic, health care, banking and military technology by controlling the mineral components (copper, rare earth, manganese) for the digital and cyber production of semiconductor chips by Taiwan and the USA. This will provide China a monopoly on chip components for electric autos, cell phones, military technology, space travel, satellites and robotics. In my Trilogy, The American Enterprise Party, the swing vote, I propose how we can win the ongoing Cold trade and technology War using the swing vote in Congress to focus on how to dismantle the China Trojan Horse.

The current problematic situation is being exposed by the new administration's policies for open borders (2 million illegals let in during a disastrous exit of Afghanistan and opening the southern and northern borders), stopping energy production by closing down the Keystone Pipeline, proposing $3.6 to 6.2 trillion dollars of deficit spending that requires thousands of billions of borrowings from China and taxation of every American. This transformation, using the power of privilege and influence peddling, certainly a conflict of interest President Biden family, turns America into a

subsidiary of the CCP, Inc., a cold war clone of Chinese communism. A true conspiracy of how Trojan Horses' work in foreign affairs.

There is no other answer to defeating the Chinese Trojan Horse, that is embedded in our supply lines and institutions, when the borders are purged, and our foreign policy is dumped into the laps of our enemies but to form a third-party resistance to progressive politics and regressive policies. That immediately and recklessly reversed the border and energy advances made by the Trump Administration. To that end the American Enterprise Party, represents enterprising Americans, where the Capitalists individually need to share and the Socialists collectively need to learn to work ethically and patriotically to ward off the China Trojan Horse.

Problem: America's constitutional Democracy is failing due to the challenge by left wing Marxists to seven basic Democracy principles.

1) Fiscal accountability for deficit spending, incurring excessive debt, stabilizing the currency and avoid inflationary legislation.
2) Leadership by patriots and marketers of the constitutional form of government based on humanism using peace as our strength of purpose not "woke" inflammatory isms.

3) Freedom of speech, protection of our citizens and borders through peace is strength and secure is humanitarian peaceful coexistence.
4) Free market Enterprise through participation and sharing of profitability and wealth based on effort, patriotism and ethics.
5) Education for pursuing the American Dream risk taking peacefully.
6) Values and lifestyle of health, happiness and prosperity for all.
7) Honoring our history and its heroes in spite of past failures.

Symptoms of Our Problems (they aren't just issues): Reaction to Fear, Conformity and Anarchy:

1) Weak leadership when it comes to disarming woke reverse racists, Marxists and anarchists, further demonstrated by the inability to respond to an international crisis in the Afghanistan withdrawal and the onslaught on our borders,
2) Crime in the cities and neighborhoods organized by gangs of domestic terrorism and foreign embedded mass destruction with fear, guns and drugs. Criminals using illegal guns is the problem not gun ownership.
3) Pandemic using fear inducing conformity as a tactic to control society and dictate American's risk-taking behavior. Socialists find that the American risk-taking culture is a deterrent for implementing the Green New deal termed FZD forward zero emissions and traffic deaths ... it uses this propaganda to change our culture not our weather.
4) Cyber hacking by our enemies attacking our financial institutions, essential businesses, livelihoods and schools using fear, extortion and bribing to steal our trade secrets that create our prosperity and their GDP.
5) Open borders unprotected, laws broken, and criminal aliens embedded in our communities and institutions by cartels and communist countries to spread terror and profit from illicit drugs and human trafficking.

6) Big media and technology infusing money-tics for dumping Trump in favor of a Biden mail in voting scam, brain washing and using propaganda tactics to create fear inducing conformity to control lifestyles, habits and voting results.
7) Money-tics used to blind the voters so they elect an identity not transparent politics with term limits where anyone can run for office and win.
8) Ignorance of fiscal accountability and the economic derivative bubble that looms over our financial and economic system where $6.2 trillion is passed for infrastructure and another $6 trillion for an annual budget that is financed by 100-year treasury notes … encumbering America for the rest of the century to insane values of our stock market, currency printing by the Federal Reserve and deficit spending loans by our enemies.
9) Tainted public education values with woke philosophies promoting reverse racism and anti-genderism as white imperialist American values.
10) An unsustainable fiscal condition using antiquated accounting and budgeting principles …. "A 1,000 billion here, a 1,000 billion there, and pretty soon you're talking real money." Senator Everett Dirksen's quote converted to 2021 trillion dollars not billions.

Solutions: Honor the constitution and democracy.

1) Leadership supporting the seven principles of our great country, by enforcing our laws, our international commitments, and following the principle that peace is strength, not running away from our enemies.
2) Voting security using legislated rules requiring voter identification, limited absentee mail-in and drop box voting and secure data tabulating systems and deadlines for reporting the results.
3) Qualified candidates for leader of the Great American Enterprise. Fewer attorneys and more small business representatives.
4) Fair representation using term limits and self-funded elections.
5) Elimination of Super PAC's and corporate intervention in elections.

6) Practice humanism and peaceful coexistence in domestic and foreign policies with regards to race and border protection.
7) Measure performance of the American Enterprise using GAAP accounting and budgetary reporting.
8) Privatizing public education and health care using Charter schools and mutual health insurance savings accounts.
9) Stop monetizing the growth of government by printing currency as it perversely enhances the wealthy with more being distributed to them through investments in the stock market and real estate that doesn't trickle down to small investors and small businesses.
10) Convert all government agencies to generally accepted accounting and budgeting principles. Enforce budgets as a percent of GDP not massive wish lists and eliminate ear marks used by a two party commitment to insolvency due to deficits and debt.

Bottom line: Five Principles of National security and profitability.

1) National guard and professional policing using problem management and reinforcement to close down criminal activities including escalation of protest into lawless riots and combating open borders.
2) Benevolence of capital and society in forming each enterprise in America to represent people working together to earn a profit and individually share in the rewards of the free market enterprise. Making education and health care a privilege earned not free, but affordable and accountable for results. So, our domestic strength is our culture of risk taking and risk capital invested in patriotic and ethical work force called enterprising Americans.
3) Our sovereign nation is protected from illicit immigration, crime in the inner cities, trade imbalances, government-imposed recessions and depressions. Our fiscal condition must be put in balance with our GDP and through accountable policies and procedures at all levels of government using GAAP budgeting and accounting principles with deficit and debt limits.

4) Reduction of fear inducing conformity, violence, vulgarity and inequality of personal wealth by sharing the spoils of America's success in the worldwide marketplace with all of the people who contribute to its success. Surprise there's no color line in free enterprise.

5) Bring the values of the shining, cleared eyed Statue of Liberty to other countries for freedom to share in the rewards of enterprise, in peaceful coexistence and cleanse our earth of humanity's bad influences and actors. Vote for the third-party candidate …

The American Enterprise Party.
www.americanenterprisepoliticalparty.org

Overcome Fear Mongers pushing conformity with Peace Makers who solve problems not compromising our strength of peaceful coexistence.

- Trade fear Mongers (such are the Adolph Hitler, Joseph Stalin, Marx, Mao Zedong , Kim Jong- I,II, un, Fidel Castro, Osama Ben Ladin, Benito Mussolini, Hideki Tajo) the puppeteers of power , for

- The proponents of humanism and peaceful coexistence. With reason minus religion equals resolution or more recently reason minus race equals peaceful resolution, with

- Peace Makers and Pacifists, (Albert Einstein, John Lennon, Mahatma Gandhi's, Martin Luther King, Helen Keller, Aldous Huxley, George Orwell, Henry Kissinger, The American Enterprise Party, Jesus Christ and God him or herself) to lead the world away from tyranny such as …

CHINA'S GLOBAL "WOLF WARRIOR" COLD WARFARE – WILL USA KEEP FIRST PLACE?

China, with the CCP, as a one-party totalitarian enterprise, while America is a gridlocked one-party oligarch arguing away its sovereignty and free market enterprise dignity, to its own destruction. Long Range Plans of CCP (Chinese Communist Party) for globalization supremacy over USA: and in the process destruction of the American democracy:

1) China's *"Wolf Warrior" Cold War"*, is to destroy American democracy and replace it with communism as the New World Order. "Wolf Cubs" are nurtured as a term of the CCP for those indoctrinated to hate and kill class enemies. Much like the Nazi Gestapo or SS officers. To do so, they are also investing billions of dollars in countries worldwide through its massive **Belt and Roads initiative** (similar to USA's foreign aid program) to take a more active role in international institutions. Solution: Close down the use of the internet for propaganda, supply lines for food supplies and stock markets.

2) *"Internet Warfare"* using their own internet, combining 5-G, AI, Cryptocurrency, Block Chain Exchange, Data Capture for Propaganda and Mind Control. Close down the use of the USA international internet.

3) *"Supply Bloc Chain Warfare"* by control of the semiconductor production by taking over Taiwan and lithium battery mining of cobalt, manganese and rare earth in Africa. China produces two thirds of the components for electric automobiles, solar panels and eighty percent of pharmaceuticals utilized by the USA. Solution: take back supply line manufacture of pharmaceuticals, hard and soft goods production and setup USA chip manufacturing with a partnership with Taiwan.

4) *"Technology Warfare"*, China has 6 million electric autos with battery lives of 5 to 8 years that equals 8 hundred thousand pounds of scrap batteries that, when disposed of, has a significant threat to the environment. CCP's anti-satellite weapons and space force have the

ability to attack USA's space infrastructure with rockets, astronauts, space vehicles, ready for the "cold" space warfare. They expect to land humans on the Moon and Mars before America does. Of course, most of their technology was stolen from the USA.

5) *"Wolf Warrior diplomacy"*, **China** using Cyber Warfare, Military Development (stealth, cruise missiles, nuclear energy), Biotechnology for Health Care and ransomware for hacking and artificial intelligence for satellite and space exploration to the moon and Mars. Estimated China hacking has transferred $350 billion of USA wealth to China's theft of trade secrets and product development of technology. The greatest transfer of wealth in history. Solution: Close down the use of the USA international internet.

6) *"Mobilization Warfare"*, Nationalism, Massive Recruitment of foreign talent. China has the largest military in the world with 2.1 million, USA third with 1.4, India second with 1.45, North Korea fourth with 1.3, Russia 1.0 million. Solution: Upgrade American Naval operations in the China Sea. Relocate Mid East troops to the Philippines, Japan, Twain and Hong Kong.

7) *"Financial Warfare"*, the yuan to become the Fiat currency (Bitcoins, Block Chain, Digital Yuan the World Reference Currency) and implement GAAP for taking over the World Order of trade and commerce. The retirement savings of millions of Americans (principally union pension funds and mutual bond market funds) currently finance Beijing's military modernization and Chinese supply chain companies that are complicit in genocide and other crimes against humanity. Solutions: Suspend all Chinese financial institutions from the US dollar network. Immediate delist every Chinese company from the New York Stock Exchange and other exchanges. Revoke the green cards and visas and place liens on the properties and bank accounts of the top 500 CCP members relatives in the USA... Grant Newsham, Epoch Times.

8) *"Propaganda Warfare"*, Social Media Control, Brain Washing, Hacking for Technology, Influence America's Social Revolution. Solution: Close down the use of the USA international internet, Facebook, Instagram, etc.

9) *"Internal Warfare"*, by the Politburo and its People's Liberation Front violations of civil rights of its members and killing of the Uighur, Turkish speaking people of interior Asia and Northern China. They also are dealing with the 350 million believers in the Tiananmen square protests central government control who have opted out of the CCP for (#*Falun Gong)* religious reasons. It's their plan to divide and conquer the CCP:

#Li Hongzhi, Chinese founder of Falun Gong writes "Pacify the External by Cultivating the Internal. If the population values self-cultivation and the nurturing of virtues, and if both officials and civilians alike exercise self-restraint in their minds, the whole nation will be stable and supported by the people. Being solid and stable, the nation will naturally intimidate foreign enemies and peace will thus reign under heaven". Li Hongzhi a sage and leader of the Falun Gong movement of 350 million Chinese who have opted out of Chinese Communist Party. Quoted from the Epoch Times, June 2021.

Solution: Clearly this is a divide and conquer approach to conquering communism that I call humanism…so we must support their efforts for human rights. Jerry Rhoads, author.

10) *"Aging Population Warfare"*, retirees will make up 40% of China's population by 2050 counteracted with the change to a three-baby limit from the two-baby limit imposed twenty years ago. While medical insurance covers more than 90% of the population, coverage is often limited to the social security program. Solution: continue to move USA's health care program to self-health and improve average life expectancy in the world ratings.

11) *"Harvesting Human Organs Warfare"*, China has admitted to harvesting human organs, for transplant, from death row prisoners and Falun Gong to provide inventory for their emergency 'human transplant" business. Reminiscent of Huxley's Brave New World, China, for "globalization to live, human agency must die for the good of the motherland". Solution: advocate against the dehumanizing use of human harvesting of organs.

12) *"Globalization of currency Warfare"*, China's goal is to replace the dollar as the reference currency worldwide being threatened by the International Monetary Fund issuing lines of credit to the world as SPR's (special drawing rights) working with China and its yuan, to float one Trillion dollars, in two trounces, for borrowing by emerging Asian and African countries.

Solution: Immediate delist every Chinese company from the New York Stock Exchange and other exchanges. The current ruling class gridlocked Congress in America is allowing China as a Trojan Horse to embed its dystopian strategy for globalization of controlling the press, the media, the wealth, the supply chain, the foreign affairs and trade with Southeast and the Western Hemisphere. All consistent with Orwellian predictions.

13) *"Drug Distribution Warfare"*, China, the one country putting highly addictive and unpredictable illicit drugs into the American bloodstream killing tens of thousands a year. The drug is Fentanyl that mostly originates in China, often moving via Mexico drug gangs into the USA, China provides money laundering to cover-up its involvement in the production of massive earnings to American gangs. This is resulting in 93,000 deaths in the USA primarily from Fentanyl.

Close our borders and supply lines for illicit drugs and drug dealers immediately and file a complaint with the United Nations.

14))"Internal Warfare", by the Politburo and its People's Liberation Front violations of civil rights of its members and killing of the Uighur, Turkish speaking people of interior Asia and Northern China. They also are dealing with the 350 million believers in the Tiananmen square protests central government control who have opted out of the CCP for (#**Falun Gong**) religious reasons. It's their plan to divide and conquer the CCP. *Solution: Clearly this is a divide and*

conquer approach to conquering communism that I call humanism… so we must support their efforts for human rights. Jerry Rhoads, author.

15) "Supply Line Warfare", 90% of the world's global trade is shipped by sea, with 70% in containers. The USA has outsourced $48 billion imports per month from China. And another $30 billion from South Korea, Japan and Viet Nam. With the supply line container ships sitting in our 20 ports averaging 10 to 80 ships or over 300 waiting to be unloaded with China having 37,311TEU's (4 containers) daily totaling 160 thousand containers on 148 Chinese vessels holding 610,000 TEU's. Being shipped to over 100 countries or 2.4 million containers waiting to be unloaded, carrying 4 per truck transported by 2 million USA semi-trailer truck drivers (68% of all freight is transported by semi's). Or by 1,000 USA trains (25% of containers) 200 per train, this creates opportunity costs of $8 to 10 trillion of GDP worldwide, installed delivery.

This is, 2.4 million containers per year loaded and unloaded by 400,000 workers with 1million sky lifts and forklifts, delivered by 2 million truckers, 167,000 rail workers, by 400,000 Fed Ex employees, 434,000 UPS employees, USPS 669,000 employees.

And stocked and shipped by 950,000 Amazon employees, 2.5 million Walmart employees, 254,000 Costco employees, 210,500 Walgreen employees stocking retail shelves. More than 6.5 million American enterprise workers making the supply chain function daily with 8 million job openings in all facets of supporting the supply chain businesses.

Solution: This is the very reason we need a change in direction away from silver lining two party politics that perpetuate polarized take down of the American Enterprise system. Both parties are lost when it comes to common sense business decisions. We now have leadership that doesn't have a clue about supply chain management. They both display some level of ignorance about shortages of inventory that will amount to a recession or even worse a disastrous depression if there is a run on the banks and stock market. If this happens America is sliding into chaos politically with the unprepared and unqualified current Administration proposing even more deficit spending with $5.2 trillion in additional debt financing over the next three to ten years.

Now the question is, can the Biden Wizard of Oz administration and Hunter Biden, who's middle name is corruption selling privilege and influence peddling, distance themselves from their past financial dealings with the Chinese government? If not, then the problem is not an issue … it's not fair business practices when our leaders have a conflict of interest by being the benefactors of China's success. It's also treason for our leaders and family members to use insider dealing to enrich themselves, that threatens our national sovereignty.

Just a conspiracy theory: If you were China, how could you convert democracies, such as the 313 million American citizens and 30 million illegal immigrants, to Marxist socialism then communism:

1) Release a synthetic virus into Democratic countries.
2) Blame the USA for developing the synthetic Covid-19 virus as a chemical warfare weapon used on China.
3) Encourage millions of Americans to vote for China's friend Joseph R. Biden selling the power of privilege and influence for codependent son Hunter Biden.
4) Refuse to investigate the origination of the Covid-19 virus.
5) Get the World Health Organization to ratify China's premise of an animal transmission that caused the worldwide Pandemic not the Wuhan lab. And advocate free global trade through influence in WTO and the UN.
6) Reject reporting of the CCP number of cases and deaths (reported to only be 4,00) while touting the success of their

own vaccine distributed to their friends in Iran, Viet Nam, North Korea etc.
7) Ride out the conspiracy theories by appeasing the Biden Administration staggering from its failure in open borders and loss of creditability in foreign affairs due to the Afghanistan bungle.
8) Biden continues to let Dr. Fauci, the person that orchestrated the gain of function weapon, used by the CCP to run the Pandemic in America with fear and to cover up his complacent cause of the Pandemic and et tu Brute' Trump in the process.
9) China is now the primary origin for illicit synthetic Fentanyl and related opioid substances trafficked into the USA. Also, it's estimated that 50% of our prescription drugs are manufactured in China. The what if conspiracy here is ... what if they lace our prescription drugs with illicit opioids or fentanyl as the Wuhan lab did with the release of the Covid-19 virus.
10) No, that could never happen in America, or could it?

Our Cold War defense or peace with strength, must first and foremost defeating the internal political infighting over capitalism and socialism bringing forth our national patriotism and humanism with the creed to marry new patriotic socialism with benevolent sharing capitalism in our enterprising and competitive work force:
- Equal opportunity for all races, creeds, sexes, religions with peaceful coexistent.
- Individualism based on freedom of speech, safety, security health and prosperity.
- Representative government with right to run for office.
- Ownership of private property with imminent domain.
- Freedoms to take a risk to fail and begin again.
- Pursuit of Profit and Investment in the Economy and Infrastructure.
- Sharing of the profits and wealth with those that contribute to the production of maximum GDP ethically and patriotically.

WILL MARXISM RULE OR WILL GOLD RULE?

The "golden rule is those with the gold rule" and the rest must serve that reality. Neither of these two political philosophies will succeed. With the American Enterprise Party representing enterprising Americans, the ten planks of Marxism proposed by Karl Marx in his Communist Manifesto, put forth in 1848 as the necessary steps to destroy capitalism in a free enterprise democratic system, will not prevail.

Are there active movements in the USA moving us to a Marxist State? Yes.

This is the current governments in Russia, China, North Korea, Venezuela, Cuba and formerly East Germany. (This represents 75% of the world's population who exist in the convoluted social order of communism dedicated to destroying democracy). With America, Canada, Israel, Germany, Great Britain, India, France, Italy, Scandinavia, Poland, Pakistan and the Ballistics with some form of democracy. Most other nations are either a monarchy, dictators or war lords controlling the gold.

Are we halfway there or not? Yes, in my opinion. What does this mean in our current situation with the pandemic, black lives matter, Trump versus Bidden, Republicans versus Democrats, Roe v. Wade and so on. With Trump losing, will Biden, Harris, Sanders, Pelosi, Schumer, AOC, take us further down the road to Marxism or will Trump supports prevail in the 2022 midterms and 2024 for the Presidency, to protect our current interpretation of the constitution by appointments to the Supreme Court and taking back the Afghanistan embassy and Bagram airport?

What do you think? Well, in my opinion, with Trump losing, the progressive Democrats will not preserve our national sovereignty and the great American Enterprise. Then we lose our enterprise based on freedom of opportunity with lower taxes and higher employment in small businesses so we can pay down the national debt, lower the trade deficit and provide equal opportunity to housing, education and prosperity. If so, China has won the first phase of the CCP versus USA Globalization

Cold War. Well, okay, will Trump run again and save us? In my opinion salvation is not the Republican party that is a coconspirator with the Democrats, taking us into this derivative bubble that's going to burst by 2024 or soon thereafter. In my opinion, the majority of enterprising Americans will vote for a swing vote American Enterprise Party to balance the power and finances. Then the golden rule is government of the people, by the people, for the people.

To stop the slide into progressive turned regressive policies, it is imperative that a third political party represent these principles of enterprise that utilizes capitalism and socialism in its very structure. That is the pursuit of the American Dream by pulling the extreme versions of those towards the middle of mutual and peaceful coexistence for our democracy in a world of conflict whose millions desire to share in our (threatened) prosperity.

See Article 13 for the preamble to the American Enterprise Party. and the bylaws of the American Enterprise Party Foundation.org. www.americanenterpriseparty.com

Otherwise, Big Brother Biden and Big Business Brotherhood thinking will push us into Marx-Lenin CCP Communist Manifesto thinking that offers Ten Planks to Defeat and Destroy Capitalism (In parentheses is where the progressive Big Brother and Brotherhood government has put USA):

What are the ten planks of Marxism proposed by Karl Marx in his Communist Manifesto put forth in 1848 as the necessary steps to destroy capitalism in a free enterprise democratic system.

1. ***Abolition of private property*** and the application of all rents of land to public purposes. (Imminent domain lost to Federalizing the wetlands, forests, offshore drilling, fracking leases, climate change property violations).

2. ***A heavy progressive or graduated income tax***. (Graduated taxation on adjusted gross income and progressive taxation on corporations).

3. *Abolition of all rights of inheritance.* (Inheritance or death tax).

4. *Confiscation of the property of all emigrants and rebels.* (Laws preventing aliens from owning property). (DEA).

5. *Centralization of credit in the hands of the state*, by means of a national bank with State capital and an exclusive monopoly. (The Federal Reserve Bank and legislation, rules and regulations). (FDIC) (FEC).

6. *Centralization of the means of communications and transportation* in the hands of the State. (FCC) (FAA) (FHA) (FMC) (FTC).

7. *Extension of factories and instruments of production owned by the state*, the bringing into cultivation of waste lands, and the improvement of the soil generally in accordance with a common plan. (EPA) (Army Corp of Engineers) (FERC) (OERE) (NRC).

8. *Equal liability of all to labor. Establishment of industrial armies*, especially for agriculture. (NLRB and Unionization of labor). (EEOC) (CPSC) (ATF) (Department of Justice) (VA) (ETA).

9. *Combination of agriculture with manufacturing industries*, gradual abolition of the distinction between town and country, by a more equitable distribution of population over the country. (Corporate conglomerates with farm quotas and subsidies). (CFTC) (FCA) (FDA).

10. *Private education for all children in public schools.* Abolition of children's factory labor in its present form. Combination of education with industrial production. (Free public education, free collage and write off of college debt, funded by property taxes, gambling taxes, sin taxes, Power Ball and Lotto).

Marx and Lenin in the Communist Manifesto laid this platform for dehumanizing the proletariat, a devil bent on the destruction of humanity. Communism declared war on humanity itself including human values and human dignity through fear, conformity and orthodoxy. Humanism, on the other hand, is a set of moral standards for human society, especially our veterans and first responders, whose patriotic work ethics are pursuing a return on their human capital using investment capital to create profits that sustain quality of life, liberty and happiness. Resulting in good versus evil, God versus the Devil, Values versus Sin ... Enterprise (the American Dream risk taking and competing for prosperity to all) versus Communism (the commune of dehumanization with mental and financial poverty).

VALIANT VETERANS

Veterans are those that live through a societal holocaust

The veteran of foreign wars
of goals and scores
scrapping on all fours
fighting off life's shores
The veteran who's treated battle wounds and sores

The veteran must have a state of mind
To diligently hunt until they find
What they seek
Whether it be to have
The strength to overcome the weak
Or make something good out of bleak

They're not afraid to try
Persistently getting up from where they lie
Battle scarred and worn
Tattered and torn till they die

Facing high noon and a dark sky
But becoming the sun on the horizon each morn
With experience and good sense
And the will to commence

A valiant veteran is the best defense
And our only offense

The **progressives (transformational politicians aka Biden, Harris, Sanders, Pelosi, Schumer, AOC, etc.)** of the twenty-first century who seem to believe in the socialistic and Marxist-Communist concepts, especially those who pass more and more laws, rules and regulations implementing those ideas, are contradicting their oath of office and to the Constitution of the United States of America. "Johann Wolfgang Von Goethe" — '**None are more hopelessly enslaved** than **those who falsely believe they are free**".

Wake up, America—Save the Enterprise Downsize Big Brother Government and the Brotherhood, Up Size Laissez--Faire Enterprise with www.usdebtclock.org as our score card, not the stock market a derivative bubble that can burst at any time. The only way to manage the future is to convert USA's systems to generally accepted accounting principles (GAAP) that monitors our budgetary system for planning and execution of our financial plans. Ironically, China is in the process of making these changes in their internal financial reporting.

Since World War II both parties have institutionalized the Enterprise with Big Brother government, public sector dominance. Big Box, Big Tech, Big Media, Big Unions, Big Pharma as the Brotherhood, labeled essential businesses by Big Brother government during the Pandemic. This takes away from State rights by justifying trillions of dollars of deficit spending and borrowing capital needed for governmental infrastructure repairs, bridges, highways, transportation and ear marks for so called "green" environment ... while for our inner cities, that are the breeding grounds for crime, injustice, drugs, prostitution, human trafficking, lawless drive by shootings, are left in squaller. All given and destined to be the root cause of social protests and riots.

We are dominated by academic issues rather than problem solving. (See Exhibit F where problem solving is nominalized by the word issue). The majority of voters are not empowered to find an accountable and competent candidate nor party. In other words, we are in a public sector government run by quack science and a Pandemic construed by a partnership of the National Institute of Health aka Dr. Anthony Fauci and China that provided a runaway virus that will be utilized by Democrats to rewrite the American constitutional government in their own image and destroy capitalism forever ... the Marxist plan is in motion in our most revered institutions of health, education and welfare.

The last target is the great American Enterprise that in effect saved millions of lives with warp speed vaccines to treat not prevent the next Pandemic used against us for political control by our one-party "winner take all "government. The prevention is in a competitive third party that stands for humanism first and politics a distant second by downsizing of big government control and upsizing enterprising Americans as the voting bloc. Preventative triaging and habit changing actions to improve the health and fitness of all individuals' rests in privatizing Health Care for All (via my book of that title shown in the back of the book) that focuses resources on holding our health, education and welfare institutions accountable for results.

It is time for the private sector to take back the Enterprise. We now have a "House of Cards" all jokers and a "Senate of Cards" all chockers creating a Welfare State of those with the power to control the handouts. Governance is by Harvard Attorneys, Harvard Professors, and Harvard endowments ... called Freak-o-Economics using the Golden Rule ... those with the golden arm shall rule by playing the Monopsony Game for destroying the constitution and the Republic while the binary two-party system fails us as Washington DC burns. The epidemy of the Roman Empire.

The Roman Empire burned its future by ignoring its collective values and patriotism. While the Senate and Emperor argued the military wasted away it's honor on meaningless wars and land grabs. America is in the same spiral.

Since the advent of the Great Society Programs, we have evolved into a culture of violence, vulgarity and disproportionate excesses of prosperity divided by politics and media. I believe this is due to the failure of the leadership of our two parties, practicing money-tics, not American enterprise values. Ask yourself, as a voter who would you pick a "better Red than dead pragmatic Republican" or a "Blue blood bleeding-heart phlegmatic Democrat" … or an "enterprising market driven American Enterprise Party Humanitarian" that wants every American citizen to be successful and healthy in pursuing the American Utopian Dream. This way we the 169 million enterprising Americans can peacefully coexist with the current uni-party "winner take all" façade by applying the politics of humanism using the standards of behavior dictated by civility, equity in results, equality in application without the use of a violent revolution. Let the progressives, Marxists, BLM, ANTIFA, racists, wokes and activists stand down and debate the future of our America the Bountiful based on the nonviolent principles of Humanism versus all the other isms.

PROGRESSIVES

*"A group, person, or idea favoring or implementing
social reform or new, liberal ideas"*
... regardless of the cost of other people's money

How can we be better
If we're all the same

Is a democracy capitalism
Or socialism or both

Is it the chicken or the egg
Is it the Republicans or the Democrats

Is it the uneven division of wealth
Or the division of Misery equally

Is it the cutting of the pork based on effort
Or the eating of the feast done by the least

Issues or problems how can anything be better
If we're all doled out our equal share ... and call it equity

Take Education ... it covers a lot of ground but
Equality won't harvest any of it

Like all political rationalization, taxes are not the solution
But crime in the cities is not our problem ... defund the police

Take wasteful Health care it's better to cover it and
Not need it than to need it and not have it ... funding is no problem

Take Defense of country it's better to waste money
And not need the WMD's than to have USA wasted ... by its friends

Take Self-reliance – to those who do only what they please …
Are seldom pleased with what they do

In the final analysis "if the good lord doesn't rule
The affairs of the people … then a tyrant's money will"

How can we be better off …
If we're all the same and getting soft

Give our brains and golf a challenge …
And all of us will be better off

Give our bodies a lift and set a goal …
We will prevent intolerance and preserve ourselves

How can we be better equal if we're all the same? …
We can't be better off if we are the lesser equally

As we will be lackadaisical meekly …
When Uncle Sam stops paying its bills weekly

The will of the many shall overcome the restrictive rules of the few or we are killing the individual Entrepreneur's spirit and economies in their intent. Adam Smith, *Wealth of Nations*, 1776: *"The general industry of the society never can exceed what the capital of the society can employ. As the number of workmen that can be kept in employment by any particular person must bear a certain proportion to his capital, so the number of those that can be continually employed by all the members of a great society must bear a certain proportion to the whole capital of that society, and never can exceed that proportion.*

No regulation of commerce can increase the quantity of industry in any society beyond what its capital can maintain. It can only divert a part of it into a direction into which it might not otherwise have gone; and it is by no means certain that this artificial direction is likely to be more advantageous to the society than that into which it would have gone of its own accord.

Hold your breath ... with the gang of 545 running our enterprise The outstanding public debt as of 31 of June 2024 @ 6:49 PM 2:35 PM CST is:

$100,393,480,897,745 trillion www.usdebtclock.org

(Source: National Chamber of Commerce, Federal Reserve and USA Budget and Management Office that claims they make accrual entries to balance their budgets, not so GAAP is nowhere to be found)

($34,783,869,292,833)
This is the recorded Federal debt that is ticking up at $388,000,000,000 per day, USA annual GDP is only $24,650,473,415,981 trillion, with debt to GDP 150% www.usdebtclock.org,

The GAAP (generally accepted accounting principles) accrual basis unfunded government pensions, entitlements, and deferred contract debt for the public sector is:

$158 Trillion Total Federal, State and Local Unrecorded Debt,

Compared to national assets $157 trillion, or $1 trillion neg accumulated negative net worth.

While the books at every level of USA government are based on cash basis of accounting and budgeting ... America currently owes more than its GDP and national assets.

Variable As % GDP	2015	2016	2017	2018	2019	Hist Avg
Revenue[13]	18.0%	17.6%	17.2%	16.4%	16.3%	17.4%
Outlays[13]	20.4%	20.8%	20.6%	20.2%	21.0%	20.3%

Budget Deficit[13]	-2.4%	-3.2%	-3.5%	-3.8%	-4.6%	-2.9%
Debt Held by Public[13]	72.5%	76.4%	76.0%	77.4%	79.2%	41.7%

Budget principles[edit] Per Wikipedia

August 12, 2021:

Democrats released their $3.5 trillion budget resolution Monday as they prepared to pass the $5.2 trillion bipartisan infrastructure bill.

- The chamber will approve the infrastructure plan as soon as Tuesday, and then move "immediately" toward passing the budget measure, Majority Leader Chuck Schumer said.

- Democrats' spending plan would invest in paid leave, child care, pre-K, community college, green energy and an expansion of Medicare, among a bevy of other programs.

- **Adding it all up and you have 10,000 billions … "A 1,000 billions here, a 1,000 billions there, and pretty soon you're talking real money."** Senator Everett Dirksen's quote converted to 2021 trillion dollars not billions.

The U.S. Constitution (Article I, section 9, clause 7) states that "No money shall be drawn from the Treasury, but in Consequence of Appropriations made by Law; and a regular Statement and Account of Receipts and Expenditures of all public Money shall be published from time to time." (The constitution needs to be amended to reflect modern day management that uses accrual accounting so the revenues earned are compared to the obligations incurred as of a date certain).

Each year, the President of the United States submits a budget request to Congress for the following fiscal year as required by the Budget and Accounting Act of 1921. Current law (31 U.S.C. § 1105(a)) requires the president to submit a budget no earlier than the first Monday in January, and no later than the first Monday in February. Typically, presidents submit budgets on the first Monday in February. The budget submission has been delayed, however, in some new presidents' first year when the previous president belonged to a different party.

The Federal and State budgets are calculated largely on a cash in and cash out basis. That is, revenues and outlays are recognized when transactions are made. Therefore, the full long-term costs of programs such as Medicare, Social Security, the federal portion of Medicaid and government pensions are not reflected in the federal budget.

By contrast, many businesses and some other national governments including China are adopting forms of accrual accounting, which recognizes obligations and revenues when they are earned and incurred. The costs of some federal credit and loan programs, according to provisions of the Federal Credit Reform Act of 1990, are calculated on a net present value basis.[14] On the accrual basis $158 trillion in obligations are not recorded on the books.

(The Federal, State and local short-term debt is $82.5 trillion, since the 50 States are reported on the cash basis, debt now exceeds assets by $1.3 trillion dollars. As a result, many are contemplating bankruptcies; California alone $573 billion, Illinois $168 billion, NY with $351 .1billion) with 15 of the largest US Cities near bankruptcy; (all reporting on the cash basis of accounting and budgeting thereby understating the debt by more than 100%).

CBO's Baseline Budget Projections

	Actual, 2017	2018	2019	2020	2021	2022	2023	2024	2025	2026	2027	2028	Total 2019-2023	Total 2019-2028
						In Billions of Dollars								
Revenues	3,316	3,338	3,490	3,678	3,827	4,012	4,228	4,444	4,663	5,002	5,299	5,520	19,234	44,162
Outlays	3,982	4,142	4,470	4,685	4,949	5,288	5,500	5,688	6,015	6,322	6,615	7,046	24,893	56,580
Deficit	-665	-804	-981	-1,008	-1,123	-1,276	-1,273	-1,244	-1,352	-1,320	-1,316	-1,526	-5,660	-12,418
Debt Held by the Public at the End of the Year	14,665	15,688	16,762	17,827	18,998	20,319	21,638	22,932	24,338	25,715	27,087	28,671	n.a.	n.a.
					As a Percentage of Gross Domestic Product									
Revenues	17.3	16.6	16.5	16.7	16.7	16.9	17.2	17.4	17.5	18.1	18.5	18.5	16.8	17.5
Outlays	20.8	20.6	21.2	21.3	21.6	22.3	22.3	22.2	22.6	22.9	23.1	23.6	21.8	22.4
Deficit	-3.5	-4.0	-4.6	-4.6	-4.9	-5.4	-5.2	-4.9	-5.1	-4.8	-4.6	-5.1	-4.9	-4.9
Debt Held by the Public at the End of the Year	76.5	78.0	79.3	80.9	83.1	85.7	87.9	89.6	91.5	93.1	94.5	96.2	n.a.	n.a.
Memorandum:														
Deficit as a Percentage of GDP, Adjusted to Exclude Timing Shifts[a]	-3.5	-4.2	-4.6	-4.6	-4.9	-5.1	-5.1	-5.1	-5.1	-4.8	-4.6	-4.8	-4.9	-4.9

Source: Congressional Budget Office.
GDP = gross domestic product; n.a. = not applicable.
a. The adjusted amounts exclude the effects of shifting payments from one fiscal year into another so that those payments are not made on a weekend.

Footnotes:

1. The above is taken from Wikipedia ... the estimated population growth of the United States in the last decade is 10 million citizens totaling of 313,857,277, plus 30 million undocumented illegal immigrants so each taxpayer's share of unfunded debt is $482,000 with ten thousand Baby Boomers retiring every day and 7,000 per week filing for Medicare. Most will end up on the streets, homeless or near homeless (currently 600,000 to 1.5 million are homeless in America, 25% are children under the age of 18) adding more to tent cities in our inner cities.

2. The national debt has continued to increase an average of $3.88 billion per day since September 28, 2007! 37 million Americans have college loans totaling $1.7 trillion dollars exceeding credit card debt . . . most will not be able to service that debt let alone liquidate it.

3. **2020 Pandemic debt of $3.8 plus $1.9 trillion** stimulus funding by the Federal Reserve printing currency or issuing Federal Reserve

Notes through the World Banking system. The funding of the lockdown unemployment driving up another entitlement. . . unemployment checks to everyone regardless of need or legitimacy. Some $400 billion going to fraudulent foreign scalpers. Concerned? Then just try to tell Congress and the White House what could be done with the $68 million misplaced in California alone!

4. Gross national income: $21.23 trillion, current prices Source: World Bank.

5. The US budget deficit hit a record $6.4 trillion for the year ended in September 30, 2020, US Congress estimates say. Total trade deficit is $912 billion with China at $305 billion.

6. The deficit was equal to 125.9 percent of gross domestic product (GDP), more than treble the 2008 level and the highest since the end of World War II. Total interest paid on total national debt is $3.2 trillion.

7. Currently the USA has negative net worth, negative working capital, inability to cover debt service out of net income and is deferring trillions in liabilities to the future. Janet Yellen Biden's Treasury Secretary and former Fed Chairman is considering a 100-year treasury bond to defer cash flow for retiring debt and its interest. We have let the Congress and US Treasury knowingly cook the books, accelerating tax collections and deferring payments, then borrowing the difference. This is the definition of insolvency leading to the declaration of bankruptcy. In American business and personal debt obligations this usually requires a Chapter 11 plan of reorganization if the organization is to survive, or Chapter 7 or 13 if it cannot survive. State and Local Governments use Chapter 10 and the Federal statute is silent on Federal Government bailouts. The constitution does not provide for a recall of an incompetent President, except the 25th amendment for health reasons, nor the filing of bankruptcy.

8. In reality, we seem to be a Republic of leftist media, propaganda, and biased reporting of the Great Hoaxes of contrived realities:
    a. Defund the police. Reform injustices by reworking bail and sentencing injustices.
    b. Open the borders to save oppressed children.
    c. Joe Biden is a moderate and transformational. Hunter Biden isn't a coconspirator with China and Russia.
    d. Democrat's base will reverse the minority caste system and maintain section 230 to protect big tech.
    e. Republicans say they want to drain the swamp while agreeing to trillions of dollars of stimulus and government infrastructure spending spread over two decades.
    f. The wokes are nominalizing our culture while plotting a black voting revolution with CRT, BLM, 1619 project, Juneteenth, open borders, open voting, packed Supreme Court, appease our enemies and a one-party "winner take all " Democrat government forever, as their agenda.
    g. Degrowth proposed in the Green New Deal as anticapitalism applied to excesses in consumption, standard of living of the white supremacists.
    h. More government infrastructure spending and the Green New Deal jobs will provide the financing of the Biden-Sanders Big Brother government and the Big Business, Big Unions, Big Media Brotherhood will provide the financing for the one-party "winner take all" totalitarian system.

Here are questions to kill these contrived hoaxes at the ballot box. How can we defund the police when we don't fund their pensions? How can we fix the infrastructure and Green New Deal when we don't fund our obligations? How can we have open borders when we don't pay our bills and immigrants are a cost not an asset.? How can we win the trade war with China when they are our supplier and bank loaning us money? How can we have the latest in weapons when we don't ever dare use them? How can we have an educated American when we don't disclose our losses and gains that cause the USA to be insolvent? How can the country ever be better if we're all the same equally and equitably? The answer is an effective competing alternative for the voters. Why because the voters would demand the following bailout plan:

The Top Ten budgetary steps to solvency: reduce State and Federal deficits and resulting debt (estimates made by author based on current costs of governing):

1. Cut government payroll and pension costs by 20% per year = $400 billion.
2. Raise government income tax rates by 10% to 15% on net worth, property and sales tax revenues by 15% per year = $2 trillion .
3. Increase rate of GDP growth by 10% per year = $2 trillion.
4. Increase employment by 20% per year = $4 trillion.
5. Decrease borrowing by 10% per year = $3 trillion.
6. Write-off debt owed to China to cover Pandemic costs = $1.2 trillion.
7. Convert State and Federal financial records to GAAP generally accepted accounting principles over a 10-year period = $15.8 trillion per year and eliminating redundancy in, regulatory agencies = $500 billion per year.
8. Limit government health care Medicare and Medicaid spending to 15% of annual GDP = $3 trillion (increase in age requirements).
9. Charge 25% foreign trade imbalances for market access fees per year = $120 billion per year.
10. Limit Defense spending to 4% of GDP = $800 billion.
11. Limit infrastructure investment to 10% of annual GDP = $2 trillion dollars in borrowing and taxation for roads, bridges, airports, 5 G telecom as the infrastructure priorities and .5% of GDP = $500 billion local opportunity zones revenue bonds for fixing the squaller in our inner cities and underprivileged small communities,
12. Defer the pipe dream of "save the earth New Green Deal" using private investment from enterprise zones tax write-offs without

debt and deprivation. Instead by using conservation of the land and earth based industries for energy research and development.

Resulting in a balanced budget by 2031 and reduced short term GAAP debt of $30 trillion by 50% = $15 trillion and long-term debt of $75 trillion down 50% by 2051= $78 trillion down from $158 trillion in 2021. This requires GDP growth of 10% per year for the next three decades. To get that degree of growth the USA must control the supply lines and technology development by merging the Western Hemisphere with Taiwan, Hong Kong, Singapore, Philippines and India into an Amerasian global conglomerate.

Milton Friedman said "capitalism and socialism are bedfellows for economic freedom as the innate connection between economics and politics. Economics is for personal freedom and capitalism is a necessary condition of individual rights in a Democracy."

Following is an example of Obama's 2013 and 2022 proposed annual budgets, shown below in billions of todays (cash basis budgeting) dollars (source: proposed Democrats 2013 fiscal budget for the next ten years)

Obviously, operating budgets are useless when using cash in and cash out as the basis for managing the Biggest and Greatest Enterprise of all time. Following is the Obama budget for 2013 forecasted to 2022 to reflect how far off the Office of Management and Budget is 50% short of realty.

Cash Expenditures:	2013	2022
Defense	$699	$788
Non-defense	600	611
Total discretionary outlays	$1,300	$1,398
Mandatory outlays:		
Social Security	$725	$1,361

Medicare	480	967
Medicaid	275	589
Other (Obama Care and other)	633	846
Total mandatory outlays	$2,073	$3,763
Cash Expenditures:	**2013**	**2022**
Interest on national debt	$230	$915
Total outlays	$3,603	$6,098
Cash Receipts:		
Individual income taxes	$1,091	$2,401
Corporate income taxes	181	501
Social Security	566	1,150
Medicare	188	355
Medicaid (state and federal revenue sharing)	-0-	-0-
Other retirement	8	13
Unemployment taxes	56	60
Excise taxes	72	157
	2013	2022
Estate taxes	8	13
Custom duties	30	52
Federal Reserve income	83	45
Other	20	100
Total cash receipts	$2,303	$4,855
Deficits (every year through 2022)	-$1,300	-$1,193
Actual deficit spending in 2020		$4.1 trillion
Cumulative deficits from 2013 to 2022		

-$8.663 trillion revised to -$81.7 trillion		
The entire budget is on the cash basis of accounting	2013 Actual Debt	2022 Forecast Debt
National debt at 2022	$14.9 trillion	$36.9 trillion
Government accounts (foreign debt)	$5.3 trillion	$10.3 trillion
Held by the public	$9.6 trillion	$26.6 trillion
Annual interest	$615 billion	$915 billion
Total Debt and 10 Year Forecast	$30.2	$81.7 trillion
	2013	**2022**
Outlays by agency (billions of dollars):		
Agriculture	$25 billion	$27 billion
Commerce	14	10
Education	64	79
Energy	17	20
Health and human services	84	95
Housing and urban affairs	43	47
Interior	12	14
Justice	28	33
Labor	14	13
State Department	.1	.1
Transportation	15	17
Treasury	13	17
Corps of Engineers	6	6
EPA	10	10
GSA	.4	1.5
NASA	19	21
SBA	.8	1.1
Social Security administration	9	11

Corporate services	1.2	1.3
Other (IRS, etc.)	20	23
War zones	163	44
Total outlays by agency	$1,258 trillion	$1,309 trillion
Cash expenditures	**2013**	**2022**
Defense	$699 bullion	$788 billion
Non-defense	$600	$611
Total discretionary cash outlays	$1,300 trillion	$6,398 trillion
Understatement of 2022 budget forecast		$5,000,000,000,000 trillion

Footnotes to a nontransparent fiscal management tool:

1. The debt ceiling will continue to be increased or removed by Congress. President Trump suspended it during the Pandemic.
2. Record deficits will continue each year as trade imbalances escalate and shipping costs from Asia become a major problem.
3. The credit rating will continue to be downgraded to C- driving interest up over $12.5 trillion per annum.
4. The Federal Reserve will continue to print money ($1.00 now worth $.17 since going off the gold standard). And base interest rates on inflation caused by the Pandemic and USA borrowing addiction. Latest hairbrained idea by the new Secretary the Treasury, Janet Yellen, is a 100-year Treasury Bond. Defer/defer/ defer disaster until the next century. How's that for skullduggery?
5. Tax reform will increase taxes on the middle-class to pay for Green New Deal infrastructure expenditures as inner cities will continue to deteriorate and crime escalates.
6. Other Biden reforms and executive orders amounting to $46 trillion over the next ten years have not been factored into this budget forecast.
7. The budget strategy that cutting entitlements will save us is false. Social Security and Medicare are Trust Funds not entitlements and

they are paying for themselves if allowed to invest funds in the economy rather than loaning the reserves to the government general fund to fight wars and develop weapons of mass destruction.
8. Medicaid is a problem due to Obama Care and cost-shifting Medicare Advantage Program benefits to state Medicaid programs using reform as the tactic.
9. Medicare is the biggest problem due to 7,000 of 77 million baby boomers filing for coverage every day and generally not healthy.
10. Social Security is the next biggest problem due to the 10,000 of 77 million baby boomers per week filing for retirement benefits every week and not preparing on their own for the future personal costs.
11. **2021 Current budgeting by the Office of Management and Budget is understating deficits by not accruing the increase in Medicare, Medicaid, Social Security recipients and Federal (State and Local budgets as well) pensions that are growing at the rate of 50% per year increases caused by aging, chronic disease and unhealthy Americans.**

Read my mind: it isn't the Old Entitlements (Medicare and Social Security aren't entitlements and don't belong to Government spending discretion) but the New Entitlements erode business profits (i.e. workers' comp, food stamps, paid leave, minimum wage, disability, unemployment wages, Obama Care, child care payments, Pandemic stimulus, etc.). The Welfare State is well stocked by the Big Brother Biden, Harris, Sanders, Schumer, Pelosi, Warren, AOC and the Squad awoke as, woke culture change Progressives, using the Marxist minority rules. AKA the Brother Hood taking away the freedoms to risk and fail bankruptcy rules so they can take over small businesses.

Politicians of both parties who want to dwell on issues (differences of opinion between the red and blue antics) rather than deal with the problems they themselves have either enacted or failed to solve. They are avoiding the reality that government's number one responsibility and purpose is to enforce the law, not just make more laws.

The problem with the budget is not the Entitlements for the elderly, impoverished and unhealthy, it's that Congress itself is expanding government for the sake of power with the thousands of new laws, ear marks and entitlements. I reiterate that rational business theory can strategically resolve the deficit problem by the following progammatic changes:

1. Cut government payroll, healthcare benefits, and pensions at all levels of federal, state, and local employees. To balance any insolvent business the first move is to cut back variable costs to the breakeven point, which typically starts with the payroll. Government payrolls around the US total of 22.7 million employees or an annual payroll of $1.3 trillion and unfunded pensions totaling $25 trillion.

2. Economize on misdirected wars, failed diplomacy policies, and pursuit of regime change for freedom for all, in spite of the reality of warlords and dictatorships, under the auspices that we can win the war on terrorism, Communism, socialism, drug-ism, etc. Stop the pursuit of liberty for all by discontinuing all foreign aid until we have balanced the budget.

3. Reduce defense spending by $300 billion by bringing troops back into our lines of defense for closing our borders, airports, transportation lines, energy sources, and clean up the city education with private Charter School delivery and infrastructure. This is being feasible with the withdrawal of ground troops replaced by cyber hacking, drone strikes, trade agreements, banking controls, sanctions on foreign manufacturing. A non-shooting cold war saves the American economy $5 to 10 trillion in five years.

4. Finance the balance of trade deficits by assessing a sales distribution fee of 25 percent of the sales created and serviced by American companies for foreign products, thereby creating 25 percent of $75 billion per month in trade deficits or annual reduction in the trade

deficits of $900 billion per year in service revenues for funding capital for small businesses in the USA.

5. Privatize and Finance healthcare through a withholding and savings program with an enterprise approach to delivering, paying, and monitoring quality-of-life programs through mutual health insurance companies that invest the funds in American small businesses. Savings in dollars and lives will save $2 trillion per year in prescription drugs, Pandemics, improvements in lifestyles, increases in life expectancy and quality outcomes for preserving life rather than health maintenance insurance that has been a failure.

6. Privatize and Finance Social Security with an increase in retirement age to seventy-five and an increase in the withholding rate to 15 percent: 7.5 percent for beneficiaries and 7.5 percent for financing single payer, privatized health care enterprise. Investment of the insurance reserves will generate billions in short term returns on investment in capital reinvested in the economy and environmental improvement standards.

7. Privatize agencies that lose money using GAAP accounting for budgeting and financial reports: for example, the post office, Amtrak, the public schools, VA, the replacements would be merged into Fed Ex, Airlines and health care systems using enterprise methods bringing capital and human capital together in an environment of competition "quality costs less". This can save up to a trillion dollars per year in redundancy and ineffective management of taxpayer dollars.

8. Incorporate OPEC (Organization of the Purchasers of Energy Countries) to negotiate with the Organization of the Petroleum Exporting Countries (OPEC). The countries to be offered stakes in the new corporation would be USA, Canada, Japan, France, Italy, England, India and Mexico and any other members desiring to control the cost of fossil fuel energy around the world.

9. Finance the affairs of the USA using a value added tax based on each taxpayer's net worth; all taxes replaced by 15 percent of net worth. Those who have profited from the American enterprise economy should pay more than those that work for those entrepreneurs and businesses.

10. Turn lawmakers into job makers, having 50 percent of the elected officials from the private sector, and for every bill passed a law must be removed. All regulations that inhibit business are removed systematically, reducing the cost of government and stimulating the creation of new products and jobs.

11. Illegal aliens need to be processed into the Social Security System with Green Cards and job training to replace a job force being decimated by retiring "baby boomers."

12. Require fair representation for the use of demonstration projects and grants for research and development funded by taxpayer monies to include a private-sector competitive input before issuing the funding. **Currently, the major research and implementation grants go to colleges and universities not the private sector small businesses who are the innovators and entrepreneurs for solving problems. All budgets must be calculated using GAAP and limited to a percent of GDP by Federal and State government agencies.**

In summary, there are trillions of dollars of savings and return on investment that can be generated when the governmental agencies are managed as enterprises for return on investment related to GDP and cash flow. Currently, taxpayers are only covering 50% of the cost of government agencies and wasted resources due to incompetent fiscal management and budget controls. The next two decades will demonstrate how close America is coming to bursting the $600 trillion bubble we are sitting on, unless we act now.

Generically, America needs fair representation of the private sector, aging Americans, middle-class taxpayers, legal immigrants and fringe groups who do not have a party. Look at the flag: red on the right, blue on the left, and white in the middle, not being represented. It has nothing to do with the color of skin but the color of money.

On the Left, we have the progressive socialist bigger is better government, (22 million employees, service unions, minorities, big business, big tech and big media). On the right, we have (the industrialists, small businesses, 200 million enterprising middle-class Americans) represented by a free-market driven American Enterprise Third Party. What we need is a coalition of the Left and Right to win the war on debt, win the worldwide trade war, with humanism and peaceful coexistence as our foreign policy.

Currently, incumbents, congressional committee chairmen, and power brokers are based on tenure with a 90% reelection rate due to no term limits; government-employed attorneys, lifetime public servants, inherited offspring, and aspiring egos representing the academic world keep the Animal Farm animals in check, now to fore defined as the intellectual elite or monarchy. It is their dominance over the last six presidents that have desecrated the constitution and budget. Now is the time for the private sector to seek and take their share of the authority since they pay the bulk of the payroll and overhead. That is what the private sector is good at, meeting budgets, making money and creating capital for growth in GDP.

Realistically we have an internal war. Welcome to the new unchecked entitlements (bribes) promulgated by our progressive socialist welfare two-party government financed by the Federal Reserve Bonds and US Treasury printing currency and 100-year cradle to grave "T Bills" printing press to further dilute the value of the dollar and stoke inflation to justify raising interest rates to member banks causing the biggest depression in 2021 and 2022 of all times:

- Pandemic bailouts $7.8 trillion over next 3 years.
- Raising Corporate and individual tax rates by 50% by reversing Trump tax cuts and upping corporate rates from 21% to 39.5%.
- $15-dollar minimum wage or $12,000 per year guaranteed annual income. 40,000 under poverty line = $4,800,000,000 billion per year for guaranteed income.
- Obama Care expansion by Biden administration costing $680 billion per year.
- Food Stamps expansion by Biden administration SNAP costs $85 billion per year.
- Increase in Federal minimum wage to $15 per hour. Costing employers $900 per employee per week totals $3.6 billion per week. $187 billion per year resulting in price increases of 7.5%.
- Public Sector employees with unlimited tenure and paid leave is a $1.3 trillion payroll per year,
- Unemployment insurance for 22 million recipients amounts to $100 million per week until the expansion by Biden administration = $600 million for 6 weeks.
- Child Care tax credit checks cut for 20 million children totaling $600 million by Biden before even filing a tax return.
- Workers' compensation insurance $48 million per year.
- Disability SSI expansion by Biden administration cost for 375,000, total disability, 110 million temporary disability and 8 million have some disability drawing $775 or per month totaling $9,300 per year. Total cost $910 million per year.
- Welfare expansion by Biden administration (child care) checks $600 million per year. SNAP increases of 25% per month increases.
- Group health insurance with COBRA paid for by businesses. 400,000 small businesses X $300 for 3 months = $900 x 20,000 termination of employment = $18 billion per year.
- Paid leave (holidays, sick leave, paid time off) expansion by Biden administration. 22 million public service employees

costs 5% increase times average hourly wage of $60,000 per year = $1.9 trillion payroll X 5% = $90 billion per year.
- Pensions for fully unionized public service employee's expansion by Biden administration. $1.9 trillion payroll times 10% per year. $190 billion per year with 3 years unfunded debt of $570 billion.
- Total cost per year, before salaries and benefits, to Government and/or businesses of $2.548 trillion per year plus public sector salaries and benefits of $1.9 trillion. Equals $4.5 trillion per year or 20% fixed overhead on $21 trillion GDP, for American Enterprises that generates a $6 trillion deficit in 2021.
- It's not the entitlements that are sinking the American Enterprise ship but the fixed cost of Government and the benefit package promised to the rest of the country. Medicare and Social Security are not entitlements but Trust Funds owed by Americans who contribute these funds from their paychecks.

How could this happen? I call these the Ten Axioms (self-evidently true) predictors of ultimate defeat.
Cooking the Pension Benefits for Government Workers:
Axion Number One:

Right now, the public sector, with the help of unionization, is holding the private sector hostage (i.e., Teachers Union and Public Service Union) when the founders of the republic envisioned that enterprise should be writing the rules of engagement and the public sector would be reviewing, reinforcing them, and engaging those principles in incentive-based taxation. Therefore, there would be no need for collective bargaining, uncontrolled benefits, perks, and automatic salary increases for public workers. The complete unionization of government employees was pulled off by the Service Union under the radar of public sector scrutiny. To make matters worse the contracts were written into law and sheltered from accountability for the review by the taxpayers.

Our K-12 curriculum is being dictated by the teachers' unions to include woke classes on1619 theory, that the discovery of America was by black slaves not white pilgrims in 1620, Critical Race Theory that white Americans are supremist by heritage and are inherently racist. Also, early education on being offered on the acceptance of transgender change, early sex education and identity inclusion in entertainment, commercials and sports. All and all this movement has turned political with the red and the blues being complacent in its incipit intentions, with apathy from the ALCU forcing diversity in our society and education when calling them issues rather than serous problems and a threat to our values, history and constitution. By banning prayer in schools, the pledge allegiance before class, religious symbols at Christmas, burning the flag at protests, tearing down statues of American heroes, burning and stealing from the haves to feed the have nots, divides the country like the Hatfield's and McCoy's fighting over what's right and wrong at the very polls that are supposed to be constitutional.

Turning Americans against each other based on unions and identity politics and the haves versus the have nots. Therefore, the teachers' unions dictate when and if the teachers will go back to in school learning and when. All based on the self-imposed low-level threat of the Covid-19 on school children. Vaccine and mask mandates. Also act as a fear tactic to illicit higher teacher's salaries and benefits which is the unions' primary reason for existence. All the more the more reason for business enterprise to learn how to share and the workers need to learn to earn for a skill to bill, ethically and patriotically. Then our individual freedoms are based on our civil rights to earn the constitutional right to work and share in the profits, as a God given reward on the risks we take.

We have allowed our fixed overhead (government labor, benefits, and pensions) to escalate beyond what our enterprise can afford and absorb: 22.7 million government employees with a $1.3 trillion annual payroll, plus "Cadillac" healthcare coverage, pensions, compensation 25% higher than the private sector with guaranteed raises, while the private sector is downsizing employment, eliminating funding for healthcare, and doing away with retirement plans with the unions emigrating into the public sector.

Currently the public sector at all levels of government *cooks the books* by operating on cash basis budgeting rather than the generally accepted accounting principles for financial reporting, that govern the private sector. As a result, tax revenues accelerated by withholding and tax estimates and expenditures deferred by budget proxy or availability of cash, thereby always creating a deficit at all levels of government, which destroys the enterprise's capability to generate profits, cash flow, and development of capital (the difference between accrued revenues and payables if applied to government accounting would show a $10 trillion annual deficit and $158 trillion debt due to unfunded government pensions and entitlement liabilities).

Cooking the economics with lawmaking: Axiom number Two:

America's investment in *wars of ideological differences and regime change* have cost America's capability to create productive jobs under the guise of national defense. Three trillion dollars spent on weapons of mass destruction never used and an annual defense budget of $800 billion per year take capital out of the pockets of the job creators. I call this *national offense* rather than national defense, which in many instances makes us as bad as our self-made enemies. Unless we resell the weapons to our enemies or our allies, the investment in weaponry does not create GDP. It creates ill-will in the very world markets that want to compete with us and have us emerge as their consumers and creditors.

Example: in 2010, the State of Illinois, a one-party "winner take all " Democrat legislature passed 300 new laws that by law have to be funded, creating $150 million in additional annual regulatory costs while having a $12 billion annual deficit and a $93 billion unfunded pension deficit. Then the merry men lawmakers decided to increase taxes by 60 percent and authorize 45,000 video gambling locations and also reserved funds from this sin tax to detect and treat habitual gamblers' diseases; all of this with four of the last seven Illinois governors imprisoned for corruption and the Speaker of the House Madigan for thirty-five years had to step down due to fraud allegations and kickbacks by Com Ed. As George Washington envisioned, "Government is not the reason. It is not eloquent; it is a force. Like fire, it is a dangerous servant and a fearful master."

Example: In 2021, former House Speaker Michael Madigan, who stepped down due to a pay for play with Com Ed, after 50 years as a member of the Illinois House and a contributor into one of five pension funds, the General Assembly Retirement System, will receive an annual pension of around $85,117, about 85% of his final salary. In July 2022 his pension will rise to about $148,995 due to 3% padding lawmakers built into the system for themselves over the years. During that time, he paid in $351,000 toward his retirement account. He will quickly start receiving far more than he put in. (In 2021 he was forced into retirement due to corruption charges). But neither investment returns nor the state subsidy have been enough to keep the state's five funds in balance. Their unfunded liabilities collectively rose from about $41 billion in 2006 to $144 billion today. As a result, the state taxpayers are now pumping almost 25 cents of every tax dollar toward its five pensions and the money is not covering the liability and is ever increasing.

Chicago based on past Democrat Mayors (mostly Richard Daily extracts) who cleaned up the ghetto version of the holocaust by building high rise ghettos then knocked them down into low rise crime infested neighborhoods costing the minorities opportunities. They also exceeded their cash in and out budgets by trillions of dollars over a forty-year reign. Leaving a legacy of squalor in the neighborhoods, gang infested and corrupt using black on black crime to avoid police control.

Currently there is only about 40% of the funding available for the promises made. Illinois, along with all the other states are in arrears to the tune of $800 billion which means the obligation is unsustainable.

The solution is made difficult because, under the radar the service unions lobbied and passed these pensions into law. The battle is yet to be raged by the taxpayers over such a bureaucratic mistake during a time when private sector pensions were being cut due to the economy.

Pearl Harbor is the reason America was able to organize and energize the American nationalistic and patriotic capital that won World War II in four years. The production of weapons and hard goods activated and capitalized on the best of America: hard work for a purpose. We must now use the same patriotic enterprise formula to win the *war on debt*. If we do not, the world leadership that is shifting to China and all of Asia will bury us in the end, next to the Roman Empire, Great Britain, Mayan Empire, USSR, Fascist Germany and Italy, the Persian Empire, etc. All had one thing in mind . . . control the world. Is that where we are or should I say were?

Cooking the economics with debt capital: Axiom number Three:

The Federal Reserve isn't a regulatory agency of the US federal government … it is a tacit regulator of its member banks. Their priorities aren't for reducing the cost of capital for the benefit of the American Enterprise. See Article four for the impact of the Fed increasing the discount rate to member banks to penalize Wall Street for the subprime mortgage arbitrage. And how they caused the depression of 2007 with inordinate increases in the discount rate they charge member banks for capital. It then rippled through international monetary system with 12% LIBOR rates bankrupting many of the smaller economies.

Example: The imbalance of trade is hitting $1 trillion per year which China now owns, by default, our productive processes, its profits, and the generation of new capital. Saudi Arabia now owns our fossil fuel energy resources. China, South Korea, Japan, India and Mexico are taking over our technology and automobile markets. Mexico, Central and South America eroding our immigration control. Emerging nations now have captured control of our American consumers with lower prices and improved quality due to the theft of our creative ideas that are not being capitalized for our own economy.

Cooking the economy with regulations:
Axiom number Four:

Why is this? Regulations, taxation, the new entitlements of minimum wage, unemployment taxes, workers' comp benefits, food stamps, disability, welfare, national healthcare, 22.7 million Big Brother government workers enforcing the stifling constraints (such as the IRS, HHS, CMS, OSHUA, GAO, THE FED, SBA, FHA EEOC, SSA, as the big business Brotherhood with gridlocked congressional committees, with no accountability), with the use of enforcement with punitive civil money penalties and felony charges that scare off entrepreneurs, the principle developers of jobs.

Cooking the economics with tax rates and tax deductions:
Axiom number Five:

Current taxation based on adjusted gross income (AGI) allows the "haves" Elite Class to avoid income taxes and allows enterprising Americans to finance the "haves'" businesses (sales taxes, property taxes, sin taxes at every level of our society are the majority). The "have-nots" invest in enterprise while the "haves" control the enterprise. To capitalize the enterprise, we should be taxing the haves' *net worth* so they have to reinvest in the formation of capital for competing with the rest of the world rather than borrowing from our competitors. Otherwise, we are truly bankrupt. More borrowing is not capital, it is an addictive habit that results in the breakdown and destruction of the risk-taking American dream. No balanced budget no cash flow, no cash flow no capital, no capital no GDP growth no ability to compete in the worldwide marketplace leaving the Great American Enterprise subservient to China, the southeast Asian and Mid East communist countries.

Cooking the enterprise with interest rates:
Axiom number Six:

Then the *war on debt* is an *investment in peaceful competition* through winning the economic war worldwide. America is the giant consumer that is supporting the entire world's productive processes. Anymore, it's not the taxpayers who pay all the bills it's primarily borrowing from China, Japan, Mexico, Canada, South Korea, India generated by the $900 billion dollar trade imbalance and Federal Reserve printing press with Treasury Notes sold to their member banks collateralizing the loans from foreign interests and the Wall Street bond market. If the Federal Reserve indiscriminatingly raises the discount rate to member banks by more than 1% America will default on its 10 and 30-year treasury interest payments. Oh, yeah now our new Secretary of the Treasury, Janis Yellen, former Fed Chairman, is considering the use 100-year war bonds to bail out the Fed and US Treasury.

Example: Deja Vu all over again. In the early 1980's the Federal Reserve and Carter Administration blamed low mortgage rates on S&L banks and punished them with 23% prime rates thereby destroying the S&L banking system that had mortgages in circulation at rates of 6% that would default all their existing fixed rate mortgages, and put the so called 745 thrift banks out of business and convicted its principal owner of fraud. Big Brother rides again with the 2007 Arbitrage Depression destroying $30 trillion dollars in home owners' equity and investors 401.k balances.

For the record, in 2005 after Greenspan's retirement, a complacent President Bush and his Treasury Secretary Paulson allowed Fed Chairman Bernanke to raise the discount rate to member banks by 500% in 2005 to 2007 causing the housing depression that swept worldwide and sunk the housing market for a decade. Then blamed the housing market and Wall Street for the Great Recession (really a depression). The aftermath was a $30 trillion hit on 401k savings accounts as Americans' housing values plummeted. (See Exhibit A the demise of the American liquidity and Article 4 Pop Goes the Monetary Balloon). This is history repeating itself.

Under President Trump we had a Fed with Janet Yellen as its Chairman sustaining the lowering of the Fed rates to 1% and on occasion a negative rate for the first time in memory. This stimulated the use of borrowed capital and more small business startups, reducing unemployment, improving wages, increasing employment of minorities and stimulating the economy as demonstrated by the Dow Jones exceeding 30,000 for the first time. How in the world could he lose the 2020 reelection by 8 million votes to Joseph Robinhood Biden and leave us in the hands of this incompetent, 47 years in the Senate, with no entrepreneurial skills, as President ... who if left unabated running the country with a teleprompter, Pelosi House, Schumer Senate and a Obama speech writer will finally sink the Great American Enterprise.

Now, under President Biden's leadership, the Democrats plan to transform America into a Socialist State, by proposing more social reform and big business Pandemic stimulus rather than infusing wealthy Big Unions, Big Media, Big Box, and Big Tech money into small business creativity. It's the new Entitlements that are further destroying the American work ethic. We need to protect the entitlements that help our elderly and needy by investing money saved on reducing and eliminating the new entitlements that strap enterprise. We no longer can just stand for free enterprise; we need to invest in the energy and patriotism of the American worker as we did in the 1940s to win a war on our very way of life and economic principles.

The war on debt in the 2020 to 2030 decade is the same type of war. It's to save the national standard of living and allowing all of the people (the have-nots) to have an opportunity to succeed, not just the elite (the haves) who can afford higher education, with jobs already secured in the public sector. To win that war, (while stymieing the charges that the White Imperialist government should pay reparation to the "Black Lives Matter" campaign and cancel our culture related to slavery and black injustices) the inner cities have to be rebuilt using small business loans and big money capital. The BLM must lead by example not by protests that unravel into uncivil riots and carnage of the very businesses that will provide the opportunity (reparation) they demand. This is called poetic justice:

WHY THE RUNAWAY CRIME IN OUR CITIES

"Too many guns or too many gangs"
"Or too few opportunities for minorities"
"Or pride in the "hood" for those of color"
"Families with a mother and father"

Who is worth their salt … it's not an issue resolver
With no bullets in their revolver
It's not having good public schools
Being administered by fools

The solution is in the hands of law makers' axes
Having the public schools funded by property taxes
Not sales taxes on enterprise and the slum landlords
Who don't pay their share with a pittance that ill affords

Hope in our public schools for the learned
Become our future by what they've earned
Pass the laws that will fund decent schools
In the places now administered by fools

The soul of our country has been sold
By the rulers of the gold … by taxing the floor
And conceal the ceiling by closing the door
Keeping them down and poor

Sales taxes will generate much more
For building better schools and morale
For those with no hope no jobs nothing in store
Spending their futures in gangs throwing in the towel

With the fatherless families
Becoming the victims of the warfare
And motherless anomalies
Becoming the grandmother's affair

While our State and Federal Governing Legislatures
Have destroyed black futures
When relegating the public schools to fail
By lawmaking a hammer rather than the nail

Taxes are an issue and appeal
Property taxes aren't the fuels
They're to repeal
Legislating sales taxes to fund the schools

Giving the teachers the tools
Administering with professionals not fools

PEACEFUL COEXISTENCE IN OUR CITIES

A problem being treated as an issue

Baltimore Detroit
Chicago Ferguson
Cleveland East St. Louis
South LA Minneapolis
Atlanta Slums USA

Life is best lived solving problems
Not just debating issues
Not giving in to obstacles
For life consists of confronting problems
And learning from them

Between two friends
There are true issues
How to raise their kids
How much sugar on their cereal?
How many drinks is enough?
Who is the favorite team?

Between two enemies
There are true problems
How to discipline children
How to get rid of discrimination
Keep the promises of a nation

Issues are disagreements
Problems demand a solution
Are you a politician debating issues
Or are you a problem maker

"Defund police remove their teeth"
"Or honor your brother that is Juneteenth"
Or a lawmaker who will compromise
Your past and your future

Are the police profiling then defiling
Do black lives matter more than gangs killing
What a pity – the problem is you not the city

To avoid honor to cauterize
An open wound that needs a suture
When humanism is in order
Peaceful coexistence for the future

That Martin Luther King
Sought as his American Dream
The color of your skin
Shall not dictate our youth to sin

Let Humanism win

Cooling the debt and heating up the economy: Axiom number Seven:

Declare war on America's debt: If you believe in the American work ethic that won World War II, but has not been the same since, needs to be reenergized into a WAR ON DEBT then lower the new entitlements (unemployment, workers' comp, disability, unfunded pensions, welfare, food stamps) protect the needed safety net entitlements (Social Security, Medicare, Medicaid) and invest the savings and revitalize the tax base for recapitalizing America's productive energies.

We are losing the war on debt (exasperated by the 2020/21 Pandemic) www.usdebtclock.org.

$21 trillion annual GNP is not growing when the unessential businesses were closed during the Pandemic. Those are the 480 thousand enterprising Americans to buck up and endure more than a year without income.

$22.7 billion overhead for government employees ($125 per year Federal employees with paid health care and pensions.

$800 billion unfunded pensions for government employees.

$6 trillion increase in annual spending and debt per year due to short falls in tax revenues due to the 2007 to 2012 depression, the 2020 Pandemic and stagnant GDP growth due to shutdowns.

$1 trillion in annual capital generation being lost by not assessing the "haves" net worth to pay down $28 trillion current liabilities and amortize the long-term obligations of $158 trillion by 20% per year or #3 trillion per year.

Read my mind or lips: it's the government fixed overhead, it's the public payroll, unionization, and public pension plans to fund punitive regulations...

Lawmakers and regulators are woke alligators *killing the golden goose.*

During the recent 2007 financial implosion and the 2020 Pandemic shutdown of nonessential businesses, created by incompetent monetary mismanagement by the Federal Reserve, the President and Department of Treasury, businesses have had to down size using the following tactics:

- Lower private sector payrolls.
- Lower private sector benefits and unfunded pensions.
- Lower private sector retirement income and savings.
- Lower productive capacity and lower quality.
- Lower productive capital, fewer small businesses, fewer new jobs.

- Lower tax revenues to fund a bloated government payroll.
- Lower investment in research and development.
- Lower home values and 401.k retirement plans.

Resulting in:

- Higher unemployment.
- Higher prices.
- Reduced value of the dollar.
- More difficulty to innovate new products.
- More bankruptcies (60,000 per month) (544,463 in 2020, 774,940 2019, 1,59,081 2010.)
- More distrust of politicians and lawmakers (88% dissatisfaction rating).
- More Government regulations and policing enforcement of those laws. With 80 million job openings created by Biden's welfare checks.
- More crime and killings in the ghettos due defunding of police movement and using enforcement rather than reinforcement.
- More collapse of the major cities' infrastructure while pushing the Green New Deal. Instead of the Green New Deal we need a Black New Deal to clean up the ghetto holocaust in the crime infested inner cities and small blighted black communities.
- More debt, deficits, lower value of dollar and higher prices = insolvency then bankruptcy.
- Contributing to financial collapse of the monetary system and stock market ($600 trillion dollars of derivatives losing value and being shorted by greedy traders for profit) with the value of the dollar losing the war to the Chinese yuan.

Yes, I'm telling this part of the story to finally educate the electorate that the political consultants tell the candidate "To never educate the voters; it will come back to haunt you when they find out the truth".

Problem: as Big Brother government grows enterprise shrinks. All the rhetoric is focused on entitlements, not on the government payroll. Medicare, Medicaid and Social Security are not the real problem because they aren't entitlements; it is the regulatory power over them that have borrowed from them to fight wars and pay public service payroll. Based on the constitution funded entitlements and criminal law are the only reason to have government in the first place.

At the same time government at all levels continues to grow. The $3.9 trillion Bush and Obama stimulus funds in 2007 and 2010 increased the number of government contracts and employees by hundreds of thousands nationwide, with a corollary increase in regulators and IRS agents. The service unions made sure their essential workers' wages increased 16 percent, their pensions grew by the same multiple, their accountability was diluted due to focus on the use of laws to restrict private business financing as more and more nonproductive workers were employed by state, local, and federal governments.

We now have 22,700,000 government employees at every level of the bureaucracy nationwide enforcing small and large business regulations with punitive infringement. That is a $1.3 trillion annual payroll, 33 percent of the annual federal government budget, and 11 percent of the $28 trillion deficits. The public sector pensions are the ripple effect of allowing unionization of public workers while increasing the public payroll, and have increased the unfunded debt twenty times the annual payroll or $800 billion unfunded public service pensions each year.

Biden's Justice department, to help fund their Green New Deal is proposing 87,000 new IRS agents to enforce a plan to have banks flag bank deposit transactions over $600 for catching taxpayers that are not reporting their income. Currently there are 76,832 IRS agents. The Wizard of Oz Biden $5.6 trillion dollar infrastructure and jobs bill proposes hiring of another 87,000 agents to catch American's legalized citizens cheating on their tax returns. Starting with monitoring each American's checking and savings account transactions over $600, using the US banks as undercover agents for reporting what accounts should be audited for criminal underpaying of their income taxes ... the current IRS budget is $12.3 billion. The addition of 87 thousand agents will cost $12 billion, or doubling the IRS budget. Assuming they find 200 million working Americans that are cheating the government out of $600 dollars per annum, amounts to $12 billion or a breakeven on increased cost, so any benefit will have to come from the 26 million millionaires and billionaires in American with net worth of $158.2 trillion ... using a tax rate of 39% on (AGI) adjusted gross taxable income rate of 12% of net worth would be $15.5 trillion. While taxes on AGI only equals $2..2 trillion in taxes compared to the 175 million taxpayers making under $400,000 times effective tax rate of 12.48% equals $1.1 trillion to pay for $5.6 trillion for infrastructure and jobs bills and annual operating costs of $6.2 trillion due to a deficit spending spree.

Our diplomats and politicians continue to placate OPEC and the costs continue to follow the imperial movements by the USA. Why not form our own Oil Purchasing Energy Countries USA, Canada, Japan, France, Italy, England, India and Mexico to allow demand to dictate a competitive price, not the one-sided formula that we now have? With the election of Joe Biden's executive orders, the liberals are playing Russian Roulette by moving to a green energy program too early by destroying America's advances in clean fossil fuel energy using natural gas and changes in carbon absorption by wetlands, farming, forest management, conservation of our green earth.

Under President Trump, using the natural gas industry, the keystone pipeline, electric autos, conservation using carbon restoration of our farm and grazing lands moved America to leadership in complying with the Paris Accord. Under Trump fossil fuels are being phased out with the rational use of nuclear power, wind, fracking to transition to managing the environment.

Doing this allowed Earth to manage itself by restoring natural habitat. In the Netflix production "Kiss the Land" highlighted by the Paris

Accord endorsement, demonstrates carbon dioxide conversion (carbon concentration offset by the carbon natural cycle absorption by plants, trees, grasslands, rain forests, etc., through photosynthesis) using farm land conservation as the solution not human standard of living deprivation.

According to Cheng Xiaonong a Chinese Studies scholar and scientist,

"Global warming has disappeared from the vocabulary of the Biden administration's climate policy. The Green New Deal's climate charge advocates fail to make the net carbon calculation by making gross carbon dioxide data as the justification for the climate change. The Green New Deal climate change advocates use gross carbon dioxide data as the political fear factor inducing conformity to attain zero emissions by 2050". Cheng further states that "these natural factors are beyond human control. However, it is unscientific to attribute all climate change to economic activities of mankind".

Example: Save the Planet, are you crazy, Mother Nature and Father time can save themselves? Do you really think that Joe Biden, AOC, the Green New Deal and the Paris Accord can change how El Nino and El Nina affect the trade winds, net carbon greenhouse affecting weather on the worldwide farmed ground, or the Pacific and Caribbean Hurricanes, the Atlantic Nor'easters, the typhoons in the South China Sea, heat and winds of the Mediterranean, the extreme cold of the North and South Poles, the heat and rainless Sharia Desert, India and China's smog and smoke stacks, Mexico's blight and poverty, Puerto Rico, Haiti, Virgin Islands, East and West Indies hurricanes and poverty, USA's forest fires, Canada's Nor' westerns and blizzards, Russia's Siberian winters, without fossil fuels and carbon burning factories that produce electricity for making solar panels, electric cars and wind mills and so-called wind farms.

Does the Green New Deal and its proponents really think the Earth can be managed by a diverse and independent society; as it did with the fear factor inducing conformity used to mismanage the Pandemic by almost destroying the very foundation of the risk-taking American Dream standard of living ... that everyone on earth is wanting by coming here? They, like we should, want conservation of their rights not deprivation of lifestyles and panic over what the Earth has been managing itself for billions of years.

Yes, we need to lower our fossil fuel energy consumption, develop safer nuclear power, remove plastic from our oceans, clean the air, the water, the soil, save the forests, restore the inner cities and we will do that by freedom of choice and enterprise not mandated by politically fear-motivated ideas that have and will not work. And more importantly commit America to unsustainable financial and economic cost of $100 trillion dollars over the next twenty-five years. When China, India, Mexico, Russia, etc. labeled as emerging economies, are noncompliant with their commitment to be fossil fuel carbon free and have not yet met their commitments to the Paris Accord. While the USA has positive reduction results and still paying more for being a member of the first world countries consortium. Yet the Biden Administration is reversing Trump's decision to drop out of the Accord for those reasons. Just another example of President Biden blindly impairing America's budget strategy to force the noncompliant countries to pay penalties on the basis of their noncompliance.

CONSERVE THE EARTH

The convenient truth is common sense
The Green New Deal is DOA by wasting dollars and cents
Hoping society will conform as Mother Nature repents
Waiting for Father Time to comply with the advents

Huffing and puffing our way through life
Fighting ourselves and our wife
Wending our way through strife
Sharpening our skills like a knife

Finding that wind has no beginning
Or end nor enough power to send
So why do we deny our sinning
And the lack of support to defend

Curtailing of the waste
And garbage of our culture
Turning our environment in haste
To a planet for the vulture

Would it be different
If life were dependent upon
The contributions spent
For the spires built under the sun

Yes produce for the harvest
Each of us is to entrust
In the system and digest
Conservation to preservation or bust

Yes the greenhouse effect
Has carbon as its shield
But the natural photosynthesis deflect
The damage that convenient truth does yield

Yes living in peace
Worldwide for mankind
While wars can cease
So the wind doesn't blow unkind

Where we are purveyors of waste management
Burying our lives in plastic
In another mound of excrement
Along with those who are climate fatalistic

Nor to an end of life

To the oceans
Wildlife with virgin wife
Void of egg and its suns
Left to the devil's knife

Otherwise we are victims
Of ourselves
Tearing out the stems
Of nature as humanity sells

Out the environment
To a windless burnt earth
Only to awake to a wind advent
Blowing across Hell's hearth

Waiting for the Savior's rebirth
To Kiss the Earth

The Biden progressives are banking on the climate change campaign (really global warming that can't be proven) and The Green New Deal will put them in control of the politics of quack science that misled the country during the Pandemic of 2020 and 2021 … Dr. Fauci still being glorified then vilified as it is becoming apparent that he had funded experimental development of a synthetic covid-19 virus in the Wuhan

Chinese lab for studying gain of function possibilities for a worldwide Pandemic and had it inadvertently infect lab workers that then was transmitted to the city of Wuhan and the world.

Then he attempted to cover it up with quack science, mimicked from the 1918 Corona Virus Pandemic, headed up by "everyone will die" task force, we got bending the curve with no calculation of risk. Forcing the shutdown, masks, social distancing, sheltering in place, PPE and hospital bed shortage and ventilator panic tactics that brought our nation under the control of one man ... not sense Hitler has a derelict misled a nation of our size.

In the meantime, the private sector continues to shrink: Axiom number Eight:

- 8 million unfilled job openings due to unemployment checks that became the right to not work and the resistance to get the mandated vaccines resulting in 17 million unemployed causing supply chains, trucking and stocking shortages. (Climaxing the fear of new variants with unemployment as high as 40 million nonessential workers during the 2020-21 Pandemic with the essential government and Big Box employees considered "hands off" for the (small)l business shutdown) (for every private sector job lost, there should have been a corresponding loss of jobs for the public sector),
- Reduction of invested capital and national wealth by 50 percent due to more and more so-called financial reform handcuffs (for the redistribution of national wealth, with reduction in income-based taxes).
- With every 10 percent increase per year in the imbalance of trade and the trade deficit of $60 billion per month (for every increase in the trade deficit there should be a marketing fee charged to those countries for using our consumer shelf space that lowers the trade deficit and our national debt).

- $3 trillion in debt to China, Japan, OPEC, and other so-called trade partners (for every increase in debt to our foreign competitors, we should charge them 5% for using our consumer market place). If it is proven that the 2020 China virus was released by the Wuhan lab the $1.3 trillion owned to China should be written off as an offset against the $6 trillion cost to USA.
- Increase in fossil fuel energy costs (for every increase in the cost per barrel of oil, we should purchase through our purchasing OPEC partners: USA, Canada, Japan, France, Italy, England, India and Mexico). Once we are energy independent, as we were during Trump's tenure, we can control the worldwide cost of clean energy ... until Biden's energy policies killed the Keystone pipeline and fracking on Federal lands to ignoring the pipeline from Russia to Germany that takes energy sales to Germany away.

90% of the world's global trade is shipped by sea, with 70% in containers. The USA has outsourced $48 billion imports per month from China. And another $30 billion from South Korea, Japan and Viet Nam. With the supply line container ships sitting in our 20 ports averaging 10 to 80 ships or over 300 waiting to be unloaded with China having 37,311TEU's (4 containers) daily totaling 160 thousand containers on 148 Chinese vessels holding 610,000 TEU;s present to over 100 countries or 2.4 million containers waiting to be unloaded, carrying 4 per truck transported by 2 million USA semi-trailer truck drivers (68% of all freight is transported by semi's). Or by USA trains (25% of containers) 200 per train,

- This is, 2.4 million containers per year loaded and unloaded by 400,000 workers with 1million sky lifts and forklifts, delivered by 2 million truckers, 167,000 rail workers, by 400,000 Fed Ex employees, 434,000 UPS employees, USPS 669,000 employees.

- And stocked and shipped by 950,000 Amazon employees, 2.5 million Walmart employees, 254,000 Costco employees, 210,500 Walgreen employees stocking retail shelves. More than 6.5 million American enterprise workers making the supply chain function on a daily basis with 8 million job openings in all facets of supporting the supply chain businesses.

- The Biden Administration has mismanaged the processing of the supply chain imports because of the Pandemic by issuing stimulus checks, rent subsidies, increases in minimum wage rates and child welfare checks encouraging workers to stay home until they are vaccinated. This unanticipated consequence has a far-reaching impact on unemployment and new job forecasts that are affecting the American GDP, that depends on having the shelves and online ordering businesses fully stocked to have an adequate inventory supply for the holidays and everyday shopping demand. If not, stagnation follows with inflation of cost and prices close behind.

- Causing a down turn of 5 to 10% in GDP could occur between now and New Year's Day of 2022 because of the shortage of supply chain labor. That, with inflation and value buying threatened by shortages of inventory could amount to a recession or a disastrous depression if there is a run on the banks and stock market. If this happens America is sliding into chaos politically with the unprepared and unqualified current Administration proposing even more deficit spending with $5.2 trillion in additional spending over the next three to ten years.

As a result, due to adverse reaction to the Depression of 2007-12, the Dodd Frank law (the Democrats allowing the Federal Reserve and its banking system to rule over free market enterprise) small businesses cannot borrow capital it needs to innovate the very solutions that bail out the bankruptcy being caused by the politicians, regulators, and bureaucracy. Big Brother Government, Big Media, Big Box and Big Tech labeled as essential Brotherhood businesses and institutions (Facebook, Amazon, Twitter, Google, Instagram, Network Media, Berkshire, Microsoft, Apple, Hollywood, Disney, Democrat and Republican Pac's and government employees, etc.) have invested $14 billion in the 2020 Presidential election; more in political action and lobbyists than research and development to prevent Pandemics or curtail, energy shortages and trade deficits. At the same time China has taken over the manufacturing supply lines charging us $1.9 billion in shipping costs. It appears that the Joe and Hunter Biden/Sanders doctrine of appeasers, pleasers and geezers on foreign policies, is based on insider money taking over American values and lively hood?

Complicated by the Corona China Virus impact on our GDP and GNP. As the tax base has fallen then flattened, and will continue to follow the irrational investment of taxpayer money by the biggest casino in the world, the Federal Reserve. Unfortunately, when the fed increases the discount rate to member banks that affect 401k, economic and home values, bad things happen.

Meanwhile the red and blue parties' *fiddle* while America burns—a strategy of *false hopes* and mosquito efforts to swat at the Goliath debt. And stall everything by using abortion as a stalemate. Why? They do not want to say the words that are the solution:

"What is the difference between a cynic and an agent of change . . . the cynic creates the problem then calls it an unresolvable issue and the agent of change defines the problem and imposes a solution."

–Winston Churchill

Solution: cut the f—king government's payroll! Downsize Public Sector, Upsize Private Sector... Free up business to grow its own work ethic and competitive technology for prosperity of its human capital.

See Volume III for the expansion of the work ethic as the solution to the loss of patriotic workers and blaming the profit motive and all the isms for loss of productivity.

Why should the private sector small businesses be expected to absorb the exorbitant cost of wasteful governmental 40% overhead? Healthcare costs are being shifted to the private worker while the public workers get free healthcare. Pension costs and raises are being taken away from private workers while the essential public workers get guaranteed union-backed pensions and wage increases. Obviously, the overhead from nonproductive government jobs is sinking the great ship *enterprise*.

I can tell you how to save the ship, do what a bankruptcy attorney or a bail-out specialist working on a turn-around would do; cut fixed overhead to the breakeven point close inefficient agencies and eliminate redundancy in the organization:

- Cut congressional and state legislative salaries by 25 percent = $400 million savings.
- Cut the number of government employees by 25 percent = $200 billion savings.
- Cut defense spending and proliferation of weapons by 25 percent = $500 billion savings.
- Cut energy costs using the purchasing OPEC to balance trade deficits with oil-producing countries = $500 billion savings.
- Repeal unaffordable pension plans and cut cost by 25 percent = $1 trillion savings.

- Cut the size of legislative salaries, benefits, and power = $50 billion savings.
- Reduce laws and regulations by 25 percent = $750 billion savings.
- Take the power of monetary policy and interest rate manipulation away from the Fed and allow markets to afford borrowed capital = $1 trillion savings.
- Conservative annual savings to Americans by lowering government payroll and debt = $4 trillion savings.

If we wait for the so-called public servants to reduce their share of the problem and continue to pass laws, we cannot afford nor need, we will not only be insolvent, but also bankrupt as a nation. (Lawmakers traditionally ignore financial responsibility by heaping on more and more laws. Every law costs a minimum of $5 million per year in government payroll to enforce the law. For example, it took billions to implement Obama healthcare reform by adding 16,000 IRS agents, 15,000 GAO auditors to police the law, and 100,000 more government employees to enforce it = $100 billion per year just to police something that would not cost us one dime.) For every law passed, it should be funded by a sunset on ten laws we really don't need.

Results':

- Fewer unneeded laws and a more active private sector in the decision making.
- Balanced federal and state budgets in four years.
- Growing stock market and dynamic capital availability to small businesses.
- A balanced budget for growing entitlements (Medicare and Social Security are saved) based on a percent of GDP.
- Voter and taxpayer taking a more active role in public service.

- Peaceful coexistence movements expanded by funding the development of investment around the world rather than weapon deployment.
- Lower energy costs and more partnerships with entrepreneurial countries who are consumers themselves.

Continuing with our Oligarchy form of governance will surely ensure the fall of America as the former leader in the world. Globally, we must realize that it is an economic war with the use of military tactics, wasted resources, that erodes our effectiveness to bring peace to those that have way less than we now have. However, shipping jobs overseas is a symptom, not the problem. Effectively, we are deploying capital to seed markets that have not existed until now, so we need to invest our capital in small information-processing businesses to serve that expanding market. Also, reinstate a President Trump policy of made in America policy and take back the supply chain controlled by China and Asian manufacturers.

And as America continues to expect to retire at sixty-five, most of the "baby boomers" will be seeking employment to supplement their lost 401(k) and pension money. We need to capitalize on this elder job corps through investing their retirement funds in creation of jobs, not socializing our economy for the "common good."

In Bob Woodward's bestselling book, *The High Price of Politics*, the binary gridlock of the last time the debt limit fiscal cliff faced Congress and the president, the red and blue collectively kicked the can down the sidetrack until after the presidential election. Now the debt limit has been temporarily suspended pending the end of the Pandemic ... or the next Pandemic. The collusion between the red and the blue will justify raising taxes for everyone and chopping entitlements. This was the strategy of the establishment ruling class all along.

Job creation's war on debt: reinvestment in the enterprise and investment in Peaceful Co-existence. The government and Federal Reserve do not create jobs. Politicians do not create jobs. Laws do not create productive jobs. Lower taxes do not create jobs. Entrepreneurs create products with capital. Capital creates the need for jobs. What creates capital … competitive, enterprising American workers?

The accumulated deficit spending for the preceding 50 years of borrowing to pay trillions of dollars of government payroll (currently 22 million government workers) and pensions is $158 trillion dollars. Taxes since Roosevelt have never paid the operating costs of the swamp but quietly encumbered America for a local drug store cash register system of cash taken in minus cash paid out that represents profit or loss for covering deficit spending to be covered by borrowing. The difference in USA, books are balanced by borrowing as the Fed sell US Treasuries to China, Japan, South Korea, etc. Or the US Treasury printing out dollars with no backing since taking our monetary system off the gold standard under Nixon. A colossal cooking of the books and forerunner of bankruptcy in free enterprise America.

Value-Added products create profits . . . Profitable businesses create more capital, jobs and prosperity. (Eliminating waste is profits … Dr. Edwards Deming):

1. Enterprising American workers and free market enterprise create *saleable* products, marketing and distribtuion services.
2. Products and services produce profits that create capital.
3. Technology creates efficiency and eliminates waste to create capital.
4. Savings create profits that create capital.
5. Lower taxes create credit, profits, and capital availability.
6. Elimination of wasted resources creates profits that create capital.
7. Lower overhead creates profit and capital availability.
8. Lower operating costs due to efficiency creates profit and capital.
9. Lower interest rates create profits and the availability of capital.

10. Raising consumer demand creates profits and capital.

What kills the availability of profits and capital? Axiom Number Nine:

1. Poor work ethic and lack of patriotism with illegal immigration.
2. Low productivity and declining quality.
3. Government regulatory intervention in all facets of business (monopsony).
4. Rising tax rates feeding inflation.
5. Lowering tax credits kills incentive.
6. High interest rates spawning inflation.
7. Oppressive government regulations adding overhead costs.
8. High government overhead (salaries, pensions, benefits, perks).
9. Unionized and lionized government workers (Teachers Union dictating work environment during the Pandemic).
10. Guaranteed government retirement with pensions, healthcare, and entitlements.
11. Open borders promulgated by Democratic States and Cities under the term sanctuary and refugee policies.
12. Value of the dollar plummets and is replaced by China's yuan as the reference currency for worldwide trade.

How to create American jobs, lower government overhead, and increase availability of capital, profits, and tax revenues

1. Tax net worth of individuals and corporations, not adjusted gross or net taxable income; and convert to shares of stock in the American enterprise that collects 5 percent from every American's net worth, not current tax rates; corporations under $5 million in annual revenues 0 percent tax rates. This represents an investment in American Enterprise. Org for

inner city development and small business expansion by good neighborhood coalitions.
2. Recapitalize American small business:
    a. Investment tax credit for technology.
    b. Low-interest, government-guaranteed bank loans.
    c. Research and development tax credits for companies over $5 million in annual revenues.
    d. Job-creation tax credit for companies over $5 million in annual revenues.
3. Lawmakers become responsible for job making using incentives.
4. American Enterprise Party becomes the third alternative. "The two wings of establishment government are flapping and the middle is dying," Sam Nunn (D), Georgia.
5. For every $1 million in capital created with a cap rate of 12 creates $12 million in available capitalization or $144 million in paying power for hiring employees to create, produce and service US salable products.
6. $144 million investment power for creating 1 million jobs creates $12 million in purchasing power.
7. $12 million new jobs annually create $3.4 trillion per year in capital times 10 years = $30.4 trillion in capita creation infused into the economy.
8. An ROI rate of return on capital of 10% for the next decade will generate $3 trillion per year for paying down the national debt in five years and produce a $7.3 trillion surplus in 10 years.
9. The value of the dollar escalates and remains the reference currency with China's yuan a distant second.

American Enterprise War chest and voting blocs:

150 to 170 million current work force.
16 million unemployed blacks and Hispanics.
20 million underemployed undocumented illegal immigrants.

77 million baby boomers who are seeking retirement.

$100 trillion net worth of Americans not being taxed

War on debt must reduce the fixed overhead:
Axiom number Ten:

- 22.7 million unionized public service employees = $1.3 trillion annual overhead payroll (INCREASE OF 3 MILLION BUREACRATS IN 9 YEARS ... 2010-2019).
- $ 4.4 to $7.3 trillion unfunded pensions for government employees.
- $28 trillion in national debt, increasing at $950 billion per week, $5.1 trillion per fiscal year.
- $158 trillion in unfunded entitlements and pensions of public officials.
- $600 trillion worldwide debt.
- 3.7 mil federal employees; $324 billion payroll: $125,583 avg. annual earnings public, $60,046 private.
- $40,785 health/pension public, $9,882 private sector. 33% of Americans make less than $24,000 per year and private sector wages have been stagnant for six to seven years until 2016 as they began to rise due to the Trump tax cuts and demand.
- 19 million state, city, township, county employees; $62,899 annual earnings, $43,589 for private sector.

	Employees			2008	2020 Labor	Inc.	2020
State, city, county	19,013,000	Avg. Salary		$47,231	$999,965,923,360	32%	$62,899
Federal gov't.	3,721,000	Avg. Salary		$67,691	$324,708,397,420	50%	$125,583
Total gov't.	22,734,000	Avg. Salary		$56,992	$1,2,674,320,780	49%	$97,691

The typical federal worker is paid 20 percent more than a private-sector worker in the same occupation. Median annual salary: $324 BILLION ANNUAL FEDERAL PAYROLL $999 BILLION ANNUAL STATE, LOCAL PAYROLL	Median annual salary:
	Federal Pvt. Diff.
Job comparison government jobs are first responders and service3 agencies … white collar essential , low turnover guaranteed longevity and fully paid for pensions.	
	$125,591 70,046 $55,545

Average federal salaries in 100 agencies exceed average private-sector pay in 83 percent of comparable 500 occupations. A sampling of average annual salaries in 2020, the most recent data, for accountants, nurses, chemists, surveyors, cooks, clerks, and janitors are among the wide range of jobs that get paid more on average in the federal government than in the private sector.

Refinancing of the American Enterprise System:

1. Capitalize the value of work in all of our lives and recreate the enterprising competitive nature of America as it was conceived by the founding fathers and mothers.
2. Deregulate the flow of capital and regulate the flow of debt; disband the Federal Reserve System, which uses taxpayer money to gamble the monetary flow to control the generation of capital, using prime interest rates. Replace it with the US Treasury under the departmental title Monetary Control.

3. Government reform by encouraging the people to do what we can, not enforce laws upon us that tell us what we can't do.
4. Tax net worth, not adjusted gross income so the middle-class is relieved of paying 90 percent of the taxes (forty-six different levels now exist and growing). This represents an investment in American Enterprise. Org for inner city development and small business expansion by good neighborhood coalitions.
5. Increase the value of the individual and enterprise values to reduce the control of the institutions (Federal Reserve, IRS, HHS, defense, energy, housing, education, healthcare).
6. Listen to the voice of the majority rather than the flagrant use of enforcement driven laws by the wealthy minority to inhibit enterprise, and by its essence ignores what the constitution has already obligated us to do so. Pursue personal opportunities to accomplish the human risk-taking American Dream.

American Enterprise Party Agenda

This isn't a movement to just another political party, it is a movement of the people for a sustainable way of life by those who believe that peaceful coexistence can be attained in our lifetime and by our human obligation to the planet. Then the pursuit of happiness, health and abundance for all who are willing to participate in that enterprising pursuit resulting in positive outcomes overriding the blind pursuit of disposable income:

1. Our enterprise is currently being run by career politicians (95 percent of whom are attorneys, central bankers, and lifetime bureaucrats), so we need to reduce the enactment of laws by government legislatures (each law enacted by state and federal governments costs the taxpayer and small businesses $5 million each). Change the label of *lawmaker* to *peacemaker* so the focus is on reduction of overhead and increased investment in productive saleable products. To do this, for every law proposed ten must be eliminated as unnecessary. As George Washington said, "Government is not the reason; it is

not eloquent; it is a force. Like fire, it is a dangerous servant and a fearful master."

2. Reduce the public sector payroll of $1.3 trillion per year for nonproductive employees who are supporting the giant enforcement and judicial machine by 50 percent over the next ten years. Convert accounting and budgeting to accrual basis to reflect the true financial condition of the enterprise.
3. Assess a net worth capital infusion from the elite, and not tax net adjusted gross income and convert to shares of stock in the American enterprise that collects 5 percent from every American's net worth. This will generate revenues even when the economy is stagnant, since it is based on our national GDP and net worth.
4. Eliminate redundant federal and state agencies that inhibit the growth of small businesses and cost trillions without accountability of verification of outcome.
5. Allow the agencies that can utilize America's tax dollars for job creation and small businesses, SBA, FHA, Fannie Mae, Freddie Mac, HUD to reduce the red tape and regulations for obtaining critical capital for small business to *win the war on debt*.
6. Lower energy costs through the buyer controls of the price of oil by partnering with other nations (OPEC for the Organization of Energy Purchasing Countries) to establish the influence of the buyers in setting the cost of barrels of oil (to neuter the complete economic control by the eastern OPEC rate setters and suppliers). And utilize our natural resources for meeting our natural need to support the American enterprising human effort.
7. Amend the Obama affordable healthcare act using mutual insurance companies that take employee withholding, matched by employer contribution, for healthcare financing through personal savings accounts reinvested in their own health and wellness into national small businesses. Mutual investment companies administer the SHIFT (Self Health Insurance

Funding Trust) of the funding paradigm from government to the private sector.
8. Equity capital generation:
   a. Lowering the 40,000 bills per year proposed with 15% becoming law annually by state, local and federal legislatures by 25 percent per year = $50 billion per year saved for investment in the *war on debt*.
   b. Reduction of the public payroll by privatizing discretionary agencies (energy, education, commerce, agriculture, NSA, health and human services, postal services, transportation, including security, by 50 percent in ten years saves $2.5 trillion over the next ten years for investment in the *war on debt*.
   c. Assess net worth of the "haves" for a capital investment that will generate up to $250 billion per year in additional revenues that can be invested in small businesses or $1 trillion over the next decade in funding for the *war on debt*. Convert to shares of stock in the American enterprise that collects 5 percent from every American's net worth.
   d. Elimination of the enforcement machine that inhibits small businesses will save $100 billion per year or $1 trillion over ten years that can be invested in the *war on debt*.
   e. Lowering the cost of oil by 25 percent over the next five years saves (fifty billion barrels per year at a savings of $25 per barrel = $1.1 trillion year in savings for American businesses over the next five years to invest in the *war on debt*.
   f. The cost of the Affordable Care Act will be $700 billion plus the current cost of $700 billion of the Medicare Part D that further makes Americans dependent on prescription drugs can be replaced by privatizing healthcare for younger Americans, and retaining Medicare and Medicaid for the aging population

will save 25 percent of $1.4 trillion that will be spent under the current reform act over the next ten years or $350 billion that can be saved and invested in the *war on debt*.

    g. By privatizing healthcare through a withholding system, the 160 million employed Americans can save $100 per month, $192 billion per year, for investment in Mutual Health Insurance to be invested in the American economy. Medicare and Medicaid can be funded through its current withholding system by eliminating the onerous regulatory system that costs $50 billion per year. Healthy Americans spending money on preventive and wellness programs will win the *war on debt*.

9. Adopt the Trump Doctrine for safe borders that was effective during his last year of the Presidency. After Biden reversed the illegal immigration executive orders of Trump it was demonstrated, how well the wall, the border protection police and arrangements with Mexico, Central and South American countries slowed the masses from overwhelming the American borders, worked. Unless this is resolved by bi-partisan legislation the illegal immigrant population growth in America that reached 30 million in one decade will fill our city streets with homeless, hopeless, uneducated, unskilled workers wanting to replace our citizens with lower expectations. How can America support the world's refugees and succeed on our own behalf when open boarders make us unsafe from cartels, terrorists imbedding loyalists in our very open society? Most will end up on the streets, homeless or near homeless (currently 600,000 to 1.5 million are homeless in America, 25% are children under the age of 18) adding more to tent cities in our inner cities.

10. Adopt the Trump doctrine of safe soldiers and peace through strength that was effective during his last year of the Presidency to correct the disastrous inhumane Biden exit from Afghanistan and southern open borders :

- After Biden reversed the verbal agreement with the Afghan government and the Taliban to come together in an enunciated peace accord contingent on the Taliban changing its policies of Sharia law for women, music and social gatherings, Biden's Secretaries of State and Defense, Commander in Chief of the Military and the President decided to close Bagram Airport and exit Afghanistan by August 31st a date enforced by the Taliban.

- Who in two months took over the Country after the Afghan administration and military collapsed under siege by the Taliban? After Bagram USA airport was closed by Secretary of State Blinken and the 5,000 prisoners released that preceded a disastrous and deadly exit of American forces that left behind thousands of Afghans and hundreds of Americans to survive on their own. Also, left behind were thousands of American citizens, hundreds of Afghan interpreters and their families, thousands of SCI and green card holders; and a new $800 million dollar Embassy, $85 billion dollars' worth of American weapons and technological warfare night gear and drones.

- In the process 13 American soldiers were killed and another 20 injured after a terrorist attack by ISIS-k who took credit for that and killing 169 Afghan citizens. Again, thousands of undocumented refugees from Afghanistan will be deposited into America and other counties. It isn't likely that the Taliban will change its colors to satisfy the Biden Administration and again will be a terrorist threat to America and its allies by teaming up with the Al-Qaeda and ISIS-k terrorists caliphate. This is in spite of China's Afghan purge for minerals from copper to manganese, to rare earth that has promised the Taliban billions of dollars to fund its government.

The *war on debt* is an America Enterprise Party initiative and must be supported by the nation's governors, who will lead the charge on the local and national debt. Without taking these drastic steps, we continue to lose the *war on debt,* as other great societies have experienced.

Implementation plan (fuse capitalism and socialism together as the enterprise of the future) using Humanism as the banner and the American Enterprise Party as the bearer)

- Downsize some government agencies and privatize others so their services are funded by private capital infusion and service fees paid by the private sector (See Exhibit B for a model).
- Retake Bagram Airport in Kabul and enforce Marshall Law on the Taliban until the thousands of Afghans and support agencies are allowed to leave in peace.
- Elect American Enterprise candidates at every level of government, who embrace the *war on debt* as their platform, starting with the governorships, who will get the brunt of the red or blue block grants for Medicaid, and moving to the state senatorial and house elections.
- Each patriotic American must participate in the *war on debt* by either working for or in the war effort.
- Support state and local officials that embrace the *war on debt* initiatives in their sectors.
- Support the National Accountability Act, which forces each state, federal, and local agency to activate and perpetuate the *war on debt*.

In ten short years, America can be back. The current national deficit of $28 trillion can be a surplus of $7 trillion, with China paid off and the rest of the world following our war on debt programs. It is truly up to the American voters as to how this gets done. Currently, a third-party swing vote **to break ties and prevent gridlock of the two-party system** at every level as the only route to national accountability and participation of voters in their governance. This is necessary, because the red and the blue flag bearers are not enacting or supporting the priorities of enterprising Americans.

Give Me Enterprise or Give me Debt

Give me liberty or give me death
These famous words come to mind as I look
Upon the progress that man has made
The car I'm driving
The highway that I am upon
The landscape highlighted by technology everywhere you look

Over there, they're building a bridge for a new highway
The heavy equipment moves the earth
Pours the concrete
And bridges another gap
Ah, the ingenuity of man
Free to create something better
Has made something from the land
The enterprise of man
In all its glory
Is the image of God
That we pray for

It's the striving for accomplishment
That makes life worthwhile
Those that do not understand this principle
Are still looking
Until they find enterprise
They shall be shallow and fallow
For they have yet to find a reason
To live

So, enterprise is the substance of life
And ironically it comes under attack
From those that have yet to find its sanctity
It is threatened by its own success

And its own unwitting stress
A stress for change and improvement
A stress for commitment and dedication
Which the weaker soil (soul) cannot activate
So as a parasite threatens
The socialist or the communist
Threatens their own life blood
They ask for something for all

Regardless of the commitment and the contribution
And want to control the enterprising soul
They take because they cannot give
In a productive manner
While looking for happiness without effort

Causing the sad state of affairs
Where a society only listens to its critics
And fails to idolize the creators
It is the first makers of de-mental-cide
The taking away of the incentives
For being an independent thinker
As a risk taker
An artist
A scientist
And a dreamer

Those that are enterprising
And do create the redeemer
Contribute and actually map out fate
This is what we should worship
Not just shallow promises of happiness
Without dedication *and work*
For to souls that believe that
All people should be equal
I'm telling the principle of
How can we be better if we are the same

The message that Jesus carried
Which is, "Ye are created by God to be equal"
To be equal in faith and effort
You shall partake in the rewards of equality
Lo, those that shall not make the commitment
Shall not partake

And with this I say to you
Strike the fatal blow to enterprise and
You've struck down what makes mankind good
So, give me enterprise or give me death
For in enterprise, I shall express myself
As there's no color line in free enterprise
But in the stifling embrace of total equality for all
I shall depress myself until I die
An unnoticed death of an enterprising soul
Which seems to be the progressive's or conservative's goal

With work as its toll

W*anton*
O*ppressive*
R*egulations*
K*ills the will of the people*

Free market Capitalism is the invention of society, not a religion, not a cult, not a dream, not a nightmare. It is the natural dynamics of risk and reward. Mankind is survival-driven and has managed to seek reward for self-esteem, creating independence by reaping the harvest of work and the willingness to compete with risk taking on debt. To interject humanism into the equation where family and community take precedence over self-wealth by investing infrastructure projects and contributions to help other Americans to deal with personal problems. This is the brotherhood of man not the Brotherhood of the Big Government regulations.

Governments, on the other hand, are the outgrowth of man's desire to control the aberrant use of capital for individual destructive purposes. But the time comes when the control becomes the reason and the result is a *Big Brother government intrusion that kills initiative for risk capital formation to fund the entrepreneurial rewards to enterprising Americans.*

> Risk and Reward (capital and workers are partisans)
>
> **R**aising
> **I**nitiative
> **S**hall
> **K**ill debt
>
> **R**aising
> **E**nterprise
> **W**ill
> **A**ttain
> **R**etired
> **D**ebt

Who would have thought that America would not be able to pay its bills and acquiesce to a Congress that is spending money that isn't theirs? It is called OPEM, other peoples' money. But continue to raise their own take through perks and pay for speaking their minds without listening to their constituency. Transparency is not accountability since the monetary decision has already been misspent. A Pandemic is not justification for killing the economy with shut downs as a solution to our institutions not finding a vaccine in 100 years. Yes, Dr. Fauci the highest paid Federal bureaucrat and Director of the Institute of Health's Allergy and Infectious Diseases with its 40,000 employees, who's 2019 salary at $417,608 exceeded President Trump's $400,000, failed America by not preventing Covid-19. His involvement with the Wuhan Lab to fund gain of function of a synthetic Covid virus that infected three Chinese lab workers that is suspected to have started the 2019 Pandemic.

Dr. Fauci may not be the blame for the panic ... that was likely caused by China. But his participation in the creation of the synthetic virus most certainly is a major health problem, since the variants are also traceable back to the Wuhan Lab release of the Corona Virus. Why is this not pursued by our Medical and Public Health department and Associations. It is the most destructive event since 1918 and will continue as the two-party politicians use it as justification for passing trillion-dollar pipe dreams, at the demise of American stability, financially and morally.

Why aren't medical doctors and practicing immunologists managing the recovery process. We now are finding out that there were and are medications that can slow down if not prevent the destruction of person's pulmonary system. Why isn't this the top priority of the Biden administration rather than defending Dr. Fauci as not a coconspirator of the Pandemic. And depending on him as Biden's chief advisor on how to prevent another outbreak, other than practicing his quack science of shutdown and deprivation to stop something our immune system can handle if we take better care of ourselves.

Yet in less than a year President Trump the entrepreneur orchestrated in "warp speed" the private pharmaceutical industry development of at least three brands and had 2 billion doses under order before he was blamed by the Democrats for the spread of the China virus and dumped as the only businessman to be ever be elected. Now, in 2021 we are back with attorneys and career politicians running and destroying our great American Enterprise.

SUM UP THIS ARTICLE

Enterprise is most certainly not free but it is freely accountable to its constituencies. How can we do this in the next decade? Using the American Enterprise Party platform to solve problems, not just vying with political speeches about issues: but implementing the following:

Ten Axioms of Success by reversing the Ten Axioms of defeat.

1. Energy costs: form our own OPEC (Oil Purchasing and Producing Energy Countries— USA, Canada, Japan, France, Italy, England, India and Mexico) to negotiate the price of petroleum worldwide. and pursue reusable clean energy over the next decade based on science not politics.

2. **Clean Energy:** phase out fossil fuels as we pursue reusable clean energy over the next decade based on valid science not politics. Create other sources of earth-based energy using natural resources and expand the use of solar resources (fire ice, fracking, harvesting sand stored solar energy).

3. **Clean Air and Water: through conservation farming utilizing and recovering the carbon back to the earth through the natural process of synthesis and atmosphere, with preservation of our rain forests, restoration of our wet lands for producing wild life, nutrients and water for consumption.**

4. **Debt:** downsize all levels of government by 40 percent and privatize FHA, HUD, post office, Fannie Mae, Freddie Mac, SBA, agriculture, commerce, education, healthcare.

5. **Deficit:** offset the balance of trade deficits and interest from borrowing from China, Japan, Korea, with a 25 percent distribution fee for utilizing the American-consumption giant market (much better solution versus tariffs).

6. **Immigration: Undocumented Aliens** should be nationalized, to replace our retiring baby boomers, by controlling the borders and giving amnesty with a requirement of speaking English, paying taxes, and obtaining citizenship within a year of entry.

7. **Taxation:** at a flat rate of 15 percent should be based on individual and corporate net worth for reinvesting in our GNP for seeding the American enterprise, thereby eventually eliminating all other taxes.

8. **Healthcare:** must be privatized and funded by withholding from the individual for private savings accounts in mutually owned private insurance companies who manage the equity through investment in the American economy and disbursements for individual claims for prevention and preservation of health in the pursuit of wellness.

9. **Entitlements:** must be honored so we do not rob from the needy for the sake of the elite's government pensions, capital hoarding, and abuse of union contracts. Medicare and Social Security are not entitlements ... they are funded by withholding, employer matching that is depositing into the social security trust fund individual savings accounts. They both should be updated reconsidering retirement age being 65. Currently retirement filing is slowing with Social Security age being increased to 67 for all new filers.

10. **Education** must be privatized as the Boards of Education are chastised for promoting CRT and 1619 project to cloud America's historical racism facts and using sexual education regarding transgender modification as justification for having genderless bathrooms and sports. Biden's Justice department is threatening to treat dissatisfied parents who are wanting a say in setting the curriculum, as domestic terrorists.

Political Détente: The bottom-line, so to speak, for America's decline financially and socially, is due to the war between the left and the right ... left is so far left it's wrong and the right is so far right it's also in leftfield. So, other identities are emerging ... nationalism, protectionism, wokeism, socialism versus fascism, liberal versus conservative, capitalism versus socialism. Why not brand and label our society as free market American Enterprise and allow the investment of capital and the rights of the enterprising Americans to be blended into the new agenda of opportunity and success for the Many and limit the power and control of the gold of the elite Few.

Political Money-tics Called Contributions: source Wikipedia

In 2008, the three main Koch family foundations contributed to 34 political and policy organizations, three of which they founded, and several of which they directed. As of 2011, Koch Industries' political action committee had donated more than $2.6 million to candidates. The Koch brothers support primarily Republican candidates and in 2010 they supported California Proposition 23, which would have suspended the state's *Global Warming Solutions Act* of 2006. The brothers pledged to donate $60 million in the 2012 election season to defeat President Barack Obama. According to the Center for Responsive Politics, of $274 million in anonymous 2012 contributions, at least $86 million is "attributed to donor groups in the Koch network".

George Soros HonFBA (born György Schwartz, August 12, 1930) is a Hungarian-born American billionaire investor and philanthropist. As of March 2021, ...

Education: London School of Economics

Soros is a supporter of progressive and liberal political causes, to which he dispenses donations through his foundation, the Open Society Foundations. Between 1979 and 2011, he donated more than $11 billion to various philanthropic causes; by 2017, his donations "on civil initiatives to reduce poverty and increase transparency, and on scholarships and universities around the world" totaled $12 billion. He influenced, the collapse of communism in Eastern Europe in the late 1980s and early 1990s,[1] and provided one of Europe›s largest higher education endowments to the Central European University in his Hungarian hometown.

Finally, for the first time in worldwide history, forever rid our earth of the Golden Rule … "those with the Gold shall Rule" replaced by "do unto others as they want you to do unto them ". Then capitalism and socialism are imbedded together as humanism competing against China, Russia, North Korea, Iran who are the 1984 communist imperialists of the 21st century. Then money-tics isn't politics it's protecting our liberties and funding our new American Enterprise.

LIFE TOO BIG TO FAIL

American values are changing …
Bigger is better
Live today
And ignore tomorrow
Pay to play
Business is business
Divorce rate up
Satisfaction down
No savings or security
America is frail and will fail

What happened to …
Small towns are better
Work forever for the same company
Be a patriot
Love thy neighbor
Pledge allegiance to the flag
Pray to God
Save 10%
Give 10%
Believe the media
Life was too small to fail

The difference is due to
Money is God
Jobs are boring
My life is abhorring
It's who you know
Not what you know or grow
College is too expensive
My vote doesn't count
Our kids are distant
I don't know my neighbors
Texting sexting kill relationships

Life was what it was … just right
How do we get it back?
Focus on family
Bring talk back to the dinner table
Play together stay together
Love our spouse for better or worse
Pride in our work each day for my pay
Bring faith in the President back into our life
Support our political leaders and police
Our security is not for sale
Then life is too big to fail

Article Two

...Marxism, Avoid 1984

- Deinstitutionalize America and humanize our culture.
- Consume our enemies—it is an economic war.
- Build coalitions with our Trading Partners.
- Give entrepreneurs a chance to create, fail and succeed.
- Honor our forefather's constitutional based past and present , risk taking and secure culture.

Due to the converging ideas and policies of the oligarchical form of government that we now have in America, I have been motivated to form a third-party movement so the voters have some original ideas and policies to consider in their voting booth and stop the evolution from the overthrow of a dictator to socialism to Marxist Communism, back to totalitarianism. Our current administration is pursuing the dreams of President Obama's father, an admitted Marxist, so a socialist America under the current Progressive Socialist Manifesto of Biden, Sanders, Warren, Pelosi, Schumer and AOC is on its way to completing the cycle.

> "The creatures outside looked from pig to man, and from man to pig, and from pig to man again: but already it was impossible to say which was which." George Orwell's "Animal Farm" and 1984 classic books on the Russian equality Revolution has become an intimate part of contemporary culture. It is an account of the transformation of Manor Farm into Animal Farm, of the brave struggle on the part of the animals to create a wholly democratic society built on the credo that all animals are created equal. Of course, as with its many counterparts in modern society, this brave struggle results in socialism, then Communism, then a new totalitarian regime and a new maxim:

"According to the seven commandments all comrades are created equal. But some comrades are more equal than others."

Accordingly, based on principles espoused in the novels by George Orwell, Jerry Rhoads formed American Enterprise Party Foundation www.americanenterprisepoliticalparty.org to raise money for a third political party called The American Enterprise Party. This third party is completely different from the Green Party, the Constitution Party, the Libertarian Party, *the Tea Party*, and the Independent Party. It is built on consumerism, not idealism, not patronage-ism, not fatalism, not communism, not socialism, not religious fanaticism not racism not wokeism but humanism. Enterprise is the lifeblood of the individual; be it learning, earning, or spending, we all benefit if we are working for the common good. For our family unit, our children's future, our own happiness founded on work ethic and the freedom to fail and get back up and try again—this is the intent of the founding fathers and mothers who fought for our freedom and won the right to coexist with those that have differences but have one thing in common: human value.

My main reasons for this effort are depicted in *Animal Farm* (see Exhibit B for a reality check on the regulatory demise of free market enterprise)

This emulates from our new appeaser President Biden and his son pleaser Hunter acting like the Boars in USA'S Farm who fail in their takeover of the USA Farm then team up with the CCP Farm to save the USA Farm from bankruptcy. By that time the distance between democracy and autocracy is blurred by wealth's power of privilege and influence peddling. Slowly but surely, CCP, Inc. merges USA, Inc. into their worldwide Wolf cold trade war takeover of the world economy.

"The creatures outside looked from pig to man, and from man to pig, and from pig to man again: but already it was impossible to say which was which." Then the American Farm through abdicating to the Chinese Farm business interests, make investments in the Chinese's economy, its stock market using NBA, Nike, California Pension funds, Face book,

You Tube, McDonalds, mutual investment funds, pharmaceuticals, and semiconductors to finance CCP, Inc's. Farm supply line marketing exploits to consolidate the USA Farm into the fold of CCP Farm.

Conspiracy yes, theory no. Why is there a trade imbalance? The theory is USA's Farm labor costs were too high and USA companies raced to Asian countries to use their cheap labor. Well, the facts show that it was the cost of government to run the USA Farm that caused the shift of wealth to Asia. This was exemplified by the tax rate of 38% to 50% and entitlements, health care cost and 22 million government workers costing $1.9 trillion per year including unfunded pensions. Ironically, it was the USA Farm's Great Society overhead that drove companies to CCP, Inc.'s Farm. Our accumulated imbalance of trade (cost of sales) for the last fifty years, resulting in our current recorded debt of $30 trillion, has sent wealth to those foreign suppliers. Who now are holding the Treasury Notes? Who established the control of the supply lines? China, Taiwan, Sought Korea, India, Viet Nam, Russia, Iran, Indonesia, Germany, Saudi Arabia, etc. Also, the USA Farm, annually pay the costs of $1.3 trillion shipping and distribution costs to get the goods to our wholesalers and retailers shelf space, without any cost to the foreign manufacturers. In effect we have shipped our technology overseas, then they sell it back to us with a markup for profit. Causing the ongoing growth of the imbalance in trade and the related debt ... USA is a giant monolithic enterprise in over its head in overhead caused by institutional government and the two-party gridlocked Oligarchy, destined to return to the bondage of third world mediocrity.

But more importantly, it's because we have lost control over critical USA industries (oil, natural gas, pharmaceuticals, automobiles, semiconductors, computers, cell phones, rare earth, steel, copper, food supplies, meat, etc.) Enabling the foreign manufacturers to reverse engineer our technology and sell it back to us at a profit. Shipped FOB destination paying the cost of container ships, port of call costs of unloading and distributing the goods to the USA Farm's shelf space. Free of charge and responsibility of FOB shipping point for the shippers. This has transferred $14 trillion GDP to the CCP, Inc. and other Asian

Farms so their GDP and our imbalance of trade debt exceeds $30 trillion. We then are insolvent and suffering from future supply line shortages, then from the influx of narcotics (fentanyl, heroin) and viruses, that is imbedded by terrorists in those 5,400 container ships that are owned by China, Japan and South Korea. And are left sitting in our 20 ports waiting for the USA Farm's distribution, marketing and cost of sales. (Side bar: Due to the Pandemic the cost of a container has gone from $3,000 per container to $30,000 overhead costs for the USA Farm to sell to its consumers).

This is more than a conspiracy, it's a total breakdown in the Great American Enterprise that has, because of this failure to do business for ourselves, the USA Farm has become the consumer for the worldwide marketplace with financing by borrowing from our competitors and printing currency that is declining n value. Leading to insufferable inflation and ultimately, stagnation. It's imperative to replace the current Animal Farm ruling class, with enterprising Americans who know how to run a business and save an enterprise from bankruptcy for the following reasons.

1. The elite, establishment ruling class of the farm is elected each term. As we get either blue or red, or now purple masquerading as change and activism, we abdicate our freedom. (The pink pigs in *Animal Farm* overthrow the dictator farmer Trump by being the most intelligent and then becoming the instigators of red inequality and blue horizons using mail in voting, unauthorized drop boxes and voter harvesting for the weapon.)

2. In the modern-day *Animal Farm*, the leadership has a conflict of interest called *money-tics*. It takes $6 billion to get elected as president, $100 million for senator, and $15 million as a house rep. So how can the common man or woman have a say when no one will return phone calls or emails unless you have donated hundreds of thousands of dollars to their campaign chests, which they get the

rights to if they are not elected. Just keep adding zeros to get inside and stay inside the belt way.

3. The ruling class results, as shown in Iraq, North Korea, Vietnam, etc., do not follow the constitution as penned by the originators of our democracy. They have spent three trillion dollars on weapons of mass destruction and tout our armies as the elite of the world without one encouraging word for peace and serious disarmament.

4. The ruling class results, as shown by the New Orleans hurricane debacle, relations with Mexico, South America, France, Italy, Russia, China, and the Middle-Eastern nations of Islam, spell imperialism and a failed regime change philosophy that we and we alone can be the nuclear power.

5. The ruling class results in borrowing ourselves, through the imbalance of trade and incurring the shipping and distribution costs, sending wealth overseas, into a $28 trillion of current debt, most of which is in the form of treasury notes to China, Japan, Saudi Arabia, and South Korea, who have been our enemies on occasion and an accumulated debt of $158 trillion www.usdebclock.org when entitlements, pensions and other obligations are booked. It is mismanagement of a diabolical imbalance of trade of $600 billion per year and the $600 trillion-dollar derivative bubble we are sitting on by committee and the Fed; not necessity or practical investment or bailout plans. We cannot run our country on the Dow Jones stock market quotes as a report card hoping our technology won't be stolen or ransom cyber hacked or our grid systems are safe from terrorist attack.

6. The ruling class inability to respond to the majority of the voters' wishes on domestic problems not issues, that relate to preventive healthcare for all, acceptable housing for all, and a quality education for all. In the meantime, our borders are not

protected, allowing illegal aliens to flood our southern borders. The deterrents as enacted by President Trump have been flushed away by the Biden Administration using human rights as the reason. Ironically this woke movement, siting white Americans as imperialist and racists, is in its application reverse racism.

7. The ruling class inability to control the money markets dictated by the Federal Reserve Bank that puts us into a planned recession to keep control over the animals in the farmyard. The Fed, a hybrid governmental entity, is not accountable for its gambling losses with American tax money. It operates as a bookie for the president.

8. The ruling class misuse of taxation for the purpose of leading the voters to believe they are against more taxes by forming new lines of taxes called casinos, gambling boats, sports betting, legalized drugs, fracking on federal properties and outsourcing American assets to foreign ownership.

9. The ruling class verbal ramblings about national health insurance, with Congress continuing to pander the insurance companies, pharmaceutical companies, the American Medical Association, etc. with diversionary tactics, with no talk of waste in the system. Clearly, 80 percent of the healthcare dollar is spent in the last two years of peoples' lives due to overmedicating the elderly, re-hospitalizing the elderly, and bankrupting the Social Security funds by governmental gaming the Medicare and Medicaid programs. This in itself wastes up to $1 trillion per year that could be used to standardize a healthcare package that would cover all Americans and have their money invested and spent on their behalf rather than on a wasteful governmental administration that uses Gestapo tactics as their enforcement strategy. If you want documented proof of this read, my book *Restore Elder Pride, Remedy Eldercide*, iUniverse, 2012.

10. The ruling class has a formulation of leadership around the institutions (idolized by the elite establishment, Big Brother government, Big Media, Big Box, Big Tech that were essential Brotherhood businesses during the 2020 Pandemic ... a monopsony patronized by Big media) and academics rather than common sense fostered by the enterprising common man. Eighty-five percent of America's businesses are manned by families, while 90 percent of the decisions made by politicians who never worked in or owned a small business and are controlled by the top 5 percent of the holders of inherited wealth.

Profile of the current national and state leadership qualities:

1. Must be an attorney, professor, or lobbyist.
    a. For every law passed we go further into debt.
    b. For every law passed we must take one off the books.
2. Must be a graduate of Ivy League or West Coast universities.
    a. For every congressman coming from a narrow ideal, money is king.
    b. For common sense to prevail we must conquer elite/caste system thinking.
3. Must be either wealthy or connected to wealth.
    a. For success, we have valued wealth, not ideas.
    b. For the pursuit of happiness for all, we must reward ideas, not just monetary values.
4. Must be red or blue in philosophy.
    a. For the tragedy the elite fiddled while New Orleans and Iraq burned.
    b. For the TVA, Roosevelt solved the Depression; for New Orleans, the TVA approach would have it rebuilt by now. There is no common sense in the elite handout thought process (TARP $600 billion and stimulus $700 billion bailout of the banks, the Fed, and the

automobile industry) in 2007 if GM and Chrysler had been allowed to file for Article 11 bankruptcy, the Fed and the banks would have had to take the hit, not the American taxpayer and the American enterprise system, and the American unemployed would have been honored and all involved allowed to start over with less overhead and debt. Zero productive jobs would have been lost and more jobs created by reducing the bank debt.

5. Must be able to raise money on the basis of a book release or past political position or family ties with political power.
   a. If you have a heritage in politics, you can raise money and get elected. How about New York Governor Andrew Cuomo who is the decedent of Cuomo family political power (Maio, Andrew and Christian) and just made seven figures on a book praising himself while mishandling of the Corona China Virus in nursing homes, hiding the number of deaths he caused and denying abuses to his female staff while getting an Emmy for his misinformation regarding the Pandemic.
   b. The Founding Fathers envisioned the common man would get involved every four years and participate in governance as a democracy. Now incumbents are reelected 90% of the time with no term limits in the Senate or House.
6. Must be willing to "go along to get along" (flexible and willing to compromise principles on issues while the problems festered in our society). For a scary real-world example, read Bob Woodward's *The High Price of Politics*, which demonstrates that the polls only vote for their reelection, not for their constituencies.
   a. Election is based on who you are, not what your stand for.
   b. Election must become a non-generational denominational run for the rights of the common man.

7. Must be younger looking and photogenic.
    a. Currently there is a disregard for aging or the private-sector businessman.
    b. In the near future, the aging class will rule despite the elitism.
8. Must be glib-tongued
    a. Those with the pulpits rule.
    b. Those with the ideas and solutions shall rule.
9. Must be a national bloomer not a baby boomer.
    a. Those who have the egos to promote their own wealth run.
    b. In the near future, the boomers will rule based on the greater good.
10. Must be vetted and cleansed of past wrongdoings
    a. If you can be cleansed, you are in.
    b. In the near future, if you are not clean you will be rejected.

Proposed national and state leadership principles and qualities:

1. Schooled in constitutional issues (problems):
    a. 50 percent coming from labor.
    b. 50 percent coming from business and education.
2. Willing to set aside constitutional issues for problem resolution (reason minus religion = resolution) by the individual:
    a. Leave abortion and its consequences to the individual.
    b. Leave same-sex marriages to the individual.
    c. Leave religion to the individual (for the same reason Church and State are separate: reason minus religion = resolution).
    d. Leave immigration to vetting the individual for citizenship to prevent our enemies from imbedding terrorists, Chinese spies, cartel and drug dealers in our mist.

3. Be willing to deal with the real national and international issues (problems):
    a. Privatized equal education for all, administered by social enterprises (for-profit businesses founded on the pursuit of outcome, not income),
    b. Privatized equal healthcare policies for all social enterprises (for-profit businesses founded on the pursuit of outcome, not income),
    c. Privatized affordable housing for all social enterprises (for-profit businesses founded on the pursuit of outcome, not income),
    d. Stand for peace, not war driven by moral incentives,
    e. Stand for democracy driven by economic incentives,
    f. Stand for freedom driven by resource incentives
    g. Stand for deinstitutionalizing America for the greater good:
        i. Department of Defense becomes the Department of Offence for Peace:
        ii. Department of Health and Human Services becomes the Department of Quality of Life; privatize healthcare and education:
            1. Parity of education: cities and suburbs with equal funding based on population, not property values, Charter schools (schools of fish not whales of indifference).
            2. Universal healthcare funded by individual savings accounts and internalized public spending using AI models of care based on individual genetic profiles
            3. Health preservation and pursuit of wellness to reduce the incidence of chronic disease and obesity; deductively utilize technology to restore function after illnesses
        iii. Department of Commerce becomes the Department of Enterprise—privatize to downsize:

1. Consume our enemies through economic warfare: build the infrastructure of emerging economies and sanction those that do not defend democracy with action. The only exception should be the Olympics and World competitions that represent one of the few positives we have in the negative world of human rights. Rather than boycotts of China or Russian world games for violating human rights, just beat them on the world trade stage by bringing back our sovereign supply lines that have either been given away or stolen. No longer making cheap labor or partisan politics as the excuse to ship our wealth off shore to competing nations. Poverty and terrorism thrive on unemployment and low standards of living.
2. Build a coalition of trading partners that choke off resources to dictators, imperialists, terrorists, and demagogues (trading partners are China, Japan, Korea, India, Britain, France, Italy, Russia, and those pursuing economic solutions rather than military solutions); from this a true forum of United Nations can be effective.
3. Tax (assess) a capital infusion from those Americans that have made their wealth from the great American consumer-driven enterprise on the basis of their reportable net worth.
4. Create the job corps for full employment for rebuilding and preserving the national infrastructure; all college graduates go into a national placement registry for small business hiring.

iv. Justice Department becomes the Department of Freedom and Equality under the Rule of Law:

1. Laws passed must be triggered by laws discontinued.
2. Immigrants must become legalized citizens systematically through nationalizing them with education and jobs to replace the retiring baby boomers so they can become tax paying citizens for pursuing the American Dream ... we must protect the borders from incursion of criminals.
3. Free trade and importation of foreign goods must be balanced with job development and capital investment in foreign countries through market distribution fees charged for using the American consumer market and use investment-based tax incentives to produce products in America.
4. First and second amendments application must be based upon the impact on society of guns and pornography that damages the mission for peace and peaceful coexistence.

v. Department of Agriculture and Conservation becomes the Department of Clean America for World Preservation to protect the environment in individual practical ways with privatized services.

4. **Reinstitute the Peace Corps** replacing foreign aid with the enterprise model of teaching the objective of work for success with a learn to earn and skill to bill values for working with emerging countries on legal and legislative infrastructures, teaching them enterprise so they too can thrive on their own human capital. "Serve your country is to serve your soul".
5. **Reinforce the standards of the United Nations** and worldwide peace initiatives, including reduction of weapons and increase in nuclear power for the greater good.

There is no perfect form of government or society. Whether it is based on comrades or associates or citizens, the equation is the same. Equality and opportunity dictate eventual human rights and the pursuit of equity earned for all. In the American Enterprise Party, the leadership must protect the rights of all citizens to pursue their right to an equal education, a challenging job, and a standard of living based on their efforts.

When government gets in the way of these objectives, the results are poverty, crime, war, anger and loss of life, liberty, and the pursuit of happiness. *Govern by the people, of the people, and for the people, so help me God* must be the credo and the outcome, regardless of the income of the elite, who shall have to abide by these principles as well if they wish to continue to prosper and compete.

In the following articles are the postulates (Axioms) and the platform for that movement that make it the party of the people (enterprising American workers, baby boomers, college students, legal immigrants, naturalized citizens, and those that want into America willing to work and pay taxes for education, peace, quality of life, and freedom to vote for effective government leaders) by the people for the people.

If we were to capitalize on the power of our natural resources (the best in the world), accumulated wealth (shared not squandered), patriotic labor force, human capital, intellectual prowess and freedom to share in the fruits we would be the super power without the necessity of labor unions, nuclear weapons, war chests, imperialistic pursuits and disregard for human life. (3,100 Americans were killed on 9/11, 4,000 have died since in Iraq and Afghanistan, while we have enabled a civil war to kill 3,000 a month in a failed strategy in Iraq and now with the withdrawal from Afghanistan we've failed again in strategy and tactical departure causing death and devastation of thousands of nationals and American service personnel, leaving our foreign policy under the Biden/Harris administration in incompetent tatters. Not only have we lost a strategic presence in Asia it leaves us vulnerable to military or economic attack by China, Russia, Iran, North Korea, etc.).

How much more proof do we need to justify a better way for the Better Good of our Planet to be founded on Humanism with peaceful coexistence in the hands of investors (capitalists) and fair representation of enterprising people (socialists) for the Better Good of the American Enterprise (corporations, entrepreneurs, institutions) and nonpartisan governance (The Red, White and Blue political parties) with tri-partisan competition for commerce around the world.

Congress and the Administration

Biting on the Edges of Disaster: The Debt Limit Fiscal Cliff and Incremental-ism:

Historically, politicians from the left to the right have never run a business and typically cause systemic problems that only business can solve. With a new president, a new administration, and a Congress of the same bent, the economy is reeling due to mismanaged or unmanaged interest rates the majority of Americans are being asked to suffer while the elite plan to dictate the use of our tax dollars while they conjure up more deficits that sink the ship. While sitting on a Big Brother government that employs a Brotherhood of twenty-two million local, state and federal employees at an annual cost of $1.3 trillion, the Congress sits in feathered nests of guaranteed wealth, playing the Monopsony Game (buyer of last resort trying to spend their way out of a problem they caused) the opposite of Monopoly that is a seller of last resort. The Brotherhood is rounded out with Big Media, Big Tech, Bid Pharma, Big Unions, Big Box businesses that monopolize their markets.

Well, American Enterprise will have to fix it, so why not start at the top and downsize the proposed spending plan to a more businesslike approach to solving what the prior administration, the Federal Reserve, and a Democratic and Republican Congress allowed to destroy consumerism in the greatest economy in the world. While China watches us self-destruct in gridlock, party bickering, squelching of the freedoms we are promised and the control of speech by social and fake news media.

Proposed Spending Reallocation Plan:

- Call for the elimination of all earmarks invest savings $100 billion in inner city development.
- Move troops out of the Middle East, use wasted funds $300 billion to police the inner cities to reduce crime.
- Downsize defense spending and missile deployment $100 billion increase investment in naval vessels and personnel.
- Reduce the size of the existing law base by 10%. $250 billion invest in forest and farmland management
- Reduce the size of the government employees by 25%. $250 billion invest in privatizing certain regulatory agency redundancy that reduces wasteful deficit spending .
- Total annual downsizes of runaway government. $1 trillion

Postscript to 2013 the year the first edition of this book. In 2016 President Donald J. Trump was a surprise winner of a very contentious campaign his four-that continued during his four-year term in office. Why, because he was hell bent on pursuing many of the ideas and principles of business applied to our staid ineffective institutions. Unfortunately, his own party disowned him for his passion for problem solving. In doing so he created a new problem for the establishment two-party system … it has to change and thus the emergence of the American Enterprise Party.

Hopefully, President Trump will not give up on his successful staging for this change and help it to happen. In updating the financial information, it has been a challenge. So, much of the changes since my pre 2013 research has to be extrapolated based on time not necessarily the latest figures since they are continually changing … however the content is still relevant and always getting much worse … enough to scare the hell out of me. If you want a full report, go to www.usdebtclock.org which is the best source of up to the second changes in the economic status of America and its States and Worldwide competitors.

It even compares, in retrospect, the performance of past Presidencies since McKinley **1900** ($2 million in national debt and $86 thousand in budget deficit with $19 billion in GDP with 10% current debt to GDP compared to Trump **2020** $28 trillion national debt, $6 trillion budget deficit, $159 trillion unfunded liabilities with $21 trillion GDP with 129% current debt to GDP).

Balance the budget by 2035;
(Focus on the core of the economic problem)

Restoring credit is the core objective to jobs creation:

1. Government SBA-guaranteed loans lower the risk to banks.
2. Government FHA-purchased foreclosed mortgages for sale or rent to former owners that were forced out by higher interest rates; rebasing the debt to current fixed-interest rates for longer amortization periods of at least thirty-five years.
3. IRS regulations to allow 100 percent tax deductions provided for sales taxes, gas taxes, health insurance premiums, fitness and nutrition expenditures, and out-of-pocket medical expenses.
4. Government HUD-guaranteed revenue bonds as loans for rebuilding inner city schools, enticing small businesses to inner city restored neighborhoods, roads, fracking leases and offshore drilling rigs with 4 percent loans for thirty-five years' amortization.

Focusing on the Sweet Spot:

1. *Reduce the risk to banks* for loans to businesses—restores credit.
2. *Puts housing back in business* by acquiring income producing properties—restores housing values to pre-2007 levels.
3. *Tax credits increase consumer purchasing* for durable goods and costly out-of-pocket health and fitness expenditures—restores consumerism.

4. *Private enterprise zones and opportunity zones with investment tax credits to rebuild the national infrastructure—redevelopment of the inner cities and public schools, privatize healthcare services, repair and maintenance of roads, bridges, public transportation, and energy production* —restores eroding foundation of our economy and standing in the world market.

Cost versus benefit	Cost	Benefit
SBA loan guarantees to businesses	$0	Stops layoffs, improve ability to increase profits, adds three million jobs
FHA loan guarantees to businesses	$0	Stops foreclosures, restores homes to income producing status, restores two million home owners back to their home
IRS tax credits for essential purchases	$400 billion	Funding for reducing health care costs and under insured share of escalating costs
HUD loan guarantees to businesses	$0	Private business stimulus for state contracts for construction of infrastructure and energy research and development costs
Total investment of taxpayer funds	$400 billion	
Re-patriot current stimulus packages	$3.9 trillion for 2020	
Health benefits to the taxpayer	$5 trillion for 2021	

Use the annual savings of $1.100 trillion for converting the paradigm from a pursuit of health care treatment and income to the pursuit of quality outcomes.

- Incentives for physicians to pursue health preservation and prevention, and reduce the dependency on prescription drugs and hospitalization of the elderly = $300 billion.

- Incentives for hospitals to utilize technology for computerizing patients' episodic care plans and databases for exchange of critical patient information on a standardized basis to all the healthcare stakeholders so the pursuit of improved outcomes can be implemented = $350 billion.
- Medication reduction, additional savings of $350 billion.
- Incentives to long-term healthcare providers to use the restorative model rather than the medical model or social model for improving outcomes.
- Universal healthcare for the uninsured = $400 billion.
- Universal healthcare for the underinsured = $200 billion.

American enterprise is what makes America better than the rest of the world is because it is financed primarily by the middle-classes with their work ethic and small businesses with their innovations. With the federal and state government intrusions this valuable asset is being destroyed, but with this plan it becomes revitalized.

Sum up this article:
The pursuit of enterprise for social welfare and capital formation using nonviolent but prudent policies

1. Overhaul of Obama Care to focus on outcomes through economic incentives using reinforcement rules and regulations.
2. Stop nation-building and regime change using foreign aid and policies based on nuclear power or military action outside our shores.
3. Create patriotism as a way to revitalization of our legal immigration policies and prevent terrorists from imbedding recruits in our mist.
4. Support the United Nations as a peace enforcer.
5. Integration of public and private sectors in setting policy.
6. If you are into the evolution rather than cultural revolution of social systems, take the time to review the content of *Zeitgeist*

Movie and *Zeitgeist Addendum*, which chronicles the events in East Germany that are changing America for the worse, forever.

Zeitgeist (German pronunciation: [ˈtsaɪtɡaɪst] is "the spirit of the times" or "the spirit of the age." *Zeitgeist* is the general cultural, intellectual, ethical, spiritual, or political climate within a nation or even specific groups, along with the general ambiance, morals, sociocultural direction, and mood associated with the current era.

The term is a loan word from German: *Zeit* (cognate with "tide") meaning "time" and *Geist* (cognate with "ghost") meaning "spirit."

This movie is a very disturbing analysis of,

- The negative impact of not confining big Government, and,
- Federal Reserve debt instruments and arbitrage interest rates causing monetary disaster and economic destruction, and,
- Unified religious effect on values, and,
- Political conspiracy of the ages leading to totalitarianism and,
- Idealistic social views of a freer spirit without constraints of individual attainment and,
- Forfeiture of our freedoms of speech, right to bear arms, legal voting, filibuster, right to choose reproductive rights and a nine-member Supreme Court and,
- Critical race theory, black lives matter and the 1619 project added to the public-school system with destruction of books, sports nick names and statues of our forefathers found unacceptable by Marxist activists to wipe out the history of 1776 constitutional government by embracing "critical race theory" and the impact of 1619 in defining the impact of white supremacy, and,
- Bankruptcy laws protecting entrepreneurs' rights to create, fail and succeed discarded for government takeover, and,

- Honor of our forefather's constitutional based past and present cultures wiped clean to be replaced with *Zeitgeist* (German pronunciation: [ˈtsaɪtɡaɪst] as "the spirit of the times" or "the spirit of the age."

In memory of the JFK era are we speaking of Camelot or avoiding Orwell's Animal Farm?

SPEAKING OF CAMELOT

Deck the halls with boughs of holly
Fa La La La La La La
Speak the vows of folly
Fa La La La La La La

We often speak of Camelot
In voices of grandeur
But more often than not
Our pursuit is unsure

We often speak of Shangri LA
With words of love
Until the ice begins to thaw
Like righteous words from above

But too often we speak of fear
In voices trembling weak
Not so are we insincere
As much as not meaning what we speak

My dreams are mine to think
Kept in perspective light
And at no time can I sink
If my hope is bright

We often speak of Camelot
Then forget that actions are facts
And more often than not
Dreams are dust in our tracks

So sing on Jester of life
A breadwinner naught
For folly is a begetters wife
And shallow words are fraught

With thought and prayers of Camelot
Be it a President who has taught
Us that it is likely or not
That happiness can be bought

Or a forgiving God
Taking away our able thought
Making reality seem like a fraud
For accepting Camelot

Deck the halls with boughs of folly
Fa La La La La La La
Speak the vows of Pollyanna
Fa La La La La La La

When all we wanted is what we sought
A family a job a home to be bought
Not a dream of whether we like it or not
For someone else's Camelot

Article Three

Capitalism Embraces Socialism

The BLM American Revolution of 2020:

Was this Anarchy "is a state of disorder due to absence or nonrecognition of authority" or equality/equity BLM Revolution "is a forcible overthrow of a government or social order, in favor of a new system". How about a counter revolution **HLM** (Human Lives Matter) pursuing humanism to replace racism and all isms?

What was the purpose of the 2020 equity revolt against America's haves by some what's and have-nots? Was (is) it for stealing or appealing for a change in the pecking order, or is it the plea of the black families suffering from injustices from police enforcement or the squalor they live in versus the safe and secure white suburbs. Or a failure in our political agendas that continue to ignore the problems of city life in the neighborhoods and slums versus the inequality of opportunity of education, health care, jobs and prosperity promised in the American Constitution. Or all of these combined to justify anarchy and/or revolution.

What was the reason for the French revolution, the White American freedom revolution of 1776, and the Black American equity revolution of 2020? It's all of the above. The many demanding the freedom they have been promised in the American constitution to be free to pursue opportunity that truly exists in all villages, cities, neighborhoods, regardless of gender, race, religion or political opinion.

Taking a look backward to the Rodney King incident and forward from George Floyd … it's not about killing cops and robbers, not anarchy destroying the America constitutional infrastructure and Rule of Law by anger, not demanding equality instead of working for peaceful coexistence in our violent world. No, it's about changing a culture of violence and fear, so all the enterprising Americans have equal opportunity in their pursuit and attainment of the American Dream. It's not about the political poles that continue to pull us apart by ignoring the problem by calling their differences as issues between the red and blue parties ignoring the fall out of the message unanswered since Rodney King and exacerbated by George Floyd and many others.

AMERICANISM IS MADE IN PIECES
The Impossible Dream

America is made in pieces
Pieces as those black lives succumb
Pieces of families in Rodney kingdom come
Pieces as George Floyd's life ceases

Along the roads to their justice and freedom

Pursuing the ultimate peace
That's illusive to those who decease
Who lose their peace of mind
Leaving their love one's behind

Only to be the victims of class warfare
And the challenges of a worldwide scare
Conflicts that won't cease
The immoral purge on peace

Sad as it may seem
Such family's no longer dream
Of what their son or daughter
Could have been that won't occur

The finality is never there
Not because we don't care
Or that it isn't fair
But in fact as reasons to despair

Why was it so important
For them to die
When the benefit is distant
In far off lands or city that belie

The importance
As benefit is negligible
When value is in an instance
Toxic as a Nazi dirigible

No facts or accomplishments
Just unjust bad sentiments
About the purpose of tearing apart
Something just to build something ala carte

Destroying hopes and futures
For stopping the wrongs of others
With the longing lasting sutures
Of fathers and mothers

Just for the making of America
A better place for semblance
Putting the pieces back together
At a funeral or in a remembrance

Of those heroes those foes
Of tyranny of treachery who forgoes
The senseless cruelty to other humans
For the sake of saving earth's spiritual omens

While in God we entrust our country
To those few soldiers of peace
Putting America together
Again, piece by piece
Family by family
Grave by grave

Who gave up their lives
For freedom that thrives
With My America Dream that they helped save
The Home of the Brave
That's Americanism

(Rodney King and George Floyd's
Deaths do not make sense as racism
Except as two large pieces of peaceful
Coexistence for the sake of the impossible dream)

It's about government by the people, of the people for the people promised in the American constitution … equal opportunity for equal effort for peace and equitable prosperity for all. It's shouting for Humanism to replace racism and all other isms. The question is who will represent this movement … the broken two-party system (capitalism versus socialism) that has created this culture or a third party representing all enterprising America for peace and prosperity not fruitless marching, destructive anarchy and the black equity revolution with no positive outcome.

My case is built on the following analytics and financial realities.

(According to the debt clock www.usdebtclock.org For the first time since World War II our debt of $30 trillion, on the cash basis, growing at $45 dollars per second or $800 billion per year, exceeds our GDP of $21 trillion that is declining at $30 per second or $500 billion per year with inflation in energy costs and supply line control by China or a negative growth rate in GDP of -$1.3 trillion per year). In accounting parlance USA can't pay its current obligations without borrowing trillions more money and is insolvent on cash basis budgeting. Plus imposing $158 trillion of GAAP unrecorded obligations facing future generations):

1. We now have legalized deficit spending when Federal and State annual taxation is only half of the current spending and obligations. Our oxymoron "lawmakers", at every level of government, just make it their passion to find new laws to pass and every law has regulations to be funded, so the spending is designed to escalate expenditures, defer payments, and accelerate tax revenues, creating concealed deficits (over 40,000 bills proposed and 5,000 new laws passed nationwide in 2010 - 2012):

    a. Now we have laws with regulations for every conceivable occurrence until the lawmakers come up with more, so the spending, by the nature of this flawed legalized socialistic structure, has to exceed any rational taxing system—so now we get more legalized gambling:
        i. Illinois now will have video gaming in 45,000 locations for electronic poker to raise 30 percent taxes on the backs of those that can least afford it, then have 25 percent set aside for treating compulsive gamblers that this maniacal philosophy creates.
        ii. Most every state is sponsoring a Lotto and Powerball legalized socialism contest to reap taxes illegally according to the First Amendment of the Constitution. Along with taxing legalized medical and recreational marijuana and sports betting.
        iii. Mayor Daley wanted casinos at every block on Lake Michigan and he sold off the Chicago Skyway parking meters, leased them back, and wants to fund his excesses using gambling and graft as the future funding mechanism. He spent like there is

no tomorrow then created legalized socialism to pay for it. Rohm Emanuel calls this *privatizing* or *downsizing the budget*; I call it selling off American assets to grow government.

iv. Supposedly we have 30,000+ gangs and 1,010,000+ gang members nationwide. Killings are escalating … black on black crime is turning ion a black equity revolution justifying reparation by rioting for purging wealth by taking it.

On the south side of Chicago, we have a war among gangs who see no future for themselves due to unemployment, lack of equal education, no affordable housing, and no future while Mayor Daley, Oprah, President Obama, Michael Jordan chased the Olympics or set up schools in Africa, then sold off the Skyway and parking meters to foreign investors then leased them back at exorbitant rates of return. Given the right to dictate the rates tolls and fees were doubled, tripled and doubled again.

b. To oversee all the legalized socialism, we have imposed on ourselves lawmakers who make laws without forcing themselves to get rid of the ten most harmful laws for every new much-needed one. As a result of this lawmaker role, we now have 22.7 million essential government workers who drain much-needed capital and demand to have full benefits, pensions, great healthcare, while the workers who produce products that create profits that generate tax revenues are being cut from the workforce at the rate of hundreds of thousands per month.

c. The resulting payroll for the so-called purchaser of last resort is over $1 trillion, with an unfunded pension debt in Illinois alone of $180 billion. Every state in the union is facing unfunded entitlements (totals over $800 billion for all fifty states) to the government workers and are willing to take it out of the Medicaid funding to perpetuate the power of the social service unions.

   d. All this heaped on us by legalized socialists such as our former secretary of labor, Prof. Robert Reich, stating that government has to be the purchaser of last resort, so the stimulus paper money can solve our depression. Dr. Reich, where is the government purchasing power coming from when the taxes from 17 million workers are being pared from the tax rolls and the employed and employers are bankrupt with no viable source of profits to generate capital to create the solution: sales of products and services generating profits from enterprise?

2. Now that the reds and blues say we have to have healthcare reform, forgetting they were the ones that invented Medicare and Medicaid, there is a purge of common sense once again for the sake of Socialistic programs. . . we must save Americans from themselves by making healthcare a privilege, not a right. A privilege that would have to be earned by better habits and acceptance of personal responsibility for internalizing and reducing the costs to all Americans by losing excess weight and being more fit? Hell no! Just more taxes, more bloat, more graft, more control by Congress for the sake of the rest of the crash dummies who need to be saved.

3. Of course, when the red and blue parties say tax the rich because they pay 90 percent of the taxes, all the rest of us (actually it's 47 percent) who don't carry our share agree they should pay more. So, the rich, most of them current or past politicians, make sure the rich are protected from any restraint or imposition when it comes to "pay to play" political action groups (American Medical Association, American Hospital Association, American Pharmaceutical Association, American Bar Association, American Insurance Association, and more importantly, the incognito American Lobbyist Consortium). In reality, saying the rich pay the majority of the taxes is the most farcical statement ever contrived by the elite, considering the following list of taxes: The fact is the top 1% don't pay the following taxes ... their companies or estates either pay them or avoid them:

a. Real estate taxes 30% of total taxes paid by 99%.
b. Retail sales taxes 30% of total taxes paid by 99%.
c. Income taxes 30% of total taxes paid by 47%%.

The rest represent 10% of total taxes paid by the lower 90%.

d. Excise taxes.
e. Gambling taxes.
f. Gaming/Lotto taxes.
g. Tobacco and marijuana taxes.
h. Alcohol taxes.
i. Social Security taxes.
j. Medicare taxes.
k. Workers' comp taxes.
l. Unemployment taxes.
m. Parking sticker taxes.
n. Gasoline taxes.
o. Estate taxes.
p. Airport and limo taxes..
q. Parking and speeding tickets and fines—just another tax.
r. Daley's sale and lease-back schemes increase costs to the taxpayer.
s. Service and renters' taxes.
t. Hidden taxes, variable Fed/bank discounts and mortgage rates, increased cost of living, declining dollar value, relocation to higher tax rate states, etc.

The fact is that when you add up all these taxes that the 169 million enterprising Americans workers' pay or conceivably could pay, puts the real share of the elite and so-called successful rich profiteers to shame. The typical worker, if they are lucky, makes $50,000 per year. By the time they pay their "fair" share, they have $15,000 left for food, clothing, education, and transportation. Of the $21 trillion GDP and $18 trillion GNP and $118 trillion net worth, these workers are the ones who produce the products that drive the economy and only 30 percent is available to them after paying the big government socialists their exorbitant share.

Creative Taxation to finance the progressives "American Jobs Plan", "Green New Deal" and its sister "Save America's Infrastructure" is opening the war on American's right to a fair wage and standard of living without regard to austerity and accountability for affordable government and its authority to commit Americans for decades not Presidential terms. What is in the wings are taxing not only consumption but personal life styles:

1. Miles driven in addition to consumption tax,
2. OLMS of Electricity used for cars tax,
3. Degrees used for heating and air conditioning tax,
4. Number of solar panels tax,
5. Tires used tax, and tax for exceeding individual quotas for amount of carbon used,
6. Pounds of plastic bottles used tax,
7. Number of gas burning vehicles owned tax,
8. Number of children in school tax,
9. Number of acres owned tax,
10. Value of stocks owned tax,
11. Number of employee's tax,
12. IRS fees for tax reviews and audits tax,
13. Immigration integrational tax,
14. When it gets convenient just tax everything 100%,

This list of legalized socialism's control will continue until the government runs out of other people's money. Then just over turn individual freedoms and continue to raise taxes for hairbrained liberal ideas … give out free fish rather then teaching those in need, how to fish (zero emissions, free health care and college, write-off college debt, support illegal aliens with health care, housing and minimum wage, justice reform, reparation, etc.). As long as we have lawmakers making laws that that have to be funded out of the pockets of the 150 to 170 million enterprising people, who have to work for a living and produce products that can be resold and generate a profit base that can be rationally taxed. Ironically, income taxes are the least invasive to personal freedoms; at least, it is based on results of an enterprise, not the whims of the lawmakers.

This proves that the well-walking wealthy do not pay the majority of the taxes, it is the minority income levels that fund everything that drives the American standard of living, government socialist spending, and congressional pork-barrel waste with sales taxes (33%), property taxes (33%) and their share of income taxes (33%). The top 50% of wealth pays roughly 50% of the all taxes as does the bottom 50% and the top 1% 3% and top 10%, 40% of income taxes.

Yet, the wealthy control the 100% of the 545 officials (100 Senators, 435 Representatives, 9 Supreme Court Justices and President) that run our country through political contributions by their holdings in corporations, investment funds, PAC's and tax-exempt foundations. For the record the Clinton Foundation net worth is more than most third world countries, as is the Gates Foundation, Buffet Foundation, the Amazon, Apple, Walmart, Exon, Facebook, Google, net worth totaling trillion dollars in intrinsic value supported by enterprising Americans who go to work every day having little or no say.

Add it up 170,000,000 struggling workers paying the bills for funding laws we don't need so the elite and socialist uni-party leaders can control all aspects of personal freedoms. And then dictating our behavior with casinos, video gambling, Lotto, legalized drugs, sports wagering and what's next? Taxes on legalized socialism for prostitution, illicit drugs (legalized marijuana), sports betting and more and more prescription drugs pushed on us through advertising and pay-for-play methods with healthcare providers. We are Rome burning while Washington has us playing Lotto with our own money.

Who is to blame is not the problem? We all are when we vote Red or Blue. The problem is their leadership stinks and is driven by ego, ambition, wealth and greed. The greed gland and corruption contempt subvert democracy. What we have now is a legalized socialized depression, not just a self-imposed recession because Americans wanted their own homes and Wall Street tricked us all into thinking that full employment, education for all, and affordable housing are within reach. No, it was the legalized socialists who decided to manipulate the monetary system to save us all from ourselves, killing the only hope most taxpayers have that their investment in a home is the credit score to fund their future retirement, which is consumerism (freedom of choice), not communism. Well, that security was devalued in the Depression of 2007 cause by monetary manipulation …

Harvard Professor "Helicopter Bernanke" (as he is called by economists) and his Federal Reserve socialist progressive cronies drove the exchange rate to banks up by 250 to 500 percent during 2005-07, thereby bursting the American standard of living bubble, causing the worst depression of all time. Then the incumbent Republican leaders tried to fix it by dumping paper money into the banks, who were sitting on variable-rate subprime mortgages that could have been paid at reasonable lower fixed interest rates and extending the term limits of the mortgages to arrive at a serviceable monthly payment.

But the Fed, with its inflation paranoia, killed the housing goose, causing a depression ripple effect of $500 trillion in derivative dollars felt around the world. Rather than letting the air out of the balloon, the Harvard socialist Professor Bernanke chose to take the situation in hand and destroy consumerism by bringing down the demand side of enterprise. Keynesian gets us again … Obama's chief economic advisor was none other than the interest king under President Carter's failed interest policies … none other than former Fed chairman Paul Adolph Volcker. D ja vu all over again. See Exhibit A and Article Four for details.

Way to go, Professor Bernanke, Secretary. Paulson, President Bush, Speaker Pelosi, President Obama, senators Harry Reid and Mitch McConnell. Legalized Socialism lives and breathes, with the Fed and government socialists running our so-called free-enterprise Democratic system with trillions of dollars of funny money misused as stimulus for bank losses, big-business bailouts, and funding the campaigns of the elite political socialists.

The emphasis on a war economy, energy panic, fear inducing conformity of global warming, pandemic and terrorism, pushing our legalized socialism agenda on the rest of the world, blaming capitalism for the depression, and running up astronomical debt with our so-called enemies (USA, Canada, Japan, France, Italy, England, India and Mexico) is giving in to the legalized socialists that now run America. What happened to peace, partnering with our allies to make the war on poverty and drugs an economical war not guns, bombs, and threats of annihilation?

Solutions (Before we do anything we need to cut the fixed overhead cost of government. First step in a quasi-reorganization is to cut the annual $1,9 trillion payroll of government employees at all levels by $500 billion, Second is to cut our energy and supply line costs by $500 billion, third cut our health care costs by $500 billion, or a total of $1.5 trillion per year or $50 per second). In reality our government has built a monolithic House of Cards. It has taken 75 years to get here and will take another two decades to fix it.:

1. Our elected officials who call themselves public servants are legalized socialists. Ninety-five percent are attorneys and/or career politicians that have rarely practiced in the business world, or their sons and daughters that are going to follow in their footsteps as the *new deal* legalized socialists. Employing millions of bureaucrats to swat down opposition while never having to worry about a payroll or Competition. Because they do not understand America's enterprise,

nor do they want to. Just tax and spend is their friend.
2. They want to blame Wall Street greed for the Main Street bleed when the truth is legalized socialism rules. So, we have to have a third-party alternative where the 170 million enterprising workers who fund the system become activists who are involved in public service to get rid of the rhetoric about how Wall Street caused the 2007 depression, so the very ones that caused it can take credit for fixing it. We need a true third political alternative called *the American Enterprise Party*.
    a. Founded on the following principles:
        i. Fair taxation and recapitalization of the American enterprise for citizens and legal immigrants.
        ii. Full employment for citizens and legal immigrants.
        iii. Private Mutual health insurance—personally funded, personally spent for citizens and legal immigrants.
        iv. Affordable housing for all citizens and legal immigrants.
        v. Equality in educational opportunities and facilities for citizens and legal immigrants.
        vi. State and federal laws and underlying regulations to be removed at the rate of ten for every new needed law passed; goal is to reduce the size of government by 50 percent in ten years. All budgets to be balanced on the accrual basis within five years.
        vii. America's energy costs driven by OPEC (Oil Purchasing Energy Countries), a coalition of oil-purchasing partners that control demand and pricing (USA, Canada, Japan, France, Italy, England, India and Mexico) as an OPEC purchasing group).
        viii. Social issues for abortion, same-sex marriages, gun control, role of religion to be excluded from the political process and left to the majority and our legal system.
        ix. Eight-year term limits for all public officials without contrived nepotism, with each American committing to a minimum of two years to public service.

1. Expansion of the Peace and Job Corps worldwide for spreading the American Dream to reduce illegal immigration.
2. Employ the unemployed from the private sector to provide infrastructure-rebuilding projects, including FEMA after natural disasters, rather than government subsidies; to be funded out of increased fair tax receipts for each state and local entities.
x. Aliens, legal and illegal, must be educated and integrated into our economy to replace the seventy-seven million baby boomers who plan to retire in the next ten years; properly educated and registered to pay taxes so they will be a valuable asset to our national vitality.

b. Each governor, each representative, each senator, each local official, each mayor, needs to consider being an Enterprise party candidate and each caucus needs to have an American Enterprise Party candidate within ten years.

c. The American Enterprise Party, based on the above principles, will gainfully represent the following enterprising American voting blocs:
   i. Baby boomers.
   ii. Union workers.
   iii. Unemployed.
   iv. small business owners.
   v. The self-employed.
   vi. The poor and aliens.
   vii. Independent Religious right.
   viii. Independent Conservatives.
   ix. Independent Liberals.

3. Utilize humanism and peace coexistence as our main weapon against fear and destruction of human life to replace 50 percent of the defense spending of $3 trillion on weapons of mass destruction we hope to never use. The mentality that it is better to have massive spending

on weapons of mass destruction and not use them, is better than not having them if we don't need them is imperialist thinking in a world that disrespects use for our imperialism.

4. We need to take the $6.4 trillion spent on wars in Middle East and Asia ($2.4 trillion for war on terror in Iraq and Afghanistan alone), post 9/11, spent on wars of our choosing and invest in emerging countries' infrastructure (economies and legal systems) before we try to convert them to our form of government. Use jobs and higher standards of living and health to combat tyranny, not bombs and guns. Plus saving the 801,000 people who have died as a direct result of fighting. Plus 335,000 have been civilians and another 21 million have been displaced due to violence.

5. The cost of a world of nation building and regime change must be redirected to America's infrastructure with education, legal infrastructure for true repairs and maintenance. The impoverished inner cities and small rural communities to be first in line for private and public investment ... the objective is to quell crime with education and opportunity to succeed in our Great American Enterprise. We have an untapped talent waiting to be released from gangs and drug traffickers using free enterprise to start new businesses in the inner cities and small struggling communities labeled as opportunity zones or enterprise zones financed by small business loans.

6. Cut the number of laws by taking ten off the legislated dole for every new priority bill passed. In doing so, cut the government payroll by 50 percent over the next ten years by privatizing half of the public agencies. Instead of cutting line items on the budgets starting with the social programs that cause the taxpayer to relent, cut the nonproductive public payrolls in every Local, State and Federal agency starting with congressional staffing budgets in Washington, D.C. that cost Enterprising Americans $1 million dollars per year for each Senator and Congressman . . . that is $545 million per year of oppressive overhead imposed primarily on small businesses and entrepreneurs.

7. Eliminate all taxes that were listed above and convert to shares of stock in the American enterprise that collects 5 percent from every American's net worth. Over the next ten years, phase out the legalized socialistic taxation methods and phase in the recapitalization method. Get rid of the thousands of pages of ridiculous tax rules and regulations and the wasted time and effort made to avoid taxes. Put the accountants and attorneys to work, helping create capital through small business loans for technology and healthcare innovations.
8. Impose a distribution fee on foreign products sold in this country for the use of our markets and distribution systems. At 25 percent of a $700 billion trade deficit with a market that is produced outside the US but sold here using our shelf space, produces $350 billion of new revenue each year. This could work to slow down the escalation of the foreign trade imbalance for the first time in twenty years and bring back American jobs as the foreign cost of labor and standard of living escalates. China's, for one, cost per unit will catch up with America's in less than a decade.
9. Every government budget must be based on accrual accounting principles, not the cash basis that accelerates tax collections and defers expenditures. Playing games with the numbers must stop and the real liabilities stated so the taxpayers know what they are funding. This is far more transparent than just after-the-fact information; it is cutting where it is financially productive, not politically expedient. Government has been cooking the books for decades, which has now pushed us over the fiscal cliff.
10. Require that every American commit a minimum of 4,000 hours in their lifetime to public service. Government of the people, for the people by the people.

Public Service needs Private Sector

Input and work ethic
To Balance Money with Humanity

I personally got concerned about our country's direction in 1992 and wrote my first proposal for the American Enterprise Party. Then Newt Gingrich and Bob Dole came out with the Ten-Step Contract with America, and I thought they were seriously going to change our legalized socialism back to a free-market enterprise economy. Unfortunately, they made things worse by decentralizing the problems to each state rather than fixing them. The state governments were handed the problem of healthcare, education, unemployment, drugs, poverty, housing, and taxation without a feasible plan for implementation.

It failed so badly that the blue Democrats swooped in with their "we can fix it from Washington" policies, which failed bringing back the Bush "red war on everything" mentality. Now we have the blue legalized socialists pushing government into every aspect of our personal freedoms, calling them the "Obama big government czars" and now the Biden czars—I call them the Gestapo! Enough is enough. As I read the news that Illinois is legalizing video gaming, legalizing marijuana and sports betting to save our bloated state government and reserving 25 percent to treat those that become addicted, I knew the time had come for the majority to stand up and say, "get the hell out of Dodge, we are taking our country back."

Then Colorado and the State of Washington and eleven other states legalized medical and recreational marijuana so we can promote both smoking and addiction. Then cure the addicts with more prescription drugs and health care claims.

Then every State in the union is rushing to legalize recreation drugs for taxation and wasted lives. All because the bureaucrats live off the welfare state by policing using surveyors, tax enforcers and auditors to use fear inducing conformity tactics to keep small businesses honest.

Then a former longtime local government treasurer of Dixon County Illinois pled guilty to fraud in federal court in Rockford for stealing $53 million from the coffers of the small northwestern Illinois city over two decades.

Then the city of San Bernardino, since declaring bankruptcy, decided to resume paying into the state pension, but the California city will continue to renege on other debts including payments to bondholders and other creditors, according to a new budget. Detroit the same situation.

Then it was disclosed that Illinois' townships continue to accumulate taxpayer dollars for no known services and paying record salaries and perks to local government officials.

Then the Illinois voters were getting a 67% tax increase to fund the ongoing fiscal disaster and its unfunded pension debt that is in arrears to the tune of $181 billion dollars while paying a retired professor $360,000 per year for his hard-earned pension and allowing State officials to double dip retirement pay and act as consultants.

To make things worse for the Rhoads family we purchased three skilled nursing facilities in 2009, 2010 and 2011 to set up three models of restorative care for the purpose of forming a franchise approach to saving rural chain operated nursing homes. The company All-American Care was founded by Jerry Rhoads after he and his son developed an episodic digital cost system based on body systems and AI computer models of care spanning the physician, hospital, nursing home, home care, assisted living, or hospice.

We renovated the exterior and interior of three old and decrepit facilities at a cost of $3 million dollars by painting the old red brick buildings white. Named them the D.C. Whitehouse after Sharon Rhoads's mother

Dorotha C. White and implemented the Caregiver Management System of care. It required a makeover of staff, programming, systems, food delivery, relationships with the medical community and the aging population of small rural culture.

Within six and half years we turned over 600 staff getting the professionalism to deliver the innovation of restorative care for the purpose of sending all admission back home or assisted living utilizing the Medicare program of rehabilitation. Then utilized Medicaid, if necessary, to provide a home like environment conducive to family and community involvement. This model of restorative care using the Caregiver Management System of Artificial Intelligence care plan models was devised by Jerry Rhoads' management company.

Rather than assist the Rhoads' in its mission the State of Iowa and Arkansas Departments of Survey and Appeal continued to harass and penalize the Rhoads' for the previous owners' failure to comply with the basics of patient care. After spending $5 million dollars to upgrade the quality and sending 57% of the admissions home the State issued violations and fines for arbitrary and capricious penalties forcing the sale of the homes. All of this in the name of democracy Russian style. See the details in Jerry's book "Failing Government Taketh Away" Xlibris 2016.

Providers Are Victims of Government Punitive "Gotcha" Surveys

Following are the three-nursing home investments the Rhoads family made to demonstrate the effectiveness of setting up franchise models for solving the nursing home debacle. 75% of the nursing homes are owned by the 20 largest nursing home real estate conglomerates partnering with the government to control the flow of $800 billion dollars in Medicare and Medicaid money spent on nursing home care (or should I say wasting?). I call this a Monopsony where the government is the purchaser of last resort because not a one of them has a owner visiting these small businesses on a daily basis and have a regional administrator (czar) visiting maybe once a month to dictate the policies and practice of the hired (care taker) administrator. Typically, the administrator isn't schooled on running a business let alone the hardest business to manage ... a small rural or struggling suburban or urban nursing home.

LITTLE ROCK, ARKANSAS (suburban)

The Rhoads' purchased this 139-bed skilled nursing facility in November 2009. It was troubled and was going to be closed. In eighteen months, we invested over $500,000 to renovate and change the culture from a warehouse for nursing home patients to a care house for human being needing health care services. Within two- and one-half months the surveyors managed to turn an incident in the facility bus into an Immediate Jeopardy violation that eventually forced us out of business. In the fifteen months we borrowed over $3 million dollars saving it for the builder who sold it out from under us then sued us for the loans he had made to get the license and Medicare certification reestablished.

Compliance to the minimum standards that I refer to in a later article are labeled F-Tags. There 400 different minimum standards that they are looking for mistakes not positive accomplishments. Having been in the nursing home business for forty years as a CPA and licensed administrator it is obvious that enforcement doesn't work because the problems are the same today as they were when I started visiting them and then owning them. It's punitive "gotcha" over reach by State and Federal Government.

WASHINGTON, IOWA (rural)

The Rhoads' purchased this 125-bed skilled nursing facility in October 2011. It was troubled and was going to be closed. In thirty-eight months, we invested over $500,000 to renovate and change the culture from a warehouse for nursing home patients to a care house for human being needing health care services. Within two- and one-half months the surveyors managed to turn an incident in the Alzheimer's unit into a Special Focus violation that eventually cost us $100,000 in fines, $100,000 in legal fees, filing bankruptcy that eventually forced us out of the nursing home business. We ultimately sold the two Iowa faculties to a chain out of New Jersey who turned them back into warehouses for the elderly.

David the ombudsman to our Washington facility always commented on the cleanliness, the professionalism of our care by restoring everyone to their highest level of functioning. He said it was so different from others.

MUSCATINE IOWA (rural)

The Rhoads' purchased this 100-bed skilled nursing facility in September 2009. It was troubled and was going to be closed. In eighteen months, we invested over $500,000 to renovate and change the culture from a warehouse for nursing home patients to a care house for human beings needing health care services. Within sixty-four months the surveyors managed to turn a minor incident in the troubled patient into an Immediate Jeopardy violation that almost prevented us from selling the facility after their enforcement action had bankrupted the business. The State of Iowa had not paid for upgrading our Medicaid rate for two years and finally settled for $900,000 so we could sell the Iowa facilities.

The ombudsman to our owned facilities or managed and consulted with (over 140 in 22 States) always commented on the cleanliness, the professionalism of our care by restoring everyone to their highest level of functioning. Judy at Muscatine said she had never seen a home so well run.

SUM UP THIS ARTICLE WITH REAL LIFE AUTHORITARIANISM

We found that the nursing home business can be changed and must be organized and owned by local operators using the franchise approach of ownership. It was our mission to build three models in Arkansas and Iowa to demonstrate using our own money that nursing homes are not the problem of the solution but of the owners and enforces using fear inducing conformity tactics to force bureaucratic regulations on small businesses.

When we purchased the three skilled facilities our purpose was to collaborate with the regulators and build a new better model. But they weren't interested ... their attitude was "just comply" or else. Compliance in surveyor terms "we've gotcha so you better comply", then you fix it while they are there and they still write you up for fines and later gotchas. In 37 years, I've never known the system of enforcement of minimum standards to improve anything particularly the care or fix nursing home problems, like we did, with them badgering us to do it their way. Example: they had their certain way of changing diapers and passing of medications and we were working to do away with diapers and reduce the 15 to 20 pills per day average being prescribed per patient to improve patient functioning. Of course, we had to fight the physician and family to do it.

The reaction by the Media and general public ... you must be doing something wrong if the surveyors write you up and fine you ... well the problem is the surveyors don't care for the patients the owners do but the surveyors have the authority to use the regulations to arbitrarily catch you doing something minor and turn into fines and threats that the media ignores.

It effectively forced us out of business with a $360,00 dollar fine for a minor infraction by an Alzheimer patient on another patient turned into a $6,000 per day fine for 40 days that killed our attempt at the last minute to sell the homes, as retaliation for an appeal I had filed with the Federal Government.

We then had to find another buyer and take a lower price. That resulted in us losing money on the transaction. And it forced us to sell regardless of the underlying circumstances which were us being pushed out for our honorable attempt to change the paradigm of filth and poor care to cleanliness and excellent care with 57% of our patients were restored and returned home.

This story is fully presented in my latest book "Health Care for All" (How to fix Nursing Homes and Prevent Pandemics), Page Turner Press, 2021.

HONOR IS TRUTH

What is truth
Is truth the sage
Naivety of youth
Or the wisdom of age

Is it the good sense
Of experience
Is it the moral code
Of each abode

Is it the golden rule
Of a spiritual fool
What is it

Could it be

It's written in the Sea of reality
By a humble man
Who made a stand
For a virtuous woman

Then love is truth
If so is it the confession booth
Between the seeker
And the speaker

Or the reflection of truth
For living loving and thinking
Virtuously
Where honor is virginity

By being accountable
For your own honor
And intent
That's truth

Some instances
Test your honor
When treated dishonorably
Surprise there's no color line in free enterprise

Article Four

Value of the dollar, Fiat Money, World Order
(Government Blunders Bursting the Housing Bubble
Causing the Great Depression
of 2007, 2008, 2009, and beyond)

It is becoming evident that the Chinese aspire to have the yuan be the reference currency for worldwide banking and commerce. In that respect they have a commitment to building a new financial system embracing generally accepted accounting principles (GAAP), using People's Bank of China, their own internet and cryptocurrency with block chain connections worldwide replacing the US dollar for investment, exchange and commerce. They also are interested in stable coins that are collateralized by the value of the underlying asset (i.e., Gold). This would require USA support the use of US or China gold to support a value-based currency. China considers this a weapon to threaten and take supremacy over the dollar. With the current financial upheaval from the Pandemic and a new Administration China is accumulating gold, developing their own internet block chain for making the yuan the new World Order of finance and banking.

Can the US and its partner the Federal Reserve Banking system confront this plan without forcing America into another Great Recession that occurred in 2005 when Alan Greenspan was replaced by Harvard College professor Ben Bernanke, Bush Administration and Treasury Secretary Paulson reacted and caused the derivative balloon to burst, rather than proactive use of the banking system to prevent mass mortgage foreclosures and bankruptcies. They saved those too the big to fail institutions and cost Americans $30 trillions of home values and their 401k plans to cover up the real cause. This, in reality, was a depression of 1929 proportions, not a recession, as it was labeled by the Bush Administration, as it rippled throughout the world of finance with the prime rate and international Libor rate soaring out of control.

In August 2008, there is calm before the storm. Then Fed races to fix the balloon they burst, the treasury plots to bribe the banks with bailout money so they keep quiet on the cause of the demise of America's liquidity (See Exhibit B for details). Then the stock market gets wind of the cover up and dives into oblivion, causing further panic in Congress, stimulating our new president Obama to attempt to spend our way out of a bankrupt economy. Who is to blame and how do we realistically fix it? First, let's define the problem so we can put together a workable plan.

In Thomas E. Woods' bestselling book Meltdown, 2009 Regnery Publishing (A free market look at why the stock market collapsed, the economy tanked, and Government bailouts made it worse) the author analyzes why the increases in the money supply and central planning of the interest rates dilutes the market place, the stock market values and the overall economy... then begs the question and gives readers answers to "shouldn't the Fed, our discount supplier of money and lender of last resort be disbanded?" And, is Laissez Faire behind all of the recessions and depressions over the last century, or is it Government intervention and fiat money with no commodity backing? Mr. Woods, an expert economist, makes the case that the free market is the healer not the cause and escalating debt based monetary policies are the root of all evil. The solution he offers is "the free market forces of production should drive prices and consumption, not vice versa".

Fact: As a fallout of the Fed using exchange rates to control inflation in the housing market and avoid a run-on member bank "TARP . . . troubled asset relief program" . . . was used as a bank bailout for those financial institutions "too big to fail". The option was to nationalize the banks or buy toxic assets from member banks. With Hank Paulson former CEO of Goldman Sachs, President Bush's Treasury Secretary, heading up the cover-up, Congress chose to become shareholders in the Fed banks rather than allow a run-on bank assets. Bear Sterns, AIG,

Fannie Mae, Freddie Mac, were saved, Lehman Bros. was allowed to fail, mergers (Citi bank, Wachovia, Goldman Sachs, Morgan Stanley, Bank of America, all talked merger) were orchestrated from the highest levels and Wall Street mortgage instruments took the fall.

But, as was the plan, the TARP funds were not used to buy toxic assets and allow the bundled mortgages to perform at lower interest rates and longer payouts but were used to expand credit to Fed member banks at the higher exchange rates and foreclosures were to abound as the housing market collapsed. $11 trillion in residential mortgages and $3 trillion in commercial paper were bought out with TARP; and an Obama $700 billion stimulus package for Wall Street companies that were too Big to Fail was passed by Congress; while "Helicopter" Bernanke Fed Chairman and Tim Geithner NY Fed chairman had the Fed cover up its bungle by lowering the inflated discount rates to member banks to 1% and millions of jobs related to the housing industry were lost resulting in the Great Depression of 2007.

Fact: Greenspan departs May 11, 2005, and the Fed rate rises under the Harvard college professor *Ben Bernanke* from 2.75 in April 2005 to a catastrophic 5.25 in June 2006, until it burst the American economic bubble in August 2007. Then the Fed reacted in an insane manner by dropping the Fed rate but not the prime rate, which had risen to 8.5 percent and allowed the mortgage banking system to collapse. Across the world, the LIBOR 12% rate then erodes the value of the dollar and sinks international trade.

Fact: George Bush and the Republicans fiddled with wars and rampant spending while the economy burned, so a Democratic Congress jumped in to save America from itself by allowing Paulsen, a retired Goldman Sachs securities gambler, to propose a bailout for the Fed and their member banks, not home owners and businesses that were going to collapse under the weight of no reasonable credit. No reasonable prospects for growth so we can compete with the foreign markets that depend on our consumers to carry the world economy. Too big to fail was the strategy and then Obama decided to bail out big business to keep unemployment rates down, but in reality, was avoiding GM, Chrysler, etc. downsizing through Article 11 write-downs that would have further sunk the banking industry.

Fact: when you kill the housing industry you kill 20 million related jobs for supporting housing . . . not since the S&L crisis has the kings of inflation fears over reacted and created an exchange rate panic worldwide. So, we should not be misled that it was all wall-street greed . . . or main street ignorance that created this contrived error in judgment that would not have happened under the Greenspan watch.

The *interest-ing* Federal Reserve Syndrome

The *interest-ing* inflating economy is that the cost of capital goes up. The Federal Reserve's mentality is to increase interest rates to control inflation. But if the cost of equity and availability of capital goes up at an escalating amount, prices cycle upward. If borrowed capital interest rates cycle upward, due to the discount rate the Fed sets for its member banks, faster than the prices can absorb, it doesn't make sense to borrow more than can be absorbed by the pricing. So, increasing debt service interest is counterproductive for stimulating economies and discouraging inflation. When the Fed does the opposite of what the economy needs, the only variable left for the business is to increase productivity of labor through increases in wages that inflates cost of living while prices cycle upward due to demand. Inflation is only controlled by a healthy economy and a strong dollar, both of which are hampered by increasing interest rates.

Therefore, the Federal Reserve, the largest casino in the world, is playing Russian roulette with taxpayer taxes for the sake of controlling the flow of monetary values to its banks and business; in other words, they are counter to economic growth under the guise that they are a reactor to, not the preceptor of healthy economic cycles. Disbanding this facade would allow prices, supply, and demand to be natural events.

Fixing the bubble

Obviously, the solution does not lie with those that caused the problem. The air in the bubble needed to be slowly released, not popped, so the solution is to restore the lending confidence through restoring the mortgages that were foreclosed and letting homeowners pay what they can so the cash is flowing and credit limits can be restored. It is not a bailout; it is undoing what the academics that run American politics caused. American businesses, on the other hand, must stop the feed on greed philosophy and step in and be the leaders. We have abdicated the world's biggest business to attorneys and bankers who have never run a productive enterprise and do not know how to manage budgets and money problems except to pass more regulations and play Monopsony games with the interest rates.

We, the silent majority, must demand changes in systems, not just policies, and elect congressmen and legislatures that get rid of laws, not pass more and more that we cannot fund. For every law passed, we incur more and more overhead cost of running the very thing that finances everything: business. It is not the just a taxing system that is the problem, it is the spending system that is wasting our resources, both human and financial. We must have a third-party alternative when we go to the polls, not the red and blue parties that have taken us to the brink of bankruptcy. Get the stimulus funds to the small businesses that innovate and create jobs and profits that support banks and big government. Disband the Fed and rebrand Wall Street and Main Street with economic leverage for small-business innovation and creativity.

We need solutions, not rhetoric. For example, China, Japan, India, and Russia should be our partners in controlling the energy costs. We need to form OPEC (Oil Purchasing Energy Countries) and dictate the supply and pricing with our demand rather than hope we find a solution at home or in the oceans. World peace should be our mission, not so-called liberty that we cannot even define. Build infrastructures with capital investment in emerging markets for the benefits of job building and standard of living equality, not greed and world dominance using military power. As for politics, we need a third party built on the working ethic of all Americans and the enterprising nature of our culture, not dictated by money and money alone. Equality in education and housing is the top priority, not equity if we have money left from the bulging spending habits of the elite.

The following table depict the Fed's history of interest exchange rates affecting monetary values and the flow of credit through member banks and the world banking system

Federal Funds Rate 1998 to 2007
Source: Federal Reserve Exchange Rate Tables

Month	2007	2006	2005	2004	2003
January	5.25	4.50	2.25	1.00	1.24
February	5.25	4.50	2.50	1.01	1.26
March	5.25	4.75	2.75	1.00	1.25
April	5.25	4.75	2.75	1.00	1.26
May	5.25	5.00	3.00	1.00	1.26
June	5.25	5.25	3.25	1.03	1.22
July	5.25	5.25	3.25	1.26	1.01
August	5.25	5.25	3.50	1.50	1.03
September	4.75	5.25	3.75	1.75	1.01
October	4.50	5.25	3.75	1.75	1.01
November	4.50	5.25	4.00	2.00	1.00
December	4.25	5.25	4.25	2.25	0.98
Month	2002	2001	2000	1999	1998
January	1.73	5.98	5.45	4.63	5.56
February	1.74	5.49	5.73	4.76	5.51
March	1.73	5.31	5.85	4.81	5.49
April	1.75	4.80	6.02	4.74	5.45
May	1.75	4.21	6.27	4.74	5.49
June	1.75	3.97	6.53	4.76	5.56
July	1.73	3.77	6.54	4.99	5.54
August	1.74	3.65	6.50	5.07	5.55

September	1.75	3.07	6.52	5.22	5.51
October	1.75	2.49	6.51	5.20	5.07
November	1.34	2.09	6.51	5.42	4.83
December	1.24	1.82	6.40	5.30	4.68

The same reaction as when Fed Chairman Paul A. Volcker and Carter drove prime rate to 23 percent and Keynesian economic theory permeated the scene pre-Greenspan days, thus destroying the S&L banking system while collapsing the housing market, then Greenspan's eighteen years of having a free-market mentality, creating availability of capital for economic growth, surpluses, and declining unemployment. Unfortunately, his retirement allowed the Keynesian academics to again take over the economy, saying that the housing market and energy cost inflation was our biggest enemy and it had to be killed by raising the fed rate, when in effect it is our government's bankrupt policies and our $158 trillion accumulated deficit, including unfunded entitlements that are sinking the ship.

The disaster was permeated by the Federal Reserve System (a public/private government entity gambling taxpayer money through exchange rates with member banks and the US Treasury) unfettered by Congress or the administration. We were told by Bernanke, Bush, and Paulsen that the Fed exchange rates to member banks had to increase to control inflation and bring down housing values and energy costs, though the cost of living was still at pre-inflation rates, because nothing else could have possibly justified them bursting the bubble. Greenspan would have let the air out slowly and a true livable recession would have been orchestrated but not the ensuing 2007 Great Depression.

What happened was the Fed rate drove the prime rate too high for the variable mortgage market (subprime is not the problem, it is the prime plus rates that occurred when the Fed raised the lending rates to 5.25 and the poor homeowners who had refinanced were stuck with monthly payments doubling to where they could not make the payments and the pompous bankers started a flurry of foreclosures that caused panic in the Fannie Mae and Freddie Mac markets, causing a tsunami effect). Rather than letting the air out slowly and deflating the housing boom and energy speculation, the new chairman, a Harvard professor, and the Republican Administration's incompetents burst the balloon for all of the American economy, which in turn swamped the international market in debt that cannot and will not be serviced. And that swamped every economy around the world with deflation.

Below are the inflation rates that the Fed was supposedly controlling with their hike from 2.8 percent in May 2005 (the end of the Greenspan era) to 4.32 percent in June 2006 when the Fed rate went to 5.25 and the prime started to escalate to 8.5 percent, with prime plus 2 for variable risk-based mortgage, ARMs, and subprime mortgages. Inflation never got over 5 percent (and that was due to energy prices) until June 2008 when the Fed, in a panic, was reducing the rate back down to 1 percent after causing not just a recession but also a run on the investment securities, which will cause a depression in jobs, tax revenues, and economic stability.

Blank cells—data not available because it has not been released by the Bureau of Labor Statistics

YEAR	JAN	FEB	MAR	APR	MAY	JUN	JUL	AUG	SEP	OCT	NOV	DEC	AVE
2008	4.28%	4.03%	3.98%	3.94%	4.18%	5.02%	5.60%	5.37%					
2007	2.08%	2.42%	2.78%	2.57%	2.69%	2.69%	2.36%	1.97%	2.76%	3.54%	4.31%	4.08%	2.85%
2006	3.99%	3.60%	3.36%	3.55%	4.17%	4.32%	4.15%	3.82%	2.06%	1.31%	1.97%	2.54%	3.24%
2005	2.97%	3.01%	3.15%	3.51%	2.80%	2.53%	3.17%	3.64%	4.69%	4.35%	3.46%	3.42%	3.39%
2004	1.93%	1.69%	1.74%	2.29%	3.05%	3.27%	2.99%	2.65%	2.54%	3.19%	3.52%	3.26%	2.68%
2003	2.60%	2.98%	3.02%	2.22%	2.06%	2.11%	2.11%	2.16%	2.32%	2.04%	1.77%	1.88%	2.27%
2002	1.14%	1.14%	1.48%	1.64%	1.18%	1.07%	1.46%	1.80%	1.51%	2.03%	2.20%	2.38%	1.59%
2001	3.73%	3.53%	2.92%	3.27%	3.62%	3.25%	2.72%	2.72%	2.65%	2.13%	1.90%	1.55%	2.83%
2000	2.74%	3.22%	3.76%	3.07%	3.19%	3.73%	3.66%	3.41%	3.45%	3.45%	3.45%	3.39%	3.38%
1999	1.67%	1.61%	1.73%	2.28%	2.09%	1.96%	2.14%	2.26%	2.63%	2.56%	2.62%	2.68%	2.19%
1998	1.57%	1.44%	1.37%	1.44%	1.69%	1.68%	1.68%	1.62%	1.49%	1.49%	1.55%	1.61%	1.55%
1997	3.04%	3.03%	2.76%	2.50%	2.23%	2.30%	2.23%	2.23%	2.15%	2.08%	1.83%	1.70%	2.34%

This giant boner destroyed the housing market that supports twenty million workers for years. From the carpenters, to the painters, to the drywall contractors, to the concrete suppliers, to the nails and mortar vendors, to the bankers, real estate and mortgage brokers, accountants, attorneys, who all feed off these small businesses, they took the fall because of the incompetence of the Fed and leadership we have put in place to run our American enterprise. Then, guess who became our treasury secretary? The chairman of the New York Fed (tax avoider), Tim Geithner. It is truly a conspiracy of politics and endemic banking, killing the American enterprise.

Deja vu …History repeated itself, because the Carter administration did the same thing in playing roulette with the interest rates in the late '70s and early '80s when the prime rate was 23 percent and Paul Adolph Volcker was the genius Keynesian economist who left the S&Ls out to sink, creating unemployment and a depression of the housing market. Don't we learn anything? (Volcker surfaced again as Obama's economic guru for the stimulus fiasco). And it was Reagan and Clinton, with the tight rein on the Fed by Alan Greenspan for eighteen years, that kept interest rates from destroying the American enterprise.

Then, as the values of homes escalated under the guise of prosperity, Greenspan would have let the air out of the balloon slowly, not the way it was done. So goes politics, destroying business for the sake of control and power. To complete the irony of this story is those that f'd up the cost of capital and destroyed equity, in retrospect, blame Greenspan for loosey goosey Fed rates … which is a coverup since Greenspan never pulled the boner that Bernanke orchestrated.

SUM UP OF THIS ARTICLE

The retirement of Alan Greenspan ignited the Depression of 2007-10 but did not cause it. His replacement, Prof. Ben "Helicopter" or "Printing Press" Bernanke floated in on a sinking ship called the Bush administration, with Paulson as its Captain Quig, and fell into the "we have to control inflation using the interest rates as our ammunition" bandwagon and burst the economic and monetary bubble! Rather than letting the air out slowly in the housing and energy markets, through slow progression of the interest spreads he let the Fed go crazy with the flagrant increases in the discount rates, thereby bursting the consumer's total balloon by making mortgage payments too high causing 3 million subprime mortgage foreclosures, and did not fix anything but his own academic ego and his desire to sell his book "Essays on the Great Depression" on how to fix a depression using the monetary supply to save "too big to fail" member banks.

In Greenspan's book, "The Age of Turbulence: Adventures in the New World", he realistically analyzes the capabilities of the presidents he worked for and found Nixon, Reagan, and Clinton adept at managing the economy, and Bush Sr. and Bush Jr. and Carter inept. Chairman Greenspan should be commended for his steady hand on the interest rudder versus such luminaries as Paul Adolph Volcker, the interest hiking king and Burns the bear market queen and "Helicopter" Bernanke the prince of tides. On the other hand, Greenspan stated that social security is not the problem . . . it is health care.

Banking and currency exchange made through the Federal Reserve System must be held accountable to the benefit of the Enterprise or disbanded. The Fed's mismanagement of the exchange rates in 2005-07, after the retirement of Chairman Greenspan caused the fall of the housing market in 2007 and burst of the mortgage bubble. Rather than gambling the taxpayers' money, the Federal Reserve System must *not* be allowed free reign with monetary exchange rates. Twenty million jobs related to housing and mortgage financing have been lost, and now we need to regenerate them by getting rid of the Dodd/Frank imposition of inhibiting regulations trying to corral Wall Street's ambitions and small businesses' need for equity capital financing that furthered the impact of the housing depression and effectively depleted capital markets for small businesses.

SPENDING MANIA CAUSED BY THE FED RATES, CURRRENCY PRINTING PRESS ANDTREASURIES AS THE DISCOUNT RATE REACHED A -2%.

2000 to 2020 was USA Playing Russian Roulette with taxpayer's future with China, Japan, Mexico, India, South Korea credit to fund enormous trade deficits.

The Bush administration (along with Paulson and Bernanke's failed Fed policies) caused the TARP $700 billion Relief (to connected investment houses and Fed member banks) Act and the debacle that was furthered by the election of Barrack Obama in 2008 and the 2009 bailout of the automobile industry American Recovery Stimulus of $720 billion and his 2012 $1.2 trillion Obama care bill.

The Bush, Obama, Trump and Biden administrations added 10,000 billion ($10,000,000,000,000,000) to the deficit spending and debt to fund bloated government and a historic Pandemic. And Obama Care is still wasting money on provider incomes not outcomes that will prevent further Pandemics. See next article for details.

Not even God can afford this insanity.

Article Five

Health Care for All, Save Medicare

SHIFT THE PARADIGM TO SELF-HEALTH
(A public-private partnership)

Prevention of Chronic Disease, Pandemics
and Pursue Health Preservation
Self-
Health
Insurance
Funding
Trust

(Medicare became law of the land, **July 30, 1965.** On this day in 1965, President Lyndon B. Johnson signed into law Medicare, which provides federally subsidized hospitalization and medical insurance for the nation›s elderly. The legislation remains an important legacy of LBJ's Great Society" initiative). Later JFK and Obama signed Medicaid and Obama care, so called entitlements to ultimately cover every American.

Government Sponsored Wealth Care (a Monopsony) is Lying to Us:

The problem isn't the Medicare law it's the thousands of pages of rules known as regulations, that twist and turn the Rule into Law by the small print and its arbitrary and capricious interpretations by patronage bureaucrats. New rules have been issued by the Biden administration on Medicare payment to physicians. That begins on page 64,996 of the Federal Register (the Federal Government's publications of the small print) and ends on Page 66,031 ... In Appendix 2, it establishes the new anti-racist plan bonus. In other words, if a physician has an anti-racist plan, they will make more money by acting as the government's enforcement arm for turning in those who are racists without proof or facts. Isn't this in itself racist in its intent and content. A percentage of their Medicare income to create and implement an anti-racist plan that entraps their staff and patients. For reporting a racist you can make more Medicare money though you ratted out an employee or patient... seems this is illegal and immoral in its intent and content. George Orwell couldn't have said it better. 2024 is 1984.

If you are over 65 and watching any TV station, are you tired of hearing the celebrity ads by Joe Namath and William Shatner on every channel or stream down service, to switch your traditional Medicare from Part A and B to an Advantage policy called Medicare Part C? What does this mean? Our Medicare financing is in trouble. It's a part of the derivative bubble that is inflated by escalating costs, as well declining health of the aging American. Medicare is based on a premise that America can afford anything and everything regardless of the cost and outcome. What is Part C Advantage Medicare? Is it to our advantage as it states in its pitch?

The pitch is to get 12 million, unsuspecting, seniors to switch their traditional Medicare to an Advantage insurance program (modifying the benefits) with all these free services based on your zip code. What in the hell does zip code have to do with your Medicare insurance? They say, it's to improve your coverage for everything from free meals to condoms (as if seniors need them). Okay that's fictious. But the Advantage program is not managed care as our Big Brother government spins it.

It's clearly Managed Cost ... what's the difference? Well, by using your zip code, to determine your coverage, there is a discount and refund of Part B Medicare based on the concept of risk pools and population health care groupings. What the heck is that? Believe me it's Fauci quack science. It's a contrived method to move every senior off traditional Medicare to managed cost Medicare. Why? Because, it isn't now affordable and the Medicare program is in financial trouble. This is primarily due to the unhealthy Baby Boomers coming of Medicare age and expecting free health care. Therefore, Medicare Advantage is contrived to cut benefits ... Managed Cost not Managed Care. The incentive for the insurance companies to sponsor the Advantage Medicare Part C managed cost program, is they get a percent of the savings. It's certainly not for better outcomes for the elderly beneficiaries or saving them money.

Since 1975, Medicare Part A has denied claims in skilled nursing homes, for billing Medicare Part A for more than 20 days, denying 80 days of the benefit period, costing the private sector billions of dollars in long term care resources. Forcing the beneficiaries to be discharged from the hospital too quickly, to nursing homes that aren't capable of providing sub-acute care. Then the elderly is warehoused in nursing homes with horrible results. Why? Read my lips ... to save Medicare and the Federal and State Medicaid budgets. This has resulted in Medicare seniors being forced on Medicaid and trapped in nursing homes for the rest of their lives. This illegal shift of the cost of care to the private resources or the Medicaid program is fraudulent.

Consequently, the government is lying on every TV ad (From November to December 7th opt in period). Big Brother tells seniors they can get all these free benefits by giving up traditional Medicare entitling the insurance companies (the Brotherhood) to cut the benefit from 100 days to 20 days. Why would they do that? Because the law and regulations specify a 100-day benefit, but this move will cut 80 days out of the benefit for hospitalization and skilled nursing care. Then a $179 coinsurance will kick in and the Part C program will not continue to pay the difference. Then private pay resources must pick it up. In effect, this deprives the 44 million entitled Medicare recipients 80% of their Part A and B long term care restorative coverage. Or trillions of dollars of benefits over the next decade. This leaves millions of seniors that could have been restored, using the 100-day benefit, convalescing in nursing homes on Medicaid, a state welfare program, for the remainder of their lives.

Under Part C, Advantage Medicare, our seniors will no longer get the proper healthcare in an average length of stay of 2 to 4 days in the hospital and only get a short 20 day stay in a nursing home before having to pick up the cost of their own care or go on Medicaid. To get Medicaid they must prove they are indigent (have spent their own money down to a burial fee of $2,500). This is a fraudulent transfer of the cost that traditional Medicare should pay for, to the private resources and forces seniors into spending down their estate to being indigent (dependent on State welfare called Medicaid).

In effect, utilizing diagnosis, procedure and zip codes Big Brother Medicare only pays what the bureaucrats decide to pay, to avoid bankrupting the Medicare and Medicaid insurance program. Wake up America Medicare pays for a code not for quality outcomes. Those rates are all based on algorithms (averages) to pay the providers their incomes not for your outcomes, that deprives the beneficiaries of their 100 days of recovery time, so they can get out of these despicable nursing homes. As for the nursing homes ... they're under funded by Medicare and Medicaid because they are the provider of last resort, on the Big Brother Medicare money chain and blamed for poor care and wasted lives sitting in wheelchairs. As usual the Medicare Advantage politics are money-tics for a quick fix of the health care funding problem.

What can the ordinary American do about it? Elect a third party that stands for the citizen's right to quality health care for outcomes not just provider incomes. This requires voting for The American Enterprise Party and its SHIFT health care program outlined in this chapter.

The Health Care Balloon

THE OVER INFLATED EXPLODING HEALTH CARE BALLOON IS THE PROBLEM ... THERE WILL BE NO RESTRAINT IN HOSPITAL PRICING UNTIL OBAMA/BIDEN CARE RATIONS THE MONEY FOR THE ELDERLY USING ACO'S, BUNDLED PAYMENT, RISK POOLS AND MANAGED POPULATIONS ... THESE ARE ACADEMIC SOLUTIONS THAT ARE NEITHER EFFECTIVE, FAIR OR LEGAL IN THEIR INTENT. (See Exhibit E for definitions for health care and governmental acronyms).

"Chemoprotective behavior, it is estimated that one-half of all cancers may be prevented by diet and life style alone". "Heart failure and diabetes can be eradicated by diet and lifestyle habits". "The majority of Covid-19 victims have underlying chronic health problems". According to the CDC, FDA and leading immunologists and epigenetic biologists.

COVID-19 AND THE 2,000 YEAR PANDEMIC WARS

- Franklin D. Roosevelt after Japan's attack on Pearl Harbor "we have nothing to fear but fear itself"

- General Patton "war is won with courage not fear ... courage is holding off fear to act not react"

- Michael Crichton "the state of fear is a political agenda"

The China Corona (Covid-19 strain) Virus changed the world of health care delivery and why prevention of chronic diseases and the pursuit of health preservation need to replace the antiquated methods exposed by the Pandemic of 2019 and beyond. Health care science needs to become more precise than having the government bureaucrats defending their failures to prepare the world for the China Virus **with a fear** inducing conformity **agend**a that pushed the world to a physical and financial tsunami exposing themselves, as the problem to be solved.

It's history that an American scientist also recreated the corona virus years ago, in an American lab, as did the Chinese in 2020, to develop a vaccine to inoculate 300 million Americans or 1.2 billion Chinese per year promoting the State of Fear inducing conformity that they contribute to the necessity to fund that agenda. A whole new industry of analyzing treatment and triage data to bend the curve on active cases and deaths, ventilators, masks, PPE, pandemic mitigation, portable hospital beds and sheltering will be put in place for when we need it to react to the next spike or surge for the flu viruses that have been with us for 2,000 years with an average duration of two years.

The main deaths being our most vulnerable nursing home patients and economy alongside less than .01% of the rest of us sheltering in place or essential working Americans. Amazingly, most essential workers are government workers, first responders or the Brotherhood Big Businesses. It is the first responders with the courage to fight off fear created by the Pandemic Task Force that are winning the war. The rest of us need to as Franklin Roosevelt said "take a method and try it ... if it fails admit it frankly and try another. Try something." "Go back to work and deal with the fear inducing conformity and deal with failure". Because the cure is worse than the disease ... et tu Brute' President Trump was right on all counts and his lack of support from his own party killed his chances at reelection ... the democrats capitalized on the Pandemic to get rid of him and install Big Brother Biden as the Wizard of Oz with his tin man fear monger Fauci, and his Vice Wizard Kamala Harris ...the first "Black brown white" Vice Wizard.

The aftermath of the failed leadership by" elections have consequences", are now starting to surface as this book hits the bookstores. With our schools being locked down, and our physicians denied the authority to treat the disease, without public Health's FDA, Institute of Health headed by Dr. Fuci, and the CDC approval, everything hinged on a "warp speed" vaccine that would enable America to resume some semblance of sanity. Though Trump's leadership, saying lock downs are a cur e worse than the disease, got him thrown out of office, he did deliver on his commitment to get a vaccine in one-year. Boohooed by Dr. Fauci and the CDC and FDA Directors his management instincts would have saved thousands more lives by invoking triage (survival of the unfit-ist) and use of approved "last resort" medications to prevent an Epidemic turning a bureaucratic Panic into a manmade Pandemic.

As a result, our children, chronically ill and elderly have borne the brunt by mandating being masked and sheltered at home. The children's virtual home-schooling for two years was a failure with lost schooling ... with the teacher's union complaisant and teachers overreacting to the low-risk nature of the virus for young healthy immune systems. Many of the problems, called issues, affected our children's and elderly's health in other ways. Teen suicides are up 15% when void of personal relationships, 169,000 nursing home deaths up 33% from normal annual deaths, general drug use up 25%, including deaths from illicit fentanyl from China, child obesity is up 10% because of in activity and no outdoor activities, crime up 25% due to defunding and Covid impact on policing, with deaths in first responders and police up 25% due to riots and drive-by shootings, health care workers up 25% as the most at risk responders working in hospitals.

All of these facts have been slow in surfacing because of the political nature of the Pandemic for mail-in voting and, the "dump Trump" actions of the Democrats. Since Biden's election, when he said he wouldn't fail like Trump did in allowing 500,000 deaths from the virus, he would kill the virus. Ironically, his first year in office, there have been more Covid-19 deaths than experienced in a Trump administration.

On top of this fiasco, China who was involved in the development of and probable release of the virus at the Wuhan lab in Wuhan, China. China's government immediately instituted a coverup of the real facts implicating Dr. Fauci who funded "gain of function" research with a synthetic DNA genetic sequencing of the virus provided by the Institute of Health to fund Wuhan research grants. On top of all this exploitation, China was the supply line for masks, PPE, medications and therapy supplies and Dr. Fauci became Dr. Dread as the head of the American Pandemic task force

... who put Trump's leadership skills out to pasture and V.P. Pence's task force leader, put Dr. Fauci's cover-up skills at work to avoid the blame of being the cause of the world-wide Pandemic. Of course, the Democrats claimed that Trump was the cause and their campaign tactics got Biden elected. Then and still, Dr. Fauci a registered Democrat, is calling the shots for the Biden and Democrat governors' mandates for mitigation, masks and vaccines. Proving that fear, is as fear does.

COMMENTARY: LITTLE KNOWN SCIENTIFIC FACTS
(Being withheld from Americans)

Since the Spanish 1918–19 pandemic worldwide there has been five pandemics taking lives, economies, dreams, hopes all created by fear. It's interesting that they too used fear and hysteria, social distancing, sheltering at home, quarantines and finally let it run its course and TYPICALLY died out during the following summer.
Following are the recorded pandemics:

- 165 AD THE PLAGUE 5 MILLION DIED
- 541–542 THE BLACK DEATH 25 MILLION DIED
- 1889–1890 THE FLU 1 MILLION DIED
- 1910–1911 CHOLERA (LAST OF SIX STRAINS) 7 MILLION DIED
- 1918–1920 SPANISH FLU 500 MILLION INFECTED, 50 MILLION DIED
- 1956–57 ASIAN FLU 2 MILLION DEATHS
- 1968 HONG KONG FLU 1 MILLION DEATHS
- 2005–2012 HIV VIRUS 15 MILLION DEATHS
- The 2009 Flu Pandemic

- Like the pandemic of 1918, this global flu outbreak in 2009 was also a H1N1 strain. The CDC said there were 60.8 million cases reported in the United States, of which 274,304 required hospitalizations.

- There were also 12,469 deaths in this country from the H1N1 Pandemic. Officials said 80 percent of those deaths were people under the age of 65.

- Dr. Megan Quinn said "the 2009 flu was remarkable in that it affected younger people more than it did older Americans. The opposite is generally the rule in pandemics".

- "People over the age of 60 had greater immunity, perhaps because they had been exposed to an earlier strain or built-up antibodies over the years," Quin said.

2019–2020 QUA CK SCIENCE DOMINATES THE CORONA VIRUS

6 MILLION INFECTED RESULTING IN 600,000 DEATHS OR A DEATH RATE OF 10% (70% PERSONS OVER 65 YEARS OF AGE AND/OR LIVING IN NURSING HOMES)

Dr. Fauci, head of the National Institute of Health, WHO and the CDC predicting 3 million deaths based on cases and hospitalization and deaths without any probability and predictability statistics. New cases are labeled spiking, reported 3% were asymptomatic but reported no positives in the statistics such as those that truly contacted Covid-19 and died from it… nor were the new cases categorized by age, location, underlying health conditions, living conditions.

The gross cases were used to continue the fear inducing conformity using a conspiracy to keep the schools and nonessential small businesses closed. Also, the rush to manufacture hospital beds and ventilators and masks and PPE (being produced by China who likely caused the Pandemic) is still keeping some businesses in business while other service industries are sinking ... awaiting the next trillion-dollar bribe labeled stimulus. How can we survive when it is supply that is missing not demand? Egg head economists still think a payroll tax holiday will fix it but fail to realize that that deprives social security funding and Medicare and Medicaid money to fight chronic illnesses.

Including the 2019–20 Covid-19 China and Spanish 1918–20 corona flu virus pandemics worldwide there have been fourteen pandemics taking lives, economies, dreams, hopes all created by fear. As such the war on pandemics continues and we keep losing to the fear inducing conformity that eventually it will take all the lives on earth. Which in fact, hasn't happened in 2,000 years and the death count of all pandemics is approximately 100 million for all pandemics, about 10 per 1,000 or the probability of .001 %of those infected die. In America alone we have some 117 million that are diagnosed with chronic disease .... 40% with more than one of 77,000 disease codes. We also have 77,000,000 baby boomers over 65 years of age with 2 million in nursing homes and thousands more in congregate housing. We have a pandemic in America of unhealthy lifestyles not just corona viruses.

Commentary: The 2019–2020 Corona China-Fauci Virus Pandemic how does it rank?

Corona China virus pandemic is the least lethal in terms of number of deaths to date but the most communicable infecting 184 countries worldwide with varying death rates averaging less than 2% and disappearing with heat and humidity. In America we are letting 2,000 years of viruses, that typically die out in two years, close downpour entire country, making the cure diabolical for our economic and humanitarian survival.

So, if age, lifestyle problems and nursing homes are the primary high risk of dying population from any flu or viral pneumonia viruses or bacterial complications, we need to focus on saving them first not trying to save everyone. Like any war you have to triage (survival of the un-fittest) the sickest to the front of the line, not everyone will get it and if they do the probability of dying is .001 % or 99.991% of the time, they get over it.

Commentary: How can we keep everyone safe?

We cannot, keep everyone safe and sound in their homes forever and expect our lifestyle to ever be acceptable. Then designate others as be essential, who are more at risk than we are sitting at home getting depressed and unproductive. The death rate is also increased by social distancing, sheltering in place, wearing masks, fearing our neighbors, not taking better care of ourselves because of the psychological effects of fear inducing conformity, mongering. When there is no proof that masks, social distancing, sheltering in place, contact tracing really work. Now that the vaccines are available thanks to the Trump Administration, Dr. Fauci is the new Biden administration fear director suggesting that double masks may work, and the mutating China virus will be worse than the Corona virus. Still no true scientific based risk data made available to the general public that unhealthy older Americans are the risk pool and the rest of us have immune systems that will win the war if we stay healthy … then everyone can be safe.

Commentary: When will it end?

When the average duration of pandemics, except HIV is two years, … most all of the viruses dying off naturally from weather conditions not conducive for transmission. In 2,000 plus years there has never been a total annihilation …. And death rates not more than .01% one tenth of one percent of human beings except the Spanish flu killing 5% of worldwide population.

In Michael Crichton's book "State of Fear" about political agendas causing tsunamis and pandemics we suspect that the Corona China virus of 2020 may have been intently caused by China. In his book Crichton sites climate change as an example of how this can happen. He quotes Mark Twain as follows: "There is something fascinating about science. One gets such wholesale returns of conjecture out of such a trifling investment of fact". And George Orwell, "Within any important issue, there always are aspects no one wishes to discuss". The essence of Crichton's or Orwell's books and their importance to the topic of pandemics is the use of unnatural causes orchestrated by political agendas can give the appearance of a real threat to all of humanity. If so, we may never know what started or ended Corona-19 when it ends in 2022.

Commentary: Why must it end?

The leadership, (the President and his 50 governors) after realizing that you win wars with courage not fear, must manage a viral pandemic and its variants with courage not a science of explicit fear tactics using negative numbers so, we enterprising Americans can reopen our defenses … positive actions produce positive hope, economies and allowing our immune system to develop its own antibodies for future pandemics. It's America's experience in the past, and in this instance, if we let science and fear inducing conformity win the war it will never end. Thus, we need to know statistics on probabilities from clinicians not scientists. For example, how many of the first responders are infected and how many get over it. These types of statistics let's all Americans that we can face the manageable risk with courage.

Commentary: Why Dr. Fauci and CDC Errored

Negative Science's wholesale conjecture is such a trifling investment of fact considering the history of the pandemics and its destructive forces. As in the past it is people who win wars not scientists.

For the History Books, quack Scientists (Fauci and CDC), without input from the clinicians, the fighters of the war, are using bending the negative statistical curves, 6' social distancing, ss mass sheltering in place, enforced quarantine. ventilators, respirators, therapeutic medicines, vaccines, PPE, masks, flattening trend lines of cases, hospitalizations and deaths … instead of stressing that there are low probabilities of those who are symptomatic or asymptomatic through casual contact are carriers who in fact infect everyone with the virus. Yet there is the implied threat that we all face death with human and inhuman contact, emphasized as fact in managing the pandemic using mass hysteria.

This is the epidemy of using a political agenda to win a war with fear inducing conformity not courage and hope personified by common sense leadership that have and will win war after war. (Our President and his governors are following the followers not their instincts). President Trump needed to follow his problem-solving instincts by having his VP to include private sector practicing clinicians and probability experts as his task force, not bureaucrats. By spreading the risk to everyone it is inevitable we will lose the war.

Commentary: How does fear force the warriors to make wrong decisions?

For example, as Governor Como famously said "we cannot triage patients we must save everyone" (triage is a medical policy that is based on the survival of the un-fittest) and ignores probabilities then continues to use negative scientific data to stimulate fear inducing conformity exacerbated by demanding 30,000 ventilators immediately to meet his thousand bed shortfalls for those that never came, while forcing hospitals to send the corona cases to nursing homes for a sure-fire increase in deaths. (By the way nursing homes aren't allowed to have ventilators since Medicare stopped paying for them in the 1980's ... I guess the governor didn't know that since he didn't involve the clinicians in his opinions, miscalculations and bungling).

Being a politician and a bully, he blames nursing homes not himself for the deaths he caused. For that he got a million-dollar book deal for corrupting the other blue state governors to do the same thing he did then got an Emmy for his ridiculous rants on the New York Pandemic for supporting the Fauci/Pence task force. Now it is reported that his staff covered up the number of deaths in New York and Dr. Fauci knew about the virus being leaked by the Chinese Lab in Wuhan under a grant to study the virility of virus and gain of function while testing it on bats

Commentary: What if this doesn't end?

As it is proceeding it has already killed our livelihoods, our courage, our relationships with family, school, sports, doctor visits, hospital interventions, entertainment, exercise, mental health, friendships, because of the fear inducing conformity tactics that have taken on a political agenda …which is "et tu Brute' "dump Trump capitalism and bring on progressive socialism." President Trump, who in my estimation was the only politician that could lead us back to our lifestyles … not the new progressive normal that leaves us in fear inducing conformity of the next spike in cases and deaths to feed political agendas.

Promising that the new normal (a nominalization of the facts) is better for Americans because of government's intervention. This smells of socialism at its worst and changes lifestyles forever awaiting the next pandemic or spike in current cases (by maintaining social distancing as a lifestyle will save us all … don't shake my hand or sneeze in my presence because you might infect me with the latest virus).

With President Trump losing the 2020 election to Joe Biden we are now faced with a Senator of 47 years supporting fear inducing conformity as the tactic to overcome what he says Trump caused. When in fact Trump saved thousands to millions of lives by using business enterprise to produce the multiple vaccines at "Warp Speed" before relinquishing the reigns to the Democrats that then try to take credit for the rollout

Commentary: What will end it?

I'm sure if President Trump and the governors would have heard my podcast, they would agree we must stop this exercise of government supporting all of its citizens with phony Federal Reserve funny money that dilutes our ability to compete with China who started the pandemic. And as this transpires China will assist (like the devil they are) us by buying up failing or failed American businesses.

Regardless of the skepticism of deposed President's "warp speed" plan for private enterprise to produce a vaccine as he predicted (by the election in November 2020) it happened. And in retrospect, despite President Biden and his surrogate Dr. Fauci taking credit for something they either caused or couldn't accomplish; the Trump vaccine has saved millions of lives worldwide and possibly the entire risk-taking American Dream from the China Virus.

Commentary: How will it end?

With the Biden Administration takeover, fear certainly will be their agenda of the Pandemic. Finally, I do believe that the hidden political agenda of the Institute of Health (Anthony Fauci), the CDC and the World Health Organization is to cover up their mismanagement of the mutating 1918 to 2019 corona China virus itself with a project to use a synthetic Corona virus to test gain of function. Is it a Chinese and Democrat conspiracy? I will answer that question with a question … who benefits the most from this political agenda of fear? Former President Trump, newly elected President Biden? Certainly, not the American people, the schools, the small businesses, the 125 million Americans with chronic diseases and the 77,000,000 baby boomers wanting to retire and file for Medicare.

You Don't Know What You Don't Know

(Governor Cuomo and the Pandemic Task Force errored)

Nursing homes aren't allowed by regulations to provide acute care. Any patient requiring hospital care for pneumonia, respiratory failure, high risk of stroke, heart failure, diabetic seizure, bariatric care for severe obesity must be transferred to an acute care hospital. As a result, nursing homes don't have respiratory therapists on staff, aren't allowed to provide ventilator care since they don't have negative air filtration rooms, 24-hour on-site RN coverage and physicians making daily rounds for continuous supervision of Covid19 interventions, evaluations and treatment.

As a result, in New York over 15,000 (1) nursing home patients in nursing homes or hospitals expired due to the decision by Governor Cuomo to require hospitals to send patients with Coved19 back to nursing homes and not accept readmissions. Across the country nursing home patients were the highest risk group and highest death rate due to Coved19. Unfortunately, the uniformed Governors used nursing homes as dumping ground for overcrowded hospitals. This not only caused deaths it exposed the other patients, the caregivers and their families to the deadly virus.

(1) As of the release of this book Governor Cuomo has resigned under pressure of his decisions on nursing homes and 12 allegations of sexual misconduct. Also, it's just been reported by Kathy Hochul, the new 'governor of New York, that the number of Covid-19 deaths for 2020 was understated by 12,000 making total 27,000 in NY alone. All other Democrat Governors are at fault also since Cuomo was coaching them on how not to manage a nursing home Pandemic.

(Then why did Governor Cuomo demand having "30,000 ventilators now and 1000 more acute care beds immediately" from President Trump along with buying billions dollars' worth of masks and PPE from China then not use them due to his ignorance, then write a book for a $4 million dollar advance, praising his ignorance and getting a unearned Emmy for his quack science TV presentations). Why because politics ran the Pandemic not health care experts or probability actuaries for true scientific risk analysis. In fact, the 27,000 deaths in NY nursing homes due to Governor Cuomo's ignorance were covered up by his Department of Public Health, to avoid lawsuits when it was disclosed that other Democrat Governors used this same tactic to kill upwards to 200,000 elderly patients and medical workers. Justice will not be served because Cuomo and others were indemnified from legal actions. This disaster has not been rectified nor reported on by any of the national media or social media.

Postscript: it is now coming out, under the direction Dr. Fauci and grants by the Institute of Health, there was a USA DNA map of the virus used to create a synthetic virus used to test gain of function in the Wuhan lab. And could have been contacted by lab workers who then spread it to others in Wuhan then to others traveling around the world. Conspiracy theory or not ... a deliberate CCP weapon on non-communist countries like USA we may never know.

Dr. Fauci, 80, who has been at the FHI since 1968, director since 1984, a millionaire, making more annual salary than the President's $4000,00 at $434,312 in 2019 and CDC, FDA, WHO are bureaucrats not Pandemic managers. And were a part of creating the problem and covering it up, by using a nonscientific solution they inherited from the last 1918 Pandemic.

If Dr. Fauci's involvement with the Wuhan Lab using National Institute of Health funding $1.50 million dollars ($826,277 from 2013 to 2019) and Eco Health study $3.75 million of grant money for musicologist (Dr. Shi Zhongli of Wuhan Virology Institute for gain of function studies to create super viruses) we may then know why he didn't bring in actuarial experts to assist in forecasting infection and death rates.

If he did, it would go a long way to explain his vacillation in not allowing the economic and health care experts to run the so-called quack bending the risk curve, the PPE rollout, the use of masks nationwide closing down the economy and schools for a year and a half. Without President Trump's "Warp Speed" idea and aggressive implementation, we would never have recovered our normal lives. Now Dr. Fauci and new President Biden want to take credit for stopping the China Virus. Irony never ends in binary two party politics.

In summary, it is no longer a conspiracy theory that we have effectively experienced the Fauci/CCP Corona Virus that escaped from the Wuhan lab either accidentally or intestinally as a CCP weapon on the free world. Then herd management was practiced by Dr. Fauci, a so-called immunologist expert while Herd immunity was pursued by President Trump using warp speed private enterprise that did save millions of lives while the bureaucracy defends how it got out of a shared gain of function experiment in Wuhan, China.

Dr. Fauci, likely as a coverup, was chief herd manager using quack science (taken from the 1918 Spanish Flu Pandemic) to mandate bending the undefined curve, social distancing, masks, testing for all Americans, quarantines, and lockdowns of nonessential businesses. This excluded big government, big box stores, big media, big unions, big media, deemed by default, essential. This left the public schools under the rule of the big Teacher's unions who demanded their members be categorized as nonessential yet should be paid in full for reduced remote learning classes. To date they are wanting every child and teacher to be fully vaccinated and wear masks against variants of Covid-19.

This was, Dr. Fauci and the CDC, WHO and FDA using fear inducing conformity as the authority usurped from the President. While Vice President Pence chaired a task force of fear inducing conformity by bureaucrats using quack science and Governor Cuomo rants about lack of ventilators and hospital beds for which he wrote a book and got an Emmy for being directly responsible for 27,000 New York state nursing home patients.

All of this without risk analysis and focusing on treating those at the highest risk (the elderly and unhealthy baby boomers) by scaring everyone that they could be infected by Covid-19 through contact not air borne droplets, inferring anyone could die from getting it off a door knob and give it anyone you come in contact with ... classic Marxist tactic against the proletariat to quell a cultural revolution against quack science. With the release of this book, we are working with a third variant as the fear factor for dictating human behavior using quack science is still driving politics while our new regime is using it at every chance to induce conformity upon American's risk-taking nature and habits.

Health Care or Wealth Care

It is quoted that Vladimir Lenin said "the fastest and surest way to convert a society to communism or socialism is through health care." With Big Brother government, Big Pharma, Big Health Care Organizations, Obama Care, Medicare and Medicaid working together exercising control for their own advantage using totalitarian rules and regulations will manage public health with fear and compromised outcomes for exorbitant incomes.

Commentary: Patient Protection and Affordable Care Act (i.e., Obama Care) Affordable: Not

Protecting the elderly and disabled: Not
Projected cost:
$465 billion for state exchanges.
$434 billion Medicaid increases.
$176 billion demonstration projects and enforcement.

$1.075 Trillion Cost for the period 2013 to 2022

Projected funding:
$414 billion Medicare cuts.
$349 billion provider taxes.
$210 billion Medicare withholding taxes and surtaxes.
$107 billion pharmacy, hospital taxes.
$68 billion fines and penalties.
150 billion Cadillac insurance taxes.
$13 billion downsizing medical savings accounts.

$20 billion taxes on devices.
$15 billion reductions in tax deduction for medical expenses.
$3 billion taxes on tanning salons.

$1.218 trillion taxes and reductions in benefits
for the period 2013 to 2022

Why Obama Care will fail: it kills creativity with regulations and enforcement that dictate and mandate compliance with averages and minimum standards of quality. The shift of the paradigm to health preservation and disease prevention will be funded through the withholding program of all employed Americans, so they can make their own decisions regarding their personal health plan.

The National Health Expenditure Accounts (NHEA) are the official estimates of total health care spending in the United States. U.S. health care spending grew 4.6 percent in 2019, reaching $3.8 trillion or $11,582 per person and $4.2 trillion, another 10% in 2020 or $14,800 per person. As a share of the nation's Gross Domestic Product, health spending accounts for 20% in 2020 due to the Pandemic an another 24% in 2021.

CMS in the report estimated that national health care spending reached $3.81 trillion in 2019 and would increase to $4.21 trillion in 2020. CMS projected that by 2021, health care spending would reach $6.19 trillion, and would account for 22% of GDP, up from 17.7% in 2018. This is excusive of the emergency spending on the Pandemic for PPE, PPP overtime pay for essential medical personnel.

Physicians	$800 billion
Hospitals	$1.4 trillion
Nursing Homes	$600 billion
Home Care	$300 billion

Pharmaceuticals	$800 billion 1 trillion on Part D drugs by 2020
Other	$300 billion

46% of these dollars are spent on chronic diseases in the last two years of Americans lives. All is spent in the pursuit of treatment rather than wellness as an outcome. Prevention is an afterthought . . . waste is never mentioned . . . why because we are practicing wealth care not true health care.

Why we lose $700 billion—and how to get it back.

By Arthur Garson Jr. from the October 8, 2008 edition of the Christian Health Monitor

"Here's the math: Our current healthcare spending is approximately $4.2 trillion (that's up from $1.3 trillion non-inflation adjusted in 2000). We waste an estimated one-third— or about $1.2 trillion— on unnecessary procedures, unnecessary visits to the doctor, overpriced pharmaceuticals, bloated insurance companies, and the most inefficient paper billing systems imaginable".

- "Saving that wasted money can begin with you and me. Medical experts say that 40 percent of our life expectancy can be attributed to lifestyle. We spend about $100 billion per year on costs related to obesity alone."

- "We must examine our role in healthcare. How often do patients visit the physician unnecessarily when a call to the nurse would have been fine? Or rush to get medication for every little cough? We spend 10 percent of all our medical care dollars in the last year of life— about $410 billion— much of which is fueled by demands from patients and families. To best understand how to deal with illness, patients need to make sure the lines of communication are open with their healthcare provider."

- "Rethinking the way, we pay doctors, would also help significantly to curb waste. Right now, many doctors have incentive to provide services, because they get paid for every one— whether an office visit or an operation. In different parts of the country, patients get two to three times as much care for the same disease, with the same result. If doctors practiced in the lower-cost way (again, with no difference to the patient), some experts estimate $50 billion in savings— just on Medicare expenses."

- "Electronic health records are one of the best ways to improve quality and cost of care. They give doctors instantaneous and the most up-to-date information on how to treat a patient), some experts estimate $50 billion in savings— just on Medicare expenses."

- "Health care is the last major USA business segment to digitize processes. Currently, there are no cost accounting for episodic processes supporting the provider prices and billing for outcomes. Currently the computerization doesn't embrace artificial intelligence modeling of standardized models of episodic care plans that connect the physician, hospital, nursing home, home care and hospice. To correct this, solutions are being offered in this Article of reorganization. This will enable the health care industry to forecast costs per patient episode to use for pricing and management of costs.

Experts at AARP estimate that the expenditures will double in the next four years and bankrupt Medicare by 2046. What is the solution? Is it more spending or less waste . . . is it more medicating or less chronic disease? If the focus was on wellness as an outcome and payment was based on that equation, we would more likely eliminate wasteful prescriptions and damaging tests that avoid a long-term fitness and nutrition program.

Health maintenance as a concept sounded good but in practice, we did not implement the concept because we did not change the method of reimbursement from diagnosis to outcome, from treatment to health preservation, from passing pills to promoting fitness. Preventive health care to be successful must embrace a payment method that reimburses for results not what I call inductive processes that now drive treatment, testing and institutionalization. . . meaning we hope that the paid for action will produce results. On the other hand, deductive processes require a care plan based on assessed problems, causes and goals for improvement or cure. Then payment can be based on the improvement and/or prevention not just effort.

The **American Health Care Association** and other long-term care professional groups are calling for a change to a deductive medicine approach for physicians, hospitals, home care, nursing homes to standardize processes and tie payment to performance. HHS (Dept. of Health and Human Services), the health care arm of the Federal government also gives support to pay for performance and evidence-based medicine. Yet the clinical professionals and their trade groups are not supporting this paradigm shift because of the focus on wealth care not health care.

Of course, everyone wants a bigger piece of the shrinking pie. My view of how to get it is P. I. E. (**P**roblem assessment, **I**nterventions and **E**valuation of outcome before we approve a provider's income). My deductive formula is problematic and programmatic. Define the root cause of the problem and apply a programmatic solution with a definable outcome. Then evaluate the results in a monetary and humanistic manor. In other words, monetize health care than digitize the process for documentation and historical recordkeeping.

Today physicians, hospitals, nursing homes, home care companies do not have to prove outcome before getting paid. They are not required by law to have a care plan that pursues outcome and do not have to prove they followed it if the bill is challenged. Unlike all other enterprises in American they are not accountable for results before they get paid. If we are to ever reroute wealth care to health care, we have to turn off the current source of resources and change the method of reimbursement to P.I.E. Every provider and American then must pursue their piece of the health care PIE using the following:

- **Computerized AI models** of care based on archive data from past experience and statistical bases for determining cause before diagnosis and outcome before payment (termed by the bureaucrats as evidenced based medicine and performance-based payment see Exhibit E).
- **Standardized terminology** and methods of care that pursue outcomes.
- **Point of care delivery and documentation systems** capturing outcomes.
- **Economies of scale utilizing technology** using epigenetics to plan and activate prevention and health preservation as a culture.
- **Electronic records** that organize the care plan and documentation around a Restorative Model not a Medical or Social Model.
- **Reimbursement methods** that pay for performance (see Exhibit E) utilizing base rates for routine services and quality incentive add-ons for improved functioning and lowering chronic diseases.
- **Universal coverage** for all Americans funded through the savings by eliminating waste (over medication, inappropriate testing, re-hospitalization of the elderly) and eliminating spend down and telephone orders in nursing homes.
- **Funding of the American Health Care Program needs to be shifted** to individual policies paid for through a withholding program for those employed Americans assigning the responsibility to stay healthy to the only level that can attain that . . . each American.
- **Investment of individual SHIFT Funding Trust savings accounts would be done** by newly formed Mutual Health Insurance Companies that are owned by its employed American mutual shareholders . . . then reinvested in the

American economy by the Mutual Health Insurance Company professional money managers held accountable to returns that exceed U.S. Treasuries.
- **SHIFT Funding of the unemployed** and catastrophic costs should remain the purview of the current Medicare and Medicaid programs.

Then we can eliminate waste through control of quality, costs and outcomes that in turn reward those that excel by preserving health, preventing chronic diseases and discharging more of aging Americans back into the community-based health care agencies.

President Obama and Biden focus on health care as the #1 priority is admirable but will not be resolved through policy tweaking or buying our way out of the waste. Any way you cut it Health Care (Wealth Care) is big business with Government purchasing treatment rather than outcomes . . . outcome driven focused on restoring the health of Americans will produce quality and save enough to insure every American. It's the author's opinion, best practices won't emerge until, we the patient, pay for outcomes not incomes.

Stated National Priorities of the New Biden Administration:

- Economy recovery after Pandemic.
- National security at the borders.
- Health Care for all
- Education avoids privatized and Charter schools.

The economy, national security and education all are related to the health of the Americans and our aging population. It touches every individual daily. That is 330 million people experiencing some form of health crisis or intervention every single second of each and every day. Either their parents, grandparents, spouses, children and themselves are having health issues, problems or death-defying decisions related to their life style, relationships and future.

Conservatively, that amounts to over a billion incidences every month and over 12 billion every year on which we expend $4.5 trillion dollars in a "treatment after the fact mode" with little if any resources spent on preservation and prevention of diseases that we very likely are caused by our lifestyles and dependence on chemicals.

My point is that the health of our nation must be the #1 priority because nothing else matters if we are not strong enough to protect ourselves or not capable of working due to poor health or cannot think clearly for learning and earning a living. The proof of the poor health of Americans can be annotated by the obesity statistics, the chronic illness impact on aging (40% have 5 or more chronic diseases), the 46 million uninsured and the 50 million under insured Americans, the increase in the unemployed at the rate of 500,000 per month during the Pandemic and the runaway costs of the current inefficient and ineffective delivery system.

To define what we are and what we are not gives us a new perspective for solutions.

What we are and are not:

- Unhealthy, overweight, non-exercising, with chronic illnesses.
- Not taking responsibility for our personal well being
- Wasting valuable resources by pursuing income not outcome.
- Not developing AI diagnostic systems of quality control and pursuing positive outcomes.
- Paying for treatment not recovery, restoration and outcome.
- Using antiquated inductive approaches versus technology driven deductive processes.

- Not efficient and effective in the delivery of value-added benefits.
- Over taxing our youth who are healthier to pay for the unhealthy.
- Not saving lives of those that most need it — the aging American.
- Bankrupting our future generations.
- Not willing to deal with systemic change.
- Destined to fail ourselves for lack of internalizing our health plan.
- Not taking steps to preserve health and our national human capital that competes and produces personal wealth.

SHIFTING THE PARADIGM ... Where should we be and how to get there:

What we should be:

- A nation of people focused on prevention and health preservation.
- Forming economic incentives to stay healthy (morale incentives).
- Standardizing and digitizing the health care processes.
- Computerizing the health care processes.
- Building AI models of quality and flagships of excellence.
- Pursuing outcomes based on best practices not just paying for input codes for incomes.
- Saving future funds through withholding for long term care needs.
- Requiring evidence of cause before medicating or treating.
- Reducing the dependency on chemicals and over medicating the elderly.

- Reducing staff turnover, absenteeism, injury and medical errors.
- Able to ensure all Americans adequately by eliminating waste (estimated to exceed $700 billion per year).
- Paying for performance at every provider level based on outcomes.

How to get there using technology development:

- National health and fitness policies— using the ISO 9000 structure.
- AI systems for integrating outcome driven processes— six sigma structures.
- Procedures for determining cause in the diagnostic stage.
- Care modeling AI tools and systems that assign the workflow and manage the workload.
- AI data bases for providing evidence for modeling care processes based on probabilities and problem assessment.
- Pay for performance criteria based on best practice outcomes with incentives for restorative results.
- Procedures for setting up quality control AI systems that provide incentives to—
    1. Reduce prescription medications and Over the Counter drugs.
    2. Reduce re-hospitalizations.
    3. Reduce staff turnover, absenteeism and injuries.
    4. Reduce the uninsured drain on Medicare and Medicaid.
    5. Reduce and eliminate Medicaid spend down.
    6. Reduce and eliminate telephone orders by physicians. Replace current practice of telephone orders with tele-medicine interventions.

- Performance measurement standards for rewarding and reinforcing the providers who perform (replace CMS enforcement and IRS fear inducing conformity tactics with Professional re-enforcement standards for each professional provider group to enforce themselves).
- Targets for economic recovery and savings—
    - Utilize personal health profiles for setting targets and measuring results for individual Americans.
    - Utilize personal health savings program for LTC and health preservation.
    - Utilize tax deductions for fitness and nutritional expenditures.
- Develop a conversion plan for making the transition and paradigm SHIFT from pay for treatment to pay for results using the "Niagara Falls method" (if the falls had to be redirected to avoid a flooding of New York city we certainly would find a way to turn off the faucet and redirect the cascading danger). This analogy may be a good formula for redirecting runaway waste and consumption of $4.2 trillion dollars that will double in 4 short years. This is what I propose:

1. Turn off the faucet at the source for funding,
2. Redirect the payment methods to pay for performance and results.
3. Redirect the flow of resources to the providers so they are not deprived of cash nor profits for their businesses.
4. Re-enforce the national standards based on professional accountability and eliminate the fear factor inducing conformity with the pursuit of quality utilizing economic incentives to attain the morale incentives we seek.
5. Stop the academic approach to problem solving by embracing best practices into the planning and conversion to a new health preservation system.

Proposed American Enterprise Health Care Program . . . **SHIFT** Self-Health Insurance Funding Trust:

- Stated National Health Care Preventive and Preservation Objectives formalized into a national Mutual Health Insurance Policy that requires all employed Americans to have an ownership (preferred stock) with shares being purchased from their savings accounts.
- Federalized withholding with employer match program from employed Americans to collect and populate the health preservation savings accounts.
- Mutual Health Insurance Companies as contractors for investing American's health preservation **SHIFT** savings accounts and paying for each American's desired expenditures for health care, disease prevention, health and wellness expenditures for fitness and nutritional plans.
- Each employed American will have an annual standardized health and fitness profile and a plan for preserving wellness and preventing chronic health problems developed for determining their dividend rate on their Mutual preferred stock holdings.
- Mutual dividends are tax exempt as are gains on preferred stock sales where the shareholder is divesting ownership of some of their investment.
- **SHIFT** savings accounts are managed by the individual within the parameters of qualified health care expenditures, wellness and fitness expenditures and programs designed to prevent chronic obesity and certain diseases. The savings accounts will accumulate for use in later years for long term care services after hospitalization.
- Medicare Part A, in its current form will continue as a safety net for catastrophic hospitalizations and terminal diseases. Medicare Part B, C and D would be disbanded.
- Medicaid will be federalized as an insurance program to only cover the unemployed . . . the expenditures would be funded by a special provision in the Federal revenue sharing.

The Cost of Administration of Obama Care:

Department of Health and Human Services employs 64,750 in 11 operating divisions with 8 distinct agencies, with over 300 web sites, with an annual budget of $800 billion that includes payment of Medicare benefits and Medicaid revenue sharing with the States . . . even the Indian health services employ 15,102 with a budget of $4.3 billion for labor and health care benefits paid. ((See Exhibit D for the misuse of power that the Department exerts through the paying agent CMS committing governmental fraud and abuse under the guise of Medicare enforcement.)

Strategic Error of Obama Care: According to the American Association of Medical Colleges, with the impact of aging America we were already going to be facing a shortage of more 150,000 doctors over the next 15 years even before Obama Care was passed. Obama Care is just going to make the doctor shortage even worse. In fact, one poll found that 40 percent of all U.S. doctors plan to get out of the profession over the next 3 years. Of course, not all of those disgruntled doctors will end up leaving the profession, but even if 10 percent of them quit it is going to create a medical crisis of unprecedented magnitude in this country. And we are still paying for illness not prevention of chronic diseases or preservation of health through diet, exercise and better life style habits.

"HEALTH CARE FOR ALL" INSURANCE ECONOMICS

All of these statistics, problems and solutions are covered in Jerry L. Rhoads' latest book **"HEALTH CARE FOR ALL" (SHIFT the paradigm, to A Public-Private Enterprise)**, published by Page Turner, December 2020

Sources: Wikipedia, internet, HHS (Health and Human Services), Jerry L. Rhoads' self-health care books. In many cases the statistics aren't 2020 yet, so make sure you give consideration to the escalating costs of

20% to 30% higher due to the Covid-19 Pandemic and the pursuit of treatments and vaccines. Regardless billions are now becoming trillions much too often.

Health Care for All mutual health insurance economics is a practice or arrangement by which a company or government agency provides a guarantee of compensation for specified loss, damage, illness, or death in return for payment of a premium. Also, "many Employers are required by law to take out insurance against unemployment or sickness".

Health insurance is a type of insurance coverage that typically pays for medical, surgical, prescription drug and sometimes dental expenses incurred by the insured.

Health insurance supplemental coverages can reimburse the insured for expenses incurred from illness or injury or pay the care provider directly. Rates are based on risk and health profile. Every health insurance plan has exceptions for what they deny payment for, subject to appeal including Medicare and Medicaid.

Generally, how does health insurance work for:

1. Fulltime Students, paid by parents until age of 26.

2. Corporate/self-employed and employees? Commercial group insurance is usually paid by employer with cost shared with employee subject to copays and deductibles and some preexisting conditions. Obama Care is a supplement to commercial health insurance through State and Federally funded affordable care act insurance exchanges.

3. Government workers? Separate insurance fully paid by taxpayers with some copays and deductibles.

4. Retired employees? Some employers have retirement health insurance benefits subject to copays and deductibles as does Medicare and Medicaid for the rest.

5. Elderly people/children who are retired or never worked? There are government benefits for disability and qualified medical care by Medicare and Medicaid if a decedent of a citizen. And all children care coverage through CHIP and SSI (supplemental security insurance).

6. Illegal immigrants? No insurance for non-citizens or illegal aliens unless an offspring of or relative of a qualified citizen.

27.9 million uninsured in spite of Obama care passed in 2012:

Before the Affordable Care Act, the number of uninsured Americans grew over time, particularly during economic downturns. By 2013, the year before the major coverage provisions of the ACA went into effect, more than 44 million people lacked coverage. Jan 25, 2019 ... excludes noncitizens and illegals

In 2018, 27.9 million nonelderly individuals were uninsured, an increase of nearly 500,000 from 2017. Since 2016 when the number of uninsured reached historic lows, the number of people who lack health insurance coverage has grown by 1.2 million due to high deductibles and coinsurance ... ... excludes noncitizens and illegals Dec 13, 2019. During the Pandemic over 700,000 came off Obama Care due to loss of employment.

What is the future of government providing free Medicare and Medicaid for all? Obama Care ... the President promised "keep your own doctor and the Affordable Care Act would not increase costs by one dime" (when effect you do lose your own doctor and it is costing trillions of dimes). Plus, most covered policies have high deductibles that have to be paid to get a doctor or hospital to take you. The future for health care as a right isn't affordable nor is health care as a privilege sustainable as it is now funded and paid for.

Historical national health expense (NHE), 2018: NHE grew 4.6% to $4.2 trillion in 2018, or $14,500 per person, and accounted for 17.7% of Gross Domestic (GDP). Medicare spending grew 6.4% to $750.2

billion in 2018, or 21 percent of total NHE. Medicaid spending grew 3.0% to $597.4 billion in 2018, or 16 percent of total NHE. Mar 24, 2020

Bottom-line: free government provided health and disability insurance for all would cost a minimum an additional $4 to 5 trillion per year and $40 to $50 trillion for the next decade.

Annual Federal tax revenues 2018 $3.3 trillion, State tax revenues $1.1 trillion or $4.4 trillion per year ... not enough in the Federal Reserve to fund free anything. We don't have enough tax revenue annually to pay for health care for all out of tax revenues. The shortfall is paid for by private commercial health insurance funded by employers and Medicare trust funds or out-of-pocket by the insured.

Health Spending by Major Sources of Funds:

Private Health Insurance (34 percent share): Private health insurance spending increased 4.2 percent to $1.2 trillion in 2017, which was slower than 6.2 percent growth in 2016. The deceleration was driven in part by slower growth in medical benefits and a decline in fees and taxes resulting from the Consolidated Appropriations Act of 2016, which suspended collection of the health insurance plan fee in 2017.

Medicare (20 percent share): Medicare spending grew 4.2 percent to $705.9 billion in 2017, which was similar to the rate of growth in 2016 of 4.3 percent. The growth in 2017 reflected slower growth in spending for Medicare fee-for-service (2.6 percent in 2016 to 1.4 percent in 2017) that was almost entirely offset by faster growth in Medicare spending for private health plans (8.1 percent in 2016 to 10.0 percent in 2017).

Medicaid (17 percent share): Total Medicaid spending decelerated in 2017, increasing 2.9 percent to $581.9 billion compared to growth of 4.2 percent in 2016. The slower growth in 2017 was influenced by slower growth in enrollment and a reduction in the Medicaid net cost of health insurance. State and local Medicaid expenditures grew 6.4 percent, while federal Medicaid expenditures increased 0.8 percent in 2017.

Out-of-Pocket (10 percent share): Out-of-pocket spending grew 2.6 percent in 2017 to $365.5 billion, which was slower than 4.4 percent growth in 2016.

Obama Care (15 percent share) Out-of-pocket spending grew 12.6 percent in 2017 to $490.5 billion, which was slower than 14.4 percent growth in 2016.

Charity Care (4% share of hospital care) due to government grants there are regulatory requirements for hospitals built utilizing government or local grants and subsidies to provide a certain percentage of charity care.

Spent on prevention lost opportunity costs:

Although primary preventive services, such as daily aspirin use and alcohol and tobacco use screenings, could have yielded net savings of nearly $1.5 billion in this analysis, the use of secondary preventive services, such as mammograms and depression screenings, actually results in net costs of almost $2 billion.

On Aug 29, 2017, according to CDC, chronic diseases that are avoidable through preventive care services account for 75 percent of the nation's $4.3 trillion healthcare spending and lower economic output in the US by $260 billion dollars a year. In other words, if we spend $2 billion dollars on prevention America could prevent $3.2 trillion in health care costs and increase economic output by $260 billion equaling $3.5 trillion improvement in GDP. To invest $2 billion dollars per year in preventive services creates wealth.

How are health care services paid to hospital, physician, nursing home, therapy, home care by insurance, Medicare and Medicaid? Is it based provider income or patient outcome? Is it by illness and episode of care or something else?

Insurance, Obama care, Medicare and Medicaid pays health care providers using codes for inpatient and outpatient services termed: DRG's (diagnosis related groups) average rate per length of stay for hospitalizations, OPPS (outpatient services or ER) and therapy visits, RVU's (relative value units) for physician average rate per encounters, RUG's (relative value units) average per diems for limited length of stay in nursing homes and OPUS (a per diem for nursing and therapy services) for home care. Unfortunately, health care continuum is currently paid based on codes not health care outcomes.

All are based on computer generated algorithms (data from past cost reports based on averages per day or diagnosis) paying for input data not output data. Since the basis for payment is based on days of stay (input data to pay provider income not outcome) there is no accountability for the degree of waste, low quality and benefit to the patient.

In other words, the providers are paid based on a symptom and diagnosis or procedure code not on the care episode itself ... there lies the biggest black hole of all ... there is no connection of the actual cost per episode or outcome to the providers pricing, profit or quality. And therefore, there is no connection of the care continuum for an episode of care from the doctor to the hospital to the nursing home to home care to hospice services. No accountability for escalating costs, prices and deteriorating quality. It is like buying a car and getting a pick-up instead for a higher price.

A History of Pay-For-Performance Plans

By: Jerry L. Rhoads, CPA, LNHA, FACHCA

(CEO All-American Care, PC, Caregiver Management Systems, Inc.)

In the 1980s, the state of Illinois had a pay-for-performance method for reimbursing nursing homes. It was labeled the performance add-on payment system using an inspection of care (IOC) survey and a Quality Incentive Payment (QUIP) survey. It was originated by Jerry Rhoads' white paper for PPS reimbursement written in 1977 for HEW and devised, with my help, by the Department of Public Health and was in use for almost ten years. At that time, I was a management consultant running, as the onsite licensed Administrator, two nursing homes in pursuit of the economic incentives for the purposes of providing a quality of life for my patients.

Prior to the add-on method, for at least twenty years (1970 to 1980), the Department of Public Aid paid the nursing homes in Illinois on a point-count system, using an assessment form that assigned a point value to the patient's deficits. The point count rate, established periodically by the Department of Public Aid, was added to a standard room and board rate for determining payment for service.

In 1974, I found out from my clients that the nursing homes allowed the caseworker to do the point-count assessment without consulting the attending physician, nurses, or therapists. The result was systemic underpayment. To combat this, my accounting firm developed an assessment form that met the standards of care for the pay-for-performance payment system. The amount of payment that the state was responsible for grew for those providers using my system, and they were better able to provide the standards of care the state wanted to purchase. In the process, I discovered that assessment and the plan of care should drive reimbursement. When the state's Medicaid budget tightened, the point-count method was replaced with a payment plan that reimbursed as a base rate for room and board plus an add-on program: if the patient needed physical, occupational, or social rehabilitation and discharge planning, the state paid add-on rates for the individualized care.

Then, in 1987, the budget was again stretched, and cost reports became the method of reimbursement. At that point, reimbursement was divorced from needs and services rendered. That was a big mistake. **Then Connie Cherin, the former assistant director of the Department of Public Health** in Illinois, entered the scene and introduced the quality incentive payment program (QUIP) and the inspection of care survey (IOC). QUIP was an add-on to the cost report per diem for room and board and the clinical survey. IOC was supposed to be an add-on based on an annual inspection of care assessment of the patient's needs met. In reality this was an effective reinforcement program with surveyors looking for provider successes not violations . . . what a difference in attitude and results.

QUIP was determined by an annual quality of care survey conducted by the Department of Public Aid case managers. The survey awarded a total of six stars for a quality performance in the environment, care planning, family and resident satisfaction, programming, survey compliance, and staffing. The payment was based on $0.50 for two stars per patient and $0.25 for the other four stars or $2.00 per Medicaid day billed during the year. IOC could amount to $10.00 to $15.00 per day add-on for meeting the needs of the patients. But it was enforcement-driven and did not fairly evaluate the true outcomes of the patients.

The IOC and QUIP programs were discontinued in 1993 and replaced by a flat cost related rate subject to an annual update of costs using an inflation factor. All of the economic and moral incentives of the previous programs were lost. The flat-rate method is in the process of being changed again, this time to a case-mix formula based on the MDS assessment. Unfortunately, this system is flawed because, once again, it only assesses 18 of the possible 102 patient problems.

To date, Illinois is the only state in the country that has had an assessment-based reimbursement system that paid for true outcomes. That system, with a better assessment instrument, should be used for all of healthcare, not just nursing homes. Why? Because the major segment of healthcare costs and problems are the results of our aging population. Federally, the reimbursement is based on income codes not outcomes.

Our Health and Human Services and CMS regulators have instituted pay for averaging algorithms for inpatients Part A services, called DRG's, RVU's, RUGs based on 77,000 ICD 10 diagnosis codes and other Part B outpatient (OPS) ancillary services using 1,400 HCPCS procedure codes and a Part D medications formulary of thousands of mediations, for review and denial of claims. These codes are all input triggers not outcome events. Nothing in the data collection, at the provider level, is based on content to support the costs or pricing or the results or outcome for the consumer's review.

Annual cost reports are required and filed by the providers to give the impression that these input reimbursement values are based on a cost related basis for determining payment for the "managed care program". Upon preadmission coverage is checked electronically by the providers with the FI's (financial intermediaries) who have the authority to deny coverage based on codes do not need, cures, prevention and certainly not quality outcomes. The right to appeal these decisions is a five-step regulatory method to discourage questioning the decisions.

Effectively, this system isn't managed care it is intended to manage and reduce cost by risk and population groupings managed by ACO's that blindly move all beneficiaries into Part C Medicare Advantage Care or Obama Care for Medicaid, uninsured, or under insured based on zip code. All deductibles are escalating, and the PPO or HMO advantage plans are so complicated that even a CPA or attorney are able to tie care to payment.

Commentary: in my and my wife's case, I swore not to ever trade traditional Medicare coverage for the Advantage Part C all-inclusive policies. But with the escalation in supplementary policies, I opted for a change to an Aetna Advantage PPO policy for one year. The next year I was needing more dental coverage and was sold an HMO Prime policy without proper contemplation. All of sudden I had to drop our doctor, who wasn't in network, after 25 years for a new primary care physician PCP and all new providers who had a contract with my Aetna policy. What a mistake ... during the Pandemic we received no services because I couldn't find a PCP in the Aetna HMO Prime network. We were trapped by the proverbial catch 22 ... no PCP no laundry. At this time, we now have a new PCP and no other providers yet after two years of red tape just so-called managed care dropped us into the managed cost category. It's a terrible mess especially when you can't get anything covered or paid for if the provider is out of network or pay a high penalty.

Outcome -Definition Formula

The current CMS QIS method of measuring quality is the satisfaction survey of the family, staff and patient. In my opinion establishing quality standards based on a piece of paper filled out by an uninformed and unhealthy community will never be the catalyst of pay for performance. In healthcare, the customer (the government) is not the consumer (patients and families), and thus the customer has no control over the spending and living habits of the consumer. The customer has to pay for services even though they are subpar. It is a rental system based on a per patient day's stay in an institution, and it won't change unless the system changes.

Quality is not like beauty. It is not in the eye of the beholder. It is very subjective needing objective proof. Instead, it must be rigidly defined and proven by documentation. There are no maximum quality standards only minimum standards that become maximums. For nursing homes in America, we are paying a deadly price for their absence. Each year,

556,000 lives are lost in nursing homes, by natural and unnatural causes. If only 10 percent are from neglect and abuse, that is 55,000 wasted lives, for which we spend precious dollars of the healthcare budget. We simply cannot afford to continue in that direction. Quality needs to be defined in terms of outcome, not income basis. The difference is simple. Outcomes can be defined using the following AI (automated standards and executable procedures):

- Using the eleven-body systems to diagnosis the problem and start the plan of care.
- Assess the degree of the medical, social and mental problems for the plan of care.
- Assign skilled interventions to teams and hold the staff members accountable using assignment sheets by shift and progress notes for improvement or deterioration,
- Evaluate the outcome goals based on predetermined numerical scales.
- Document progress using P.I.E. format (P=problem, I=Intervention, E=evaluation}.

For each activity of daily living (walking, bathing, dressing, grooming, toileting, etc.), determine the patient's initial deficit level and set a goal, using a numeric scale like the following:

4 = total dependence.

3 = extensive deficit.

2 = moderate deficit.

1 = minimum deficit.

0 = independent.

Then report progress in each activity using numerical values. Let's say we have a patient with three problems, a program of interventions for each problem, and a set of outcome goals for each program. If the patient cannot walk, talk, or feed himself, he will be placed into an ambulation program, with assigned interventions for the clinicians and goals to measure progress against. Let's say our patient had a 4 in walking, a 3 in talking, and a 1 in eating when initially assessed. Our plan would be for the patient to have a zero in all these activities upon discharge from the programs. If, after the first thirty days, the patient was evaluated as a 3 in walking, a 2 in talking, and a 0 in eating, he would obviously need more restorative services to attain the discharge goals set upon admission. All staff types, including the physician, must be informed during the restorative process of the patient's status and prognosis for discharge.

The system is simple but very effective. But it is never used by physicians or hospitals, rarely by nursing homes, and only occasionally by therapists. *Without a commitment to restorative care, how can we expect people to ever get better?*

Ultimate Standardized Payment Methodology

Of course, in order for this preformatted AI system to work, we must also institute a standardized payment methodology, based on outcome. Here are the steps that must be taken:

1. Privatize a "Health Care for All" with personal savings accounts in Mutual Health Insurance Companies who process and pay claims.
    a. Combine Medicare and Medicaid for catastrophic care.
    b. Provide a standardized benefit package.
    c. The plan is fully portable since employee pays the premium.
2. Provide coverage for all Americans, including:
    a. The unemployed.
    b. Legal aliens.
    c. Government employees.
3. Charge premiums based on the health profile of each covered life, putting people more in charge of, and responsible for, their health-based destinies.
4. Provide cradle-to-grave standardized benefits.
5. Withhold premiums from employees and employers.
6. Provide a 100-percent tax deduction for all out-of-pocket expenses for:

    a. Medical-related expenses (travel, ambulance services).
    b. Fitness programs.
    c. Screening programs.
    d. Nutritional programs.

7. Utilize the Caregiver Management System of standardized Enterprise Models of episodic care plans as set up by Caregiver Case Managers using the standardized cost accounting module and pricing module. The breakeven point analysis module is a function of the cost and price modules. The data collected from the system will be used for staffing patterns, pharmacy management, labor management, medical supplies inventory management and overhead absorption.

Currently the regulatory process has evolved into a Gestapo compliance approach to forcing providers to care more, cost less, and be more effective in their management systems. If they don't comply based on some 400 F-tag care assessment categories, they are subject to civil money fines and put on probation for punitive "get out of jail" violations. The providers are intimidated not constructively allowed to improve.

However, the design of the infrastructure for delivering the care is not conducive to the effective forms of labor management and computer processing. The standards for regulatory and provider compliance outlined above will go a long way toward organizing the infrastructure for efficiency and quality control. Quality measurement can only succeed if it is tied to performance based on scoring patient functioning, staff accountability and quality of life.

Criteria For Outcome Driven Payment (An Enterprise AI Modeling System)

Of course, everyone wants a bigger piece of the shrinking pie. My view of how to get it is P. I. E. (**P**roblem assessment, **I**nterventions and **E**valuation of outcome before we approve a provider's income). My deductive formula is problematic and programmatic. Define the root cause of the problem and apply a programmatic solution with a definable outcome. Then evaluate the results in a monetary and humanistic manor. In other words, monetize health care than digitize the process for documentation and historical recordkeeping.

According to Dr. W. Edwards Deming the guru on using analytics to measure productivity and quality outcomes, has proven, by eliminating waste and mistakes where problems begin, reduces production costs improves quality and profits. "In contrast outcomes planned are different than outcomes measured, and mistakes corrected," His genius was his definition of quality as a production line free of wasted time, human error and measured output. In other words, waste is profit and human errors are quality failures. Using an Enterprise AI Modeling system for health care is a deductive process that starts with the eleven body systems diagnoses connected to the related medical, dental, mental health and social problems that have model care programs attached. Is in effect quality control that reduces cost, improves profitability and customer/consumer satisfaction.

Dr. Deming, if he were alive today, would be advising us to pursue higher profits by eliminating wasteful clinical practices that permeate the wealth care market. Quality control, which is Deming's proven method, is not counting a provider's mistakes and fining providers or rewarding providers for lower incidences of deaths or passing aspirin in the emergency room . . . it is restoring function to the highest level, preserving health and preventing chronic illnesses then discharging successful outcomes back to the community. It is modeling and blue printing the care based on scientific computer data not individual art forms of treating symptoms not defining causes then treating. The application of ISO 10,000 standards and Six Sigma processes must be applied in this business, or we will all be working to support America's aging population in bigger and bigger institutions.

While turning off the faucet to reroute Niagara Falls may seem trite it is relevant when it comes to moving wealth care to health care. Today physicians, hospitals, nursing homes, home care companies do not have to prove outcome before getting paid. They are not required by law to have a care plan that pursues outcome and do not have to prove they followed it if the bill is challenged. Unlike all other enterprises in American they are not accountable for results before they get paid. If we are to ever reroute wealth care to health care, we have to turn off the current source of resources and change the method of reimbursement to P.I.E. Every provider and American then must pursue their piece of the health care PIE using the following:

The programs have proposed interventions by staff type, by shift. For each problem there is a stated improvement, prevention, palliative, maintenance or sustaining goal that becomes the planned outcome. Then the evaluation of progress is measuring the change in the patient's condition in the context of the base line deficit and the targeted goals. A pay-for-performance reimbursement system would:

1. *Pay operators more if the patients are well enough to go home.* This would provide incentive to get the patients better and out of the facility. Word would spread fast. These operators would become models, the local facility of choice.

2. *Pay employees more to restore patients and purge hidden costs.* When the incentive is to get patients better, the result is improved morale, better attendance, lower turnover, improved patient safety, lower theft, lower insurance costs, fewer injuries, and higher profits.

3. *Pay operators more if the right number of staff are doing their job 100 percent of the time.* Know what the workload is, and pay for getting the team function done on time. Time management systems are needed to blueprint the process. Modern computer software can map out the process and assign the work. Pay fewer productive staff more instead of paying more nonproductive people less.

4. *Pay operators more if they use the Medicare program to pay for restoring the patients to their highest functioning level.* This is better than taking them off of Medicare and putting them in a wheelchair paid for by Medicaid.

Understand the Medicare insurance policy and get the Caregiver Management System to create the documentation help you need to meet the Medicare 100 day stay per "spell of illness" review standards.

5. *Pay the nurses, aides, therapists, social workers, and restorative staff more if they follow proven models of care triggered by comprehensive assessment tools.* The standardized MDS assessment form only triggers 18 problems, and the elderly clearly can demonstrate up to 102 nursing diagnosis problems. Better tools would help them identify all of those Medicare coverable problems. If the typical 100-bed nursing home did this, they would be $500,000 ahead in revenue and $250,000 ahead in profitability *in the first year*! This would go a long way toward repairing the facility, providing better care, paying additional staff benefits, paying staff adequately, and achieving environmental respectability.

6. *Pay more for attending physicians that are involved in the implementation of the care plan at the nursing home.* The attending physicians would be expected to make the rounds, intervene in the control of medications, oversee quality control and restorative care by monitoring the active care plan, participate in utilization review, and keep the patients out of acute care. And the skilled nursing facility could bill as a part of utilization review for their time!

7. *Pay operators more if they have zero-defect surveys.* Being ready for a survey every day should be a minimum standard, not a hurdle. That readiness would represent the true mark of quality. This is done by assigning staff team members responsibility for the survey "F tags" that are holding them accountable for completing the task and documenting the interventions with quality outcomes.

8. *Pay operators more if they use computers for all paperwork and not just the financial business.* Modern Caregiver Management computerized tools are available to assist in planning and assigning interventions that lead the staff and patient to an outcome. Assessment using MDS is just the minimum; comprehensive assessment should embrace the nursing diagnosis list of problems (NANDA).

9. *Pay operators more if they are a six-star provider in their market. Reap the rewards for being the best.* Make it your objective to become the leading

facility in your community. Be the one that shifts to a new caregiver management paradigm and integrates with other healthcare providers. Change the infrastructure and lead the families and patients to a quality of life that can be replicated by others.

Proposed Congressional Mandate:

- Set criteria for episodic evidence-based evaluation, intervention and QUIP payment.
- Require that Caregiver Management Modeling Systems be utilized for costing, pricing and outcomes.
- (QUIP) Quality Incentive Payment based on improvement of or solving patient problems.
- Evaluation of outcome based on standardized caregiver enterprise models of care,
- Relate incentive payments to prevention, wellness and health preservation,
- Aging patients must be in fitness add-on programs.
- National health statistics published on number of patients discharged back to community and/or restored to higher levels of care.

Bottom Line is Connectivity Across the Continuum of Care:

Using episodic standardized cost accounting data for provider pricing allows the case management system to connect interoperability, accountable outcomes and shared medical records from physician office to the hospital to the nursing home to home care or assisted living, or independent living or hospice. The data base then is a moving picture, across all stakeholders including the Federal government, of the patient problems, interventions and outcomes justifying provider incomes. The analytics from this type of system is the transparency needed to be able to budget by patient, provider and population grouping. It is then managed care not just managed provider cost and continuing unsustainable increases in national health care costs as a percent of GDP. This format is then used to digitize processes using global health care maps for drilling down to root cause of the problems. Then formulate the plan of care triggered by relational data management of interventions by skill level, mediations, and estimated outcomes.

Published References:

Mary Telsa-Nayak "Nursing Home Exemplars of Quality, Charles Thomas publisher, 1988 ... source of Illinois Department of Public Health's QUIP quality incentive payment.... Implemented in 1980's by Connie Cherin, the former assistant director of the Department of Public Health in Illinois and Jerry L. Rhoads, CPA).

Jerry Rhoads, author of eleven health care books: Eldercide (Remedy Eldercide, Restore Elderpride, iUniverse, 2012, Restore Elderpride (second edition), iUniverse, 2014, Never too Old to Live, Xlibris, 2015, America in the Redzone, iUniverse, 2016, Lifestyle for Aging, Xlibris, 2017, The Boomers are Coming, Xlibris, 2014, Failing Government Taketh Away, 2015. The Monopsony Game Xlibiris 2014, How to Live Forever (Memoir of a 60 year marriage) Lettra Press, 2019, Health Care for All, Page Tuner Press, 2021 ... and this book makes eleven.

WARP SPEED CHANGES TO HEALTH CARE
(A Public-Private Partnership for Warp Speed Changes to Health Care)

Currently, the worldwide data demonstrates that America is 38th in quality and number #1 in costs per capita and as a percent of GNP. While Singapore Medisave program is the best health care system in the world. #1 in quality with the lowest costs per capita and percent of GNP. A country of 5 million people has a collaborative approach that bases provider income on patient care outcomes and preventive health care profiles. It is just the opposite of Obama Care.

It's built on a platform of individual responsibility for health preservation, prevention and wellness. Individuals pay for their own health preservation and preventive care. It is an Enterprise model similar to my SHIFT system. It embraces savings accounts, spending decisions by the individual and a payment system managed by the Government. There are safety nets for the elderly and free health care for the poor who are responsible for their own health and wellness profile.

Is socialized medicine the solution to high cost and low quality or Medicare for All or the Public option or Biden Care? Or my proposal of personalized Restorative Care managed privately by everyone based on patient quality first and managed provider cost second? Having a partnership with the government regulatory oversight for accountability and quality, prevention and wellness. Individuals pay for their own health preservation and care. It is an Enterprise model using a SHIFT (self-health insurance funding trusts) system. It embraces savings accounts, spending decisions by the individual and a payment system managed by the Government. There are safety nets for your own health and wellness profile.

What would this public private partnership look like? First and foremost, each American must accept responsibility for their own health and welfare. In the book and my other self-health books I make the case for internalizing our own health by accepting a role in its funding and holding providers accountable for their costs, pricing, quality and profit. Now we externalize that responsibility since we aren't' the consumer ... we are a third party in the equation when we don't pay the bill. Simply put, we are subservient to the government payor systems (Medicare, Medicaid, VA and regulated private insurance). For us to have a right to quality health care we must first commit to being as healthy as possible for our own good but also for the better good if we are to expect the best preventive and health preservation services.

Whether it is using American Enterprise and our government for warp speed in developing vaccines and treatment in solving the Corona China Virus Pandemic or saving lives with better preventive health care services or by preserving our individual health we must act in sync for the better good. To accomplish this, we must use our government resources and private entrepreneurial skills to collaborate in a public private partnership developing solutions to national health problems … this is the strength of our democracy,

Following is such a partnership and why it's necessary for our individual sake for the sake of the country's financial viability and how it can be done. Yes, the Pandemic is changing America's understanding of our current antiquated health care system and that it needs to change. But more importantly, each of us must change our lifestyles to manage our underlying habits and relationships to be afforded longer lives, needed incomes and better outcomes.

The Best Healthcare System in the World (excerpt from Mr. Rhoads' book entitled Failing Government Taketh Away, Xlibris, 2014):

The small country of Singapore of 5 million has the best health care system in the world. It's a Public-Private Partnership. Practicing an Enterprise Model of preventive health and delivery system labeled Health Care for All.

As an example of Government and Private businesses collaborating is the very successful Medisave system in Singapore. An Asian country of 5 million. The system was developed by Private business and Government working in collaboration.

The author's SHIFT the paradigm system is like this Singapore Healthcare System that is the most cost effective and efficient and quality driven solution in the world today. They are number 1 in quality and number 1 in lowest cost per capita. While America is number 1 in highest cost per capita and 38th in quality indicators.

Singapore's Stated Philosophy:

The Ministry of Health collaborating with the providers believes in ensuring **quality and affordable basic medical services** for all.

At the same time, the Ministry promotes **healthy living** and **preventive health programs** as well as maintains **high standards of living, clean water and hygiene** to achieve better **health care for all**.

Structure and Budget

Singapore's healthcare system is designed to ensure that everyone has access to different levels of healthcare in a timely, cost-effective and seamless manner.

Healthcare Services and Facilities

Healthcare services are accessible through a wide network of primary, acute and step-down care providers.

Healthcare Regulation

The Ministry of Health and its statutory boards regulate both the public and private providers of healthcare in Singapore.

Quality and Innovation

To ensure that patients are treated safely with good healthcare standards, the Ministry strives to promote better quality and innovation through various initiatives.

Schemes & Subsidies

An introduction to the healthcare system in Singapore. Medisave, introduced in April 1984, is a national medical savings scheme which helps individuals put aside part of their income into their Medisave Accounts to meet their future personal or immediate family's episodic hospitalization, day surgery and certain outpatient expenses.

Find out more about Medisave.

MediShield, introduced in 1990, is a low-cost catastrophic illness insurance scheme. It is designed to help members meet the medical expenses from major or prolonged illnesses from which their Medisave balance would not be sufficient to cover. MediShield operates on an episodic copayment and deductible system to avoid the problems associated with first-dollar, comprehensive insurance. The premiums for MediShield is payable by Medisave.

Medifund is an endowment fund set up by the Government in April 1993 to help needy Singaporeans who are unable to pay for their medical expenses. This fund acts as a safety net for those who cannot afford the subsidized bill charges despite Medisave and MediShield coverage. Medifund was established with an initial capital of S$200 million and capital injections will be made when budget surpluses are available. The capital sum currently stands at $1.7 billion. The interest income from this capital sum are being utilized to finance the needy.

ElderShield, introduced in September 2002, is an affordable severe disability insurance scheme designed to help Singaporeans meet with episodic expenses incurred in the event of severe disability. ElderShield premiums can be paid with Medisave or cash.

Other subsidy schemes

The Interim **Disability Assistance Programme** for the Elderly (IDAPE) scheme provides episodic financial help to needy and disabled Singaporeans, who were not eligible to join ElderShield due to their age and pre-existing conditions.

The **Community Health Assist Scheme** (CHAS) is one of the Ministry of Health (MOH)'s programs to help provide accessible and affordable medical and dental care to Singapore Citizens. Patients receive episodic drug subsidies based on their paying status and the scheme under which the drug is covered (e.g. Standard Drug List, Medication Assistance Fund, inpatient drug subsidy, etc.). Some drugs are subsidized only for specific clinical indications.

The **Caregivers Training Grant** (CTG) provides caregivers with an annual grant of $200 for each care dependent to attend AIC's pre-approved training programs. It aims to build the caregiver's capabilities in caring for the physical, social and emotional needs of the care recipients.

What are the metrics that prove Singapore's health care system is working better than any other approach in the world?

Singapore's life expectancy is superior:

National Life Expectancy

1. Singapore 82.
2. Australia 81.5.
3. Canada 81.2.
4. Japan 810.
5. France 80.5.
6. Sweden 80.5.
7. Switzerland 80.5.
8. Germany 79.5.
9. United Kingdom 78.5.
10. USA 78 (38th in quality and declining)

Singapore's costs (excludes the cost of the Pandemic) as a percent of GNP is superior to all countries especially America.

Health Expenditures … National % of GDP.

1. USA 19% (highest in per capita costs).
2. Singapore 3.25% (lowest in per capita costs).
3. Canada 9%.
4. Japan 8%.
5. Germany 10%.
6. United Kingdom 8%.

Sum Up of the Article:

By privatizing health care, the Government's share of the spending is reduced to a manageable level and accomplishing the objective of having a public option and a single payer system using the savings accounts administered by the Government while the episodic spending decisions are left with the individuals.

The savings accounts are the backbone for this Enterprise Model of health care because it introduces episodic supply and demand and competition to the equation. This does not occur in America where someone else is responsible for making the buying and paying decisions. Where an insurance company or the Government pays the bill, the individual does not internalize the necessity to stay fit, practice wellness habits and hold the providers accountable for the cost of quality of care and life style services.

The Author's Proposed **SHIFT SYSTEM** (Self-Health Insurance Funding Trust) embodies the Singapore Enterprise Model and will produce the same results that are being demonstrated in Singapore.

Article Six

USA Enterprise is Laissez-Faire

Deming Says Waste is Profit labeled an Operating Cost

Dr. W. Edwards Deming, a household name in Japan, became the prime catalyst behind the incredible success of the Japanese industry. In fact, since 1951 the Deming Prize has been the most coveted and prestigious award among Japanese corporations, like the Malcolm Baldrige Award for quality in business in the United States. Today (1990), Deming is finally becoming a household name in his own country. The lessons he has to teach American business are more urgent than ever.

Just how different is the Deming management method? Compare just a few of the many differences in beliefs between conventional organizations and Deming organizations:

Conventional company or governmental entity

- Quality is expensive.
- Defects are caused by workers.
- Buy at lowest cost, sell high.
- Fear and reward are proper ways to motivate.
- Play one supplier off against another.

Deming company or governmental entity

- Quality leads to lower costs.
- Waste is cost.
- Most defects are caused by the system.

- Buy from vendors committed to quality.
- Fear leads to disaster.
- Work with suppliers as business partners.

Deming rules applied to health care:

Healthcare in America is in a financial crisis due to wasteful business practices:

1. Inductive medical model processes utilized by the clinicians.
2. Lack of use of technology to assist in setting up inductive processes.
3. Pursuit of treatment without research.
4. Pursuit of diagnosis without evidence.
5. Pursuit of least invasive approach without a care plan.
6. Use of rule-out theory without determining cause.
7. Quality indicators and measures are not outcome based.
8. Payment is for pursuit of treatment, not outcome.
9. Funding is by employer, not employee.
10. Control of funds is by government, not private business.

Healthcare using Deming rules would be entrepreneurial and cost-effective

1. Deductive quality-control processes using models of care.
2. Use of technology to access models of care based on problems.
3. Pursuit of outcome based on electronic research tools.
4. Pursuit of outcome based on assessment, evidence, and cause in developing the plan of care.
5. Payment based on quality-of-life outcomes for each problem.
6. Funding for universal healthcare done by employee savings accounts.

7. Disbursement of funds by private mutual insurance companies that invest savings accounts.
8. Individual premiums set based on health and fitness profiles.
9. Major tax deductions allowed individuals for fitness, nutrition, natural health remedies for health preservation.
10. Major tax deductions for screening for prevention of chronic diseases.

Deductive Processes

Inductive clinical processes are defined as the pursuit of treatment with no known destination. Deductive clinical processes are defined "as setting a destination and pursuing an outcome using a blueprint of care." It starts with an assessment of the patient's problems (physical, emotional, social, and spiritual) using an assessment instrument that is comprehensive, not minimal as we now have with the government tools. The use of the NANDA (nursing diagnosis) problem list cross-tied to the medical diagnosis (ICD-9 codes) gives us a modeling tool bar none. Linking the patient's holistic problems to the doctor's medical diagnosis enables the entire process to be standardized.

For example, an eighty-five-year-old stroke patient with diabetes, COPD, and hypertension has the following problems:

- Can't walk, talk, dress, bath, feed self, nor toilet or groom self.
- Can't remember, sequence thoughts, nor use fine or gross motor skills.
- Can't ambulate with device or assist and is afraid of falling.
- Can't generate enough strength to reposition self in bed.
- Can't manage own medications.
- Can't breathe normally without a device.
- As a result, is depressed, incontinent, has skin issues, has pain, is overweight, and is combative.

The outcome destination is to return home with spouse. The deficit and outcome measures are related to walking, talking, dressing, bathing, feeding (diet controls), grooming, getting out of bed, ambulating with a walker, remembering room name, date, and room location, deep breathing, asking to go to the toilet with assist of one, and complying with diet and taking of medications. These are all called activities of daily living (ADLs).

If we are practicing inductively, the staff is directed by getting things done for the patient, making the beds, keeping the room clean and uncluttered, with the nurses passing medications and doing skin treatments. The routine is focused on keeping the patient fed a controlled diet, clean, and dry, along with avoidance of further skin breakdown. Therapies have their own plan with separate responsibilities of providing short-term treatments until they subjectively decide that the patient has reached their potential. Then they are turned back over to nursing for ADL maintenance. Also, there is an attempt to involve the patient in activities and religious functions. The last thought is to plan on discharge or independence, because that is not the (outcome) goal. Unfortunately, this is the practice in the typical long-term care facility.

If we are practicing deductively, the staff is directed by the interventions that are planned to restore the patient to his or her highest level of functioning for discharge back home with the spouse. How would that impact care?

First we would have a problem list:	Current Status		
Problem	Deficit	Goal	Progress
Walking	4	1	3
Talking	4	0	3
Dressing and grooming	4	2	3
Bathing	4	2	4
Toileting	4	1	3

Reality orientation	4	0	3
Depression	4	1	3
Skin breakdown	4	0	0
Respiratory	4	2	2
Medication management	4	3	3
Pain management	4	1	1
Noncompliance with diet	4	2	2
Total Score	48	14	30

There are twelve distinct problems with twelve distinct outcome goals. To be able to measure the deficit, progress, and the goal, we will use numerical scales promulgated by the government's minimum data set (resident assessment instrument).

      4 = Total dependence.
      3 = Extensive assistance required.
      2 = Minimum assistance required.
      1 = Supervision.
      0 = Total independence.

After thirty days of therapy, fourteen days of low rehab nursing, and thirty days of restorative programming (patient is cued to perform this themselves), the patient has progressed from a forty-eight (totally dependent) to a thirty, which is still about halfway to the expected outcome of fourteen. Thirty would equate to extensive assistance, while fourteen would require some professional supervision (a home care aide with oversight by a nurse) when the patient goes home.

Obviously, the patient requires more intensive skilled services. Seventy-four of the one-hundred-day benefit under Medicare Part A has been exhausted, with twenty-six remaining. The prognosis is all the goals will be met by day one hundred. If that is not accomplished, then Medicare Part B is available for limited services and the nursing restorative programs can be continued and paid for by long-term care insurance, private funds, or Medicaid (case mix).

Deductive Systems

If the nursing facility has 100 patients that have a combination of chronic diseases along with medical problems that are being treated at the hospital, it is impossible to manage the care without a very functional care-planning system that focuses on outcomes, not paperwork and income. The design of such systems typically has been left up to the clinicians who do not think deductively. In medical, nursing, and therapy schools most of the time is spent on how to pursue treatment, not outcomes. Until the focus in medical and emotional training is driven by the pursuit of outcomes, the schools will continue to graduate a good part of the problem.

Care plans should be the center of the clinical world. Deductive programming forces the processes to be thought through and irrelevant procedures eliminated. For example, why would all patients receive vital signs, head-to-toe assessments, and checklist care whether they need it or not and have their urinary, skin, exercise, companionship, life interests ignored? Why, because the facility gets paid whether the patient gets better or not. Nursing homes are not a housing alternative; they are medical service businesses, and they take money for that purpose but rarely deliver it.

Even though it is a regulatory requirement that every patient have a functioning care plan, it does not require that it be efficient, productive, and quality driven. The staff knows it isn't, the families know it isn't, the surveyors know it isn't, so why not make it a Deming rule that the system be fixed so the staff can like their job, stay, and get something productive done each day. This is where outcome means income.

The perfect system, that I will call a *case-management system*, puts the patient's problems in the forefront and the outcomes in the back-front.

What must we do to get this person restored to their highest level of functioning so they can have a life? Is that too much to expect for $150 to $550 per day. That is $4,500 to $16,500 per month and that is $54,000 to $198,000 per year. Come on, there should be no excuses for not providing what the patient needs to be restored to their highest level of functioning.

Case management, in fact, does what was proposed in the explanation of deductive processes. It produces results for the money. It is not the reason for doing it, it is the result of doing it. Case managers (nurses or therapists) can fix all the defects in the nation's nursing homes if allowed to organize the care into manageable units of service measured by units of outcome. It is as simple as that. It is top management's responsibility to let the staff do it.

Electronic Research Tools

Every computer today has access to a vast research tool: the Internet. You Google it and you will find an answer. But most providers would rather be told what to do and what they can't do rather than look it up and make an interpretation that helps their caseload.

Pursuit of Outcomes (Quality of Life)

Research in healthcare must relate to determining root causes of problems, not just symptoms. Typically, the clinician is not tapping into the electronic search engine for help on determining the root of the problem, leaving much to guess. It is my position that we must pre-format the care, so we know what to perform and when. If the cause is not determined and the outcome is not predictable, then the care is still an art form; anyone can do that. When the cause is determined and an outcome predictable, the care is a science and only a professional can do that.

Quality of life for an aging society is much different from sports injuries or drive-by shootings. The elderly person is suffering from a multitude of ailments that are determined by genetics, lifestyle, drug usage, and habit patterns. Until each individual is personally responsible for the cost of their care, they don't really care about cost.

To control costs is an individual equation, not an enforcement or containment issue. A healthy American is a cost-effective American. They don't sop up billions of dollars in chronic episodes at the ER. They don't swallow billions of dollars in pills that all have side effects. They don't spend down and become wards of the state the rest of their lives. They don't suffer from depression, alcoholism, drug-ism, etc. So, outcome starts with the income of each individual American. If they can see an economic benefit in their pocket today for staying healthy, they will make the effort. If someone else is paying the bill, they will procrastinate into the emergency room and continue to deteriorate.

Funding: Who Must Pay the Bill?

That's the $4.2 trillion question. By 2020 we will be spending 30 percent of the gross national product on healthcare if we don't stop the guessing and wasteful business practices. The politicians all want someone else to pay the bill while they have their cushy healthcare coverage. The Republicans propose that every American be their own insurance company; the Democrats propose that the government increase taxes so they can increase spending. While the *Deming-crats* say, "What about the waste in the system?" If the $600 billion per year in resources wasted were preserved, there would be enough money. And if there is enough money, you can bet we have enough staff time being wasted to get it all done in record time. All it takes is Deming-like leaders.

Let's review, lest you forgot:

- Quality leads to lower costs.
- Most defects are caused by the system.

- Buy from vendors committed to quality.
- Fear leads to disaster.
- Work with suppliers.

Okay, what is the fire drill?

1. First, we must define quality (no indicators or measures that count mistakes—how many of this "defect" and how many of that "defect") in outcome terms (how many patients were restored to higher levels of functioning; how many are being discharged to home- and community-based programs).
2. Revamp the inductive systems using deductive systems.
3. Require that the providers define the quality of the products that they buy and then expect them to be defect-free.
4. Get rid of the fear inducing conformity factor of an enforcement mentality by CMS.
5. Electronically link up with the provider networks utilizing standardized systems and terminology.

This, coupled with a change in America's attitude that we are healthy until proven otherwise, must happen or we will all be sicker from pills and irrelevant testing. Granted, not everyone is responsible for themselves, but the majority are until the system tells them that there are safety nets, so don't worry about the cost of healthcare, the employers or the government will take care of it for you. Ha-ha, I looked for the enemy and the enemy was me. It is simple; to cut costs, cut the incidence of chronic disease by preventing it. Each and every American can do it through diet, exercise, and effort. If they don't, we all will be in a 1,000-bed nursing home, suffering from bankruptcy.

Savings Withholding Accounts

Yes, individual SHIFT (self-health insurance funding trusts) withholding savings accounts are pretax deductible and accumulate a return on investment; administered by the employer, like a 401k plan, not by the government. The fund is portable and invested by mutual insurance professional investors. Then the healthier person has more left for after-care and retirement. For the unemployed, we will have a workable Medicaid fund. For catastrophic illnesses we will have an affordable Medicare fund. Everything else will be a withholding program for long-term healthcare.

A national healthcare policy with defined benefits and an Enterprise Funding (Mutual Health Insurance Companies where the beneficiaries own the company) approach. It has to work because America works on the same basis . . . fund as you go along by forced savings and improved utilization by staying healthier . . . because it makes us all money. Deming would love us all if we can meet the Japanese culture of business . . . or maybe we should just let the Japanese run our health care business.

Premiums

Rate setting will be the most scientific endeavor since the premiums will be based on the beneficiary's health, not utilization. That health profile will be the basis for annual rate setting and altered with significant changes in condition. In concept, the healthy person gets the better coverage for less premium and can save more by not over utilizing their savings account.

Tax Deductions for Health Preservation and Wellness Costs

All health-related costs that exceed 75 percent of the current individual savings account balance and fitness expenses are 100 percent deductible from adjusted gross taxable income. Fitness embraces workout facilities, nutritional foods, annual physicals, and screenings. Health preservation and wellness is the next trillion-dollar industry.

Prevent Chronic Illnesses

The highest cost in healthcare is the five chronic diseases (diabetes, cardiac, respiratory, stroke, obesity). Prevention of those would save Medicare $100 billion per year. Of course, we are spending a pound for every ounce of prevention that is not practiced. Economic incentives (personal health savings accounts and tax deductions) are the only way to get Americans' attention and commitment to be healthy. Dr. Deming, if he were alive today, would tag healthcare management with the "waste of the year" award. His advice would be the same as above, organize for quality, save money, and reinvest in those Americans that will stay healthy. The unhealthy ones will have to pay more and have less.

Currently, $4.2 trillion dollars is spent on low to marginal healthcare services in the US. The uncontrollable outlays are as follows:

- Physicians $800 billion
- Hospitals $1.2 trillion
- Nursing homes $600 billion
- Home care $300 billion
- Pharmaceuticals $1 trillion ($1 trillion on Part D drugs by 2020)
- Other $300 billion
- Total expenditures in 2010 $4.2 trillion

Of that amount, 80 percent of those dollars are spent on chronic diseases in the last two years of Americans' lives (bureaucratically termed *end-of-life care*). All is spent in the pursuit of treatment, rather than wellness as an outcome. Prevention is an afterthought; waste is never mentioned. Why? Because we are practicing *wealth care*, not true healthcare.

According to AARP this black hole will get deeper, to the tune of $4 trillion by 2020, and my estimate is more like that much by 2011, because the REFORMERS want to add the uninsured, the underinsured, noncitizens, and the unemployed to our staggering health economy, funded by enormous borrowing; and in my opinion, there still will be no viable solution in place.

So, what is the solution? I propose the American Enterprise Mutual Health Care Program:

1. Clearly stated national healthcare preventive and preservation objectives formalized into a national mutual health insurance policy that requires all employed Americans to have ownership (preferred stock), with shares being purchased from their SHIFT savings accounts. We can computerize the whole process if we standardize the benefits and payment methods. Let enterprise set up the standards and comply with them for profit.
2. Federalized withholding with employer match program from all employed Americans to collect and populate the health-preservation SHIFT savings accounts. Let the government collect it but not spend it!
3. Mutual Health Insurance Companies as contractors for investing American's health-preservation SHIFT savings accounts and paying for each American's desired expenditures for healthcare, disease prevention, health and wellness expenditures for fitness and nutritional plans. There can be no competition in healthcare if we want results. Government will continue to throw good money after bad care if enterprise does not intercede.
4. Each employed American will have an annual standardized health and fitness profile and a plan for preserving wellness and preventing chronic health problems developed for determining their dividend rate on their mutual preferred stock holdings. As long as we separate payment from the person, we will not get a reduction in spiraling costs (a.k.a. waste).
5. Each unemployed American citizen will be covered by Medicaid that will be federalized as an insurance program to only cover the unemployed. The expenditures would be funded

by a special provision in Federal revenue sharing. Illegal aliens will not have insurance or health benefits.

6. Medicare Part A, in its current form, will continue as a safety net but only for outlier payments related to catastrophic hospitalizations and terminal diseases of the elderly and disabled. Medicare Part B, C, and D would be disbanded, and the Part A method of payment will be changed to include economic incentives based on restorative-care plans and outcomes. The funding for this benefit will continue to come out of the Social Security trust funds.

7. Individual SHIFT health savings accounts are managed by the individual preferred shareholder within the parameters of qualified healthcare expenditures, wellness, and fitness expenditures and programs designed to prevent chronic obesity and certain diseases. The SHIFT savings accounts will accumulate for use in later years for long-term care services after hospitalization.

8. Mutual dividends are tax exempt, as are gains on preferred stock sales where the shareholder is divesting ownership of some of their investment.

The Balance Sheet and Income Statement of American Health

Why We Can't Trust the Government (health care is a right, Medicare for All and Obama Care isn't working)

If you are depending on the politicians and the government to fix it, take a look at the last twenty years. The rhetoric is the same: contain and refrain from driving up costs but keep those tax dollars coming or we won't be able to pay for those pills and tests and bypass surgeries.

In theory, the government is us. I say "in theory." Have you tried to get your friendly senator or representative on the phone lately? Good luck.

They are too busy to listen to the public. That is why they have deflectors called *aides*.

To make universal healthcare or universal anything work it cannot be administered by big government or big business—it is corrupt now. What is needed is a concept where the individual does have control over funding and disbursement of healthcare and education dollars, but only upon presentation of their need. Otherwise, the money will be peeled off for some other gamble and nothing left for paying the bills.

In ten years, using this paradigm SHIFT to pay for an outcome system, we can generate $12 trillion per year in resources as the 200 million workers contribute as little as $500 per month investment in their mutual insurance preferred stock. That is, without giving the effect of a return on the investment made by the mutual insurance company's infusion of capital into our economy. Many of the companies receiving infusion of capital are the providers of health preservation and preventative services to meet the demand of the seventy-seven million baby boomers coming into that market.

This enterprise solution will also eliminate the insane policies of the political left and right that have driven our country to the brink of bankruptcy (we have $158 trillion in debt if the entitlements are recorded on the cooked government books) and made us vulnerable to our economic enemies, who are far more ominous than a few terrorists whom the politicians use as fear factors inducing conformity to keep the Middle American at bay. By using the American Enterprise Mutual Insurance Company as the catalyst to change, in ten years we would be self-funding aging, health preservation, elimination of chronic diseases, and a quality of life that leads the world to better health. More importantly, by putting enterprising America at the center and having cost-effective services emanate from the center, we will create two million to five million more jobs per year to service the mutual insurance company's shareholders. It is a self-perpetuating business approach to a political nightmare.

A 2012 White Paper
Pay for Performance
Replace Enforcement Minimum Standards
With Maximum Re-enforcement Standards
Incentive Payment Replaces RUGs and Case-Mix Formulas
By Jerry L. Rhoads, CPA, FACHCA

My Story (175-175-175): from the many to one.

At a skilled nursing facility, I took on, which was decertified and called "Death Valley" by the surveyors, there were 207 beds with plummeting occupancy. It had 175 patients that did not want to be there, 175 families who did not want to come there, and 175 employees who did not want to work there—quite a big undertaking.

Within five days of taking over without even an administrator's license, a ninety-three-year-old contracted patient drowned in the whirlpool while a foreign therapist charted behind a privacy screen. The next day I was on TV trying to explain the accident, which the attorney general called neglect and criminal abuse.

My attitude of "I am going to fix this mess" and a forgiving family got me through to the next big problem. After that and for the next six months it got worse: 200 percent turnover, 25 percent absenteeism, 50 percent absenteeism on weekends, theft of patients' valuables, air conditioning that broke down for two weeks. Surveyors were there every day with their humidity and temperature thermometers, just waiting to shut us down.

My staff was made up of legal or illegal immigrants who weren't properly trained nor effective but wanted what I wanted. I had Polish bed makers, Mexican housekeepers, Filipino LPNs, East Indian night staff, Black American CNAs, white RNs, Hispanic dietary staff, many of whom were probably not legal aliens. Not a team, but a group of workers focused on paychecks and their departments, not on the patients. I found out that I didn't have the quick fix and probably made things worse by doing nothing but reacting to family, patient, staff complaints.

Even an ineffective leader sometimes does nothing and becomes a leader. During a snowstorm that November, only half the staff showed up for work and for seventy-two hours the facility ran better without troublemakers and thieves. Since the Director of Nursing didn't show up and my assistant director o nursing was on the phone wanting direction, I suggested that they organize as teams and focus on priorities, such as feeding, dressing, medications, treatments, etc.

When I got there the ADON, and lead aide had organized the staff into teams and were performing as they never had before. Priorities were done first, and busywork was shelved. After the snowstorm, it dawned on me that before the storm all of the staff only worked half a day; and after, half the staff got more done in a day than they did in a week before. Quite an eye-opener, so much so I decided we were not going back to the old ineffective departmental structure but were going to stay with the teams set up in my absence.

> To do this required that I know what the root cause of the complacency and apathy in our team. Teams have been a part of my whole life growing up competing for a position being the smallest on the field or floor. So, I decided to become a nurses' aide, a housekeeper, a dietary aide, a maintenance man, a social worker for each shift for a day to learn their problems. After contacting scabies and giving them to my wife it finally dawned on me that we had tribes not teams. From that time on "we many" would work as one for a common goal ... "Serve our patients is to serve our soul". The rest is history.

In conclusion, this epiphany changed my view of the infrastructure of nursing homes. As teams only focused on the patients' priority problems and organized to implement the care plan interventions, we achieved efficiency and effectiveness never before attained. Productivity was based on outcomes we could get reimbursed for and quality was a byproduct of our control of the processes. By our next QUIP (quality incentive payment) and annual survey we were recertified and received a clean survey with five of the six stars of quality awarded exemplary providers, which meant more money for better quality.

The byword for this miracle I experienced is taking a staff with no purpose and turning it into a team with a purpose is better utilizing my human capital was enterprise. My realization that our staff was handcuffed to antiquated management awoke with the snowstorm. From that day on I implemented "learn to earn and skill to bill" programs to provide each staff member a career path to their American Dream.

This was built on the program I learned at Arthur Andersen & Co. Each person was the center of their life's aspirations and goals. All I had to do, as their boss, was to activate them in an organization of winning not losing to their job performance. In other words, doing their jobs with excellence and effort as their goal, we all were winners ... and in the process the patients received quality of care and improvement of their lives. Out of this grew my pay for performance program based on "skill to be bill and learn to earn" career plans that evolved into the so called "Death Valley" environment being replaced by a six-star facility that was the envy of our competition and the joy of our patients and their families.

Unfortunately, this could not last forever because the facility, after I fixed it, was sold by the owners who exercised their lease/purchase clause. They then were able to acquire the facility then sell it for a profit of $1.2 million and I was replaced as the Administrator (by a chain operator who reversed all of the organization and physical changes that we had accomplished) to save money and the facility was returned to a warehouse for the elderly.

My staff was devastated and thought the new owners were crazy for firing the coach taking them to the Super Bowl (their words at my departure party where they gave me a trophy for believing in them).

It was again not a care house for restored patients so they could return home or to the community, but the typical nursing home allowed to operate due to the chain operator's political contributions that allowed them to avoid closure. By knowing when the surveyors were coming and staffing up to look like they are complying with the minimum standards of care, where it's acceptable to have odor and understaffing, because they are highly rated by a flawed system of systemic low quality of life for the elderly.

Out of this experience comes my educated opinion:

(Another epiphany I had was to pay the performing providers (See Exhibit D) on service excellence. Why not pay fewer efficient staff more for providing quality work, rather than more staff less for whatever they decide to do or not do?)

At the root cause of the quality problem is the current regulatory minimum standards for skilled nursing facilities that promotes mediocrity by using them to penalize and use civil money fines to incriminate the providers:

- 37.106.601 minimum standards for a skilled nursing care facility: general
- 37.106.605 minimum standards for a skilled nursing care facility: staffing
- 37.106.606 minimum standards for a skilled nursing care facility: prescription drugs
- 37.106.640 minimum standards for a skilled nursing care facility: infirmary

- 37.106.645 minimum standards for a skilled nursing care facility: developmentally disabled
- 37.106.650 minimum standards for a skilled nursing care facility: kidney treatment

Presently, control is futilely tried and attained through threats, penalties, fear tactics inducing conformity, and less reimbursement. In my opinion, this approach makes care worse. It does not deal with the problem; it deals with symptoms. Poor care is due to lack of economic incentives to provide a quality of life for those who are forced to accept the alternative lifestyle in nursing facilities. And there is not any educational training to assist nursing facility providers in improvement; the government and the provider are at opposite ends, a "we against them" scenario, using subjective intimidation as opposed to a more democratic environment where both the government and providers are working together to achieve quality care.

It is not the patient's desired home, and staff need stability, not threats; organization, process development, and control, not more people; tools for efficiency, not more hours; models of care designed to address problems and achieve goals, not guessing what should be done; more involvement with the medical community, not a cursory visit by a physician every thirty days skilled, and ninety days non-skilled, with phone orders galore.

A proposal for maximum standards that reward excellence:
The cliché "minimum standards become maximum quality" certainly applies in many nursing homes. Since there are no incentives to do better than minimum, there are no reasons to exceed what you have to provide to minimally pass a subjective, arbitrary and capricious survey process, rather than a survey process based on factual data.

Survey happens once a year, around contract renewal dates, so it is supposed to be totally a surprise visit. The surveyors are typically former nursing employees who are allowed to subjectively interpret the minimum standards during their visit.

Nursing home management is given ten days to develop a plan of correction for those violations noted by the surveyors and the Fire Marshall. If the plan is accepted, the state has the option for doing a follow-up survey or accepting the correction plan through a desk review.

Nursing home reforms have been promulgated and directed toward additional or revised deficiencies for years. However, very few facilities are held financially accountable for providing quality outcomes, which can be reviewed from statistical and factual data. The root problem here is the system pays for treatment and medications not restoring the elderly so they can return home of to assisted living. As a result, the population in nursing homes are relegated to a remaining live on Medicaid on a maintenance program, not restorative with measured outcomes. It's all about guaranteed income to the providers not positive outcomes for the patients.

What could be the maximum standards and how this would impact quality by using incentives to excel not penalties for violations and deficiencies?

- 37.106.601 maximum standards for a skilled nursing care facility: general. A facility should be clean, without odors, and provide adequate space for patients, families, and visitors; would receive one of six stars of quality.
- 37.106.605 maximum standards for a skilled nursing care facility: staffing. A facility would utilize care plans for determining the number of staff based on the care plans; would receive one of six stars of quality.
- 37.106.606 maximum standards for a skilled nursing care facility: pharmaceuticals. A facility should institute a drug-reduction program involving attending physicians and pharmacies; would receive one of six stars of quality.
- 37.106.640 maximum standards for a skilled nursing care facility: hospitalization. A facility should reduce the incidences

of rehospitalization by at least 25 percent each year, receiving one of the six stars of quality.
- 37.106.645 maximum standards for a skilled nursing care facility: dementia and Alzheimer's. A facility that institutes psycho/social programming receives one of the six stars of quality.
- 37.106.650 maximum standards for a skilled nursing care facility: activities of daily living optimized. A facility that institutes restorative and retraining programs for all patients receives one of six stars of quality.

QUIP (Quality Incentive Payment)

Incentive reimbursement would be tied to the maximum standards of care and six stars of quality, while a minimum base rate would apply to the minimum standards of personal care.

For example, the minimum base rate would consist of:

- Actual cost of room—includes physical plant cost, depreciation, interest on debt, real estate taxes, insurance, utilities, maintenance of plants, common-area cleanliness, and infection control, etc.
- Personal care services provided every patient—includes meals, continence supplies, laundry, housekeeping, safety in general activities
- Personalized activities—includes recreational, spiritual, social, and educational activities

Maximum daily rate would consist of the base rate plus add-ons (as needed based on assessment):

- Occupational rehab and restorative care—therapy and nursing retraining programs for ADL deficits, upper and lower extremity exercises

- Physical rehab and restorative care—therapy and nursing retraining for ambulation, transfer, bed mobility, toileting, strengthening, fitness training
- Social rehab—therapeutic clubs, enterprise activities, discussion groups, card groups, gourmet club, church groups, Bible study
- Psychological rehab—groups for wanderers, smokers, cancer survivors, stroke survivors, demented, confused, withdrawn, prone to falls, overweight, underweight

Outcome-based reimbursement must pay for performance proven by documented results. More patients restored and more discharged back to the community.

Annual quality incentive payment based on a survey by state to determine degree of compliance toward quality maximum standards (designed to document the providers doing something right and rewarding them for quality of life).

- Award first star: Evaluate the effectiveness of the facility's care-plan implementation based on the documented assessed problems, programs, and outcomes for each patient's stay
- Award second star: Evaluate the effectiveness of the facility's staff-management program based on the turnover rate, absenteeism rate, theft rate, fall rate, number of complaint surveys
- Award third star: Evaluate the facility's effectiveness in reducing drug dependence and managing drug interactions based on documented occurrences and outcomes
- Award fourth star: Evaluate the effectiveness of the facility's management of the attending physician's orders and reducing the number of unnecessary hospitalizations, ER visits, and misdiagnosed testing based on documented occurrences and outcomes

- Award fifth star: Evaluate the effectiveness of the facility's management of the psychological needs of the dementia, confused, and Alzheimer's patients
- Award sixth star: Evaluate the effectiveness of the facility's skilled nursing restorative and rehab programs, including the therapists

This method has been demonstrated in Illinois. The add-on and QUIP programs were instituted in the State of Illinois in the 1980s by the Department of Public Aid under direction of Connie Cherin. I managed nursing facilities during that time, and my staff and I were in pursuit of quality every day, based on a variable rate and the annual QUIP survey. Proposed daily reimbursement model (evidence based, pay for performance):

1. Base rate, actual costs per day from latest facility cost report, $62 per day
2. Personal care services
   - TOTAL PERSONAL CARE: $23 per day
3. Hospitality and personal services, $85 per day
4. Add-ons based on a comprehensive physical, mental, social, and psychological assessment, and plan of treatment using outcome scales to measure progress or decline
   - TOTAL REHAB: $65 per day
5. Annual quality incentive payment (QUIP) survey, potential bonus based on survey results
   - TOTAL QUIP: $25 per day
6. Maximum rate attained maximum standards: $175 per day
+ Pass through of actual costs for medications above a certain outlier per diem
+ Pass through of actual costs for durable medical equipment above a certain outlier per diem
+ Pass through of actual costs for medical supplies above a certain outlier per diem

Restorative modeling methodology:

The pass-through costs would be at actual billed costs plus a handling purchasing and accounting fee of 5 percent. The only guaranteed rate is the base rate and personal services. All other program services are add-ons, and the annual QUIP survey values the bonus to be paid for each star.

Enforcement, civil money penalties, tort reform, negative incentives can be eliminated by using the reinforcement and collaboration approach and accept that the providers are not going to be paid unless they perform and be prepared to prove the claim with medical, emotional, and social proof of outcome.

In the book *Freakonomics*, the authors propose moral incentives are the way we would like things to be and economic incentives are the way things are. They then propose we can use one to get the other if we are smart.

201-201-175, the rest of the story

After the snowstorm and our next QUIP survey, we had 201 patients who were happy to be at Fox Valley, 201 families who would come to the facility, and 175 staff who wanted to work at the facility. Yes, we added an average of twenty-six patients to our census (all Medicare qualified) and sustained the same staffing levels due to efficiency, 20 percent turnover rate, 5 percent absenteeism rate, and a fall rate below 5 percent. At Death Valley, the solution was giving the staff a purpose and they will give you quality. We were then proud to be called Fox Valley, a six-star facility.

Bottom line:

This enterprise model (restorative processes) is designed to save Medicare and Medicaid dollars by restoring the patients, rather than housing residents. This model over the last twenty years has resulted in 44,000 more discharges home and money saved for those who only implemented 25 percent of the model. If instituted as the restorative model, replacing the medical model and the social model, billions can be saved on inappropriate medications and wasted lives sitting in wheelchairs, in diapers, with no future. I would predict the baby boomers will not pay their taxes and their Medicare withholding for this type of care.

Post Script: At Fox Valley after the snow storm, my staff was still made up of, possibly illegal, immigrants who were now effective and wanted what I wanted . . . pride of workmanship and getting people better so they could return home . . . we were not homemakers but game-changers. I still had Polish bed makers, Mexican housekeepers, Filipino LPNs, East Indian night staff, Black American CNAs, white RNs, Hispanic dietary staff, but many were learning to speak English and wanted to seek a career in health care while preparing for citizenship. A cohesive team focused on the patients, not a gang of workers just focused on paychecks and their departments.

Unfortunately, this success could not last forever because the facility was sold and I was replaced as the Administrator by a chain operator who reversed all of the changes, we had implemented to save the facility. So, the patients could no longer return home or to the community. As a result, it was regressed back to a Medicaid warehouse for the elderly. My staff was devastated and thought the new owners were crazy for firing the coach taking them to the Super Bowl (their words at my departure party where they gave me a trophy for believing in them). From there I was hired as the contract Administrator for another 206-bed skilled nursing home that had lost its Medicare and Medicaid certification. By this time, I had a template for solving the same problems experienced and solved at Death Valley. In 22 months, the results were the same but better financially. This enabled the owner to sell it to a local chain operator and I moved on. The facility was turned back into a warehouse in spite of the staff revolting. In the next twenty years my consulting company, Caregiver Management Systems, turned 141 facilities around using this formula. We then formed All-American Care, Inc. and purchased three skilled nursing facilities documented in an earlier Article.

MORAL OF THE ARTICLE:

Dr. W. Edwards Deming, the lessons he has to teach American business are more urgent than ever. Jerry Rhoads, author of this book isn't a household name in nursing homes, but his policies and practices are well documented in this book and his other 9 self=health brand books document and support how his 40 years' experience in the nursing home business, is predicting the future.

When I started writing the book in 1991 The American Enterprise Manifesto was a manuscript that has evolved into this rendition. My purpose was to offer an alternative to a two-party system that had evolved into a 1984 version of an Oligarch. Obviously, with the impact of the worst Pandemic since 1918 we are changing everything to fit an old agenda called how to get rid of capitalism and replace it with socialism (Marxist style). This where big government (Big Brother) and the Brotherhood (big business) become everyone's benefactor, supported by an all-knowing symbiotic uni-party, one voice Congress (Brotherhood) promising to fulfill everyone's dreams and needs. In contrast The Great American Enterprise takes us back to the forefather's dreams and needs of freedom, peace and respect for the individual's volition and responsibly to live a happy, healthy and prosperous life. Characterized by ...

Ronald Reagan (1911-2004) (President of the United States 1981-1989)

- "Entrepreneurs and their small enterprises are responsible for almost all the economic growth in the United States".
- "Government exists to protect us from each other. Where government has gone beyond its limits is in deciding to protect us from ourselves".
- "Government does not solve problems; it subsidizes them".
- "Government's first duty is to protect the people, not run their lives".

Article Seven

Humanism and Peaceful Coexistence

(National Political Priorities)

American the beautiful, America the bountiful. America the leader for peace. America the free enterprise. America the government of the people, by the people, and for the people. Are these values safe? Is it the representation of free market enterprise in that scenario? America the bountiful is dependent on enterprising Americans being represented for their part in governance. Thus, we need fair and effective leadership and representation of the small-business owners, the hard workers, the wage earners, the providers of care and support staff, the elderly, the disabled, the forgotten minorities that merely get lip service from the reds and the blues. We are the twenty-first century advocates of smaller government and bigger business segments, supported by fair taxation, resulting in recapitalization of the American enterprise to fulfill the American Dream.

With a gridlock Congress and a society in turmoil the principles of fair representation are tainted. Black Lives Matter voters claim the white privileged are racist and the WASP'S claim they are systemic color blind with truth somewhere in between. This leaves the binary "winner take all" Presidential race and congressional seats just a pass through for incumbents. Unless you have mail in voting for the first time, uncontrolled drop boxes and harvesting of votes in the cities leaving the results in question. Toss in the George Floyd hate crime and police being blamed for injustice by the inner-city crime wave, led by the BLM, ANTIFA gangs, concerned protesters turning into rioters and thieves … the politician's set them up to fail and enforcement became impossible if they aren't indemnified; then those rioting demanded they be defunded. Have we elected the people that believe in and pursue solutions to problems rather than debate their differences (so-called issues)? Do They represent their constituency or their reelection? Hell no! Take the following opinion poll and see where you stand, because *if you don't stand for something you will fall for everything!*

National Political Priorities

Tell me yours:	My ranking	What is yours?
Energy independence	5	
Interest rates on debt	3(a)	
Infrastructure, Inner city crime and ghettos	4	
Poverty in the World	c	
Liberty and justice for all	2 (b)	
Peace at all costs	13	
Education choice	9	
Housing for all	9 (a)	
China, Russia and Iran	1	
Guns	2 (c)	
Jobs for all versus unions	6	
Taxes an effective use of wealth	9	
Illegal Immigration	2	
Economy	3	
Healthcare (Medicare/Medicaid)	7(a)	
Social Security	8	
Retirement of Baby Boomers	7(d)	
Life Expectancy	7 (c)	
Health Care For All	7(b)	
Family and love life	c	
Global warming (climate change)	12	
Abortion	c	
Gay marriage	c	
Racism, wokeism, reverse racism	2	
Religious rights	c	

The C's stand for constitutional issues that have been or will be resolved through civil legal actions and Supreme Court decisions. They should not be political issues. The S is for science to figure out before society takes drastic actions other than personal energy savings. The remaining ten priorities are not political issues, they are economic problems that politicians need to take a definitive stand on.

See Exhibit F for an exercise of issue versus problem. Also "no worries" is being replacing problem in our everyday vernacular. Eventually every conversation will be a political compromise.

Quotes from Pe Healing of America, by Marianne Williamson on the Brotherhood:

"Corporate soul, do we have one? "The forces that drive the US economy are drunk on power. They swagger, they deny, they justify, they intimidate. That's what drunks do. The American people must stop wimping out, and awaken from our codependent stupor. We must not allow the American political system to become little more than the servant of dominant economic interests."

"Citizen-based politics: A citizen-based political culture would have a different collective nervous system from the culture we have now. Our current leadership plays into our immaturity, often acting as immature as we, promising us everything during campaigns, then delivering very little after the election."

"Blood money: Money is, at heart, the great moral problem of our time. America must have a very serious discussion with itself about the wisdom of allowing the market to drive us. From the left and from the right, voices are beginning to rise up to protest the market's unbridled power. We can no longer afford to look the other way, as American economic interests systematically compromise our societal values."

Rhoads on Big Brother and the Brotherhood:

Isn't it overwhelming to consider the problems each of us face and collectively abdicate to our government who then treats them as debatable issues to be tabled for study, so we forget about them? When we personally are not starving, being shot at, live in our own house, have a job that enables us to pay our bills and taxes, deal with gas prices, and are domesticated, our concerns are about those close to us and leave the rest to those who don't really care about anything but themselves.

Then we lose our job, our house, and can't pay our bills, then the priorities change instantly, dramatically. We then must consider poverty, living on the street, owning a gun for protection, updating our education, competing with illegal immigrants for money, welfare, unemployment benefits, food stamps, fee healthcare, with survival as our future.

Ironically, each of us must deal with the circumstances that face us now; the future is another time warp, so priorities take a new twist and the politics don't matter. All of this is resolved through true change of leadership to those who have the values of the majority in mind, because thought changes everything while talk stalls the change of anything.

So, are you listening, Joe, Kamala, Bernie, Elizabeth, Mitt, Paul, Mitch, Harry, Chuck, Nancy, whoever you are in Congress and the White House? Your list of priorities is not mine, nor are they really yours. If you ignore how the enterprising Americans' world works, because it is that group that pays all the bills and your salary, retirement benefits, and healthcare. Listening to us is not a reality unless we buy our way in. Your inner circle is a circle of Oligarch wagons set up to keep the masses out.

All we have for the ebb of change are promises; as usual, our political expectations are focused not on our priorities. Spending billions on the following is not what enterprising Americans want:

Another cold war with China, Russia and Iran. We must focus on what we have that they want:

1) Food supply, R&D for technology, staples.
2) Energy, global franchises.
3) Capital and stock exchanges.
4) 5-G, military technology and internet control.
5) Colleges and Universities for embedding and talent.
6) Supply line control with FOB shipping cost.

China sees us as an intimidating war machine:

- The war machine (cost of wars in today's dollars):
    - Korea $341 billion.
    - Viet Nam $738,
    - billion Persian Gulf $102 billion,
    - Iraq $812,758,193,633,
    - Afghanistan $2.6 trillion,
    - Bosnia $1.2 billion,

    About $5 trillion spent on wars of no return . . . the cost of peace is much more productive.

- $500 million embassy in Iraq, $800 million in Afghanistan.
- Unlimited $780 billion annual defense spending, $85mbillion lost in the Afghanistan retreat.
- Wasteful $4.2 trillion healthcare costs.
- Manipulated interest rates (the Fed 2005-6 popped the balloon when it should have let the air out slowly; now the professor of controlled economics wants to take credit for fixing a disaster he caused).
- Debt $30 trillion financing on federal and $1.2 trillion state budget deficits bloated by overemployment. www.usdebtclock.org

- Unfunded obligations of $158 trillion using GAAP accounting.
- Underfunded:
    - Inner-city repairs and maintenance.
    - International peace corps movement.
    - Public and private education for underserved inner city schools.
    - Housing for underserved classes.
    - Available well-paying Jobs for all.
    - Small-business tax reduction and low-cost capital.
    - Preventive Health, Fitness and wellness programs.
    - Roads, highways, bridges infrastructure.
    - 5G Technology and GPS surveillance protection from private R&D investment.

In other words, take the $10 trillion Green New Deal infrastructure funding over the next decade focused only on political priorities and invest in:

- Black New Deal: Replacement of eroding inner-city infrastructure (slum neighborhoods, transportation, schools, etc.) Hundreds of thousands of homeless are living amid filth, excrement and disease in the nation's urban sidewalks and tent cities "Victor Harmon". Employ gang members to be a part of a community is "Serve your country is to serve your soul".
- Technology that solves fossil fuel energy sources (solid state batteries, harvesting energy from fire ice, sand, etc.)
- Peace corps reactivated for entry level into government "Serve your country is to serve your soul".
- Full employment:
    - Deployment of job placement.
    - Public works programs run by private businesses.
    - Inner-city development for enterprise zones.
- Comprehensive healthcare using Self-Health principles.

- Modified retirement funding and planning.
- Reduce national debt 10 percent each year.
- Enterprise zones and technology investment tax credits.
- Affordable housing and private education for all Americans by eliminating red lining and invest in family-based homes.

This movement to avoid national bankruptcy due to health care and manipulated interest rates forecast to happen by 2021 needs to make the following priorities known to those who claim to have the means to fix it:

- Reduce government employees 10% per year replaced by privatized agencies enforcing reduced regulations that have incentives to manage for outcomes not incomes.
- Pass a bill (law), kill a law and its regulations (instead of lawmakers we need peacemakers).
- Form a coalition of USA, Canada, Japan, France, Italy, England, India and Mexico as our own OPEC (Oil Purchasing Energy Using Countries) to control production and prices through distribution quotas and demand pricing.
- Universal healthcare long-term care insurance funded by employee withholding accounts invested in mutual funds and distributed at the discretion of the insured. Shift the paradigm to Self-Health.
- Retain traditional Medicare for the retired Americans: Part A, and Part B; discard Part C and D with a Self-Heath program.
- Retain Medicaid for the unemployed and disabled.
- Pursue peace and negotiate with the Arab countries and Israel to economize the use of oil as an alternate to emission free energy.
- Close the borders and legalize immigrants recruited to replace aging Americans, must speak, write, and function in English, pay taxes, and vote.
- Balancing federal and state budgets by outsourcing the budget to professional financial planners then holding government accountable to a balanced GAAP budget.
- Investment tax credits for technology:

- o Healthcare preventive and preservative AI costing and pricing models for body systems.
- o Biotech for chronic disease detection and treatment.
- o AI Management systems for managing business processes.
- o Electronic satellite communication systems.
- Fair tax on foreign products sold in USA (tax the producer, not the consumer).
- Rename Health and Human Services to Quality of Life, the joining of enterprise and healthcare preservation and prevention outcomes, and delivery pricing supported by episodic cost accounting.
- Rename Treasury Department (IRS) as National Wealth Depository.
- Rename the Defense Department to Offense for Peace Corps.
- Rename the Justice Department to the Constitution Department.
- Rename the Commerce Department to the Enterprise Department.

By 2030 this approach will recruit more talented Americans to public services and dilute the dominance by the elite and legal ties to nepotism.

Enterprise is the solution; it is not free but frees Americans to create wealth while unfettered government ties the hands that feeds it. When wealth is given as entitlements, it soon disappears.

Following are the postulates and platform for that movement, that make it the party of the people (baby boomers, college students, legal immigrants', Dreamers, naturalized citizens and those that want into America willing to work and pay taxes for education, peace, quality of life and freedom to vote for effective patrician government leaders).

If we were to capitalize on the power of our labor, intellectual prowess and freedom to share in the fruits we would be the superpower without the necessity of nuclear weapons, war chests, imperialistic pursuits and disregard for human life (3,100 Americans were killed on 9/11, over 7,000 have died since in Iraq and Afghanistan, while we have enabled a civil war that killed over 1 million combatants and collateral civilians in a failed strategy in Iraq and Afghanistan).

It is estimated that 1.8 million Iraqis, another million from Afghanistan, 2.5 million from Mexico, South and Central America have been displaced to the USA and neighboring countries, (10.6 million were displaced internally to America in the last two decades 2000 to 2020). With nearly 100,000 Iraqis fleeing to Syria and Jordan each month. Since those wars, more American soldiers have taken their own lives than killed in action . . . 22 commit suicide per day from post-traumatic syndrome. Is it worth our youth and innocent civilians to force our values on others in the name of fear of terrorism, regime change, nation building and pursuit of the American Dream? Give humanism and peaceful coexistence a chance!

How much more proof do I need to justify a better way for the Better Good of our Planet. When government and politics get in the way of those objectives the results are poverty, crime, war, anger, and loss of life, liberty and the pursuit of happiness. Government of the people, by the people, and for the people must be our principles, as well, if we wish to compete economically with China and other emerging nations.

Twenty-first century liberty requires a third political party that represents humanism with peaceful coexistence first, human rights second, government infrastructure third with the rule of law democracy and constitutional government providing the platform and free market enterprise the funding of R&D for advanced technology to rid our earth of waste with conservation not deprivation. Frankly, Mother Nature manages herself if we get out of the way. The practical Green New Deal is using capital to fund common sense conservation of our wetlands, farms, forests, seas, and human capital to have jobs that produce an outcome not just guaranteed income.

Ten commandments for peace and prosperity:

1. Law: Legal and justice infrastructure with consistency among states and countries ... all lives matter including the police and suspects.
2. Order: conformity to a definition of a human's right to protect themselves ... 300 million guns is not necessary for personal protection if we let justice prevail.
3. Democracy: voting is a right; education and healthcare are privileges to be earned ... privatized education to provide opportunity not conformity.
4. Free speech: expression of personal beliefs until it gets vulgar and promotes violence in our entertainment and daily living.
5. Housing: affordable and available to all wherever they can afford and qualify for a mortgage and can pay what's lent or rent.
6. Diplomacy: based on peaceful coexistence, not war financed by winning the economic war being conducted worldwide with China, et. al.
7. Security and safety: use of negotiation, not threats, use of reason, not more weapons of mass destruction nationally and internationally. Leaving religion out of the conflicts if possible.
8. Partnership between Public and Private "Health Care for All": universal coverage for prevention and preservation of life... a book by Jerry Rhoads, Page Turner Press 2021.
9. Private Education: equal opportunity for all to pursue the American Dream based on traditional diverse values and constitutional culture.
10. Employment: have a goal for full employment with job and peace corps pursuing technology for jobs, jobs, jobs. "Serve your country is to serve your soul".

Ben Franklin said, "They that can give up essential liberty to obtain a little safety deserve neither." Our national security and safety are more dependent on our attitude toward peace than the threat of war.

Ten commandments for fiscal fitness:

1. Eliminate wasteful lawmaking:
    a. Pass a law, kill a law and regulations.
    b. Transparency of GAAP budgets versus spending
    c. Bills must fit budget.
    d. Legislatures paid incentives if budgets are balanced.
2. Privatized education Charter principles:
    a. School boards focus on elimination of wasteful practices.
    b. All schools standardized for facilities and equipment.
    c. Funded by sales taxes and private tuition.
    d. Funded by a gaming tax on gambling, liquor, and professional sports.
3. Privatized healthcare using Self-Health principles:
    a. Providers must eliminate wasteful practices using episodic cost accounting, pricing and GAAP budgeting.
    b. Hidden costs must be exposed for elimination.
    c. Funded by withholding for universal long-term healthcare.
4. Pursuit of Full employment for diversity of the job corps:
    a. Job corps for unemployed to repay and maintain public properties and repair after natural disasters.
    b. Learn to earn with rights to equal opportunity through STEM education, SAT scoring, and diverse curriculum.
    c. Skill to bill on a worldwide free market-based economy.
5. Taxation based on increased net worth:
    a. Limited to a flat tax on the base and increase in net assets of individuals and companies.

b. Tax credits and incentives for:
      i. tuition for higher education,
      ii. catastrophic healthcare costs,
      iii. education sales taxes paid,
      iv. job and peace corps employment.
6. Constitutional issues left to Supreme Court decisions:
   a. Abortion no longer a political issue left to personal beliefs.
   b. Same-sex marriages accepted.
   c. Religion kept out of political arena ... diversity is earned.
   d. Rights to bear arms limited to laws and rights of the victims.
   e. Due process of law determines new legislation and disposes through sunset of unneeded laws.
   f. Immigration made legal by commitment to due process.
   h. Limit the court to nine justices.
7. Economic war to pursue peaceful coexistence in commerce and sovereignty of free countries:
   a. Systematic arms reduction globally, nationally, individually.
   b. Peaceful coexistence with emerging societies.
   c. Build infrastructures worldwide with capital and peaceful investments of America's wealth in enterprise and benevolence.
   d. Universal health preservation initiatives using tax incentives and penalties for better health outcomes for citizens and legal immigrants.
   e. Build on self-determination:
      i. Education is a privilege not to be wasted.
      ii. Health care is a privilege not to be wasted.
      iii. Jobs are sacred and should be available for

every American, of every extract and legal immigrants.
            iv. Affordable housing must be available to all Americans and legal immigrants regardless of location.
        f. Trade deficit must be eliminated by bringing production of products back to the USA and charging for access to our consumer-based economy:
            i. Distribution fee charged on foreign products.
            ii. Energy coalition to control the price of oil.
            iii. Alternate sources of energy tax credits provided for exploration and innovation.
8. Leadership objectives to pursue financial stability:
    a. Peaceful coexistence must be the mission.
    b. Economic incentives to accomplish moral incentives.
    c. Free trade with a balance based on market consumption and distribution.
    d. Education must be number one priority for immigrants as well as nationals.
    e. Housing must be affordable and credit available to all who work.
    f. Healthcare for all through a withholding account for each American who works ... the unemployed must have incentives to graduate from higher learning for STEM or trades.
    g. A tax system for growth and parity of all Americans, including a reinvestment of wealth in small businesses that create wealth.
    h. Convert books to GAAP and balance the Federal and State budgets over the next decade.
9. ISO 9000, 12,000 and Six Sigma standards for America:
    a. National healthcare policy,
    b. National education policy,
    c. Economic expansion plan,

d. American Enterprise Party for offering an alternative to the two-party establishment system.
10. Peace in the Middle East:
    a. Withdrawal of troops stop regime change philosophy.
    b. Maintain a peace corps dedicated to building a legal and legislative infrastructure acceptable to the Middle East leaders. "Serve your country is to serve your soul".
    c. Refocus military on peaceful coexistence and safety of the world.
    d. Support the Arab states in their position on setting up legal and economic entities (reason minus religion = resolution) on nonreligious grounds.
    e. Support Israel as a sovereign State that is willing to coexist with the sovereign Arab States including Palestine.
11. In our 193 embassies, consulates, and diplomatic missions around the world that are already funded and functional, could also be staffed by the Peace Corps to:
    - Promote peace and stability in regions of vital interest,
    - Creating jobs at home by opening markets abroad,
    - Helping developing nations establish stable economic environments that provide investment and export opportunities,
    - Bringing nations together to address global problems such as cross border pollution, the spread of communicable diseases, terrorism, nuclear smuggling and humanitarian crisis.

Administrative Policies:

Separation of powers... government and religion are to be separate... when are we going to get it that the world has to let go of its perceived religious differences or peace is not attainable!
Reason minus Religion = Resolution (the algorithm for Peace)

- Reasoning—to talk to another to cause a change of mind.
- Religion—a personal set of institutionalized religious beliefs, attitudes, and practices; a cause, principle, or belief held to by faith and order.
- Resolve—to find an answer, determine, decide; the action of solving or reasoning.

Reason minus Racism = Resolution (the algorithm for Equality)

We must build legal infrastructures first and foremost with capital and human rights invested by the peace corps and job corps. "Serve your country is to serve your soul".

These are the objectives of the ten commandments.

Stand for peace, utilizing economics rather than imperialism. What are the subjective of the ten commandments? Save lives by building relationships founded on moral and human rights.

Why? Because peace is the result and enterprise is the reason.

Peaceful coexistence in a world of conflict. America must be the leader and example of freedom. We must be neither dove nor hawk. In the world, we must be the eagle that soars for peaceful coexistence of divergent societies. But it also must be for all religions teachings to personify our GOD:

Pursuit of happiness.
Economies of scale.
Aging American power.
Constitutional consumption.
Enterprise Party.
Full employment.
Universal Health Care.
Lives and enterprise matter.

Good.
Offers.
Democracy.

Implementation Programs

Pursuit of happiness

Invest defense budget savings in equal educational opportunities for all (reinstitute a worldwide peace and job corps), invest legislative savings (pass a bill, kill a bill) to reduce family dysfunction (save the nuclear family to reduce 50% divorce rate in the US). Make friends dilute enemies with the power of enterprise— it is an economic war not a military exercise. Only sell weapons of mass destruction to our allies. Look for a balance of power to contain our adversaries in cyber space, ransom ware and outer space deployment of weapons.

Economies of scale

Team up with, if conciliatory, China, Russia, India, Japan, Germany, Britain, France, Italy for control of the energy market and reduce the imbalance of trade with the Middle East, replenish the aging workforce with legal immigration programs (must speak, read, pay taxes, and think American). Consumption is our strength; our markets are the weapons for leading the dissidents to a higher standard of living not destruction of God's creation.

Aging America

Reduce institutionalization of the elderly for planned prevention of chronic diseases using artificial intelligence for modeling of care, cost and outcomes for pricing and incomes. Eliminate employer and tax-based healthcare funding using individual withholding accounts and institute a standardized universal Self-healthcare policy for all Americans based on health profiles and prevention protocols. Deinstitutionalize the care of the elderly using restorative care principles versus custodial care.

Constitutional consumption

Economic health incentives for moral reasons fitness, weight controls, reduction of prescription drug use, and re-hospitalization of the elderly; balance trade deficits by charging a distribution fee for foreign products marketed and sold to the dynamic American purchasing power.

American Enterprise Party

Offer a swing vote third alternative to the establishment binary two-party system that will focus on America's middle-class, aging population, youth, and small business as a strong voting consensus that America must build on peaceful coexistence and enterprise, not money and the elite. The dominant stripe in the flag is white, red is to the right, blue is to the left, and white is the diverse middle-class representation.

Create private enterprise jobs for reclaiming forests, repairing infrastructure, fighting and preventing natural disasters (i.e., TVA for America's response to nature). Devise a tax system that is based on net worth, not income or purchasing power (the death tax becomes a reinvestment of capital of the wealth that is generated through the enterprise of all Americans). Put individuals in charge of their own individual healthcare spending accounts to eliminate the middlemen (get government and insurance company overhead and profits out of the equation) who profit on illness, not wellness.

Annual investment comes from savings

Current national debt is $28+ trillion (as high as 30 trillion after funding the 2020 Pandemic, funded by federal securities that are held by foreign countries and Wall Street investors. Current accrued deficit that includes entitlements is $158 trillion, national net worth is $157 trillion—America is on the verge of being insolvent. This is being covered by the Federal Reserve US Treasury printing more currency to fund Big Brother and the Brotherhood diluting the value of the

American dollar in the world market. Inflation follows this strategy then deflation then stagnation. The 2021 dollar is worth 68 cents compared to 2020 while it will be worth 25 cents by 2030 with the Biden administration. Solution: downsize government upsize enterprise … let our free-market economy solve the problem not law makers and regulators but establish rules and regulation for valuing crypto currency.

Why? Funding of misdirected military efforts and wasteful government spending:

- Middle East = $500 billion per year funding Israel.
- Funding of defense ($3 trillion spent on nuclear weapon stockpiles) = $500 billion per year.
- Waste in healthcare system due to bureaucracy and no standardized benefit package = $600 billion per year.
- Imbalance of trade = $800 billion per year.
- Interest on national debt = $ 600 billion per year.
- Total amount spent on questionable non-peace-driven initiatives = $1 trillion per year out of a total budget of $3 trillion per year.
- $17 trillion wasted on post Ben Ladin regime change.

Annual reinvestment of savings

- +$200 billion for education parity (charter schools for inner cities).
- +$150 billion to reduce divorce rates by financial counseling and remediating broken homes relationships.
- +$300 billion to build refineries in coalition countries and find alternative energy resources.
- +$100 billion to educate and integrate legal immigrants (the new job corps).

- +$500 billion to convert to deductive pay for performance evidence-based medicine and institute health preservation as a national program.
- +$150 billion to set up withholding-based individual healthcare accounts and tax deductions for health preservation costs.
- +$600 billion to invest healthcare savings in universal coverage for all Americans.
- + $200 billion in tax incentives for Americans to innovate and build technology.
- +$300 billion in tax incentives to expand American GNP and replace declining workforce.
- +$150 billion to finance the peace and job corps.
- Total reinvestment = $2.150 trillion per year based on peaceful coexistence Nixon and Kissinger style.

SUM UP THIS ARTICLE:

It is enterprising Americans that need the political representation of enterprise. America is beautiful due to enterprising Americans being represented for their part in governance. Thus, we need fair and effective partisan leadership and representation of the small-business owners, the hard workers, the wage earners, the providers of care and support staff, the elderly, the disabled, the forgotten minorities that merely get lip service from the reds and the blues. Effectively, this voting bloc pays all the bills by making the wealth in America that needs to reinvested and used to paydown the massive debt and fund the deficits until the reorganization pays for itself with GAAP budgets.

We are the twenty-first century advocates of smaller government and more startups and small business segments, supported by fair taxation, resulting in recapitalization of the American enterprise to fulfill the American Dream. The Red White and Blue in the flag will represent the three-party representations with enterprise being depicted as the stars and white stipe and Red stripes on a Blue background.

USA National Anthem
(Star Spangled Banner is our heritage and salutes our diverse veterans)

Say, can you see
By the dawn's early light
What so proudly we hailed
At the twilight's last gleaming?
Whose broad stripes and bright stars
Through the perilous fight
O'er the ramparts we watched,
Were so gallantly, yeah streaming?
And the rocket's red glare
The bombs bursting in air
Gave proof through the night
That our flag was still there
Oh say, does that star-spangled banner yet wave
O'er the land of the free and at the home of the brave

MY INDEPENDENCE

Independence what does it mean

Give me liberty or give me death
Give me freedom at any cost
Better dead than red
Dialogue of the idealist

Maybe
Sentiments of a cynic
Maybe
Emotions or an evangelist
Maybe
Platitudes of a pragmatic

Maybe
Just maybe
It's the feeling
Of being free to express reservations
Without condemnation

The feeling of being able
To throw your arms around an
Idea and make it come true

A feeling that you can express yourself
To a listening ear seeking independence
Maybe the entrance instead of the exit

It may be the top instead of the bottom
It may be the sunrise instead of sunset of an alternative
It may be the cream instead of the sediment

Independence is the positive rather than the negative
The summit rather than an event
Independence is a real sense not pretense

As is freedom of speech
Right to bear arms
That fall victim to government overreach

Rather than a purple issue
Independence is a real problem
When the politicians use a tissue

And table the problem as under study

To avoid the solution when the problem is them
Proposing 40,000 bills per annum
And making war with an atom

Thus, we declare our independence
From Big Brother and the Brotherhood
Embodied in the Gang of 545 that run our future
With no accountability

No fidelity or finality
Downsize Government Upsize Enterprise

Article Eight

Honor the Flag and Our Leaders

Red, White, Blue Stars, and Stripes

We have three colors in our American Flag, red and white stripes with a blue field with white stars: stars and stripes forever. The red and blue are represented in our political arena, but the white is not. It is not the color of skin that I am talking about, it is the representation of enterprise in that scenario. America the beautiful is dependent on enterprising diverse Americans being represented for their part in governance.

Thus, we need fair and effective leadership and representation of the small-business owners, the hard workers, the wage earners, the providers of care and support staff, the elderly, the disabled, the forgotten minorities that merely get lip service from the partisan reds and the blues. We are the twenty-first century advocates of smaller government and bigger business segments, supported by fair taxation, resulting in recapitalization of the American enterprise to fulfill the American Dream and protect our sovereignty with diverse citizenship.

Ten questions for voting Americans

The following questions are meant to present facts to the voters in making their decisions on who their leaders will be, the same or different, based on substance:

1. Are you happy with $786 billion annually being invested in the military buildup while our soldiers are put in an "only shoot if not shot at" mode with inferior equipment and endgame? Or

with $3 trillion invested in weapons of mass destruction that are never used.

2. Are you happy with the 200,000 of our youth being sacrificed to war? When those who make the decisions on deployment keep their children at home?
3. Are you satisfied with healthcare for the elite essential government employees that does not cover forty-six million Americans and wastes $600 billion per year on overmedication, re-hospitalization, and imprisonment of our elderly and disabled? While our government officials have full coverage and better benefits than any CEO while, making $50,000 more per year then private sector employees.
4. Are you supportive of a government that practices imperialism and setting up military governments under the guise of liberty, homeland security, a quality for all in pursuit of one world government called regime change, while spending endless resources on military weapons?
5. Are you satisfied with education for the elite that underfunds inner city schools for the sake of war and military buildup in uneducated countries and does not make a commitment to the workers that there will be affordable housing for all Americans? And with Congress and state legislatures continually upping their salaries regardless of the economy and rebase education on failing budgets, not GAAP budgetary outcome?
6. Do you accept that a military solution will win over oppressed and poverty-dominated dictators versus investment in economic infrastructures that create jobs and productive economies not building missile sites in and around Europe?
7. Are you convinced that our only solution to energy is to be self-reliant or fossil fuel free by 2050? Or maybe a consortium of USA, Canada, Japan, France, Italy, England, India and Mexico could control the distribution of world energy resources? Our own OPEC: oil purchasing economic control. Fossil fuels requiring oil must be replaced by natural gas so USA can be energy independent.

8. Are you convinced that the Middle East's (Arab) rejection of Israel is worth dying for ... when only reason minus religion = resolution? The Trump doctrine was to make peace not war and orchestrate a two-state solution to the Palestinian versus Israel crisis. That since has been reversed by the Biden administration and results in President Netanyahu being replaced by a moderate.

9. Do you believe national and world natural disasters (i.e., New Orleans, Hurricane Sandy, Takako, Miya go, Japan, Jakarta, Indonesia, earthquakes, tornados, floods) should be managed from Washington, D.C.?

   Or should a local TVA (Tennessee Valley Authority) approach employ teams from those areas, using those who have lost jobs, businesses, and futures to rebuild and restore the damage, funded by portions of the money being wasted on military buildup and destruction and rebuilding of Iraq? Shouldn't public works and inner-city rehabilitation infrastructure projects come first, not last?

10. Do you support a government that has twenty-two million Federal and state unionized, lionized employees who have sweet pensions, salaries and perks? Then mismanage $6 trillion Federal Budget and another $10 trillion State and Local Governments' budgets for the sake of special interest groups, academia, and lobbyists? While much needed social and medical research programs go under- or unfunded?

We are asked to choose, in an election year that proposes two establishment candidates who have little to no business qualifications, are a part of the problem, and only know how to govern with taxes and more laws. Well, I cannot and will not lower my standards and sell out to the elite. Isn't red, white, and blue indicative of needing a third party between the red party and blue party? Call it the swing vote **to break ties and prevent gridlock of the two-party system** at every level. A white party, no color of skin excluded or intended, or more appropriately the American Enterprise Party, standing for the working class, the entrepreneurs, and the risk takers. Not the risk makers, representing the lawyers who defend superfluous laws and never propose to get rid of those we don't need. Not the lawmakers, who have heaped 555,000 laws on us in the last twenty-four years and proposed over 40,000 in 2012 and pass thousands that dilute our Freedoms, all of which have to be funded through taxation and primarily debt.

America is in a bind big time, having a monetary system that allows the Federal Reserve to destroy the economy in seven months by doubling the Fed exchange rate (remember the S&L demise) in less than a year, causing a crash (depression) in the banking, capital markets, and housing industries under the guise of subduing inflation, (Under 5% at that time). Then taking credit for saving us by funding a $793 billion TARP paper Fed printing machine that further destroys our financial future. That, my friends, as the McCain Republicans would have us believe, was Mr. Greenspan's doings; however, my friends, Mr. Greenspan kept the books for nineteen years better than Bush and Bernanke could ever "cook them," with turn coat Treasury Secretary Paulson collaborating in the destruction of certain investment bankers that he hated and saved the ones that were "too big to fail", unto which, the big deficit spenders gave birth.

With the 2020 elections in the books and Donald Trump being unseated by Joe Biden both houses effectively are in Democrat's hands. Standing by are Chuck Schumer and Nancy Pelosi, second-guessing them-selves and wringing their hands, hoping no one realizes that Congress has historically spent us into a bankruptcy ... with Obama's eight years misspent naively feeding his ego with promises even God could not keep.

Why wasn't there talk about laying off some of the twenty-two million government workers or cutting Congress' salaries or foreclosing on the White House. Why? Because it is the problem of the middle-class homeowner-taxpayer, not the binary two-party establishment system we have fostered. Bankruptcy is not foreboding in our constitution ... yet. There is now chapter ten (eleven in the private sector) in the institutional parlance. But there is no legal process for the bankruptcy of a sovereign nation, so the technical answer to legality is no. But for necessity of saving our currency and control of the World Order we must have new blood leadership ... not 90% reelection of red and blue incumbents with a 12% satisfaction rating and then their heirs inheriting the mantel of money-tics governance that blinds our liberty and freedom.

My fellow Americans, as every president since Roosevelt has promised and never delivered, we need to reduce government, lower taxes, and not borrow to fund our future. Neither political party has delivered. Therefore, we need an alternative.

The American Enterprise Party is a sincere and effective third alternative to take the best of the current two-party establishment system and removes the worst to form a true political opportunity center for all classes in America. It goes beyond the influence or confluence of money, connections, and graft to open the future to the talents of all enterprising American citizens.

If you can work and want opportunity, then support this new concept. It embodies the American spirit of hard work, family security, and homeland peaceful coexistence that I call humanism. This is where the difference lies from the Democrats and Republicans, who represent serving the public left and right elite and then don't even listen to the public. You only get an ear if you are a major contributor with influence or a lobbyist with connections.

The new American Enterprise Party uses a platform of GAAP economics that funds the social and moral imperatives for citizens, which are:

- Enterprise employment for all.
- Quality education for all.
- Affordable housing for all.
- Stable family values for all.

- Quality health preservation and care for all.
- Peaceful coexistence for all.
- Participation in the political and governing process for all. American citizens (get rid of second and third generational domination of the Congress and state legislatures) and give to your party by being involved.

More importantly, will you support a third party that answers these questions with a "peaceful coexistence and a peace corps" approach to diluting terrorism and military conflicts? The economic solutions can and must bring peace, jobs, education, and housing to the people of the world or we will continue to have dictators, nuclear weapons, oppression, starvation, and control by the money managers and those that feed off unfeeling bureaucrats.

Do you think we can change the paradigm by using the voting blocs to move the opinion and attitude of Americans, so they influence the appointment of the President, the Congress, Governors, and local public officials? The following are the groups that can move us to a truer version of constitutional democracy that defends peace, not fighting for oil and gold for respect.

Voting blocs:

- 77 million baby boomers.
- 36 million AARP members.
- 40 million registered Republicans.
- 60 million registered Democrats
- 11.6 million union members.
- 1.7 million physicians.
- 2.0 million nurses and therapists.
- 20.5 million factory workers.
- 75 million foreign nationals (including 21 million illegal aliens).

- 46 million uninsured.
- 50 million underinsured.
- 75 million religious' factions.

My Vote, Your Vote

As an American voter, do you approve this message:

- We have not moved Iraq and Afghanistan to democracy.
- China, Iran, Russia, North Korea are our main enemies.
- Our base economy is solid, but our obligations are horrendous … the stock market isn't our report card.
- Healthcare must be universal.
- Homes must be available to all citizens and aspiring citizens.
- Education will be equal for all based on effort and talent.
- Jobs must always safe and sound as the backbone of our economy.
- The GAAP budget must be balanced.
- Gays can be married, transgenders are equal.
- There will be no illegal abortions.
- Guns for protection with policing as our life insurance.
- Criminals must pay for their crimes.
- We are not the world savior or liberator.
- Interest rates are for stabilizing investment capital not rewarding big banks for satisfying the bank examiners.
- Making sure our aging population is happy and doing well.
- Obesity is bad habits and a disease of the mind.
- China is not at our mercy since the US is not too big to fail.
- Illegal immigrants are not welcome … we must protect our borders and our national security free of imbedded terrorists.
- Saudi Arabia, Israel, Pakistan, and Argentina are our friends, or are they? If not, then a third-party swing vote **to break ties and prevent gridlock of the two-party system** at every level must

make sure our foreign affairs aren't based on foreign bribes or Hunter Biden's Lobbyist fee.

Hear me as a Democrat or Republican; there is no problem we can't solve, because as politicians and diplomats we are prone to cause the problem and then take credit for solving it; by keeping the masses at bay with lack of say and money. Just ask the Federal Reserve, that created the credit crisis by popping the derivative balloon and now wants to take credit for saving us by issuing paper instead of value from our GDP consumption driven economy.

Who are you kidding? The majority of rational voters don't really believe any of the rhetoric and approved messages, but we are kept at bay with town hall meetings because we have no say and inflated resources. Can we call our friendly senator? Hell no. Can we go see them and express our real opinion? Hell no. Not unless we throw real money their way. So, what can we do?

Well then, I, Jerry L. Rhoads as President and founder of the American Enterprise Party, make this proclamation:

- Iraq and the Arabs are not our problem unless we believe they are.
- American nationalism and regime change, and foreign aid is not working for us and never will.
- Our economy is weak and unstable due to poor leadership and cooking the books.
- Healthcare is wasteful due to paying for illness not wellness and is not solution driven but money driven.
- Homes and hope can be lost due to the Federal Reserve policies.
- Equality in education should come before wasteful defense spending on weapons of mass destruction.
- Jobs come from sound economic leadership, not protectionism; capital creates jobs, not politicians.
- The budget will never be balanced with attorneys and politicians

- passing laws and not un-passing laws and regulations to avoid building debt beyond the means of any future society to fund.
- Gays and transgender's have the right under the constitution and our democracy to choose their lifestyles.
- As do mothers or unwed women with unwanted pregnancies that must provide placement of the unborn and complete the adoption papers to do so,
- Why should everyone pack a gun if we have equal education, full employment, and a dynamic economy?
- We must become the leaders for peaceful coexistence and the pursuit of happiness.
- Interest rates must be a function of supply and demand, not bankers and speculators with elite-contrived theories about an enterprise they do not know how to run.
- We have to have legal immigration to replace our aging population and seek full employment with expanded enterprise and profitable businesses. But not the sanctuary for every refugee seeking the American Dream.
- Our aging Americans must support late retirement and self-health practices.
- Obesity is a disease of the mind due to inactivity and bad habits . . . it must be eradicated for Americans to thrive.
- New Orleans and the East Coast hurricanes must be rebuilt out of the savings from reduced wasteful spending for defense and congressional healthcare and pensions sweetheart-ism.
- China will own us if we keep borrowing from them and telling them where to go, ignoring their tactics in southeast Asia and the world of currency and trade.
- Any legal immigrant should be welcome if they pay taxes, speak English, and become a citizen, because we will need them to work to support the baby boomers who are seeking early retirement even though they cannot afford it (economically this keeps resources in this country to pay down State and Federal debt).

- Russia, Japan, China, India, South Korea, Mexico, Canada, should be our trading friends and, in a coalition, to control the world's energy sources, not just threatening the so-called axis of evil by building missile sites in Poland and South Korea.
- Israel needs to be on the side of peaceful coexistence within two state borders, even though they don't control the economics of the Middle East with their capitol in Jerusalem,

AXIS OF PEACE

Jesus Christ
A story much told
Seasons spiced
With legends old

It's told he was born
Like you and me
In the early morn
From Immaculate virginity

It's told he lived his mortal life
For his sisters and brothers
Enduring the cross's knife
As a sacrifice for others

It's told he died a poor man
With the richest epitaph of all
Known as the last command it's told
"The righteous star shall never fall"

It's told he rose to his beginning
From whence he was born
Having sacrificed for our sinning
He is forever the child of Christmas morn

The mortal guiding light
From God's only begotten son
The everlasting Star is Bright
A mortal game of chess he won

Against war and its upheaval
As cultures promoting violence
Labeled as Axis of Evil
Aka Russia, China and Jihadists

The Communist Dream suppresses freedoms as a sin

Lo it's true his star shines on
All faiths that believe war must cease
Labeled as Axis of Peace
Aka America, Ukraine, NATO, UN

The American Dream defends freedoms as a win

Ten more questions for the discriminating voter

1. Are you happy with attorneys running the country, making thousands of laws each year that require taxpayer money to fund with no laws being removed to lighten the load and balance the budget or second and third generation politicians controlling the economy, public institutions, and mail-in voting systems?
2. Do you support a government that is irresponsible by continually creating budget deficits of $6 trillion to $10 trillion per year and an accumulated deficit of $30 trillion ($158 trillion on the GAAP accrual basis) financed by selling our future to China, Japan, Saudi Arabia, Russia, South Korea, and others that have invested in U.S. Government securities for funding the budget shortfall and the trade deficit?

Pre Trump trade deficits:
- China trade deficit facts:
- August 2012, $44.4 billion.
- Annualized $532.8 billion.
  Japan trade deficit facts:
- February 2012, $19 billion.
  Total trade deficit for 2011:
- $560 billion.
- China alone, $295.5 billion.

Post Trump Trade deficit for 2020:
- Total trade deficit $66.61 billion per, month approaching $900 billion annually.
- China's share has decreased to $38 billion per month but still will top $600 billion per year.
- Japan $217 billion annually.

Effectively America is borrowing money to import foreign products to consume while the exporting countries are making money by importing or producing America's technology for export to America. They make money twice and are sinking our ship doing so. We must bring the supply lines back to America ASAP. The 39.9% Biden corporate tax rate is definitely a deterrent to keeping America Great.

More importantly, how do you feel about other countries owning the rights to our real estate and businesses due to irresponsible financial management if the federal government cannot service its debt; in other words, what happens if we cannot pay back the $28 trillion ($158 trillion when you add entitlements) in accumulated budget deficits and the accumulated trade deficits? President Trump was the first leader of the US that is a businessman who would have in time tamed the imbalance of trade with the rest of the world.

The Biden Harris administration is at the mercy of runaway trade deficits and have no acumen to slow down the exchange rates deterioration and monetary drain to Asian technology and foreign automobile companies. Fortunately, the NAFTA agreement was canceled but the shift of economic power is still going to Asian interests. The Trump Administration was getting close to a deal with China and the Asian consortium on trade, tariffs and balancing the America's deficit. Also, fortunately the trade pact between the US, Canada and Mexico was signed and ratified March 2020 just after the Pandemic closed the borders. Then Biden opened them wide for every conceivable race, religion, drug cartel, drug users, criminals, Covid carriers, human traffickers and masses of unaccompanied underage minors. At the same time the ICE patrol had their authority taken away with a moratorium on deportation. Insanity had been triggered by a crazy progressive view that this would feed their indiscriminating voting machines for taking back and keeping the White House at any cost. Of course, in the et tu Brute' process Trump was Dumped and Biden-Harris-Fauci skidded in on a Pandemic banana peel mail-in vote. Inheriting a false positive leadership role as the Wizard of Oz Biden and Dr. Fauci, his chief of fear, with Harris as Dorothy the border czar managed from behind the screen by the speech writer Bernie Sanders and the tin man Schumer and the Lion Pelosi, putting Toto in a dog pound on the farm owned by Aunt Em and Uncle Henry of the AOC squad.

3. Do you support the concept of human rights pushed upon other countries that we do not practice domestically or internationally (i.e., China, North Korea, Iran, Syria, and Russia)?

4. Do you believe that America has the exclusive right to nuclear weapons (WOMD), military buildup, and nuclear energy sources while wailing on other countries under the guise of fighting terrorism? Then defrocking the United Nations on solving these problems, while building missile sites in Poland. Trying to intimidate Russia, Iraq, Afghanistan and North

Korea with sanctions.

5. Are you for funding woke public education and social rehab programs using gambling and sin taxation (i.e., casinos, lotteries, smoking, sin taxation, etc.)? Are you in favor of selling our tollways, ports, airports to foreign investors then leasing them back to collect a hidden tax from our taxpayers? Resulting in inflated pricing to make a profit off the American taxpayer.

6. Are you for having a country being ruled by Big Box, Big Tech, Big Pharma, Big Media as the Brotherhood and special-interest groups for the sake of their agendas. Such as the Progressive Party, Democratic party, Republican party, green party, constitution party, libertarian party etc. Using the congressional committee structure that promotes their own party on the basis of tenure and patronage which puts our country in the hands of *elito-crats* who do not reflect the opinion or priorities of the enterprising American public?

7. Are you impressed by elections that are based on negative TV advertising, digging up dirt to avoid substance because there is no depth to the candidates except their ability to raise MBZ's (millions of billions and zillions) to run? What happened to public service for the sake of the public?

8. Are you happy with the money managers, committee chairman, stock markets having all the say when it comes to social and economic issues (problems) that impact every American? While insider trading is rampant during a bullish stock market with the Pelosi's and Schumer's profiting in the millions by buying and selling hot and cold stocks such as Robin and such short sales stocks.

9. Are you willing to stay uninvolved because you don't want to make waves or have the money or afraid to stick your neck out?

10. Most importantly, do you have any degree of confidence that your say or vote really counts when it comes to policy?

In reality, the last two questions are the first questions that the public must answer if we are to be able to form a third party and change the *Animal Farm* (George Orwell's roadmap to cultural warfare) and 1984 form of government to an enterprising government for the people, by the people, and of the people!

In my opinion, if you accept

1. That two-party establishment system is working and,
2. That our leaders have the health, education, and welfare of the majority of middle-class, ordinary, hardworking Americans in their minds when they vote and,
3. That our leaders are not practicing "feed the hand that got you there," and,
4. That our leaders rating at the polls are not their accountability standards, "to just go along to get along".

   ... you have been bamboozled.

You now work for the new form of progressive socialism that just burst our economic bubble because we taxpayers were overheating the economy. *Ha*, what a way to keep us scared and working harder. Just ask yourself, do you really think the following officials represent your personal views? Can you get them on the phone or by mail and voice your opinion?

- Bush(es), Kennedy(ies), Romney, Daley(s).
- Dole(s), Gore(s), Gingrich(s), Clinton(s).
- Grassley(s), Rangel(s), Thompson(s), Blagojevich(es).
- Obama, McCain, Cheney, Palin, Trump.
- Bidden, Harris, Pelosi, Schumer, McConnel, Sanders, Warren, Fauci or AOC and her Squad.

Or do they misrepresent their own intentions and practices for the sake of what Sam Rayburn suggested to LBJ, "go along to get along," because America has lost its founding principles to money-tics. Six or nine hundred billion dollars spent to elect a president and almost a trillion spent to keep the public at bay is what we now have. While letting our slums fester, our unemployed and uneducated kill each other, touting Lotto as the way out, legalizing casinos on every block, legalized recreational marijuana, outsourcing our parking meters and tollways to foreign investors, legalizing the manufacture and sale of assault weapons, creation of weapons of mass destruction under the guise of combating terrorism, frisking every child and adult before they board an airplane, letting the Internet promote pornography and violence. Is this really what the majority of Americans want? Or is "Washington Burning" Roman Style?

GO ALONG TO GET ALONG

Sam Rayburn gave this lore
To President Lyndon Johnson as the only
choice When he became a Senator
If he wanted a voice

Go along to get along

Have you ever come upon a problem
Rather than face it head on
You put a bridge over it
Until its gone

Maybe you have or not
That's been my ploy to plot
By calling a problem an issue
So I can bury the result in a tissue

This is called that human way
Pacify the politicians say
Don't confront
That impossible stunt

You'll only waste away your desire
To fight fire with fire
To me this is building bridges too long
When you have to circumvent the right for the wrong

Why not meet that obstacle head on
Closing the night and raising the dawn
Surely this is the way to honesty
Thereby avoiding the temptation to serve only me

Along life's path there are many bridge builders
Calling themselves coy for their story that bewilders
What has become of good intentions to seek
Truth and goodwill without fear to speak

Have we gone so far as monogamy to fool a girlfriend
Without caring who what or when
If we have we're foolish for as even a dog knows
You can fear the Wiley Coyote despite
The color of his clothes

Funny it's not but surely, we've known lies
As a horse feels fear on his thighs
Those bridge builders so adept
May fall for truth if its kept

I'm not saying don't feel an understanding
Just know where you start and why you're landing
And your bridges won't be too long
They'll be fair and founded on strong

To get along to go along

An infrastructure and security partisanship
Righting any wrong
Preventing gamesmanship
Just to go along to get along

If not, have you tried to call, write, or speak personally to your senator or representative (Federal or State or Local) about these problems (not their issues and disagreements among themselves) only to get a twenty-nine-year-old aide who is a recent graduate of Georgetown Law School, who takes notes and buries your input? Well, I have and that is why I have formed the American Enterprise Party as a third swing vote alternative that listens to the majority, not the elite minority.

That could change the questionable voting systems and solve problems, not just tweak the policies by debating the issues between the red and the blues. That will fix problems, not just talk about the "party line" perception of the issues. Interestingly, issues are disagreements among the "haves," not solutions to problems of the "have-nots," and our current establishment politicians' dwell on issues, not problem solving, because they are the problem. That's applying "go along to get along" politics at its worst.

Ironically, our deposed President Donald J. Trump, an excellent businessman, broke the chain of established politicians but they in turn broke his back with the good ole boy tactic of harvesting votes and choosing to believe a conniving scientist covering his butt ... effectively we have been Fauched. No, there is no doubt that the Democrats, with complicity of Republicans, and Dr. Fauci and Vice President Pence's bureaucratic task force, using a 100-year-old Corona China virus to roll out uncontrolled mail-in, drop box and harvested voting that threw our nation's future out with the 80 million harvested mail-in-votes, that Trump predicted would sink his reelection and our ship ... which it did.

In retrospect if President Trump would have had an ounce of humility, he would still be our President… based on results he was a 9 as a rally cheerleader an 8 and as a head coach at best a 1 when selling his plan and building on a winning team. It was all about his "accomplishments" that he thought had already put him on Mount Rushmore. Even Lincoln wouldn't beat him out for the fifth spot.

We now have the same ole attorney, senator, politician Biden mismanaging America in a hurricane of debt and deficits compounded by 330 million people growing at the rate of 10 to 15 million legal and undocumented illegal immigrants in the next decade.

America, the preemptive leader of the free enterprise world, with its enterprising workers, is in an identity and economic war with itself for peace and prosperity. Pogo said it best, "I looked for the enemy and found it is us."

Will former President Donald Trump run again in 2024. In my book Americana, Page Publishing 2016 he does run and is beaten by Andrew Cuomo and Hilary Clinton as his running mate. I was certainly wrong about that pair but not about President Trump's resurrection to prominence in the following excerpt from that novel revisiting George Orwell's 1984 in 2084.

> CNN/FOX News (2024) – Former President Trump, having recovered completely from his stroke changes his Republican Party affiliation to the new American Enterprise third party due to the total failure of the Republican Congress to pass legislation to downsize government and upsize enterprise. Due to the disruption in the Republican leadership, presidential candidate Donald Trump lost the 2024 election to Andrew Cuomo, a democrat from NY and his running mate Hillary Clinton. He managed to pull 25% of the vote and Congress remained Democrat and perpetuated the ineffectiveness of two-party politics.
>
> President Trump and the American Enterprise Party, as swing vote party, garnered 25 percent of the electoral college votes putting the two-party system in jeopardy. The new third party then called for

constitutional amendments on redistricting the Electoral College. Former President Trump presented the American Enterprise Party's platform to the voters in a formal presentation on C-SPAN, CNN, Fox News, Facebook, YouTube and Google News: resulting in the Preamble to the American Enterprise Party

We, as the representatives of enterprising Americans, who need fair representation, form a contrasting political party that moves America away from the great society programs to a freedom to work for the values assured by the American constitution and to have the following equal rights and opportunities that best serve enterprising Americans' 'sovereignty and preserve health, happiness, and prosperity for all:

Which, I paraphrase in the book, the American Enterpris4e Party representation, boils down to having equal freedom to speak, vote, education, work, pay my share, reproduce, have a family, a home, a future and as a voter have an input on our countries policies and regulations, so help me God.

SUM UP OF THIS ARTICLE:

How can we not have a third party to keep the other two parties functional and honest? No different than a referee or umpire. Two stripes in our flag and government is like two strikes and we are out of positive partisan decisions that affect us all. Do away with tenure in committees and subcommittees and deal with problems not issues. Then "Get along to go along" is the motto not the reverse. Then everyone's vote gets something rather than no one getting anything but just another failed Roman Empire.

YOUR VOTE COUNTS

Article Nine

... Leadership, American Creed and Patriotism

Who Captains the Ship?

- Why would we reelect the very parties that got us into a bankrupt position?
- Why would we believe that the red and the blue parties act in our best interests?
- Why would we choose to bank our future on the past faults of these establishment elitists?
- Why wouldn't we find someone that represents enterprising Americans?
- Why wouldn't we vote for enterprising officials?
- Why wouldn't you now Vote for someone that believes in Humanism and peaceful coexistence for a better good. Someone that is a dark horse from the middle American independent philosophy who has been one of the enterprising Americans that pay all the bills, creates the wealth for the elite Few and as the Many, want opportunity to live well, sleep well and be happy.

Who would you choose to lead the great America enterprise away from debt, deficits and cancel culture towards peaceful coexistence where capitalism and progressive socialism are not competitors but partners in pursuit of humanism?

I repeat, since the advent of the Great Society Programs, we have evolved into a culture of violence, vulgarity and disproportionate excesses of prosperity divided by politics and media. I believe this is due to the failure of the leadership of our two parties, practicing money-tics that blinds our Statue of American liberties that enterprise values guarantee us.

Ask yourself, as a voter who would you pick a "better Red than dead pragmatic Republican" or a "Blue blood bleeding-heart phlegmatic Democrat" … or an "enterprising market driven American Enterprise Party Humanitarian" that wants every American citizen to be successful and healthy in pursuing the American Utopian Dream.

CURRENT CAPTAINS

Joseph R. Biden, Current President,
Harris, Pelosi, Schumer, Sanders,
Warren, the Squad

FORMER CAPTAINS

Donald J. Trump, Past President Pence,
McConnel, McCarthy, Pompeo,
Mnuchin, Barr

Existing Qualifications: wealthy, over 35years of age, a citizen, a resident for at least 15 years, a Harvard trained attorney, a career "go along to get along" politician. Donald Trump broke the barrier by running a business while the rest are law makers and regulators at best. It became evident with the election of a businessman we were finally in the problem-solving mode for jobs, equal trade and foreign policy agreements. And he was disgraced for acting like a businessman in the arena of World trade, foreign affairs, national security, patriotism, military and defense. He made enemies on both sides of the aisle tweeting his way through a Pandemic and bad press and fake news losing a questionable mail-in voting election with 75 million Red voters demanding a second term and the 81+ million Blue voters wondering who's on first.

Because Biden wasn't their first choice, not even last choice but the only choice. Now they are wondering, will he last four years, after a basement campaign and a teleprompter as his safety blanket. Using the Biden-Sanders play book (manifesto) it appears that all of Trump's gains swill be reversed as America's future wains into self-destruction.

With 70 executive orders and policies further sinking the financial ship, an ill-advised $1.9 trillion pork barrel liberal anchor (on top of $3.9 trillion stimulus thumb in the dike) plus job killing cancellation of the Keystone pipeline is further sinking the hopes of our legalized citizens. Since Biden and Sanders want open borders as a wing and prayer approach to legal immigration and legalized blue sanctuary cities and States lining up every refugee in the world that will be coming to our doorstep wanting in to share in the spoils that aren't there. This, and the Afghanistan debacle, increases the risk of terrorists, drug dealers, super spreaders of the Pandemic, embedding themselves into our society for later voting and revolutionary activities. Who wins? Americans or the cartels, the Marxists, the terrorists, the communists, the fascists or the environmentalists? Or is it President Biden, as the appeaser, pleaser, geezer for his son Hunter's money laundering schemes?

Now the Republicans, asleep at the switch, find that the transformation crew of Biden, Harris, Pelosi, Schumer, AOC has blown the country wide open for takeover by revolutionaries from both sides of the aisle. Marxist BLM, ANTIFA, progressive liberals on the left and WLM white lives matter too, conservatives, evangelicals, the stock market and the Fed on the right both declaring gridlock, filibuster, vaccination mandates, and fake news for their 2022 mid-terms and 2024 elections. Fake news is designed to kill the factual pursuit of mass media and daily news. Freedoms are subverted into attacks on the greater good. The identity is assigned to individuals regardless of underly facts, as white supremist, racist, anti towards collective pluralism. That we will do together, it then destroys the past with the new socialism of new government-based news media.

It's no longer the Red Republicans against the Blue Democrats that tell voters what to do. It's the Big Tech, Big Box service businesses that produce no GNP that have the power of the dollar and internet for political influence. With those opponents nobody wins and the country continues to spiral into violence, vulgarity, excessive wealth of the Few, deficit spending, 1,000 billion here and a 1,000 billion there according to Everett Dirksen is a LOTTO debt that is certain bankruptcy.

Oh, and also with HR1, S1 and ranked voting bills sanctioning mail in voting, drop boxes and harvesting votes, sixteen-year-old voters and more legal or illegal immigrants of color there are more new voters to keep the Blues in charge forever. With the green new deal, tax hikes, cancel culture approach to endemic racism, a packed supreme court to overturn Roe v Wade, govern without the filibuster and changes to the electoral college brings America to the doorstep of the ten planks of Marxism to dump capitalism as our future Americania (Orwell's version of Oceania in 1984). AKA as totalitarianism.

What are Biden's qualifications, 47 years in Senate, 4 years as Vice President. Per the Epoch Times, historically he spent two years in third grade after being determined below average intelligence. His college grades and class standing were barely passing. He finished near the bottom of his law school class and admitted to plagiarism and received an F in a particular class for doing so. Plagiarism has been alleged numerous times including his 2021 inauguration speech using President Clinton's saying "And we'll lead not merely by the example of our power but by the power of our example" and in campaign speeches use of Lincoln's "of better angels of our nature" and use of Lincoln's characterization as America's discourse not leading to "disunion" and Obama's "doesn't see Red states and blue states, only sees the United States" in the inauguration speech. A proven weak and demented mind proves a weak man inside, isn't up to the job.

Kamala Harris on the other hand graduated from Howard University and the University of California, Hastings College of Law. She was elected as Vice President after a lifetime of public service. Prior to that she was elected District Attorney of San Francisco in 2003. In 2010 She was elected California's Attorney General and over saw the largest state justice department in the country. In 2017 she was sworn into the U.S. senate. During the campaign of 2020 she was cast aside early on but ginned up her resume by being both an Asian and Afro American and also use her gender to garner second in command. Neither President Biden or Vice President Harris have ever had real job experience in enterprise or the private sector. Her performance through the first 800 days has been rated as poor with a incompetent response to being assigned by the Wizard of Oz to deal with the open border crisis and to date has done nothing to slow the tidal wave of illegals coming in at the rate of 200,000 per month ... she giggles anytime she is challenged on her performance ... and is another plagiarizer using the Martin Luther King story about saying as a baby all she wanted was "freedom." Since then, she has disappeared behind the "teleprompter" government scene.

If you are a tried-and-true blue or red voter you've taken sides before and after the election while the middle is wondering who captains, the ship and where are we headed with the government taking away more and more of our personal decisions. Maybe with the after math of the Pandemic we will have to measure the captains based on results not party affiliation.

It's either America the Great American Enterprise will overcome Big Brother and the Brotherhood, or it succumbs to overreach by government, as Orwell predicts for Oceania in 1984. Then saves the planet from the China Virus and cloning as Huxley predicted in "A Brave New World". If not, we cannot survive or pay for this much government with no fiscal accountability for our leaders acts. As the very essence of our constitution states neither of those two alternatives can happen if we have a third-party swing vote **to break ties and prevent gridlock of the two-party system** at every level, holding the other two parties accountable for their extreme policies and results.

DARK HORSE (DH) WHITE HOUSE

*Ride a dark horse
Seek a White House*

*Chain a trigger
Rope an elephant
Kiss a Cobra
Fight a Gorilla*

*Who are you kidding
When you're a dark horse
As if you're bidding
And gambling against the House*

*It's a loser's hand they say
Stakes too high
Pick 'em up and back away
For it could be do or die*

*Out front are the money players
Holding pat to hands of gold
Not even the Pope's prayers
Could force them to fold*

Running up the polls
Taking down the competition
Most chasing the leaders paying their tolls
Chancing logic with reason

Thinking possibly just maybe
A fast-dark horse
Could catch up on his own money
By engaging the Hispanic force

Build a fence
Make them pay
Never did make sense
Until he'd said he's doing it anyway

Dirty money, drug funding
Even the Clintons got clean
Before being caught under dunning
Allegations of the White-Water scene

The Dark Horse pursues White House superiority
A beacon in the scenario
When the beam of the silent majority
Lit up his Sombrero

Mexico decided to step up
And play the big game
Rolling the dice into a cup
Of the Dark Horse with no name

Now running to and not from
Passing the faster horses on the rail
To fight the forces of the Kingdom
The Dark Horse pledged his tail

The race got close and mean
All the other horses ganged upon
The Dark Horses' Queen
Tearing her apart before dawn

She gave in to the masses
Exposing the Dark Horse to blight
No longer kicking asses
DH fell out of sight

The campaign came and went
DH rode in on the wind as a stag
Without the Party's consent
He held up the third-party flag

No longer was it just
The red and the blue
It was another party thrust
Into something brand new

When the election was enforced
It was the White House
Needing the Dark Horse
To out run the rest of the course

The moral to this story is
Give the Donald a chance
To do his show biz
And he will win the Big Dance

So the Dark Horse can prance
Taken down by Fauci to steal his second chance

THE WORLD IS SHOUTING

The world is shouting for leadership
For a dynamic captain of the trip
The masses crowd around
Rally against those dictating the crown

They're looking for someone who can show
Them how to run and let freedom grow
And take it or leave it to a gun
Or controlling the grueling sun

Towards a worthwhile earth
Befitted with comfortable worth
Tough few are willing to step out front
To use their shield to absorb the brunt

Most want to stay back in the pack
With full bellies and an unthreatened sack
What the world needs most is leadership
Someone to take the reins and the helm of the ship

Guiding them through those rocks
The canals and the locks
Into the quiet peaceful sea
Where all can feel the joys of being free

What the world needs most is a courageous quest
It needs those who are willing to risk
Themselves for the sake of being blest
With the responsibility to lead in the midst

And the teeth of the storm
But still keep their attitude and ploys
Somewhat warm but above scorn
This is truly separating men from the boys

Without the sin of the military toys
And sinister weakness of what it deploys
For if you're going to accept and step with the baton
You must be willing to take on the bomb

When your defenses are gone unwilling
And if God's willing you to avoid the killing
And standup for the pyramid of life
Having led the troops through the battle and strife

Hail to the leader
Society's entrepreneur and feeder
Hail to the chief
Hail to the one who could absorb the grief

Of being alone
Yet being the granite and the stone
Upon which the institutions of life are shorn
While heroes are made the leader is born

Is Donald Trump or Joe Biden this leader

Does he have the courage to be honest
Sincere without fear of conquest
While upholding America's quest …
Land of the free and the best

If your answer is yes you must vote
If your answer is no you are the heir of Billy's goat

Trump, stump, grump never humble or hip
All rhyme with Trump's persona to gamble the ship
Biden the appeaser, geezer, pleaser for bigger is better
What is the true man demented or a gloating go-getter?

To find out we may have to put someone else in command
How about the giggler Kamala the Czar of the open borders? No way you say, maybe...

More than likely as a third-party dispatcher
We need our own Margret Thatcher
Who is quoted as saying ...
"Socialists traditionally make a financial mess
They always run out of (OPM) other peoples' money"
Putting the honey before the Queen bee's nest
And the King's conquest

While Enterprising Americans, voting for the American Enterprise Party, want to be the best

Vote for the American Enterprise Party candidate.

Can a dark horse third party win an election in a free country and a land of opportunity? Probably not, unless the country is bankrupt and continues to slide into mediocrity due to complacency, as we are right now. In 1992 Perot purchased a place in the race as the Reform Party then bowed out when the heat got too hot for, he and his wife, and was accused of mudding the waters so Clinton got elected over the incumbent Republican. Since, a third-party candidate hasn't threatened any race in any State or Federal office except for Bernie Sanders, who has declared a Social Democrat, only to lose to Hillary Clinton, a progressive and now dark horse Joe Biden supposedly a moderate.

How do they stack up as a replacement for a President Trump who stepped on the ruling classes' toes but was very effective in problem solving versus compromising on the issue of the day?

Even then the Trump rally train was off its track where, currently the USA has negative net worth, negative working capital, inability to cover debt service out of net income, and is deferring trillions in liabilities to the future. He basically, didn't enunciate a distinct plan for draining the swamp and killing the woke alligators. As a result, both parties have knowingly let a gridlocked uni-party Congress cook the books, accelerating tax collections and deferring payments, then borrowing the difference. This is the definition of insolvency that in business circles results in bankruptcy. This usually requires a Chapter 11 plan (Chapter 10 for government entities) of quasi-reorganization if the organization is to survive. This has been Trump's modius operandi when he overextended in his peripheral casino and golf course business outside the real estate side of those risky ventures.

Then, if we don't raise some equity capital from investors or generate corporate profits, we are destined to liquidate our natural resources to our creditors. How do I know Chapter 11 ... well like most entrepreneurs I have been that route and have thrived again despite perceived failure by my competitors? The bankruptcy code is unique to American businesses ... for the very reason that America may have to choose that route, though not legally ... just fail to pay entitlements and defer, defer, defer ... requiring tax and more taxation to hold off Chinese US Treasury bond holders by creating a 100-year bond instrument to defer debt to the next century, an idea of our new Secretary of the Treasury and former Fed Chain-woman, Janet Yellen. (That's an American Nightmare killing off the American Dream for the rest of the 21st century).

If the red and blue parties want to dwell on issues, not problems, and detract and deflect by trying to reinterpret the constitution, let the white party (the dominant stripe in the flag, not the color of skin) move in front of the majority as a swing vote **to break ties and prevent gridlock**

of the two-party system at every level and lead America back into the black (not the color of skin, but being financially solvent). To do this, we must be proactive and also move past the independents, the Green Party, the Tea Party, the Constitution Party, the Green Party, the Libertarian Party, the Communist Party, the Socialist Party, the Workers Party, the Whigs, etc.

These are all founded on economic control, not on enterprise. Ninety percent of Americans are enterprising but not represented economically. Go to the American Enterprise Party blog and web site to read about a real reorganization of America and avoid the fall of the Great American Enterprise. www.americanenterprisepolitcalparty.org .

"On the right you have the pragmatics, the aggressors, the opportunists, the elites from Yale and on the left you have the progressives, dreamers, intellectuals, theorists, professors, legal gurus, constitutionalists and in between you have those poor undesirables who are hard-working middle class, hoping for a chance at the pragmatic like American Dream." Quote by a professor of economics that is truly a visionary for the American enterprise movement.

This same economics professor made a statement that he had never failed a single student before, but had once failed an entire class that insisted that Obama's socialism worked and that no one would be poor and no one would be rich, a great equalizer. The professor then said, "OK, we will have an experiment in this class on the Obama's plan". All grades would be averaged and everyone would receive the same grade so no one would fail and no one would receive an A . . .

After the first test, the grades were averaged, and everyone got a B. The students who studied hard were upset and the students who studied little were happy. As the second test rolled around, the students who studied little had studied even less and the ones who studied hard decided they wanted a free ride too so they studied little. The second test average was a D! No one was happy. When the 3rd test rolled around, the average was an F.

As the tests proceeded, the scores never increased as bickering, blame and name-calling all resulted in hard feelings, and no one would study for the benefit of anyone else. All failed, to their great surprise, and the professor told them that socialism would also ultimately fail because when the reward is great, the effort to succeed is great but when government takes all the reward away, no one will try or want to succeed.

As the late Adrian Rogers said, "you cannot multiply wealth by dividing it." And as the dark horse supporter Jerry Rhoads says "how can we be better if we're all the same sitting at home afraid to take a risk in a risk-taking world of free enterprise…?"

Right now, our enterprise ship captain is Joseph Biden a 47-year establishment Senator, Kamala Harris, the giggler, a career liberal politician, and imperialist Nancy Pelosi, a sulky Chuck Schumer, has been Bernie Sanders, professor Elizabeth Warren all lifers and grifters in the game of money-tics that blinds voters to the intrinsic value of liberty and freedom of free market enterprise. Will we be safe with the bureaucracy growing faster than the business, with governance by philosophy rather than practical management of the Great American Enterprise, built by risk taking entrepreneurs not politicians or regulators.

Will build back bigger government be better or is the economics professor right that you cannot multiply wealth by dividing it among those who don't contribute effort and then take advantage of opportunity that America promises. For the first lesson in financial failure by the establishment two parties go to the US debt clock app www.usdebtclock.org for a vision of a country on the verge of imploding and our nearest competitor China exploding.

Does it bother you that the 40 to 70 executive orders signed by our new captain and his crew will make the debt clock burst at the seams and swamp the swamp with new woke alligators as a bankrupt economy and financial condition take decades to repair, if at all. As they say in sporting circles, maybe we need a different quarterback and a GAAP generally accepted accounting system because we have been losing ground since Roosevelt, who started us towards the progressive and socialistic nightmare, rather than the American Dream as pitched by all the Democrats and Republicans for a century.

If the red and blue parties want to dwell on issues, not problems, and detract and deflect by trying to reinterpret the constitution, cancel our culture then let the white stars and stripes party (the dominant stripe in the flag, not the color of skin) move in front of the majority and lead America back in the black (not the color of skin but being financially solvent). To do this, we must be proactive and move past the wavering Independents, the Green Party, the Tea Party, the Constitution Party, the Libertarian Party, the Socialist Party, by being founded on economic and financial control and become the swing vote **to break ties and prevent gridlock of the two-party system** at every level in the Senate and House as the American Enterprise party. I repeat, it splits the independents away from the Democrats and the Republicans to join the swing vote **to break ties and prevent gridlock of the two-party system** at every level so neither has a majority. So, a third party does not assure any of the three parties a 51% majority allowing for the filibuster to hopefully mean better legislation and laws.

Ninety percent of enterprising Americans aren't represented economically. Go to the www.americanenterprisepolicalparty.org to read about a real reorganization of America to avoid the rise and fall of the Great American Enterprise.

I reiterate: It's as simple as bringing capitalism and socialism together into an Enterprise party that collaborates in unison making hay with our successful business enterprises every day. It takes capital to start and sustain an enterprise and it takes human capital competing to make it work. So, we effectively, as a third-party, have found the secret to consensus between capitalism and socialism driven by humanism to downsize government and upsize enterprise.

What if we vote for the third-party candidate?

I liken the current situation in American politics and business to the one depicted by Orwell in *Animal Farm* (and later *1984)* where the dictator (Donald Trump) is run off the farm so the smarter boars and pigs (Biden, Harris, Pelosi, Schumer, AOC and the Squad) could garner the support of the comrades for equality until the farm could not meet its output quotas, and then it becomes a socialist state until the farm no longer could afford to pay equitable wages, and then it becomes a Fascist state to control the underpaid and unpaid workers. Then due to the need to trade with their neighbors, the elite intellectual management teamed up with the other dictator farmers for the good of the Few owners, not the greater good of the worker animals. Sounds strangely familiar, doesn't it?

Also, In Orwell's book 1984 about a dystopian government run by Big Brother and the Brotherhood, he portrays a society that is controlled by mind alteration and fear. Destroying freedom and the will of the people to fight back for the sake of relationships, personal opportunity and love of family that sustains wellbeing. It then becomes a society of human robots. Where:

- **War is Peace**
Ignorance is Strength
Slavery is Freedom

Also, in the book "A Brave New World" Aldous Huxley predicts a dystopian society that does away with gender and diversity by using manufactured birthing and human development to eliminate issues (problems) of human interactions. To test this on a village of savages (BLM and ANTIFA) it was the plan to convert it in an evolutionary model to The Brave New World. Once exposed to this plan, the vector of change was the Savage of the Old World was to embrace and accept the brave new utopia ... but suddenly he realizes the love of his life and his old-world ways were the victim and takes his own life rather than be the benefactor of this version of the Brave New World.

As an example: Our Congress during the Great Recession of 2007 misused the monetary resources by taking taxpayer money and gambling them away on our capital system. Then blames Wall Street (our enterprise system) for the problems that the Federal Reserve caused by playing Russian roulette with the exchange rates for member banks. Then had the US Treasury fund those "too big to fail" with borrowed money from China and newly printed loans to the Government, that we do have an updated version of 1984. Also, we have a Brave New World of finance and a dystopian version of 1984 justifying how Big Brother miscalculates and covers it up with the Brotherhood of Big Banks and Big Business.

Then we dissipate capital and devalue the housing market to save the stock market, investment and corporate giants causing America's consumption-based economy to spiral downward. Not the Great Recession but the Depression of 2007. To correct this mistake, the Bush and Obama Administrations fertilized the economy with borrowed stimulus funds that flowed readily downward to member banks to stop the spiral. Rather there were reforms that sucked more tax dollars upward and printed more borrowed dollars for stimulating public service projects, depriving corporate giants of investment capital for spending on research and development of products for small business, that essentially crashed our gross national product, stock market, personal home values and retirement 401k plans. As a result, the two parties failed to downsize government and privatize our institutions, using capital infusions from the wealthy tax payers and their foundations.

As government forces resources upward, business shrinks; as resources are disbursed downward, business thrives. In the middle you have the enterprising American's, the wage earners, the taxpayers, the consumers, the risk-takers, the entrepreneurs, the voters without a true representation of their efforts, needs, and dreams. Also, a loose Biden illegal immigration policy and weak protection of our border's sovereignty shall dilute the pursuit of opportunity promised in our constitution. Until attaining citizenship, a legal immigrant must speak our national language and submit competitive qualifications for the job opening and employment, compared to an aspiring candidate with or without a green card.

Therefore, we need to downsize government and upsize enterprise using the principles of a successful business. This great American society can only prevail if we need to decentralize and seed downward monetary resources to the individual brains, hearts, and souls. The great American Dream can only be stimulated if we guard the monetary seeds do not squander or smother them using the Federal Reserve as savior and the American dollar as the victim of inflation and wasteful government policies.

Government is necessary to percolate our economy, not overregulate it. Government is only necessary to protect the individual's rights to be free to think, work, and succeed as the seed for evolutionary GDP growth.

Government is necessary to define the greater good, not enforce it; recognize the good, not divorce it; organize our defense, not build fences against it. Government must be founded on the participation of the private sector, not the wasteful and inappropriate nesting of public officials.

Government must not exceed the authority of the individual's rights and freedom to choose and live a fruitful life without regard to color, creed, religion, sex, gender, or will birth, with the opportunity to attain an education, a job, a home, a future, and a say in their governance.

THE FREEDOM TO BE YOU

Ours is the right to be alive
Ours is the right to think for ourselves
Ours is the right to live
Our life as we decide

Ours is the right to be good or bad
And to protect those that tried
But were bound to lose
Their freedom to choose

Ours is the right to earn our daily bread
Ours is the right to forgive trespasses
Ours is the right to avoid temptation
Ours is the right to forgive transgressions

And deliver ourselves from evil
By freedom to change

Ours is the kingdom, the power
The glory forever
Ours is God in heaven peace on earth
Good will to ourselves and others
(As you treat yourself you treat as brothers)

The freedom to be you

Then heaven comes to earth
For those that have peace
Theirs is the heaven of a peaceful mind
A peaceful kingdom
A peaceful power in kind
A peaceful glory that is won

With the freedom to learn and earn a career
By fighting the war for one's self-worth
Winning the freedom from fear
By the hope of peace on earth
Good will to (men) who fight sin
And protect to win

Our Father's Kingdom
The Power
And the Glory
Forever
Amen

(Then I am an enterprising citizen of America
the great American Enterprise)

Why must we reform our existing government and the exercise of destroying the great society for Congress' piety? We need to preserve our past and improve the future:

1. Government must be returned to "of the people, by the people, for the people" (town hall government is not what we need or want).
2. Downsize the government and privatize certain of our institutions so we save our economy. Money is not the reason we work but the result of our freedom and opportunity to succeed on our own entrepreneurial and democratic will.
3. Give peace a chance. The militarization of our foreign policy must be directed as peacemakers, not peace for-sakers.
4. Redirect foreign aid to domestic aid to seed our small businesses, the jobmakers for renewal of our inner cities using enterprise and opportunity zones.
5. Replace the moniker of lawmakers with jobmakers by reducing encumberment and confinement of the flow of capital for enterprise designed regulations.

6. Tax net worth (a reinvestment of capital to pay down debt using wealth as the basis), not forty-six different facets of taxing the enterprising workers to seed the wasteful, dominant, ineffective, and uncaring government.
7. Replace the Federal Reserve Bank with the US Treasury Department that won't gamble taxpayer money to control the economy and destroy supply and demand. Save the honor of the dollar by stimulating the economy using generally accepted accounting principles for our taxation and budgeting systems.
8. Privatize the promotion of a healthy America. It should be the individual who internalizes the cost and determines if the pricing provides a quality outcome in relation to the price, not the Government payer. We must stop overmedicating and underdiagnosing health problems and pay for outcomes, not just incomes.
9. Reorganize the electoral process so the majority rules and encourage the expression of the third-party voice as the middle stripe between the red and blue stripes a binary (gridlock conspiracy) in the American flag.
10. Elect government officials at all levels based on problem-solving initiatives, not speeches on issues between the red and blue stripes' domination of our disappearing individualized spirit.
11. Direct the fifty governors that we want them to take up enterprise over regulations as their banner, eliminating all obstacles to our future GNP. Basing it on enterprise, not sin taxation, gambling tax, sale and lease back of American property to foreign interests, managed competition, and indiscriminate public costs for pensions, perks, special deals for state officials.
12. Create a list of enterprise analytics for evaluating the success of each State in comparison to other States, giving out Gold Stars to those State who excel at governance and economics by producing profits and surpluses for their citizens. For example, comparative, crime rate, abortion rate, teen pregnancies, number of guns, graduation rate, GDP rate, surplus, research and development.

In summary, we must act now before we become an impure version of other great societies that failed to reverse the dominance of the many by a few. The opportunity is the vitality of the enterprising American for the youth, the elderly, the disabled, the dreamers, the entrepreneurs, and the seekers of peace.

Therefore, the voter must take a personal interest and an active part in our governance. The proposed platform of the American Enterprise Party is based on the constitutional rights to pursue individual opportunities for work, education, housing, procreation, lifestyle, and the pursuit of happiness. To do this, 50 percent of Congress and legislature in the country need to be seated by the private sector.

We must move away from any ideology that dissipates our American Enterprise. We must honor it for the sake of individual rights to decide, ability to perform, desire to procreate, receive equal opportunity for housing, education, and jobs. We must again fertilize our economy with the American enterprise principles constituted by Washington, Lincoln, Jefferson, Hancock, Franklin, Adams, Henry, etc. As they envisioned, there would be new blood infused by the voters, so all aspects of the nation would be duly represented. Those rights no longer exist, nor will they again until we interject opposing alternatives.

New jobs, lower taxes:

Every political ad by career politicians promises more jobs and lower taxes but status quo on our existing strategy of deregulation to save us from ourselves, using a state of fear as the tactic. But they do not propose any real solution to the current depression of small business. That's where the job losses due to the Pandemic are the most compelling, and according to HOYLE that is where the job increases have to be. In the author's opinion, Donald Trump became the only President since Ronald Regan that understands business economics and free market enterprise.

Now we have President Biden signing América's future away with the stroke of a pen to reverse the gains made under President Trump. In his first two weeks in office, he signed Executive orders to close down the Keystone pipeline, restricting fracking, obliterating the use of fossil fuels, and 40 other policy orders agreed to in the Sanders' socialist Manifesto to get elected. The most controversial is the promise to do away with the Trump tax cut and stop building the Border Wall and call one and all to our sanctuary country.

Currently, 85 percent of 46 different taxes most of which are property and sales taxes are paid by small businesses and their employees. However, only 10 percent have any political or economic influence. Sixty-five percent of the new jobs are created by small businesses. But 60,000 small businesses startup per month and 60,000 go bankrupt per month with no government or banking support. So, the solution for recovery is to stimulate small versus big. The current stimulus was designed for "too big to fail" thinking by Harvard, Yale and Princeton grads while the cost was borne by small businesses through taxation, loss of jobs, loss of capital, and more regulations.

Where has common business sense gone? Where? In the campaigns of career politicians that have never run a business, sweated a payroll, or invented a product.

The Small Business Administration was initiated to stimulate entrepreneurs and supply risk capital for small businesses. Now it is overregulated and underutilized for its original purpose. HUD, Farmers Home Loan, FHA, Fannie Mae, Freddie Mac, government grant programs, all are designed primarily to fund Trump-style real estate ventures. If you want to fund an idea, you must go to the venture capitalists, the public stock market, angel investors, or your country club pals and family members, all of whom want a 30 percent return on a marginal investment.

In other words, most potentially great ideas, like the American Enterprise party, never get funded ... see my "Go Funding" account the American Enterprise Party, then tell your friends and neighbors to support this movement. The shrinking role of small business is eroding America's dream of having its people strive for personal wealth. In America, the farms are now big business for corporations who will pyramid until there is no human capital being utilized. Big business is being created by consolidation in pursuit of economies of scale that squeeze out competition and only result in higher costs and lower worker esteem. Deja vu . . . Animal Farm rides again and 1984 governance is right around the corner.

Remember, post-war Russia, Italy, Korea and China went through the ascension of the politburo taking over Bolshevik farming and industry for the common good. Now they are pursuing the pseudo-capitalistic dream. The monarchy of British design built a phenomenal worldwide reach using colonial capitalism, then destroyed it through over taxation to pay for the kingdom. The rise and fall of the Roman Empire were driven by a plan to acquire productive land and govern while the emperor and the senate only wanted to govern. History is repeating itself here in America. Et tu Brute as Donald Trump was impeached twice by the House of Representatives and acquitted twice by the Senate before being deposed of his Presidency through a voter assassination of the rule of law. Julius Caesar, pontifex maximus of Rome was assassinated by the Senate and House of Nobles for overreaching land grabs, indebting Rome beyond its means to support. In each instance, the people were left without the leader that was to solve the divided society of violence, vulgarity and excess wealth. The replacements, Pompey and Biden leave Rome and America in Marxist hands that destroyed Rome's democracy forever and America's for the rest of the century. Unless an effective third party, using the swing vote, to bring civility and accountability as the principles driving the economy and institutions.

History tells these stories, and as we in American repeat them, the politicians and bureaucrats promise reform (defer to a committee then subcommittee), which eventually means more regulations and government on the faulty premise that our economy can recover from any recession, even a Pandemic shut down depression.

Well, Adam Smith, George Washington, Thomas Jefferson, and even Karl Marx consulted would predict the fall of America based on the dominance of governance for the sake of power, not for the sake of productivity and value-added services. Only small business truly deals with this equation of supply and demand. Enterprise does not embrace overregulation, over taxation, waste of natural and human resources by paying for nonproductive government jobs, political rhetoric, and fear inducing conformity for the sake of control. That's why the American Enterprise Party calls the USA a free-market capital and social enterprise.

We need creativity, not rhetoric. For example, create added revenues by charging China, India, Japan, South Korea, Mexico, etc. a distribution fee of 5 percent of their sales for utilizing the biggest consumer markets in the world (American consumers) rather than giving them a free market so they can profit, grow their GDP at our expense, then loan us money to provide them a service and technology network, at no cost.

So, the solution is simple:

1. Fund idea generation through lending to and investment in the grassroots of enterprise and reduce dependence on taxes and more on profits that generate capital for investment.
2. Fund small business startups and expansion with adequate capital formation.
3. Fund and privatize SBA, FHA, FHL, HUD, etc. for the sake of small business, not Big "Brotherhood", Big Media, Big Box and Big Tech consolidation.
4. Reduce taxation by 50 percent on small businesses; tax net worth, not net income (Eventually replace flat taxation with incentives to increase GDP):
    a. Income taxes.

b. Sales taxes.
   c. Property taxes.
   d. Sin taxes.
   e. Energy taxes.
   f. Estate taxes.
   g. Embargoes.
5. Privatize certain government agencies for the sake of investing entitlement resources in the economy (investment through controlled strategies); a 6 percent annual return on investment in our economy results in positive cash flow to pay down our negative debt financing:
   a. Healthcare savings accounts for workers.
   b. Social Security funds collected by government and invested into 401(k) mutual funds.
   c. Taxation (collection and accountability.)
   d. Eliminate the costly healthcare enforcement structure, replace with pay-for-performance payment based on reinforcement and accountability tactics, not punitive-based civil penalties.
6. Reduce laws and regulations by 50 percent
   a. OSHUA.
   b. CMS, HHS, GAO, OIG.
   c. IRS.
   d. EEOC.
   e. Environmental agencies.
   f. Limit laws passed to one, eliminating ten.
7. Require fair representation of the chambers of commerce using the www.usdebtclock.org for grading governance at the Federal, State and Local levels:
   a. Remove PAC for campaigns.
   b. Fifty percent of the legislature/Congress should be private-sector representatives.

c. Reduce the dominance of Congress by attorneys and big-business special interests who use former politicians as lobbyists.
8. Privatize government agencies that are losing money or in a deficit position:
    a. Post office.
    b. TSA security force.
    c. Health and education.
    d. Commerce and agriculture.

What would this do? It would take from the big and give to the small. Decentralize and economize. The very concept of many doing way more than a dominating few will kick "butt." Within five years of implementing these principles, unemployment will be resolved, full employment can be a goal, so could lower crime rates, divorce rates, teenage pregnancies, war deaths. Baby boomer financing can be lowered due to our economic health and wealth. Within 10 years America will be out of debt and fulfilling the promises we make for "keeping America Great".

Principles of True Change:

Problems	Solutions		
	Red Republican Party	Swing Vote American Enterprise Party	Blue Democrat Party
1. Budget deficits/ debt Ceiling/credit rating	Cut Social Security and Medicare	Cut govt. payroll	Raise taxes
2. Education results	Vouchers	Cut govt. payroll	Raise taxes
3. Discretionary spending	Cut earmarks	Cut govt. payroll	Raise taxes
4. Government pensions	Cut entitlements	Cut govt. payroll	Unionization
5. Foreign aid	Bribe for policy	Eliminate	Up bribes

6. Defense spending	Increase weapons	Eliminate WMD	Increase fear factor
7. Forty-six different taxes and regulatory redundancy	Shift debt to states	Cut state payrolls	More taxes
8. Unemployment	Cut taxes for big businesses	Increase small business capital	Raise UE taxes
9. Healthcare	Vouchers	Pay for outcomes	Raise taxes
10. Social Security	Raise retire age	Cut govt. pensions	Raise taxes

The Freidman idea that Vouchers are the solution is a false positive: meaning that government shifts the responsibility to the states and/or the private sector without changing the real problems of flawed public policy and little private involvement in setting public policy.

1. Support the American Enterprise Party for the unrepresented, by the private sector, to balance budgets as a true alternative to government for the elite, by the elite, and to the elite's benefit.
2. Elect governors to the American Enterprise Party for they are being dumped on by the national parties for the sake of practicing politics as usual and avoiding the true solutions. Only the governors can make true change at the grassroots. Cut the redundancy of regulatory agencies between Federal and State governments riding State and Federal budgets of waste and excess regulations.
3. Establish that the flag represents this country's greatness. It has three colors for a purpose. It is more than red and blue; it is also white in the middle for a reason, a purer alternative for the middle classes, the aging Americans, the minority interests, the unrepresented small businesses, and more than ever the financial position of the multigovernmental entities who are not now accountable. Transparencies only show us the errors in strategy and tactics. It is too late after the horse is out of the barn and dead from over consumption.

4. Elect government officials based on private sector experience and eliminate the tagline *lawmakers*; it should be job and peacemakers. Rather than squeeze small business to death with unnecessary regulations, help fund capital needs with true debt instruments based on performance. All government contracts must be based on pay for performance formulas.
5. Provide America with a true alternative to conservatives and liberals as a party of enterprising Americans that are the majority of taxpayers who have little, if any, representation in the governmental budget process and have no means for fiscal accountability but provide 75 percent of the funding from forty-six different national and state taxes.
6. Make education a higher priority than our so-called national defense fear system so our best minds can devise protection for our inner-city infrastructure to protect our transportation system, our energy systems, grid systems, our computer networks, our vulnerable elderly, and unemployed/underemployed under privileged masses, and more importantly, allow us to compete in the world markets. It is an economic war, not a shooting war, that will allow us to lead the world to peace and prosperity. China and other socialist and communist parties are there waiting for America to fail then pounce with cyber hacking and fear mongering.

SUM UP THIS ARTICLE:

As the image above shows, I wrote Volume II of The American Enterprise Party book subtitled "The American Enterprise Manifesto" that exposes the depth of the swamp and the dire financial predicament weighing on our future generations. This must be dealt with now as America slides into the depths of the swamp, as did other great societies in the past. I've been told it will never happen because it takes billions, trillions and zillions to compete for any office let alone the presidency. Well, 330 million enterprising Americans create $21 trillion GDP per year and create wealth for 22 million millionaires and 814 billionaires so why not invest their equity (wealth) in paying down the $158 trillion in unfunded debt, rid ourselves of half of the 22 million government workers that cost 40% of fixed overhead wasted on redundant laws and regulations to be able to compete with China our ominous competitor.

- Why would we reelect the very parties 90% of the time that got us into a bankrupt position?
- Why would we believe that the red and the blue parties act in our best interests?
- Why would we choose to bank our future on the past faults of these elitists?
- Why wouldn't we find someone that represents enterprising Americans? www.americanenterprisepoliticalparty.org
- Why wouldn't we vote for enterprising leaders and country men and women?

Why wouldn't you now Vote for the unknown stranger! Someone that is a dark horse from the middle American independent philosophy who has been one of the enterprising Americans that pay all the bills, create the wealth for the few and want opportunity to live well, sleep well and be happy. Why because what we have isn't working and this may just be the solution. Well worth a true alternative considering that the binary two-party Congress may be gridlocked forever and the deficit/debt clock is broken, the alligators own the swamp and Humpty Dumpty Biden can't be put back together again.

Article Ten

American Enterprise Economics (Drain the Swamp, Reign in Big Brother and the Brotherhood)

What is our Socio-Economic Legacy?
"Apathy is worse than sympathy, empathy, allergy or a short eulogy"... Jerry Rhoads

> **L**everaging
> **E**nterprise
> **G**oes
> **A**gainst
> **C**ivil obedience
> **Y**es, even with the Rule of law

Blue Economics:

Under Keynesian theory, cutting government spending hurts economic growth. Obama, Biden and his advisors are Keynesians; they believe that government spending creates jobs and grows the economy as the purchaser of last resort. That using the Federal Reserve banking system to print money for the US Treasury notes and set interest rates controls inflation and increasing taxes to balance the growth of the federal budget will stimulate job growth, though it's hiring more government workers, adding no cash flow to the American GDP. Now, with Biden's Build Back Bigger, by reversing all of Trump policies is growing government at an accelerated pace. As the swamp is flooded with new woke entitlements and welfare checks. Creating 8 million job openings due to the Pandemic incentive to stay at home and demand their $300 per month stimulus unemployment checks.

Red Economics:

Under trickle-down economic theory, increasing taxes hurts economic growth. President Trump, Reagan, Dr. Laffer and their advisors were trickle-down advocates. They and current Republicans believe that cutting taxes creates jobs and grows the economy by giving entrepreneurs, small businesses, and risk takers more capital to create jobs. And that the continued growth of big government is a byproduct of unacceptable taxes and entitlements but support runaway lawmaking and punitive regulations.

Under President Trump the taxes were cut, corporations began retuning production back to America and the stock market reached record highs. Unfortunately, President Trump used the Dow Jones stock market quote as his report card as it reached record highs. He attributed that to the tax cuts and return of manufacturing and investment back to the USA. He failed to also use generally accepted accounting principles for managing the budget and legislation. In reality the stock market is the biggest contributor to speculation not supported by fiscal accountability and GAAP earnings per share for the underlying 500 enterprises making up the daily total $600 derivative risk balloon. This derivative bubble was safer with Trump than it is Biden, purely because he had run and started businesses. He also learned how to utilize the bankruptcy rules when he was insolvent. He utilized bankruptcy rules in his cassino businesses to enable the capitalist to restart the business and the socialist/workers to retain their jobs by downsizing fixed overhead and cutting inefficient labor. Biden and his cabinet are lifetime bureaucrats, not entrepreneurs. Neither are Nancy Pelosi, Chuck Schumer. Kamala Harris, Bernie Sanders and AOC. This derivative bubble encompasses the worldwide economy with China the most dynamic in its plans and goals to unseat America as the leader in most economic indicators. To his detriment, President Trump intimated he would drain the swamp but didn't have the time in a four-year term to get-a-round to it. The swamp and its alligators just got much bigger with the Biden/Sanders sell out mentality.

American Enterprise economic formula:

Bigger government creates smaller business enterprise, smaller government reduces bigger business enterprise, downsizes government, privatizes regulatory agencies, and economizes the cost of government thereby creates the dynamics of enterprise, which is jobs, jobs, jobs, with GDP and stock market growth as the result. Through reduced government overhead, the deficits are eliminated, national debt is paid down, and America's needed entitlements are intact.

To do this, capital is required, both human and monetary. So recapitalizing America's enterprise by using investment taxation for those who have high net worth will capitalize small businesses, entrepreneurial initiatives, and funding risk takers who will save the Great American Enterprise. By combining risk capital and human capital (merges capitalism and socialism) into the enterprise party, splits the two-party system with swing voting representing free market enterprise versus the left and right extremes that are pulling America closer to Marxism and pure Socialism called communism.

The free-market Enterprise economics of supply and demand is the original Adam Smith Wealth of a Nation are still representative government but uses the swing vote **to break ties and prevent gridlock of the two-party system** at every level to balance the budget, create wealth, hold government accountable for job making not just law making. It is truly a vision of a better world for all people regardless of race, creed, gender, religion and business acumen.

IDEALS

"Ideas die a natural death, Ideals live forever"

*No God ever crossed my t's
Or dotted my i's
It's up to me to pray
Then do it my way*

*Faith helps but doesn't heal
No it merely gets the will started
Headed up a hill
So procrastination can be thwarted*

*Into an admission of mortality
As I'm no legend
"Can this ideal really be me"
And proprietor of such a regimen*

*Being a soaring light to suggest
On a ground of darkness
That religion surging in my chest
Is from a God of action to bless*

*Loaded with ideals it seems
That the fears of saints
Are cast into the sea of dreams
Churning out life's constraints*

*Until dreams become mere schemes
Giving reality it's worth and naught
In a world of ISIS and Marines
Casting a shadow and humility of what*

It means to be real not an ideal
That enables me to feel wheel and deal
Make my way and buy a meal
Making real my ideal

Vision of a Better World:
The American Enterprise Party Credo

Look toward the sky of tomorrow
Feast on the setting sun
Let us look for a better harrow
Swear yes to human vanity undone

Dream not of the dying
But cherish the fruit of the living
With eyes not shut to crying
But forthright with open giving

Find and seek the manner
To which the vision of a better world
Is in the heart of the beholder
With an enterprising nation's flag unfurled

As politicians and lawmakers lose sight of the practical
Common sense and peace prevail
The common man as the job maker must scale each obstacle
With a better version on a grander scale

Yet thus a third party will be formed
With its foundation of simple and practical economics
As an answer and divorce of the elite's control scorned
In its place, a modern form of enterprise must be affixed

With fewer divorces, less crime, higher education, higher employment, better GNP, Better standard of living for all, lower drug usage, lower teen pregnancies, more human resources, more affordable homes, and fewer unwanted children.

Yes, my version of a better world is in the heart of a mother and the hope of a grandmother, not man's version in the theory of diversion calling problems issues to go along to get alone
by the pseudointellectuals to their own ways and means.

This vision is what I call *Mancology*, the science of managing human value in an enterprising society. This results in more human capital and less government intervention that will enhance our country's stature and influence worldwide.

Let the reformed institutions, laws, and regulations redirect our energies into the livelihood of hard work, family life, and peaceful love for our fellow man, replacing the negative forces with positive opportunities for

A better world.

Government reform

- Do we need entitlement reform?
- Do we need tax reform?
- Do we need financial reform?
- Do we need healthcare reform?
- NO, we need government reform!

Monday, August 8, 2011
Charley Reese's final column for the Orlando Sentinel
545 vs. 300,000,000 People
(*The Orlando Sentinel* has given the American Enterprise Party rights to reprint Charley's viral article.)

Politicians are the only people in the world who create problems and then campaign against them.

Have you ever wondered, if both the Democrats and the Republicans are against deficits, WHY do we have deficits?

Have you ever wondered, if all the politicians are against inflation and high taxes, WHY do we have inflation and high taxes?

You and I don't propose a federal budget. The president does.

You and I don't have the constitutional authority to vote on appropriations. The House of Representatives does.

You and I don't write the tax code, Congress does.

You and I don't set fiscal policy, Congress does.

You and I don't control monetary policy, the Federal Reserve Bank does.

One hundred senators, 435 congressmen, one president, and nine Supreme Court justices equates to 545 human beings out of the 300 million are directly, legally, morally, and individually responsible for the domestic problems that plague this country.

I excluded the members of the Federal Reserve Board because that problem was created by the Congress. In 1913, Congress delegated its constitutional duty to provide a sound currency to a federally chartered, but private, central bank.

I excluded all the special interests and lobbyists for a sound reason. They have no legal authority. They have no ability to coerce a senator, a congressman, or a president to do one cotton-picking thing. I don't care if they offer a politician $1 million in cash. The politician has the power to accept or reject it. No matter what the lobbyist promises, it is the legislator's responsibility to determine how he votes.

Those 545 human beings spend much of their energy convincing you that what they did is not their fault. They cooperate in this common con regardless of party.

What separates a politician from a normal human being is an excessive amount of gall. No normal human being would have the gall of a speaker who stood up and criticized the president for creating deficits. The president can only propose a budget. He cannot force the Congress to accept it.

The constitution, which is the supreme law of the land, gives sole responsibility to the House of Representatives for originating and approving appropriations and taxes. Who is the speaker of the house? John Boehner. He is the leader of the majority party. He and fellow house members, not the president, can approve any budget they want. If the president vetoes it, they can pass it over his veto if they agree to.

It seems inconceivable to me that a nation of 300 million cannot replace 545 people who stand convicted—by present facts—of incompetence and irresponsibility. I can't think of a single domestic problem that is not traceable directly to those 545 people. When you fully grasp the plain truth that 545 people exercise the power of the federal government, then it must follow that what exists is what they want to exist.

- If the tax code is unfair, it's because they want it unfair.
- If the budget is in the red, it's because they want it in the red.
- If the army and marines are in Iraq and Afghanistan, it's because they want them in Iraq and Afghanistan.
- If they do not receive Social Security but are on an elite retirement plan not available to the people, it's because they want it that way.

There are no Unsolvable government problems.

Do not let these 545 people shift the blame to bureaucrats, whom they hire and whose jobs they can abolish; to lobbyists, whose gifts and advice they can reject; to regulators, to whom they give the power to regulate and from whom they can take this power. Above all, do not let them con you into the belief that there exist disembodied mystical forces like "the economy," "inflation," or "politics that prevent them from doing what they take an oath to do.

- Those 545 people, and they alone, are responsible.
- They, and they alone, have the power.
- They, and they alone, should be held accountable by the people, who are their bosses.

Provided the voters have the gumption to manage their own employees. We should vote all of them out of office does not reelect 90% of them and clean up their mess. What you do with this article now that you have read it is up to you. This might be funny if it weren't so true. Be sure to read all the way to the end.

Obviously, we need government reform, not more taxes, because government has already taken the voters' livelihood and wasted it.

An Ode to the American Taxpayer by Charley Reese

Tax his land,
Tax his bed,
Tax the table,
At which he's fed.
Tax his tractor,
Tax his mule,
Teach him taxes
Are the rule.
Tax his work,
Tax his pay,
He works for
peanuts anyway!
Tax his cow,
Tax his goat,

Tax his pants,
Tax his coat.
Tax his ties,
Tax his shirt,
Tax his work,
Tax his dirt.
Tax his tobacco,
Tax his drink,
Tax him if he
Tries to think.
Tax his cigars,
Tax his beers,
If he cries
Tax his tears.
Tax his car,
Tax his gas,
Find other ways
Taxes to pass
Tax all he has
Then let him know
That you won't be done
Till he has no dough.
When he screams and hollers;
Then tax him some more,
Tax him till
He's good and sore.
Then tax his coffin,
Tax his grave,
Tax the sod in
Which he's laid...
Put these words
Upon his tomb,

> "Taxes drove me
> to my doom..."
> When he's gone,
> Do not relax,
> It's time to apply
> The inheritance tax.

The middle-class pays 95 percent of the taxes, not the elite or wealthy, as we are led to believe. Not the Big Media, Big Box and Big Technology corporations... following are the taxes enterprising Americans pay that Big Brother government squanders:

1. Accounts receivable tax,
2. Building permit tax,
3. CDL license tax,
4. Cigarette tax,
5. Corporate income tax,
6. Dog license tax,
7. Excise taxes,
8. Federal income tax,
9. Federal unemployment tax (FUTA),
10. Fishing license tax,
11. Food license tax,
12. Fuel permit tax,
13. Gasoline tax (currently 44.75 cents per gallon),
14. Gross receipts tax,
15. Hunting license tax,
16. Inheritance tax,
17. Inventory tax
18. IRS interest charges, IRS penalties (tax on top of tax,)
19. Liquor tax,
20. Luxury taxes,

21. Marriage license tax,
22. Medicare tax,
23. Personal property tax,
24. Property tax,
25. Real estate tax,
26. Service charge tax,
27. Social Security tax,
28. Road usage tax,
29. Recreational vehicle tax
30. Sales tax,
31. School tax,
32. State income tax,
33. State unemployment tax (Suta),
34. Telephone federal excise tax,
35. Telephone federal universal service fee tax,
36. Telephone federal, state and local surcharge taxes,
37. Telephone minimum usage surcharge tax,
38. Telephone recurring and nonrecurring charges tax,
39. Telephone state and local tax,
40. Telephone usage charge tax,
41. Utility taxes,
42. Vehicle license registration tax,
43. Vehicle sales tax,
44. Watercraft registration tax,
45. Well permit tax,
46. Workers' compensation tax.

Still think this is funny.

Not one of these taxes existed 100 years ago, and our nation was the most prosperous in the world. We had absolutely no national debt, had the largest middle-class in the world, and mom stayed home to raise the kids.

What in the heck happened? Can you spell "politicians"?

I hope this goes around the USA at least 545 times! You can help it get there! (Charlie Reese's article did resonate around the world and became one of the most read, in history).

This ends Charley Reese's final column for the *Orlando Sentinel* and begins the American Enterprise campaign for equal representation and/or voting power to not just create problems but prevent them or solve them.

Lawmakers are Job Breakers

I loathe the term "lawmaker." To me it means more laws, attorneys controlling every facet of society, more cost and less profit to generate capital to fund small businesses that do in fact create jobs. It means more infrastructure government jobs or contracts and fewer productive jobs. In Illinois the lawmakers continued to make 300 laws while the state had $189 billion in debt and $500 billion in unfunded pension debt. They then increased taxes by 67 percent and borrowed $4 billion to pay their own pension costs and increase their own salaries by 16 percent during the great recession. This, in fact, is the second Great Depression that is bankrupting America.

Ironically, the tagline *lawmaker* is an oxymoron. They are in fact *job breakers* and *debt makers*. Why wouldn't we want them to be peacemakers? We should discard the social culture that we need more laws and leaders who exercise their rights to their own welfare not ours. We the middle-class, unemployed, poverty-limited Americans are in fact the majority controlled by this minority. The Tea Party, the Occupiers, the extremists, are being led into bankruptcy because of flawed political processes.

In fact, what is transpiring in the legislative process is socialization and demobilizing the national capital structure of our nation's enterprise and demonizing the police and military. To save the enterprise, the Americans who use it for productive work and use it to pay their bills must not listen to the problem makers, but to our own common sense. It is a third party, the American Enterprise Party, whose platform is not free enterprise nor pure capitalism. It is a political platform of investment in the enterprise system that the Founding Fathers set up:

1. The first plank in our move to reorganize America should be taxing net worth, not net income or net purchases. In this manner the Americans who have capitalized on the great consumer machine due to America's work ethic and use of the enterprise should share their wealth to sustain the enterprise. What impact would this have?
    a. Jeff Bezos, Bill Gates, Elon Musk the world's wealthiest individuals, would be expected to pay tax on his use of the enterprise and its consumer base.
    b. Warren Buffet would be expected to share his wealth with those that worked in the enterprise that he helped to develop so the rest of us can expand the enterprise, rather than giving it to a nonproductive charity that takes capital out of the enterprise.
    c. America's GNP capitalized is our net worth in the world economy and would produce a gross national net worth of a negative $-31.3 trillion (USA assets $158.3 trillion less $189.6 USA liabilities). USA is in the hole based on GAAP is a negative $-31.3 trillion = insolvency and unable to sustain the Enterprise. Needs $100 trillion in equity capital to avoid bankruptcy.
    d. Convert to shares of stock in the American enterprise that collects 5 percent from every American's net worth would produce $5 trillion in annual national revenue that can be used to pay down the national debt and seed the enterprise with equity capital for small businesses that will sustain the enterprise.

2. The second plank in our reorganization of America should be using surpluses that will be produced by this taxing system to

save the consumer powerhouse that the rest of the world uses at no cost.

    a. We should be charging China, Japan, India, Germany, Russia, South Korea, Mexico Canada a distribution fee, not trade tariffs but user fees, for accessing our consumer markets. This will help reverse the $800 billion annual decline in the balance of trade that has been going on for twenty years. A 25 percent charge to those countries for the imbalance of trade of $70 billion per month would produce a $840 billion distribution fee base. At 25 percent per year, $240 billion would be collected for use of our consumer markets.

    b. The portion that is not consumed by our government agencies has to be earmarked for infusing capital into the small businesses that create the products that the rest of the world will manufacture and resell into our enterprise.

    c. After paying down our national debt at $1 trillion per year, $1 trillion in surplus can be used to supplement the distribution fee charged to our foreign producers. All of this capital should be infused into the development of small businesses that create the sixteen million jobs we need to attain full employment.

3. The third plank to reorganizing America is to downsize the government machine that has been built up since World War I.

    a. Currently we have twenty-two million government employees costing us $1.3 trillion per year in labor costs and unfunded pension and healthcare costs of $25 trillion per year.

    b. By downsizing and privatizing government agencies we provide more private sector jobs that create capital for the private sector, and those employees will create more net worth and more tax revenues from capital conserved to sustain the enterprise.

c. If we were to privatize agriculture, energy, transportation, education, security, healthcare, post office, and commerce, we would save $200 billion per year in overhead costs, thereby creating eleven million private-sector jobs to operate the American enterprise more efficiently and effectively.
d. If we were to only eliminate the redundancy of Federal and State agencies that currently exists, we would save $100 billion and eliminate 10 million government jobs that can be replaced with fewer regulations and more private reinforcement for quality and less fraud and abuse.

4. The fourth plank is our approach to energy and foreign affairs. First and foremost, we must give peace a chance. Currently the $47 billion per year in foreign aid is not creating any goodwill; rather, we should be investing in foreign infrastructure and investing our newfound capital in these countries to create more consumerism and improved standards of living that grifting can never accomplish.
    a. At the same time, we are spending $750 billion per year on war, calling it defense, of which $3.3 trillion has been spent on weapons of mass destruction that we hope we don't have to use, plus billions per year policing the world that wants us to keep our noses out of their cultures. Our share of the UN budget is 22% of $5.4 billion every two years and World Health Organization $ $893 million for two years and NATO 22% of $ 6.9 trillion = $2.9 Trillion every two years. President Trump was in the process of reducing the expenditures for these foreign aid organizations.
    b. Once we have established ourselves not as lawmakers but as peacemakers, not international lawbreakers, we can team up with other oil consumers to control the cost of energy by forming our own OPEC (oil

purchasing energy countries). We can have a coalition with USA, Canada, Japan, France, Italy, England, India and Mexico and Mexico produce competing energy solutions that will control the escalation of the Arab OPEC offerings.

5. The fifth plank is the salvation of entitlements as the only real reason to have government in the first place. Social Security, Medicare, Medicaid, and healthcare aren't entitlements but trust fund not budgetary items; the abuse that has been conceived by too many rules and regulations. If the Enterprise were allowed to innovate, these entitlements can be more practical in the application of their funding.
    a. For example, healthcare expenditures must be based on outcomes, not incomes. Paying for performance at every level of government means a paradigm shift away from lobbyists to accountability, not transparency after the horse is out of the barn.
    b. Unemployment must be eliminated by capital infusion into small business, workers' comp must be eliminated by safer working conditions, using more capital to make productivity our goal, using technology to computerize and standardize processes, thereby eliminating waste before it is factored into our enterprise. Private sector employers must improve safety programs, pay incentives and promote equal pay for equal skills. Public sector employees must have the same benefits as the Private sector. And the Public sector employees must be accountable with incentives for preventing fraud and abuse in government.
    c. Stop illegal immigration at the borders using former President Trump's deterrents such as the building of a wall, agreements with Mexico and other central and south America to detain refugees with better policies and less trafficking of drugs and workers. Also,

establish a pathway to citizenship for those 30+ million undocumented immigrants that includes speaking English, learning employment skills and paying taxes.

This platform of the American Enterprise Party is to provide solutions to problems rather than frivolous debating of issues and stall tactics by promoting reform and never reforming anything. The difference is that we are dealing with priorities rather than disagreements between the reds and blues. We do not waste our time and energies rethinking and trying to remake the constitution; the Supreme Court is in that business.ABortion, same-sex marriages, freedom of speech, poverty in the world, liberty and justice for all, imminent domain, gun control, retirement, entitlements, life expectancy, family and love life, gay marriage, racism, religion are all inalienable rights, not political issues. So, a vote for the fictious stranger is a swing vote for common sense.

It is said the older worker does not dwell on perks but on what works, ego replaced by will go, seed instead of greed, teamwork for the good of the business, not just personal success. The definition of enterprise we are looking for is in Webster: readiness for daring action and initiative. This has nothing to do with age or physical strength but everything to do with effort, attitude, and fulfilling a need. Like an older woman and her man, there is no demand that cannot be met with love.

SUM UP THIS ARTICLE

Our personal freedoms are being threatened by the lawmakers making laws we do not need. I am not a gun bearer or a gun defender; however, I want the freedom to create and debate if I do not agree with the government's interpretation of the constitution. Having reread Orwell's *Animal Farm* before I wrote the American Enterprise Party Platform (see Article 13 for the plan for reorganization of the American Enterprise for and the formation), it became apparent that we are evolving from the constitutional version of America to the institutional version of America's infrastructure. Control of the monetary system is the intent of our current Congress, governorships, city councils, and local agencies. With the help of the Federal Reserve Bank, the interest rates have been used to keep the majority dependent on the minority.

Government, by its nature, unless stifled, will tell us what we can't do, not help us do what we can do—irony at its worst. What the American Enterprise Party does is gives a "we the people" the alternative to exercise the true value of voting, change for the sake of saving the economy, not for the sake of saving the monarchy.

THE END OF THE WORLD

I thought it was the end of the world
But the world didn't end
I thought I was dead to rights
But I wasn't dead

I thought I was guilty
But I wasn't charged
I wanted to hide
But no one was looking

Except fear of my own fear
And doubt which had come to rest
Upon my shoulder
And across my chest

I thought it was the end of the world
But the world didn't end
I thought it was too much to handle
But even that did pass

No more scars than mental anguish
No more suffering did I have to languish
Then thoughts of why I should be giving
The last rites of the end of the world

But the world didn't end

Matter of fact each day
it was on the mend
It was on an upward trend
Though from my perspective

The hill was insurmountable at times

I kept my eye on the target just ahead
Shying away from doubts and dread
But eventually everything worked out
Not exactly with a yell and a shout

But at least things were coming about
So, my lesson was to be unbound If
you get down you never know
When that pendulum will turn around

So, don't give up and don't count yourself out
Don't give in to fear and doubt
Because the end of the world
Thought to be a one-way route

Down but never out
Just before it turned about
Vote America Enterprise Party (VAEP)

YOUR VOTE COUNTS

Article Eleven

Quasi Reorganization of the Institutions

(Chapter 11 Bankruptcy Statute . . . Private sector)

Reorganizing the Great American Enterprise using Chapter 10, of the Bankruptcy Statute For public institutions and Tax-exempt Organizations

The Real Crash (America's Coming Bankruptcy), by author Peter Schiff, St. Martin's Press, 2012

> "Taxpayers pay government workers whose money goes to government unions whose money goes to the campaign of politicians who approve more taxpayer money for the unions who then contribute more to politicians".
>
> Paraphrased. . . "But unlike most unions government unions are negotiating with people who are spending someone else's money (politicians). Un-beknown to the general public 22.7 million government workers making salaries of $1.3 trillion per year were unionized, lionized and pens ionized with taxpayer debt. At $25 billion per year in unfunded pension debt it does not take long to sink the ship. America is insolvent, cannot pay its priority bills and will file for Chapter 10 bankruptcy (quasi reorganization) or go through dissolution and start over".

Using the tactics of the bailout used by Governor Romney's company (Bain Capital) America will have to downsize the fixed overhead, lower variable costs to the breakeven point and sell off or close those services (agencies) that do not make a profit or are bloated before excessive Government faces dissolution. Then the wealthy will have to infuse equity capital to market, produce and sell profitable services to the rest of the world and be run like an profitable Enterprise.

Principles of reorganization of America's insolvency:

1. Every unemployed private-sector employee requires the layoff of a public employee.
2. For every law passed, at a minimum ten laws must be discontinued.
3. Corresponding cuts in congressional salaries and benefits as being experienced by the private sector.
4. Downsizing of government-funded programs to reduce inflation.
5. Eliminate the Federal Reserve Board . . . let the market dictate price and equity.
6. Management of interest rates to be done by the U.S. Treasury, private and public members on a National Economic Board of Directors.
7. Revamp the taxation system to infuse equity capital into America's debt amortization based on individual, corporate and not for profit institutions net worth.

The Enterprise Needs to Reorganize:

Problem	Real Solutions
Healthcare reform	Self-health funding and spending
Economy	Deregulate all facets of business
Jobs	Fund small businesses using reduced taxes
Taxation	Tax net worth, not net income
Size of government	Cut payroll, pensions, perks, unionization
Foreign policy	Give peaceful coexistence a chance
National security	Educate and eradicate fear as a tactic
Energy	OPEC (Oil Purchasing Energy Consortium)
Entitlements	Change retirement age/pay aging workforce
Governance	Half of governance employs private sector
Human rights	Constitutional rules not politicians or judges

While American business and American workers were forced to downsize because of the 250% percent increase in the fed funds rate from 2005 to 2007 that popped the housing bubble, forcing America into a depression to slow down the economy, government grew by 16 percent in employment numbers and 20 percent in cost. It is time to deal with the economic problems, not political issues.

Un-cooking the Books

Economic problem: America, at all levels, is insolvent and bankrupt. (Following is an estimate of the degree of the problem using accrual basis accounting)

1. 22,700,000 government employees nationwide
    a. Average salary of $60,000 per employee
    b. Average pension liability per employee $250,000
    c. Average healthcare cost per employee $5,000
2. Annual cost of governmental labor $1,511,000,000,000
3. Annual unfunded cost of governmental pensions $5,555,000,000,000
4. Annual cost of governmental healthcare $111,000,000,000
5. Too many laws not yet funded:
    a. Current state laws that have yet to be funded   100,000
    b. Current federal laws that have yet to be funded 50,000
    c. Total yet to be funded laws on the books   150,000
    d. Average annual cost of a law $5,000,000
    e. Annual cost of laws to USA economy on
       the accrual basis of accounting $7,500,000,000,000
6. Federal, State, taxation at every level
    a. Business $800,000,000,000
        i. Income taxes,
        ii. Sales taxes,
        iii. Property,
        iv. Sin taxes,
        v. Gasoline,

      vi. Social Security,
      vii. Medicare,
      viii. Five others for local government
  b. Individuals (same list) $2,500,000,000,000
      i. Income taxes,
      ii. Sales,
      iii. Property,
      iv. Sin taxes,
      v. Gasoline
      vi. Social Security,
      vii. Medicare and sixteen others/ local government
  c. Total annual reduction in all taxes $3,300,000,000,000
  d. Infusion of equity capital assessment $5,000,000,000,000
7. Annual cost of government using accrual basis of accounting
  a. Labor, $1,111,000,000,000
  b. Defense, $800,000,000,000
      i. i Iraq. $100,000,000,000
      ii. ii. Afghanistan. $5,000,000,000
      iii. iii. Other occupations. $1,000,000,000
  c. Healthcare, $111,000,000,000
  d. Enforcement, $100,000,000,000
  e. Unfunded pension, $5,000,000,000,000
  f. Unfunded laws and enforcement, $7,500,000,000,000
  g. Unfunded entitlements, $1,000,000,000,000
  h. Annual cost of government using
    accrual basis of accounting, $15,728,000,000,000
  i. Annual operating loss of big government, ($11,928,000,000,000)
  j. Current national debt,   ($30,700,000,000,000)
  k. Annual deficit level on the accrual
    basis of accounting,   ($27,428,000,000,000)

1. 300 million people have $124 trillion unfunded debt or $1,092,59 per taxpayer and incurring $85,000 per year deficit per person, bankrupt by any estimate.

Economic solution: stop excessive government and reinvest savings in small businesses.

1. Downsize government employment at all levels by 15 percent per year for three years.
    a. Savings each year for three years, $450,000,000,000
2. For every law proposed ten will be eliminated
    a. State level 2,000 eliminated per year, $100,000,000,000
    b. Federal level 12,000 eliminated per year, $500,000,000,000
3. Multiple levels of taxation and enforcement are eating up capital for small business—eliminate,
    a. 10 percent of taxes at all levels, $600,000,000,000
    b. Privatize healthcare, $600,000,000,000
4. Annual savings re-invested in the American Enterprise, $1,850,000,000,000
    a. Annual return on investment 10 percent $185,000,000,000,
5. Total reduction of debt per annum $1,170,000,000,000
6. Twelve capitalization rate, $ 14,040,000,000,000
7. Leveraged period to balance America's future. 10 years

The above estimates are predicated on current population growth and utilization of national resources, but by factoring in the baby boomer and illegal aliens' eventual impact on tax revenues and healthcare usage, the above figures could be underestimated by as much as 50 percent, making it even more imperative to move now to reorganize our country's excesses of Big Brother authoritarian government structure. The American Enterprise Party is founded on each and every American to be heard if they personally commit some of their time to being involved in public service to replace the Brotherhood mentality.

We, the people, are being deceived by Big Brother, by big business, by minority interests. To rationalize and nationalize our priorities, we risk being the next Roman Empire. Are we going to be the next Rome, China, Russia, N. Korea, Cuba, Venezuela, Great Britain, the former Mayan Empire, or the leading Enterprise in the World? Or will we amplify Georg Orwell's 1984 by 2084. Or will individual freedoms truly prevail? "Of the people, by the people, for the people" that is currently dead; just try to reach your senator or congressman or governor by phone to deal with problems while they debate issues.

PS: Obviously I have taken the liberty of using the educated WAG method to put some perspective in the seriousness of the situation. If you can improve on these thoughts and numbers please step up and help the cause. If we don't do this the spin doctors and lobbyists will continue to dominate the media and our future. Jerry L. Rhoads, CPA, creator of the American Enterprise Party

I repeat, I have developed the platform with a campaign strategy of becoming the "swing vote party" **to break ties and prevent gridlock of the two-party system** at every level by eliciting legalized voting support from all Enterprising Americans from the left, right and the middle to solve the problem that Big Brother Government and Big Business Brotherhood cannot solve without us. By being the following backbone of the Great American Enterprise.

1. The seventy-seven million baby boomers and 13 million voters of color.
2. The 100 million middle- to low-income enterprising American families to vote for doing away with the control of our country by the elite Few for the Many.
3. See Article 12 for strategy where we must sell our party to the forces that control the media, the internet to educate and involve the patriots that still dwell in every community and business.

(It must start now before we have leased out our entire country to the Chinese, Koreans, Japanese, Germans, Mexicans, Indians and Arab countries by borrowing to fund our national debt and imbalance of trade. Already we have mayors, governors, senators, representatives supporting gambling casinos, power ball, State lotto games, sports betting, setting up video gaming in our places of business and leasing of our ports, highways, parking meters, bridges to fund ever-increasing deficits and ineffective trade agreements).

The Enterprise Party swing vote **to break ties and prevent gridlock of the two-party system** at every level is a practical application of the democracy envisioned by our forefathers by turning the tables on the very system that is destroying the American risk taking, constitutional infrastructure.

SUM UP THIS ARTICLE:
Give Me Work (Enterprise) or Give Me Debt

In Aristotle's book on Poetics there are three political forces:

- A monarchy rests its future on the past, makes no plans for tomorrow.
- A tyranny rests it future on wiping out the past and making its version of the future.
- A democracy rests its future on past tradition and staid politics, while money never rests.

None of the three predominant forms of social systems (capitalism, socialism, communism) or political parties (red, blue or white) embrace accountability to the masses unless there are laws, rules and boundaries with consequences... but they must be applied by a true Rule of Law without prejudice and discrimination...
- But with a third swing vote party **to break ties and prevent gridlock of the two-party system** at every level the enterprise

rests its future on creativity and profits, with greed harnessed for the better good not just the affluent few.
- Work is the balance... jobs and worthwhile effort are the fuel to the pursuit of the American Dream, peaceful coexistence with our allies as well as our enemies. Free Market Enterprise governed by enterprising Americans who bring capitalism and socialism together every day of every year, termed Humanism, pursuing profit for the people, by the people, of the people so help us God.

BLACK OR WHITE

(Does it matter)

Race relations are based
Not on color
But on love thy neighbor
Without regard to race or pallor

Sisters and brothers feeling their way
Black red yellow or white we're all people
Humanity facing each new day
Standing in wonder before the steeple

Pose that find the happy heights
Heights of courage come what may
Remember why we must have human rights
Opportunities found not gone astray

All roots go deep in our land of mortal humans

Roots recalled will not decay
Roots that even guns can't slay
Fighting to find the pride of bygone kin
Pose beginnings though some are to delay

Begin the ending parody
For to be the most one destined must be least
Warriors employers and Tom Sawyer beware
Beware if our self-held feelings betray

Because truth can't be ours if ourselves are untrue

Masking and hiding our real griefs
Believing you fool all being politically correct
Pen in the end you've lost to misspent beliefs
Corrupting your offspring with its affect

Eulogy
Black or white we are human and have regret
As did the proud Mandingo don't forget
Pose proud lash marks that ignorance beget
Come from what we believe not threat

Let's confess then profess
Equal opportunity now is a solution to the matter
With peace beating in our chest
Making black and white human lives better

Before we all fall to the widow maker

Article Twelve

American Enterprise Politics

"We should reject big government and look inside ourselves for all the things that built this country into what it was." . . . Glenn Beck
"Power tends to corrupt, and absolute power corrupts absolutely" . . . Lord Acton

"Big Government turns everyone into liars and cheats" . . . Jerry Rhoads

Whoever thought the www.usdebtclock.org would show 22 million government employees fully unionized and lionized for hanging on to their pensions, wage increases, perks without an ounce of accountability. Well, that is where the private sector finds itself: seventeen million unemployed, a $30.7 trillion national debt, an unfunded pension plan of $8 trillion for the bureaucrats, who are getting upward to 16 percent automatic wage increases, and above all a $6 trillion annual budget deficit that will get worse forever unless the private sector takes back America.

Our irresponsible, red and blue Congress thinks it is sufficient to have town hall meetings and transparency and a Trump super tax reduction committee that will come back with a so-called balanced approach to entitlement cuts and tax increases by taking away the middle-class deductions for mortgage interest, state income taxes, charitable contributions, and claim they have saved $1.3 trillion over the next ten years. While there is no true growth in the economy though the stock market continues to rise as the major predictor of overindulgence, the trade deficit continues to grow and America is insolvent then bankrupt.

The private sector needs to take back America using the enterprise model for taxation, foreign trade, spending, and incentives to small businesses. Convert to shares of stock in the American enterprise that collects 5 percent from every American's net worth.

- Taxation can be simplified and vilified by using a 5 percent capital infusion rate on net worth of individuals and corporations. This will raise $5 trillion per year in revenue and have the well-off pay American workers for their participation in generating that tax base. This is not redistribution of wealth; it is sharing with the workers that helped the wealthy get there. So, a net worth (wealth tax) is the only fair way to capitalize the enterprise. Actually, this will increase GDP and GNP by making America financially healthy for the first time since World War Two.
- Governmental payrolls will be reduced by 25 percent by privatizing the following agencies:

    - 50 percent of defense transferred to corporate bidders.
    - Farm Bureau takes over Agriculture.

- Mutual insurance companies take over healthcare services.
- Education services run by local Charter School trade associations.
- NSA privatized as the Aeronautical Trade Association.
- EEOC privatized as human services companies.
- OSHA privatized as a Preventive Health and Fitness Insurance company a wing of the US chambers of commerce.
- Judiciary privatized as federal and state courts.
- Justice privatized with policing and crime stoppage local reinforcement incentives based on the Rule of Law and constitution.

- Congressional workforce, salaries and benefits reduced by 40 percent.
- Federal Reserve banking system becomes the U.S. Treasury Department. The foreign trade deficit must be their focus using the US dollar value to attract trade and supply lines back to the homeland by devaluing the China and southeast Asia hold on manufacturing of pharmaceuticals, electronics, automobiles, soft and hard goods.
- Small business administration privatized and operated by National Chamber of Commerce; capital will be disbursed from savings to the applicants for R&D for creating new and competing products for exportation to the Chinese, Japanese, German, Korean, Russian, Mexican, Indian, Canadian and Arab countries as untapped markets. By balancing the trade deficits our national debt is reduced through natural economic supply and demand free market principles . . . i.e. upsized American Enterprise.

How Can We Accomplish This?

The power of the internet and the social media (twitter, face book, etc.) to make the American Enterprise Party virile and must be harnessed for educating Enterprising Americans on the details they do not know about. The existing problems and solutions need to go viral into every home and business campaigning to elect the American Enterprise Party stable of senators, House of Representatives, governors, state legislators, and local officials. The seasoned politician will tell you "Don't try to educate the voter during a campaign" . . . well look where that got us . . . dumbing down enterprising Americas is their strategy for ongoing control of enterprising Americans . . . not freeing the American Enterprise from excessive Government overhead.

Enterprising Americans must vote for private sector officials to replace the lawmakers with peacemakers, job makers, and responsible financial experts that know business and enterprise. This brings in a school of fish to replace the Big Brother whale we have allowed to take over America for its own behalf and allow the private sector to profiteer by making changes in our infra- structure and problem solving with respect to:

1. Job creation incentives using equity capital and lower Government overhead.
2. Debt reduction, revenue generation and equity development.
3. National and local economy using generally accepted accounting principles.
4. Accountable accrual basis budgetary processes.
5. Accountable accrual-based Government institutions.
6. Accountable accrual-based privatized Educators.
7. Gross national product using GAAP.
8. Accountable accrual based foreign trade and aid policies.
9. Accountable accrual-based Peace actions.
10. Accountable accrual based National defense.
11. Accountable accrual based National security agencies.

12. Accountable accrual based National health initiatives.
13. Accountable accrual based Housing and inner-city restoration.
14. Enforce diverse voting rights and virtual control using ID's and in person voting.
15. War on crime in the cities as function of restoring our inner cities with investment in infrastructure, small businesses, schools and patriot-sizing the gangs as enterprising citizens.
16. Respect and defend our first responders as heroes not Niro's fiddling while ANTIFA runs the game of protests escalating into riots for theft and profit.

Job creation is a function of capital for small businesses to innovate and create new products. (There are 158 thousand small to medium businesses employing 148 million workers and only 14,000 corporations employing less than 15 million workers). Taxation using net worth balances the playing field for the workers who make it happen. Economies of scale come from downsizing government overhead and privatizing capital formation. Budgets are used to subsidize profits that can be reinvested into capital formation outside of the Federal Reserve control over interest rates. Government institutions then can be those that protect entitlements and safety nets for the workers.

The public education system needs to be privatized and standardized for higher learning more than the 3 R's, by exposing our youth to STEM studies, the political sciences and the way Social and Government systems are supposed to work. The leftist programs for 1619 project, the critical race theory need to be focused on the 1776 reality history for declaring America's independence and development of the constitution so the emancipation proclamation and civil rights amendments could be passed. Establishing that Americans aren't racist not xenophobic but the attack by woke progressives, BLM, ANTIFA reparation-ists and rioters who believe history should be rewritten are practicing what they claim white America has done to them.

GIVE PEACE A CHANCE

Hand me your weapons
Hand me your cause
Now contemplate your sons
Think of your daughters as you pause

Is it worth the price you pay
To confront your fellow man
With fists clenched to betray
Peaceful days in each other's land

I don't believe
You believe it's right
To forsake those you conceive
Your children, just to fight

With only selfish banners to carry
Think and ponder
Why is it necessary
To ravage God's wonder

Why not throw down
Your pride; from your side
Make peace your sound
Before we all have died

What do we have to lose
That we haven't already lost
It is our choice to choose
Peace rather than the holocaust

On this Earth at any cost

For in peace

Lives don't cease
Love and friends abide
Before religion and principle all have died

As a belief in the same God's absolution
That Reason minus Race and Religion = Resolution

Give Peace a Chance

With the following principles:

- Gross national product is dependent on America's labor costs and costs of government being reduced by 25 percent through technology, lower healthcare costs, lower unemployment benefits, reduced workers' comp claims so hard product generation is brought back to America.
- Monetize the benefits of foreign trade, foreign aid, balance of trade so our past deficit spending is globalized by charging emerging nations a 5 percent distribution fee for selling their products into the American consumer markets.
- Give peace a chance by making our national security and defense based on profiling our enemies and setting up preventive technology to replace the current "check everyone" system at the airport.
- Computerize and standardize the national healthcare systems and only pay for best practice outcomes, not just input based incomes.
- Subsidize the housing markets by removing red lining and Jim Crow laws for John Crow opportunities changing the dominance of banking regulators and paranoia regarding private sector controls.

In Summary, now that we know it is the $3 to $4 trillion spent on nuclear weapons, $18 billion on a scrapped star wars system, two wars that cost the Americans $1 trillion to $3 trillion in dollars and lives, a healthcare system built on treatment, not outcome. That our leaders, mostly attorneys and third-generation lawmakers merrily pass more legislation to spend more money we simply don't have, we have a call to action for comprehensive change in the way we govern, legislate and enforce laws, rules and regulations.

This country was imagined to be dynamic through the replacement of the senators and representatives every four to six years, so we have equal representation of all Americans; rather, we have no term limits, except the President, nepotism, political incest and control of the monetary, productive, and distribution system by the huge Government, conglomerates and institutions that are in the pockets of the gang of 545. Literally a Big Brother Monopsony with a Monopoly Brotherhood. It is time for establish term limits of three for the house and two for the senate and rid our government of nepotism

Stop the madness using our current antitrust laws enforced by the Justice Department, before we totally erode our natural resources and waste valuable business vitality that could be spent on research and development rather than on lobbyists and campaign funding. Therefore, as the manifesto proposes we face a need for comprehensive overhaul of Government at all levels.

Recapitalize America Tax Net Worth and Save America

The Shared Equity Program downsizes government and upsizes American business. This represents an infusing of equity capital as reinvestment in American Enterprise. Org for inner city development and small business expansion by good neighborhood coalitions.

Save America
Help Small Diverse Business
Accumulate
Real
Equity

Cut government labor costs

22,700,000 Government employees reduced 15% per year until annual payroll and benefits are less than 10% of annual GDP.

Cut government overhead costs

- Guaranteed Union Pensions.
- Lobbyist Perks.
- Health Care benefits.
- Excessive Pay Raises.
- Pork Barrel legislation.

I. Shared equity formation allows America to protect its enterprise through reinvestment of wealth into the enterprise by converting reinvestment to shares of stock in the American enterprise that collects 5 percent from every American's net worth:
   a. Taxing net worth shares the wealth with the middle to lower class workers who enabled the wealth and the wealthy. Five percent of the gross net worth of $100 trillion would generate upward to $5 trillion per year in American annual revenue stream.
   b. Instead of Bill Gates, who has a net worth of $60 billion dollars, avoiding income taxes by donations to nonproductive charities, he would pay $30 million per year in share equity to recapitalize America. He is reinvesting his capital into the very enterprise system that generated his wealth. His return is his increase in net worth generated by seeding American business that creates jobs and value.
   c. Warren Buffet would then have to share his $50 billion wealth by having $25 million reinvested in saving America's enterprise system.
II. At the same time, America needs to restate its financial position and report on an accrual basis (GAAP):
   a. Cutting government labor costs of $1.3 trillion by 25 percent would generate $400 billion annually in savings,

    b. The 25 percent overhead (unionized pensions, perks, healthcare, raises) related to that cost would also be saved; this would generate another $100 million in savings from discontinued annual perks to government employees,

III. Transparency is not responsible cost management since it happens after the fact:
    a. The increase in revenues and reduction in direct labor and overhead costs would generate an annual profit of $2.5 trillion, thereby eliminating the Accumulated $16 trillion deficit in seven years and lowering debt service by $500 billion per year and unfunded pension and healthcare costs by $150 billion per year, further building a surplus for future generations.

IV. Scandals should be utilized as the catalyst to enacting much needed Government Reform through decentralization:

"Scandal is an action or event regarded as morally or legally wrong and causing general public outrage: The outrage or anger caused by such an action or event."

Examples of scandal in the Obama Administration:
- Benghazi, where or where was our *Secretary of State as the talker.
- IRS scrutiny, why just conservatives.
- AP subpoena is the height of invasion of privacy for leaking information.

Examples of scandal in the Biden Administration:
- Close down of Bagram Airport.
- Leaving military equipment $85 billion.
- Leaving the Embassy behind $800 million.
- Leaving hundreds of Americans and interpreters behind.
- Letting over 2 million immigrants come through the border without vetting, inoculation against the Pandemic and means of supporting themselves.
- Closing down the Keystone Pipeline and supporting the Russian Pipeline to Germany condemning the USA'S energy

independence that died on Biden's arrival based on the Green New Deal that has yet to pass the Senate for funding.

Examples of scandal in our American culture:
- Big Brother Government's role in our lives:
    - Invasion of privacy using whistle blowers and WikiLeaks type tactics.
    - Over regulation of businesses.
    - Punitive tactics blaming the private sector for every problem using anti-business laws.
    - Race protests that always escalate into riots, destruction of private property and disregards police sovereignty.
    - Allowing social media to subjectively shut down the freedom of speech for selective political and social priorities.

Examples of scandal in our Monetary and Financial condition:
- The gold standard is gone and so is the dollar's control of the international monetary system. The fiat American dollar has lost 85.4% of its value since the exit of the gold standard in 1971. Gold and precious metals are competitive threats to the floating fiat dollar underlying monstrous deficit spending and Fed debt instruments. Any revaluation of the floating dollar requires more debt financing and floats the interest boat into insolvency.
- The US dollar is being replaced as the world's reserve currency by the Chinese yuan, Euro currency, Asian interests, Russian strategists, Middle East dominance of energy sources, South America's economic agenda.
- Capital flight from equity to debt increases costs and reduces profits furthering the slowdown of GDP growth, limiting jobs and expanding unemployment and under employment.
- Obama Care converted health care from a business model to a bureaucratic model without regard to the 77 million baby boomers who are the unhealthiest Americans and wanting

their benefits at the age of 65 . . . a tsunami not a bounce over a speed bump.

Foundation of American Enterprise Party: Declaration of Independence (Government Reform Platform)

Reprint from the Declaration of Independence, paraphrasing the power that the Constitutional Congress usurped from the King of England and the United States of America individually need to take back the right to enterprise as their code and creed for fiscal and social responsibility.

By replacing in the Declaration of Independence the subject from *He the King of England* to our current monarchy the *Congress*, you will find how our rights are being usurped by the pursuit of money and war rather than the pursuit of peace, freedom, and happiness for all. To recover the intent of the Declaration of Independence, we must reestablish the rights, will, and hopes of the people, for the people, by the people with a government that stands for peace, freedom of choice, and allowed to act on the enterprise of their own work, play, and voice.

The King of England (American Congress) has refused our assent to laws, the most wholesome and necessary for the public good.

Congress has forbidden our governors to pass laws of immediate and pressing importance, unless suspended in their operation till our assent should be obtained; and when so suspended, has utterly neglected to attend to them.

Congress has refused to pass other laws for the accommodation of large districts of people, unless those people would relinquish the right of representation in the legislature, a right inestimable to them and formidable to tyrants only.

Congress has called together legislative bodies at places unusual, uncomfortable, and distant from the depository of their public records, for the sole purpose of fatiguing them into compliance with our measures.

Congress has dissolved representative houses repeatedly, for opposing with manly firmness our invasions on the rights of the people.

Congress has refused for a long time, after such dissolutions, to cause others to be elected, whereby the legislative powers, incapable of annihilation, have returned to the people at large for their exercise; the State remaining in the meantime exposed to all the dangers of invasion from without, and convulsions within.

Congress has endeavored to prevent the population of these states; for that purpose, obstructing the laws for naturalization of foreigners; refusing to pass others to encourage their migrations hither, and raising the conditions of new appropriations of lands.

Congress has obstructed the administration of justice by refusing our assent to laws for establishing judiciary powers.

Congress has made judges dependent on our will alone for the tenure of their offices, and the amount and payment of their salaries.

Congress has erected a multitude of new offices and sent hither swarms of officers to harass our people and eat out their substance.

Congress has kept among us, in times of peace, standing armies without the consent of our legislatures.

Congress has affected to render the military independent of and superior to the civil power.

Congress has combined with others to subject us to a jurisdiction foreign to our constitution, and unacknowledged by our laws; giving our assent to their acts of pretended legislation:

- For quartering large bodies of armed troops among us
- For protecting them, by a mock trial from punishment for any murders which they should commit on the inhabitants of these states
- For cutting off our trade with all parts of the world
- For imposing taxes on us without our consent
- For depriving us, in many cases, of the benefit of trial by jury
- For transporting us beyond seas to be tried for pretended offences
- For abolishing the free system of English laws in a neighboring province, establishing therein an arbitrary government, and enlarging its boundaries so as to render it at once an example and fit instrument for introducing the same absolute rule into these States
- For taking away our charters, abolishing our most valuable laws and altering fundamentally the forms of our governments
- For suspending our own legislatures and declaring themselves invested with power to legislate for us in all cases whatsoever.

They too have been deaf to the voice of justice and of consanguinity. We must, therefore, acquiesce in the necessity, which denounces our separation, and hold them, as we hold the rest of mankind, enemies in war, in peace friends. We, therefore, the representatives of the United States of America, in general, assembled, appealing to the supreme judge of the world for the rectitude of our intentions, do, in the name, and by authority of the good people of these states, solemnly publish and declare, that these United States are, and of right ought to be free and independent states, that they are absolved from all fiscal allegiance to the federal government and that all political connection between them and the state, is and ought to be totally based on enterprise.

And that as free and independent states, they have full power to levy, conclude peace, contract alliances, establish commerce, and to do all other acts and things which independent states may of right do. And for the support of this declaration, with a firm reliance on the protection of divine providence, we mutually pledge to each other our lives, our fortunes, and our sacred honor to the Republic for which it stands, one nations indivisible with liberty and justice for all. Mandated by the American Enterprise Party Articles of freedom for all.

Commentary:

In George Orwell's classic book "1984" possibly *the* most definitive dystopian novel ever written he takes us to a world beyond imagining, where the totalitarian government uses video cameras to watch everyone's home life and work habits then imposing fear inducing conformity of reprisal to keep everyone subservient by killing the dissidents and offenders. The Government has **absolute power** in Oceania which includes the United Kingdom, where the story is played out. As you read 1984 you will meet many recognizable characters, themes, and words which have become part of **our everyday life**. Where Big Brother knows all, sees all and controls all. Written in Orwell's inimitable journalistic style, *1984* is a tribute to a man who saw the true dangers of historian Lord Acton's (1834-1902) statement: *"Power corrupts; absolute power corrupts absolutely."*

Even more frightening is *Ray Bradbury's novel Fahrenheit 451* set in a bleak, dystopian future with Guy Montag as a fireman. In his world, where television rules and literature were on the brink of extinction, firemen start fires rather than put them out. His job was to destroy the most illegal of commodities, the printed book, along with the houses in which they are hidden and the people that read them. This extinction of learning was in fact practiced by Asia Communists in the Twentieth Century until personal freedom fighters emerged to protect the Aquarian Entrepreneurs that ruled the world for hundreds of years. And as a result, China, South Korea, India and Japan are now emerging as Enterprising societies.

FINALE: To reign in the evolution to Big Brother Government and the Brotherhood and its regulatory impediments to personal freedoms as depicted in Animal Farm, 1984, the Hunger Games, Fahrenheit 451, Zeitgeist, etc. the Great American Enterprise must prevail. Then as the American **Enterprise wins over Conservatives, Liberals, Kings, Dictators**, Socialists, Communists, Constructionists, Constitutionalists, and Incrementalists the world can capitalize on a revitalized work ethic that is dedicated to investing the national wealth in our individual human assets.

SUM UP THIS ARTICLE

Declaration of Independence

In America people are independent
Due to a Declaration in 1776
Due to the Constitution in 1774
Due to the Civil Rights Act of 1964
Due to World Wars I and II
Due to the First and Second Amendments

So why do we feel inhibited by Government
Is Enterprise really Free
Since each American is an Enterprise
And most laws are to inhibit this dynamic
With 40,000 bills and 5,000 laws being passed each year
By lawmakers who vote their own agenda

Not ours any more

What exactly is ours
Is it our right to work?
Is it our ambition?
Is it our dreams?
Is it our responsibilities?
Is it our FREEDOM to vote?
Is it my American Dream?

Then why do we feel helpless
It is not our authority
It is not our preference
It is not our risk that counts
It is not our decision to go to war
It is not our opinion on peace

Not now

Freedom is a right
Freedom is a necessity
Freedom is our only weapon
Against power and poverty
Against enforcement
Against Tyranny

Will Americans let go of freedom
Will Americans go down peacefully
Will Americans lose independence
Ask yourself if you want 40,000 laws per year
Ask yourself if you want lawmakers endlessly making laws
Ask yourself if you have given up or will stand up
For your independence and freedom that won't wait

Your individual answer collectively will determine America's fate
So, now make your pledge of allegiance to a government
For enterprising people, of enterprising people, by enterprising the people
... the American Enterprise Party Creed
American Enterprise Party Matters (AEPM)

Article Thirteen

The Articles of Incorporation and Constitutional Bylaws

Mission Statement

For the sake of the nation's survival as a leader in the world, the private sector must take an active role under the laws needed to govern moderate and reformative principles of American enterprises by resurrecting the intent of the American Constitution and Declaration of Independence by creating a new third political party alternative. The American Enterprise Party is that alternative using the swing vote **to break ties and prevent gridlock of the two-party system** at every level for parity and resolution of deep-rooted problems facing the Republic. No longer will the President of the United States and a government of 100 senators, 9 Supreme Court Judges, 435 Congressmen and 22.6 million government employees rule 330 million enterprising Americans without fair representation of enterprising Americans and effective leadership. What is at risk . . . The health and wealth of our nation to be shared, based on individual effort, by all.

ARTICLES OF INCORPORATION

- Whereas, the country of America has forsaken the pursuit of happiness, peace, and love of fellow man, and
- Whereas the states have been led by lawmakers who stifle the American enterprise system, and
- Whereas our current public officials are not accountable to the private sector and feel transparency is enough, and
- Whereas the gridlocked no consensus Congress of the United States of America has ground down our national vitality and ability

to create jobs and fulfill the risk-taking American Dream, with burdensome taxes, laws, rules and regulations, and
- Whereas, the majority of enterprising Americans want rebirth of constitutional government, we the people hereby erect a new political party founded on the following principles:

1. Peace in the world in policy and actions.
2. Government by the people, of the people, for the people.
3. Less government intervention in all facets of life.
4. Recapitalize our American enterprise for its enterprising people.
5. Liberate the creators of jobs, knowledge, justice, and the gross national product for all its citizens.
6. Restore the health and wealth of America.
7. Share in the wealth in proportion to effort and contribution to its making.

We as the representatives of the enterprising Americans, who need fair representation, form a contrasting political party that moves America away from great society programs to a freedom to work for the values assured by the American Constitution and to have the following equal rights and opportunities that best serve enterprising Americans and preserve health, happiness, and prosperity for all:

1. Propagate and promulgate family values.
2. Pursue STEM and higher education.
3. Have home ownership.
4. Pursue full employment.
5. Have health and wellness services for all.
6. Pursue happiness without malice of race, gender, religion or creed.
7. Have an opportunity to share in prosperity for all.
8. Free to innovate new economies and businesses uninhibited by arbitrary and capricious laws and regulations.

9. Support the concept of three-party rule and a swing vote **to break ties and prevent gridlock of the two-party system** at every level of democracy that the majority rules.

We as the representatives of the American Enterprise Party move and agree to the following health and wealth enterprise platform:

1. Recast the current income tax and estate tax system to recapitalize the American enterprise system based on 5 percent of individual net worth as an equity infusion to refinance the enterprise.
2. Downsize government at all levels by spinning off public services to private enterprise that is accountable to its private sector shareholders.
3. Impose an up to, 25 percent sales tax on distribution fee on foreign sales that utilize the American enterprise consumer market.
4. Pay down the national debt by assessing an infusion of capital from net worth and eliminating all burdensome taxation that impedes the growth of America's economy.
5. Eliminate the complexities imposed by bureaucratic rules and regulations.
6. Turn lawmakers into job makers and peace makers.
7. Improve the health values through Self-Health wellness programs and economic incentives for individuals to have earning their own health annuity by staying well.
8. List all college graduates in a National Job Corps Registry for resurrecting R&D technology for creating enhancements to the Great American Enterprise.
9. Preserve the existing entitlements for the aging and poor by amending Obama Care for the oppressive and costly pursuit of treating illness. Replacing treatment with the pursuit of wellness outcomes. This paradigm SHIFT can be funded by eliminating the new entitlements for minimum wage, workers comp, unemployment, welfare and guaranteed pensions . . . those

being replaced by a system of personal investment accounts reinvested in the American enterprise.

10. Engender the war on debt through reduced deficit spending on weapons of mass destruction, public pensions, perks, and guaranteed compensation packages for the public sector.
11. Form the Great North American Enterprise Union with Canada and Mexico for free flow of legal immigrants, energy resources, and jobs according to attaining citizenship and use of English as their primary language.
12. Form OPEC (Oil Purchasing Energy Countries) to negotiate with *OPEC (Organization of the Petroleum Exporting Countries)* pricing on oil products to control waste and overutilization of our world's energy resources. Using clean energy goals to become independent of fossil fuel emissions using conservation America should protect it natural resources as the end game.
13. Amend the Green New Deal so it recognizes the Earth's history of controlling itself if we as passengers comply with conservation of our carbon transfer into the atmosphere and better management wasteful practices (i.e., find a recycling system for plastics ... see example on page 19 regarding Myles Petron, age 18 and an entrepreneur in Canada utilizing plastics recycled as building materials).

We, as the representatives of working Americans, will dedicate our time to three-party governance at all levels of the American society through reduced dominance of money-driven politics, utilizing the Internet to elect private-sector candidates using term limits to populate the governance with private sector candidates for:

1. Governorships.
2. Legislative and congressional seats.
3. Mayoral positions.
4. County commissioners.
5. Township supervisors.

The representation and leadership will require a two to four-year commitment by all American citizens to participate in the reformation of our Founding Fathers' American enterprise dream. The reformation of America at all political levels must move to:

1. Ensure freedom of speech.
2. Freedom of self-preservation and personal defense.
3. Freedom to pursue knowledge and opportunity.
4. Freedom to determine one's own healthcare and wellness program using self-health lifestyles.
5. Freedom to propagate family units regardless of sex, race, or creed.
6. Freedom to contribute to foreign relations based on the world's peaceful coexistence and building international relationships and infrastructures for enterprising individuals around our planet.
7. Freedom of choice of educational facilities and patriotic and ethical curriculums.

The time has come for the private sector to take back America, the great American enterprise that populates consumerism and allows workers worldwide to form a coalition and consensus of ideas, ideals, and opportunities for all. The war on debt and destruction of human lives for the monetary benefit of the few must give way to a transformation of all governments where the involvement of the many will replace the power of the few, where the imposition of money as the flag bearer will give way to knowledge, and the transformation of the world's war on hunger and poverty will be generated by enterprise for job creation and self-preservation, not socialism or any other -ism.

Signed this day of and year _____

By the Board of Erectors of the American Enterprise Party
                Chairman: Jerry Rhoads
                Vice Chairman: Sharon Rhoads

Secretary: Alec Stephens
Treasurer: Kip Rhoads
Counselor: Mark Levin (proposed AAL)
Consultant: Donald J. Trump

Proposed Advisors:
Donald Trump potential candidate on policy and accountability.
Henry Kissinger on détente and peaceful coexistence.
Rudy Giuliani attorney general on crime and secure borders.
Dr. Arthur Laffer on taxation for enterprises and individual net worth.
Michael Pompeo on foreign relations and China's capitalism.
Hershel Walker race relations and voting rights.
Elon Musk environmental problems and solutions.
William Bennet education curriculum and Charter schools.
Mark Levin constitutional amendments and electoral college.
Tucker Carlson media relations and social media accountability.
Warren Buffett foreign trade and trade imbalance.

The American Enterprise Party is based on the proclamation of economic and moral values for the majority of American citizens . . . we hereby revitalize the American worker's jobs for peace not more laws and development of weapons of mass destruction . . . incorporating the mission of building "Peace through Strength" not destroying the fabric of human existence and be the leaders towards a free, healthy, prosperous and peaceful world. Our intelligence and ideals will take us there if we understand that ideas are the fruit of thought and solutions to problems are the result of change and confronting fear inducing conformity, thereof.

Twelve-step implementation plan:

Timing: after the 2024 presidential election and the State of the Union Address, regardless of who wins, we will announce the formation of the party and the ten-step plan with the platform published in Jerry Rhoads' book *"The American Enterprise Party"*:

1. Publish the American Enterprise Party Platform.
2. Form the American Enterprise Party corporation.
3. Obtain 504 foundation tax exemption status.
4. Elect a board of directors.
5. Announce the formation of the party in media.
6. Sign up participants in the formation of local grassroots members.
7. Post videos, blogs, Tweets, and information on the American for Enterprise website on the Internet, announcing the party's platform and objectives.
8. Elicit national press coverage and media coverage for key party members.
9. Announce Jerry Rhoads as the party's candidate for governor of Illinois in 2024.
10. Survey and canvas fifty state governors for their interest and involvement.
11. Sign up key State legislators who represent the private sector for membership.
12. In 2024 have a candidate for American Enterprise Party announce for the presidential race.

American Enterprise Party Platform

(An excerpt from the book Man*cology: The Science of Managing Human Value* by Jerry L. Rhoads, CPA, July 1992, second edition July 2007, third edition July 2012)

Third Party Platform (The Merging of Capitalism and Socialism as the formula for the party of Humanism)

Operating under the premise that the two-party system in America has narrowed to a one party "winner take all" called the *elito-crats*, who govern by the money for the money and not by the constitution. We must go back to the government "for the people, by the people, of the people with life, liberty and justice for all." The definition of Humanism.

1. Authority: the constitutional right of human beings, regardless of color, gender, creed, nationality, or religion to pursue enterprise, morality, happiness, and good fortune.
2. Foundation: constitutional amendments:
    A. All Americans are created to be equal with the opportunity to pursue equality in educational, economic, and religious endeavors.
    B. All Americans have the civil right to an education by an institution of their choice.
    C. . All Americans have the civil right to an enterprise as long as it is pursued legally with ethics and morality.
    D. All Americans have the obligation to participate in the process of governing themselves if they wish to receive their civil right to an education and economic freedom.
    E. All Americans have the obligation and responsibility to use guns for protection only and participate in collecting and banning military weapons for personal use and sale on the open market.
    F. All Americans have an obligation to support world peace efforts, utilizing the economics of peaceful coexistence where human value promulgates nonmilitary actions to replace arms buildup and disregard for human life.
    H. All Americans have an obligation to practice self-health principles as it is a privilege of self-sacrifice.
    I. All Americans have the right to live in comfort and good health with safety and happiness as the goal.
3. Structure is founded on *Americanism* as the ethical political and economic philosophy. This is the science of managing *Americrats* (ethical workers) human capital value. The third-party ticket is *Americratic (*ethical political party*)*, requiring the direct participation of Americans to accept the responsibility of governing themselves through a modification of the established practices using constitutional rule of law as the platform.

4. Strategy of the third party is to offer Americans who believe in the constitutional right of opportunity to participate in establishing a structure and systematic process that pursues the intent of our Founding Fathers. This strategy will be founded on the following principles:

   A. Authoritarian processes will be decentralized in government and business. This is a movement back to the identity of the individual and a movement away from large government and conglomerates who have not met the emotional nor economic needs of the individual.
   B. Organizations will be encouraged and taught Mancology so the processes are understood and reconfigured for the benefit of building the skills and productivity of the individual. This will require analytics of the functions and the authority of the individual to produce and effect their own future.
   C. Productivity statistics and unitary analytics of cost and benefits of the output versus the input will be posted for all of the functions to review and evaluate.
   D. The recapitalizing and financing of government will be based on simplified taxing methods for the American enterprise by converting reinvestment to shares of stock in the American enterprise that collects 5 percent from every American's net worth:
      (1) 5 percent flat* tax on individual net worth at the Federal level.
      (2) 5 percent flat* tax on corporate net worth at the Federal level.at the Federal level. * Flat tax standing for a reinvestment as an infusion of capital in the American Enterprise to pay down current debt service.
      (3) Zero income tax on individual at the state level, only 5 percent sales tax on individual's consumption.

(4) 5 percent flat tax on businesses' net worth at the state level, less credits for jobs, investment, research, and development.

(5) 0 percent capital gains tax, 10 percent investment tax credit at federal level.

(6) 5 percent investment, jobs, and research and development tax credits at state level.

(7) 0 percent tax on estates and gift taxes dated prior to new tax system (a $250,000 floor and a $1 billion ceiling); zero estate and gift taxes after net worth recapitalization assessment (tax) implemented.

E. The competitive data analytics of the United States in the world market will indicate the value of the individual value and productivity toward national goals. The criteria would consist of:

(1)) Gross domestic and national product broken down into the component gross state products that make up the whole.

(2) SAT scores by state.

(3) Employment rates by state.

(4) Crime rates by state (number of guns and shootings).

(5) Divorce rates by state.

(6) High school graduation rates by state.

(7) Teen pregnancy rates by state.

(8) Literacy rates by state.

(9) Abortions by state.

(10) Balanced operating budgets using GAAP.

F. The system of financing the American enterprise reinvestment will come from the following changes in the American results:

(1) Balanced trade deficits (imposition of a 25 percent distribution fee for use of American consumption market to offset the imbalance in pricing in foreign markets)

(2) Absolving problems requiring American intervention in other countries' internal affairs, except as it directly affects U.S. security.

(3) Improved worker productivity equating to improved quality and a resultant reduction in the cost of delivered product.

(4) Emphasis on worker skill development (learn-to-earn programs); this investment in the individual Americrat is the cornerstone of Mancolgy (work ethic).

(5) Small business financing must be the responsibility of a deregulated banking industry and aggressive tax credits, which promote small-business enterprise as the solution to worker dissatisfaction and unemployment, which is the result of corporate misuse of human value by not sharing in the wealth form their endeavors.

(6) Dissolution of the Federal Reserve Banking system and complete deregulation of banking for small-business private investments.

(7) Complete the Border Wall to secure America for planned and managed integration at strategic border clearing stations of migrants that apply for Social Security numbers, English-speaking coaching, and apply for citizenship, subject to a waiting period. (Replace sanctuary cities and states with accelerated citizenship for immigrants.

(8) Balanced operating budgets using GAAP.

G. A balanced federal budget through the following initiatives:

(1) Foreign aid phase out for those countries that have a foreign trade surplus with the U.S.

(2) Foreign aid (capital investment in an economic infrastructure) phases up for emerging markets (Mexico, Africa, Middle East, Central and South America, etc.) that commit to peaceful coexistence pledges through the United Nations Security Council.

(3) Realignment of defense spending so it focuses on computerized alert systems and tracking of foreign weapons deployment. Total phase down of the military complex with the objective of more effective foreign policy built on economic power and peaceful coexistence initiatives versus military power, being the goal. Improve satellite and drone defenses for safe and peaceful coexistent protection of our citizens.

(4) Realignment of entitlement programs to the use of enterprise plans and tax credits for SHIFT withholding accounts for self-funding the individual's share of the cost of financing individual healthcare needs and costs:

  (a) 100 percent individual tax deductions for health insurance costs
  (b) Job-based tax credits for small business.
  (c) Rethinking of retirement age and preservation of Social Security based on personal choice, not a date or an age (sixty-five due to increased life expectancy may be too early). Personal accounts managed by professionals may be a way to disconnect this from government mismanagement of the benefits. (Late retirement versus early retirement may be a cultural change in administering the Social Security benefits).

(5) Sunshine laws for all legislative programs (pass a bill, kill a bill, review ten other bills for termination or extinction).

(6) Limited terms for congressional seats at state and federal level while discouraging generational nepotism for reelections.

(7) Redistricting of congressional seats based on a revised federal revenue sharing criterion:
  (a) Gross state productivity.
  (b) State employment rate.
  (c) State SAT scores.

(d) State high school graduation rate.
(e) State literacy rate.
(f) State divorce rate.
(g) State crime rate (number of guns and shootings).
(h) State teen pregnancy rate.
(I) State abortion rate.
(j) Balanced operating budgets using GAAP.

H. Balance state budgets through the following initiatives:
1. Restructure welfare (great society programs) into great enterprise programs based on "learn to earn" functional job corps to clean up the inner city and instill pride in the traditional neighborhood culture.
2. Institute incentive tax credits for investment in:
   A. Full employment job credits.
   B. Equal private and charter education revenue credits.
   C. Affordable housing credits.
   D. Capital investment in inner city businesses.
   E. Research and development projects.
   F. Mutually owned health insurance networks.
   G. Private Charter School educational opportunities for minorities.
   H. Drug rehab centers and Planned Parenthood counseling.
3. Pass sunshine laws and limited terms for the legislature (for every law passed, an old law must be removed so the funding of the new law can be affordable, and ten others reviewed for termination or extinction).
4. Flat tax schedule on individuals of 0 percent of gross spendable income with a 5 percent sales tax on consumable type items.
5. Five percent flat tax on business net worth, less incentive property tax credits, plus a 5 percent value-added

tax for financing private education and drug rehab centers and Planned Parenthood counseling, thereby eliminating personal property and real property taxes for funding education.
6. Federal revenue sharing based on each state's:
    A. Gross state contribution to GNP.
    B. Employment rate.
    C. SAT scores.
    D. High school graduation rates.
    E. Literacy rate.
    F. Divorce rate.
    G. Teen pregnancy rate.
    H. Crime rate (number of guns and shootings).
    I. Adoration rate.
    J. Balanced operating budgets using GAAP.
7. Redistricting members of national congress based on the above success contribution formula, getting away from population-related representation and electoral college disparities.

I. National drug management programs administered by states:
1. State-financed private investment in drug rehab centers program.
2. State-financed private investment in family counseling centers program.
3. Offer job incentive property tax credits to businesses that assist and employ recovering alcoholics and drug addicts.

J. National prison management programs administered by states:
1. Implement enterprise job-placement incentives to inmates for skill development and release learn to earn programs.

2. Establish private enterprise counseling incentives for institutional rehabilitation and job placement.
3. Offer job tax credits for employment of recovering inmates.

K. National abortion management programs administered by state:
1. Expand sex education and Planned Parenthood through investment in private enterprise counseling centers.
2. Establish criteria for freedom of choice centers, requiring enrollment in counseling in first trimester (Lower abortions rate).
3. Establish pro-life and free to choose campaigns focused on sex education and Planned Parenthood counseling.

L. National (universal) healthcare quality control program administered by the private mutually owned health preservation companies specializing in evidence-based medicine and pay-for-outcome processes (utilize a withholding program for individual savings accounts for "aging insurance," with investment and distribution by private enterprise; paradigm SHIFT self-health insurance funding trust to manage the resources).
1. Disconnect healthcare funding from the employer and connect to individual responsibility incentives. Options for employer equal match).
2. Set up a standardized health-preservation package of benefits administered by private enterprise (mutually-owned health insurance companies that invest the funding and process the claims) on the basis of the improvement of fitness and the prevention of chronic diseases.
3. Tax deductions for each individual's long-term care insurance fund. Rates are based on each person's fitness and health profile.

4. One hundred percent tax deduction to individuals for fitness, nutritional, and weight-management costs, regular screening exams and annual physicals.
5. Deregulate healthcare providers except for licensure and reimbursement audits. Replace the Department of Health and Human Services with the Department of Quality of Life.
6. Eliminate preexisting-condition clauses and waiting periods.
7. Establish a reinsurance fund for the high-risk pool of individuals who have catastrophic episodes or are underinsured.
8. Do not ration health claims under Medicare and Medicaid programs to critical illnesses for the elderly and the uninsured/underinsured but require that the payment thereof must be based on the basis of outcome, not provider income.

M. National educational management programs administered by the states:

1. Standardized SAT scoring.
2. Federal requirement for revenue sharing using an approved curriculum based on 75 percent STEM technical development and 25 percent personal development courses.
3. Graduation rate methodology.
4. Invest in inner city educational reform 75 percent jobs in city enterprises 25 percent personal development for American culture and arts.
5. Counseling for learn to earn, skill to bill, Mancology principles, and local business to rally minorities to nationalism.
6. Encourage the educational focus on the STEM curriculum (science, technology, engineering and

math) and technical studies but with a more aggressive approach by deregulating the businesses so they can more readily employ such specialized graduates in the pursuit of new technology in the applied sciences and use of liberal arts in the practicum of Free Market Enterprise using the Founding principles of Mancology, the science of managing human value replacing capitalism, socialism, racism, ism isms ism's with humanism:

Humanism behavior: development of the personal being:

Axiom one: human values must be learned through traditional family structure and morals exemplified by the parents in the home environment and in the teachings at school and in constructive social agencies for counseling families on such. This is founded on the principle that the value of individuals is the result of each person's constitutional right to pursue happiness and freedom based on their personal commitment to remove all self-imposed obstacles. Our investment in human value can be gauged by the traits of humility, fortitude, positive attitude and willingness to be a team member or leader for the good of the country.

Work ethic and patriotic values are what determines human value in a social sense and it must build on personal worth and a productive work environment. Early retirement is not the mark of a success in America but the value that is brought to the job, and late retirement may mean a more productive and valuable aging process. In this vein, the concept of Social Security may have to be based on an age related to personal decisions, not a specific age or date.

Political behavior: development of political systems:

Axiom two: humanism value must be based on the economic realities of our enterprise system. The enterprising American "learn to earn and skill to bill value of the individual is what each can contribute to the sum total of the society's worth in the world marketplace. This is the gross national productivity founded on the principles of supply side versus demand side economics. The following formulas make up the logic for choosing supply side over demand side economic and political theory:

Demand side economics: Government is expanded to create jobs that do not produce products. The earning power created by these jobs erodes the profits of the businesses through more taxes. The result is less productivity from the workforce because of the emphasis on cost cutting (reduced investment in job training, R&D, and marketing) rather than productivity to meet increasing demand, which would have been created by job training, R&D, and marketing. All of which erodes quality of the input and output units of production. The investments that would result from higher returns do not occur because of the lack of retained earnings, capital, and purchasing power.

This will result in an economic strangulation of resources that America needs to be able to compete in a world economy, that is doggedly in pursuit of the American Dream.

Supply side enterprise economics: Government is shrunk to create jobs in the private sector, which produces more and better products at lower costs because of the incentive for workers to earn more and pay less in income taxes. The founding principle here is that less government involvement in business enterprise will result in more available profit resources for paying off debt, the expansion of job training, R&D, and marketing of American products to a world economy. The formula is:

- \<More business deployment\>
  less government employment =
- \<More production\>
  less waste per unit of production =
- \<More jobs\>
  less unemployment =

- <More quality>
  less cost per unit of sales =
- <More profits>
  less taxes per unit of sales =
- <More capital>
  less erosion of balance of trade =
- <More markets>
  less erosion of GNP =
- <More resources for eliminating the budget deficit based on GAAP to pay down debt
- <More capital from higher profits and equity = payment of debt and balanced operating budgets using GAAP
- Growth in GDP and GNP as a percentage of the current stock market, price index and cost of living.

Disband the term *lawmaker* and replace the process of lawmaking with peacemakers and job makers. All laws must be economically feasible as well as socially needed so that we do not continue to kill the goose that lays the golden eggs for the sake of the interests of a minority who do not participate in the development and sustenance of the enterprise. We are not meant to be a welfare state but a state with welfare as part of our national responsibilities to the better good. Participation is the reward for human effort, value and integrity.

Business reform: organizational development of human capital as added value to the enterprise for philosophical change:

Axiom three: Mancology is the science of managing human value for the good of the individual, who will make a commitment to self-development and change of negative attitudes toward their fellow human being. Mancology is a philosophical commitment that the organization's value comes from each of the individual humans that participate in the pursuit of the corporate goals and objectives within the context of each person's goals and subjectives. Thus, emerges the *management by subjectives*, a managerial and political theory that embodies Drucker's MBO and Maslow's hierarchy of individual needs and emotional desires. This embodies the enterprising American's "learn to earn and skill to bill" values. From this important plank of the platform will emerge sharing in the wealth that is up till now controlled by the ruling class elito-crats making mandated rules, who themselves break at will. Masks, vaccines, insider trading, sheltering at home, quarantining since they are all essential workers.

Social reform: personal development for society changes:

Axiom four: Enterprise is the solution to social and political divergence, which a society needs when the value of human beings is eroded by the destruction of the family unit, social mores and morals, and the sanctity of self-esteem. Enterprise is built on the concept of family values and "learn to earn and skill to bill" work ethic lived in healthy and happy conditions.

Constitutional reform: governmental development for patriotic nationalism:

Axiom five: The American Constitution is the mechanism for change and de-institutionalization of the enterprise system, as regulated by a decentralized government with indicators of human value. The use of unionization for the benefit of the public sector must meet the same criteria as the private sector in using collective bargaining for the benefit of the public domain, not the public officials.

Transparency is not enough when the lawmakers become union makers and the enterprise suffers with overloaded fixed overhead and unaffordable benefits for the public sector paid for by the private sector.

For the safety of peaceful citizens put gun control initiatives in the hands of the private sector, not in the hands of politicians, so the elimination of military weapons in the marketplace can be policed and such weapons confiscated.

The need to repatriate inner city gangs to clean up their neighborhoods for the good of their families. The family unit has to be brought back together in strengthening of our most valuable assets ... human effort and pursuing education and a productive position in the Great American enterprise, is the American Dream.

Metrics for measuring States government reform effectiveness (ratings from first to fiftieth will be used to allocate revenue sharing):
- Gross state productivity.
- Unemployment, jobs created and employment rates.
- Literacy rate (by region and districts).
- Divorce rate (by region and districts).
- SAT scores.
- Crime rate (by region and districts).
- Teen pregnancy rate (by region and districts)
- Inflation, minimum wage, cost of living rates.
- High school graduation rate (by region and districts).
- College graduation rate.
- Crime rate death by guns rate (number of guns and shootings) (by region and districts).
- Balanced operating budgets using GAAP.
- Conditions in the inner city and small marginalized small rural communities (by region and districts).

Political reform: institutional development for democracy:

Axiom six: The American Enterprise Party would be managed by Americrats who are trained and schooled in the science of managing human value at the local and state level, utilizing the constitution as the guiding text for change and financial viability in the marketplace. This new political party would run for office at every level, and carry with them the new wave of human dignity—*Mancology*. The third-party candidates would move the country toward a three-party, a swing vote **to break ties and prevent gridlock of the two-party system** at every level as an alternative at the state and national level. The governorships and the presidency would be the targets before the senate and house are being represented by Americrats as the merger of capitalism and socialism into humanism for the better good becoming the redemption of extremism politics in America.

Axiom seven: Change will be instituted by third party swing vote, and not by the traditional special interest lobbying groups dictating to the Congress what the minority wants for the majority. For the only viable way for America to continue to be a leader in world politics is to demonstrate economically that democracy works and is the direction in which all governments must move in order to improve the value of, and the resulting standard of living of each and every human being:

- Removal of laws when making laws will : focus on economic feasibility as well as moral and social issues.
- Removal of political campaigns being financed for public hangings on the TV and Internet media . . . debates on problem resolution not just two-party issues are the only topics allowed for public exposure.
- Removal of political contributions being used for public exposure negative campaigns . . . limited to debates and problem resolution that are topical to the voters involving the third-party balance.
- Removal of generational inheritance of the political office.
- Removal of laws guaranteeing incumbency by redistricting the voters and imposing term limits.
- Removal of tenure being the basis for committee chairs and passing term limits for Congress.

Axiom eight: SHIFT (Self-Health Insurance Funding Trust) of the paradigm in healthcare to deductive pursuit of outcome from inductive pursuit of treatment based on a method of payment that requires definable episodic outcomes. Physicians, hospitals, nursing homes, home care, hospice, clinics, etc. must be standardized using deductive models of care based on problem assessment, programmatic interventions, and evaluation of outcomes using ISO 10,000 standards. From this paradigm, the use of "evidence-based medicine" and "pay for performance" can be attainable along with transparency, interoperability of data, and control of quality:

- Create a universal healthcare policy for all Americans.
- Actualize the importance of quality of life based on health preservation as a national priority to replace the expediency of sacrificing lives with the following program of preventing chronic disease, thereby saving cost and lives (amend Obama Care to enact the following principles):

    1. Reimburse more for wellness and less for treating illness; take away incentives to keep the elderly dependent on a wheelchair and over medicate.
    2. Elimination of "personal spend down" to access Medicaid; do not turn the self-reliant into wards of the state.
    3. Federalize Medicaid into a true safety net for the uninsured and underinsured
    4. Standardize Medicare as the true safety net for the elderly and disabled.
    5. Initiate personal withholding savings account for long-term care insurance and disconnect funding from employment.
    6. Require all healthcare providers practice the Six Sigma principles of eliminating waste using standardized processes, customized care plans, point-of-care computers and the requirement that the patient must be seen before a physician's orders can be executed. Currently 90% of orders are given over the telephone without examination or evaluation of outcome.

    7. Provide 50% premium credit reductions for personal fitness, nutrition, health screening, and health-preservation costs expended by each taxpayer.

- Quantify national savings objectives by replacing the current enforcement regulatory system with a re-enforcement system that coaches' providers on efficiency, cost effectiveness, quality control, and productivity, utilizing technology and computerized models of care. Eliminate Centers of Medicare/Medicaid and replace with CQL . . . Centers of Quality of life.

Diplomatic reform: foreign policy for development of worldwide commerce:

Axiom nine: SHIFT emphasis from protectionism and fear inducing conformity to nationalism and peaceful coexistence with the world. The United Nations should be the catalyst to empowering each member to be both enterprising and peacefully conduct business on a worldwide platform. All members sign a pledge of peace and peaceful coexistence with its members and a worldwide plan for financial stability. Any nation not willing to sign this declaration shall not be active in the world marketplace:

- Stop pushing nation building and regime change until there is an opportunity to assist in implementing infrastructure. Allow United Nations to head up banking of resources to assist financially struggling nations rather than the world banking system. Those ready for change can be cloned by the UN for peaceful growth, an entrepreneurial expansion of their legal infrastructure.
- Enable peace corps development of commerce as the solution to terrorism. "Serve your country is to serve your soul".
- Spend less on arms buildup and more on capitalizing businesses, creating jobs, and market development.
- Develop OPEC (Oil Purchasing Energy Companies) consortium for purchasing petroleum from oil-producing countries.

- Champion and conduct arms reduction of weapons of mass destruction and outlawing the use of "over the horizon" missiles and drones for military purposes.
- Create national and worldwide enterprise (opportunity) zones and set up local small businesses in all third-world economies.

SUM UP THIS ARTICLE:

If I Were President (a fantasy at my age, since all I run on is my treadmill, but at 81 I can still have this risk-taking American dream).

Leadership Reform:

Axiom 10: It's easy to criticize, hypothesize, visualize, epitomize productive thoughts and opinions. Here's mine ... change our culture of violence, vulgarity and excesses to Humanism. So goes the aftermath of the contested election of 2020. Since the country is split into two waring parts as Congress fiddles while America is burning literally and figuratively, the victim of overindulgence with an insolvent under pinning. Our weakness in reinforcing justice and policing will do us under as the criminals become emboldened and take more and more advance upon our safety and security on the streets of our cities. And the problem of homelessness has to be eradicated through intervention for marginalized citizens and immigration management by providing private housing, education and job training as a private enterprise pursuing profit from more competent and effective entrepreneurs and their socialized work environment.

Therefore, the POTUS' bully pulpit is an enabler to exercise collective leadership and opinion. Since I don't yet have one, I'm going to create my own looking for consensus of ideas, goals and solutions.

First of all, no one is totally ready and competent to be President of a country of 330 million diverse and enterprising Americans. That being the case how can we collectively work together for common goals? What are the collective goals? Are there 330 million different visions of a better world or a consensus of what we all want that becomes our vote to achieve because we passionately need it! Is it a happy family, a healthy lifestyle, a prosperous livelihood, a friendly neighbor, a fulfilling job and a vote that counts?

If it is, listen up because I going to make a proposition to achieve these individually and collectively to replace what we are now experiencing as a nation of violent behavior, vulgar vocabulary and unequal resources because of unequal opportunity due to poor leaders and poor role models. Our America is a result of just the opposite. Our silent majority are now calling for a change in that culture. Let's review a plan for peaceful change. First, our behavior is our own responsibility so changing that is our personal commitment to change the culture of violence. Secondly, our entertainment is violent and vulgar so why not shut down those instances we all find harmful to peaceful coexistent by being disgusting and uncomfortable. Thirdly, is it more financial security we want or an equal chance at the risk-taking American Dream of a happy marriage, healthy home and a fulfilling family as our life's American Dream. If it is, how do we get there under the current circumstances?

We are now facing a Pandemic of fear inducing conformity threatening our livelihood and health, along with the changes that our society is demanding of our institutions. These are the result of two- and one-half centuries of development. How can we change these divergent and conflicting goals unless we agree on the changes we want? Do we want a better justice system? Do we want a better health care program? Do we want more resources from our work ethic.? Do we agree that our current leaders aren't taking us there? If so, what can we do? Change our leaders or give in to the current state of affairs? Well, I'm just one voice saying we have to change our leadership regardless of our political affiliation because it is the underlying problem ... we have lawmakers making more laws taking away freedoms, the red and the blue defend our establishment two-party system, protesters seeding revenge with dark money, defunding our police security blanket, politicians ignoring the blight in our inner cities and small rural communities while bankrupting our future with financial bailouts using welfare checks. The problem isn't racism, fascism, capitalism, socialism or any other ism, ism, isms, it's not honoring the virtues of Humanism!

The solution is to pursue Humanism as the national patriotic campaign. It must be driven by the votes of enterprising Americans that pay all the bills, fight all the wars and make capitalists wealthy beyond their dreams and needs ... the 200 million enterprising Americans who are not represented nor compensated adequately by a system that glorifies violence, vulgarity and excess compensation in entertainment, sports and our social media. It's the golden rule ... those with the gold shall rule. Why not the other golden rule ... do unto others as you want to be treated.

The vision of a better world would be to create a third political party that pursues enough votes to become the swing vote **to break ties and prevent gridlock of the two-party system** at every level for every political decision made by the Congress and State Legislators to bring the current proponents of the extremes towards a balanced middle of society. Not left or right, not red or blue, not progressive or socialist, not fascism or communism, but American Humanism. We want to individually have an opportunity to prosper and be happy with our future peaceful dealings around the world including the conservation of our environment and peaceful coexistence with our trading partners and competitors. Read my lips ... it's an economic war not a shooting or bombing war. Give peace and prosperity a chance.

How can this happen. First let's agree on a very important fact. Capitalism is not the enemy of Socialism and are waiting in the wings as a third American Enterprise political party. Then we can acknowledge they work together every day in every business. I'll call it humanism in enterprise and it has to have capital to startup and sustain its equity and it has to have human assets to implement and sustain its profitability. So why do politicians pit one against the other as conservative and liberal, while assigning each to either the left or the right bending the curve towards the extremes for stirring up the voters.

With successful enterprises being the foundation of the American economy, then the extremes of an establishment two-party system must be pulled towards the middle-class small businesses that populate our shopping centers, internet trading and commerce with the rest of the world creating standards of living to pay all the bills and taxes to sustain what I call the Great American Enterprise. That's the master we all must serve not 545 people (100 senators, 435 congressmen, 9 supreme court justices and 1 President) who now run everything with money-tics that blinds our politics using the golden rule … those with the gold and media rule.

To reiterate: The George Soras influence at the national and community levels is tainting our justice system where there has to be consequences for committing crimes at the misdemeanor entry level as well as the felon level. At the other extreme, progressives want to discharge half the three million nonviolent convicts to be pardoned then catch and release later, as they fall to recidivism, so they can vote... or better yet go back to the "stop and frisk" successful reduction of all crimes, implemented by Mayor Giuliani. Now with the Wizard of Oz Biden we have an appeaser, pleaser and geezer looking the other way for the crimes of his son Hunter, BLM and ANTIFA.

The political theory here is to create a swing vote party **to break ties and prevent gridlock of the two-party system** at every level called the American Enterprise Party that, with as few seats as 5 to 10 in the Senate and 10 to 20 in the House, representing enterprising hard-working enterprising Americans. I repeat It splits the independents away from the Democrats and the Republicans so neither has a majority. So, a third party does not assure any of the three parties a 51% majority allowing for the filibuster to really mean better legislation and laws.

The third party's platform balances the budget by privatizing agencies that are redundant with all the State Governments and rids every layer of government to "pass a bill kill one standing law and regulations" and taxation becomes a reinvestment of excessive wealth to pay down the unserviceable national and State debt. We not only "drain the swamp" we tame the alligators that are exposed or kill them with a bill calling for defunding them. In a decade, as Margert Thatcher did in England, a third party can kill the idea that Big Brother government solves social problems and higher taxation with obtuse borrowing pays for it.

I wrote a book entitled The American Enterprise Manifesto in 1991 updated in 2012 and now The American Enterprise Party Trilogy that exposes the depth of the swamp and the dire financial predicament this put our and future generations in, that must be dealt with now as America slides into the depths of the swamp, as did other great societies in the past. I've been told it will never happen because it takes billions, trillions and zillions to compete for any office let alone the presidency.

Well, 330 million enterprising Americans create $21 trillion GDP per year and create wealth for 22.6 million millionaires and 885 billionaires so why not invest their equity (wealth) in paying down the $158 trillion in unfunded debt, rid ourselves of half of the 22 million government workers that cost 40% of fixed overhead wasted on redundant laws and regulations to be able to compete with China our ominous cold war threat and economic competitor.

I hope by now, as a discriminating voter, that having a third party representing the Great American Enterprise is a necessity for fiscal and spiritual values of the majority of enterprising Americans. And, it very effectively splits the independents away from the Democrats and the Republicans so neither has a majority. So, a third party does not assure any of the three parties a 51% majority allowing for the filibuster, Electoral College, a swing vote **to break ties and prevent gridlock of the two-party system** at every level including the Supreme Court and our State legislatures to really mean better legislation and laws. While retaining government by the people, for the people, of the people.

"I pledge allegiance to my Flag and the Republic for which it stands, one nation, indivisible, with liberty and justice for all". "To protect our values, constitution and memorials of past heroes of the constitutional government of diversity and ethnicity".

IVORY TOWER

(When I worked for Arthur Andersen & Co. an accounting firm we called the final say the "ivory tower")

Abuse of the seat of power
Sitting in an ivory tower
Away from the humdrum and the cower
Just sitting on the seat of power

Misuse of status
Abuse of the right to lead honestly
What a mess when it's not about us
And the seed to integrity

Pe stem of competence in spite of fear
And the roots of principles held true
So your honor is what we need to hear
Not just to praise you

Abuse of the seat of power
Is sitting in the ivory tower

Sifting platitudes out of the shower
Believing only what you're told
Looking in the mirror with face of dower
Never venturing outside the fold

Pe fold of isolation at the top of society's gradation
Just to feel the height of adulation
Ah you say that is the leader's station
He's above and beyond the ordinary creation

For if he were to stand down with the lower
Alongside the peasant and the poor
Waiting for their score
Anticipating what is in store

He might just have to accept reality
And understand why there's history
Feeling what it's like to just be
Overwhelmed by mediocrity

But no there is abuse of the seat of power
More for the high that it brings
From the isolation in the ivory tower
Like a kite without strings

Just flying high saying look at me
Not stopping to make a mental note
Pat in the land of the free
I'm the reason poor people cast their vote

It is not to jack me up on this seat
It was to provide a semblance of leadership
So they could admire the importance of my feat
Being the captain or the helmsman of the ship

Yes it was someone to admire
More than the ordinary can perceive
But not so high or higher
As to be out of touch and deceive

Because when the seat of power is out of touch
Pen there is abuse
And there's no in between to provide a crutch
For the taint of the mortal recluse

With the abuse by a Joe Biden
Or a Xi Jinping
Of that seat of power
Yes oh yes that's my concern
Burn down the ivory tower

Cast your vote
Cast out that seat of power
Choose a leader for the boat
Hear ye extricate the ivory tower

Vote with your gut
For if you happen to pick a goat
With your head or butt
We shall all end up in the moat

With collective voting renewing the ivory tower
As enterprise shuns its dower
Void of the ivory cower
And its failure to empower

Pe higher power …
Government by the people, for the people, of the people

Volume Two After Word

America's future hinges on more of the private sector taking back responsibility for its fiscal and social health. It may seem radical now to turn our political and legislative system upside down, but it will take decades to do it so now is not too early. New and creative thought is needed at all levels of the public and private sector if we are to continue as the leading nation in the world. The failed establishment binary two-party system has become antiquated and inbred. The control of many by few is destined to further tank our Enterprise. As a people we allow the IQ (intelligence quotient) to set the rules when it is the EQ (emotional quotient) that pays for them... this is not working... nor can it work as depicted in Animal Farm; human greed enters the picture, and all good intentions fall to egos and each person's livelihood.

I am sure there will be much controversy over these egos and livelihoods but for the individual's Good, Government cannot be the reason for our existence. It has to be the result of our persistence to be individually free of arbitrary and capricious rule making and allow creativity to prevail. Our standard of living, work ethic (attaining the American Dream) and patriotic leadership for world peace and pursuit of happiness should be the justification of the end result... not our individual instinct to control our destiny with money... it must be generated by our faith in a higher authority, our national patriotism and individual work ethic as our commitment to world peace that will pay all the bills.

This is predestined if we believe in the essence of the Lord's prayer:

Our Father who art in heaven, hallowed be thy name, thy kingdom come, thy will be done, on earth as it is in heaven, give us this day our daily bread, and forgive us of our trespasses as we forgive those who trespass against us, lead us not into temptation, but deliver us from evil, for thine is the kingdom, the power and the glory for ever and ever. In God We Trust. Amen

It is thought that 2 over billion people around the world recited the Lord's Prayer at Easter. So, it is religion and race that binds us together and yet pulls us apart so let reason minus religion or race be our resolve with peaceful coexistence in the Kingdom of God's One World Enterprise be our outcome. God Bless our American Enterprise and our enterprising and ethical American workers. www.americanenterprisepartypoliticalparty.org

From many to one we "serve our country to serve your soul".

LET FREEDOM RING

Living in the now
Dwells on a goal
From many to one we
"Serve our country to serve our soul".

Placing our bets
Minding our debts
Respecting the vets
Living just plain living
Needs to blend all three

If we're going to be happy
Yes Siree
Give it our all
For no regrets

With no inflexible mind sets
Offers plenty of outlets
For living and giving
By paying back personal debts

Also banking that gets
Later return on the risky bets
Showing up on my pay checks
As life and limb intersects

As for foreign wars
And domestic quarrels
The early responders
Deserve honor for being the doors

Opening for and backing the veterans
Who deserve our gratitude
To amend our ineptitude
To restore them to their prior servitude

But not living in their past
That dwells on regrets
Living in the future
Dwells on mind sets

Honor thy debts to
Thy vets advents
And for those events
That lets freedom ring

Of thee I sing

FOLLOW THE FOLLOWERS

Those who don't follow
Their own thoughts
Only follow the
Thoughts of the ones
They're following

Lining up following
The followers
Over the cliff
Through the closing door

With them a circle is a circle
A square is a square
A box is a lock
On political correctness

Creativity and leadership
Is relegated to the elite
With the blind and meek
Following the followers

To the never lead land
Of poverty racism wokism cynicism
Hopelessness Homelessness
A commune a gang a clan

Jones Town or Manson
Put us all in a line of
Followers following
The followers to their doom

Into death and prison
While being a follower
Shouldn't relegate
Us to Watergate

It only can state
That we all have a responsibility
To lead our life to
Our own fate

So don't wait for a leader
Step up to the front of the divine
Lead the followers to a meter
It's your time to be at the front of the line

"President of the Many to the Order of One"
As God blesses those who serve
Their country to serve their own soul

PRAY IT FORWARD

Separation of Powers but
Reinstitute prayer in the schools

My will be done
My acts be told
Thy flock shall abound
As a magnet to the fold

The law of attraction

This to be magnetized
This to be a shepherd
For the love of you vitalized
Please us now and pray it forward

Belief in mankind as a positive force
To perform our humble work
Sharing our self to the righteous purpose of good
The cause and effect of our energy

Is the cost of life
For the good of praying, it forward
Pass on the lifeline to others
And you shall have the good life
Though you must perish of flesh

Get behind me and pray
It forward
Project your own good
For the good of others

Then Lead me
Follow me
Or get the hell out of my way

Exhibit A

BIG BROTHER BIDEN SWAMPS THE SWAMP

BALLOTPEDIA (Underlines are a Cross reference to Google Data Search for the documents)

As of June 9, 2021, President Joe Biden (D) had signed 54 executive orders, 23 memorandums, 98 proclamations, 21 notices = 196 edicts reversing President Trump's policies and forming a Biden/Sanders Democrat Socialist Party.

Each of these presidential documents is different in authority and implementation. Executive orders are directives written by the president to officials within the executive branch requiring them to take or stop some action related to policy or management. They are numbered, published in the *Federal Register*, and cite the authority by which the president is making the order.[1][2]

Presidential memoranda also include instructions directed at executive officials, but they are neither numbered nor have the same publication requirements. The Office of Management and Budget is also not required to issue a budgetary impact statement on the subject of the memoranda.[3]

In his 2014 book, *By Order of the President: The Use and Abuse of Executive Direct Action*, Phillip J. Cooper, a professor of public administration at Portland State University, wrote, "As a practical matter, the memorandum is now being used as the equivalent of an executive order, but without meeting the legal requirements for an executive order."[4]

Proclamations are a third type of executive directive that typically relate to private individuals or ceremonial events, such as holidays and commemorations.[3][5]

This page provides a list of the executive orders, presidential memoranda, and proclamations issued by Biden in reverse chronological order. The following lines indicated by underlines can be accessed if you are using the electronic version ... otherwise you can go to the BALLOTPEDIA (Cross reference to the documents) website and read them and weep. This certainly is an act of the Wizard of Oz (Big Brother Biden) telling the "Tin man and the Lion" (Schumer and Pelosi) to have "Dorothy and her pet dog Toto" (Harris and Sanders) to prevent Trump tornados on the "yellow brick road back to Washington D.C." will now be just right.

- **Executive orders** (reversing Trump administrative policies for immigration and the Keystone Pipeline and Afghanistan)
- **Presidential memoranda**
- **Proclamations**

June 2021

- Executive Order on Protecting Americans' Sensitive Data from Foreign Adversaries (June 9, 2021)
- Executive Order on Blocking Property And Suspending Entry Into The United States Of Certain Persons Contributing To The Destabilizing Situation In The Western Balkans (June 8, 2021)
- Executive Order on Addressing the Threat from Securities Investments that Finance Certain Companies of the People's Republic of China (June 3, 2021)

May 2021

- Executive Order on Advancing Equity, Justice, and Opportunity for Asian Americans, Native Hawaiians, and Pacific Islanders (May 28, 2021)

- Executive Order on Climate-Related Financial Risk (May 20, 2021)
- Executive Order on the Revocation of Certain Presidential Actions and Technical Amendment (May 14, 2021)
- Executive Order on Improving the Nation's Cybersecurity (May 12, 2021)
- Executive Order on the Establishment of the Climate Change Support Office (May 7, 2021)

April 2021

- Executive Order on Increasing the Minimum Wage for Federal Contractors (April 27, 2021)
- Executive Order on Worker Organizing and Empowerment (April 26, 2021)
- Executive Order on Blocking Property with Respect to Specified Harmful Foreign Activities of the Government of the Russian Federation (April 15, 2021)
- Executive Order on the Establishment of the Presidential Commission on the Supreme Court of the United States (April 9, 2021)
- Executive Order on the Termination of Emergency With Respect to the International Criminal Court (April 1, 2021)

March 2021

- Executive Order on Establishment of the White House Gender Policy Council (March 8, 2021)
- Executive Order on Guaranteeing an Educational Environment Free from Discrimination on the Basis of Sex, Including Sexual Orientation or Gender Identity (March 8, 2021)

- Executive Order on Promoting Access to Voting (March 7, 2021)

February 2021

- Executive Order on the Revocation of Certain Presidential Actions (February 24, 2021)
- Executive Order on America's Supply Chains (February 24, 2021)
- Executive Order on the Revocation of Executive Order 13801 (February 17, 2021)
- Executive Order on the Establishment of the White House Office of Faith-Based and Neighborhood Partnerships (February 14, 2021)
- Executive Order on Blocking Property with Respect to the Situation in Burma (February 11, 2021)
- Executive Order on Rebuilding and Enhancing Programs to Resettle Refugees and Planning for the Impact of Climate Change on Migration (February 4, 2021)
- Executive Order on the Establishment of Interagency Task Force on the Reunification of Families (February 2, 2021)
- Executive Order on Creating a Comprehensive Regional Framework to Address the Causes of Migration, to Manage Migration Throughout North and Central America, and to Provide Safe and Orderly Processing of Asylum Seekers at the United States Border (February 2, 2021)
- Executive Order on Restoring Faith in Our Legal Immigration Systems and Strengthening Integration and Inclusion Efforts for New Americans (February 2, 2021)

January 2021

- Executive Order on Strengthening Medicaid and the Affordable Care Act (January 28, 2021)

- Executive Order on the President's Council of Advisors on Science and Technology (January 27, 2021)
- Executive Order on Tackling the Climate Crisis at Home and Abroad (January 27, 2021)
- Executive Order on Reforming Our Incarceration System to Eliminate the Use of Privately Operated Criminal Detention Facilities (January 26, 2021)
- Executive Order on Ensuring the Future Is Made in All of America by All of America's Workers (January 25, 2021)
- Executive Order on Enabling All Qualified Americans to Serve Their Country in Uniform (January 25, 2021)
- Executive Order on Protecting the Federal Workforce (January 22, 2021)
- Executive Order on Economic Relief Related to the COVID-19 Pandemic (January 22, 2021)
- Executive Order on Establishing the COVID-19 Pandemic Testing Board and Ensuring a Sustainable Public Health Workforce for COVID-19 and Other Biological Threats (January 21, 2021)
- Executive Order on Protecting Worker Health and Safety (January 21, 2021)
- Executive Order on Supporting the Reopening and Continuing Operation of Schools and Early Childhood Education Providers (January 21, 2021)
- Executive Order on Ensuring an Equitable Pandemic Response and Recovery (January 21, 2021)
- Executive Order on a Sustainable Public Health Supply Chain (January 21, 2021)
- Executive Order on Ensuring a Data-Driven Response to COVID-19 and Future High-Consequence Public Health Threat (January 21, 2021)
- Executive Order on Improving and Expanding Access to Care

and Treatments for COVID-19 (January 21, 2021)
- Executive Order on Promoting COVID-19 Safety in Domestic and International Travel (January 21, 2021)
- Executive Order on Ethics Commitments by Executive Branch Personnel (January 20, 2021)
- Executive Order on Preventing and Combating Discrimination on the Basis of Gender Identity or Sexual Orientation (January 20, 2021)
- Executive Order on Protecting Public Health and the Environment and Restoring Science to Tackle the Climate Crisis (January 20, 2021)
- Executive Order on Ensuring a Lawful and Accurate Enumeration and Apportionment Pursuant to the Decennial Census (January 20, 2021)
- Executive Order on Revocation of Certain Executive Orders Concerning Federal Regulation (January 20, 2021)
- Executive Order on the Revision of Civil Immigration Enforcement Policies and Priorities (January 20, 2021)
- Executive Order on Organizing and Mobilizing the United States Government to Provide a Unified and Effective Response to Combat COVID-19 and to Provide United States Leadership on Global Health and Security (January 20, 2021)
- Executive Order on Protecting the Federal Workforce and Requiring Mask-Wearing (January 20, 2021)
- Executive Order On Advancing Racial Equity and Support for Underserved Communities Through the Federal Government (January 20, 2021)

Memoranda issued by Biden

Presidential memoranda are similar to executive orders, but they are neither numbered nor have the same publication requirements. The Office of Management and Budget is also not required to issue a budgetary impact statement on the subject of the memoranda.[3]

June 2021

- Memorandum for the Secretary of State on the Delegation of Authority Under Section 1217(c) of Public Law 116-283 (June 8, 2021)
- [1] (June 4, 2021)
- Memorandum on Establishing the Fight Against Corruption as a Core United States National Security Interest (June 3, 2021)

May 2021

- Memorandum for the Secretary of State, the Secretary of the Treasury, and the Secretary of Energy on the Presidential Determination Pursuant to Section 1245(d)(4)(B) and (C) of the National Defense Authorization Act for Fiscal Year 2012 (May 19, 2021)
- Memorandum on Restoring the Department of Justice's Access-to-Justice Function and Reinvigorating the White House Legal Aid Interagency Roundtable (May 18, 2021)
- Domestic Policy Presidential Directive – 1 (DPPD-1) (May 6, 2021)
- Memorandum for the Secretary of State on the Emergency Presidential Determination on Refugee Admissions for Fiscal Year 2021 (May 3, 2021)

April 2021

- Memorandum for the Secretary of State on the Emergency Presidential Determination on Refugee Admissions for Fiscal Year 2021 (April 16, 2021)

February 2021

- Memorandum on Advancing the Human Rights of Lesbian, Gay, Bisexual, Transgender, Queer, and Intersex Persons Around the World (February 4, 2021)
- Memorandum on Revitalizing America's Foreign Policy and National Security Workforce, Institutions, and Partnerships (February 4, 2021)
- Memorandum on Maximizing Assistance from the Federal Emergency Management Agency (February 2, 2021)

January 2021

- Memorandum on Protecting Women's Health at Home and Abroad (January 28, 2021)
- Memorandum on Restoring Trust in Government Through Scientific Integrity and Evidence-Based Policymaking (January 27, 2021)
- Memorandum on Redressing Our Nation's and the Federal Government's History of Discriminatory Housing Practices and Policies (January 26, 2021)
- Memorandum on Tribal Consultation and Strengthening Nation-to-Nation Relationships (January 26, 2021)
- Memorandum Condemning and Combating Racism, Xenophobia, and Intolerance Against Asian Americans and Pacific Islanders in the United States (January 26, 2021)
- Memorandum to Extend Federal Support to Governors' Use of the National Guard to Respond to COVID-19 and to Increase Reimbursement and Other Assistance Provided to States (January 21, 2021)
- Preserving and Fortifying Deferred Action for Childhood Arrivals (DACA) (January 20, 2021)
- Reinstating Deferred Enforced Departure for Liberians (January 20, 2021)

- Modernizing Regulatory Review (January 20, 2021)
- Regulatory Freeze Pending Review (January 20, 2021)

Proclamations issued by Biden

Proclamations are executive directives that typically relate to private individuals or ceremonial events, such as holidays and commemorations.[3]

June 2021

- A Proclamation on Black Music Appreciation Month, 2021 (June 1, 2021)
- A Proclamation on National Homeownership Month, 2021 (June 1, 2021)
- A Proclamation on National Ocean Month, 2021 (June 1, 2021)
- A Proclamation on Great Outdoors Month, 2021 (June 1, 2021)
- A Proclamation on National Caribbean-American Heritage Month, 2021 (June 1, 2021)
- A Proclamation on National Immigrant Heritage Month, 2021 (June 1, 2021)
- A Proclamation on Lesbian, Gay, Bisexual, Transgender, and Queer Pride Month, 2021 (June 1, 2021)

May 2021

- A Proclamation on Day Of Remembrance: 100 Years After The 1921 Tulsa Race Massacre (May 31, 2021)
- A Proclamation: Prayer for Peace, Memorial Day, 2021 (May 28, 2021)

- A Proclamation on Honoring the Victims of the Tragedy in San Jose, California (May 26, 2021)
- A Proclamation on National Maritime Day, 2021 (May 21, 2021)
- A Proclamation on National Safe Boating Week, 2021 (May 21, 2021)
- A Proclamation on National Hepatitis Testing Day, 2021 (May 18, 2021)
- A Proclamation on Armed Forces Day, 2021 (May 14, 2021)
- A Proclamation on National Defense Transportation Day and National Transportation Week, 2021 (May 14, 2021)
- A Proclamation on Emergency Medical Services Week, 2021 (May 14, 2021)
- A Proclamation on World Trade Week, 2021 (May 14, 2021)
- A Proclamation on Revoking Proclamation 9945 (May 14, 2021)
- A Proclamation on Peace Officers Memorial Day and Police Week, 2021 (May 7, 2021)
- A Proclamation on Mother's Day, 2021 (May 7, 2021)
- A Proclamation on National Hurricane Preparedness Week, 2021 (May 7, 2021)
- A Proclamation on National Women's Health Week, 2021 (May 7, 2021)
- A Proclamation on Military Spouse Appreciation Day, 2021 (May 6, 2021)
- A Proclamation on National Day Of Prayer (May 5, 2021)
- A Proclamation on Missing and Murdered Indigenous Persons Awareness Day, 2021 (May 4, 2021)
- A Proclamation on the 60th Anniversary of the Freedom Rides, 2021 (May 4, 2021)
- A Proclamation on Older Americans Month, 2021 (May 3, 2021)

April 2021

- A Proclamation on the Suspension of Entry as Nonimmigrants of Certain Additional Persons Who Pose a Risk of Transmitting Coronavirus Disease 2019 (April 30, 2021)
- A Proclamation on Law Day, U.S.A, 2021 (April 30, 2021)
- A Proclamation on Loyalty Day, 2021 A Proclamation on Loyalty Day, 2021 (April 30, 2021)
- A Proclamation on National Teacher Appreciation Day and National Teacher Appreciation Week, 2021 (April 30, 2021)
- https://www.whitehouse.gov/briefing-room/presidential-actions/2021/04/30/a-proclamation-on-national-building-safety-month-2021/ [A Proclamation on National Building Safety Month, 2021 A Proclamation on National Physical Fitness And Sports Month, 2021] (April 30, 2021)
- A Proclamation on National Building Safety Month, 2021 (April 30, 2021)
- A Proclamation on National Foster Care Month, 2021 (April 30, 2021)
- A Proclamation on Jewish American Heritage Month, 2021 (April 30, 2021)
- A Proclamation on Public Service Recognition Week, 2021 (April 30, 2021)
- A Proclamation on National Mental Health Awareness Month, 2021 (April 30, 2021)
- A Proclamation on Asian American and Native Hawaiian / Pacific Islander Heritage Month, 2021 (April 30, 2021)
- A Proclamation on Workers Memorial Day, 2021 (April 27, 2021)
- A Proclamation on World Intellectual Property Day, 2021 (April 23, 2021)
- A Proclamation on Earth Day, 2021 (April 22, 2021)
- A Proclamation on the Death of Walter Mondale (April 20, 2021)

- A Proclamation on National Park Week, 2021 (April 17, 2021)
- A Proclamation on National Volunteer Week, 2021 (April 16, 2021)
- A Proclamation on Honoring the Victims of the Tragedy in Indianapolis, Indiana (April 16, 2021)
- A Proclamation on Pan American Day and Pan American Week, 2021 (Aprill 13, 2021)
- A Proclamation on 160th Anniversary Of The Unification Of Italy And The Establishment Of United States-Italy Diplomatic Relations (April 13, 2021)
- A Proclamation on Black Maternal Health Week, 2021 (April 13, 2021)
- A Proclamation on National Fair Housing Month, 2021 (April 11, 2021)
- A Proclamation on National Former Prisoner of War Recognition Day, 2021 (April 9, 2021)
- A Proclamation on National Public Health Week, 2021 (April 5, 2021)
- A Proclamation on Days of Remembrance of Victims of the Holocaust, 2021 (April 4, 2021)
- A Proclamation on Honoring United States Capitol Police Officers (April 2, 2021)
- A Proclamation on World Autism Awareness Day, 2021 (April 1, 2021)

March 2021

- A Proclamation on Month of the Military Child, 2021 (March 31, 2021)
- A Proclamation on Second Chance Month, 2021 (March 31, 2021)
- A Proclamation on National Cancer Control Month, 2021 (March 31, 2021)

- A Proclamation on National Donate Life Month, 2021 (March 31, 2021)
- A Proclamation on National Child Abuse Prevention Month, 2021 (March 31, 2021)
- A Proclamation on National Sexual Assault Prevention and Awareness Month, 2021 (March 31, 2021)
- A Proclamation on National Financial Capability Month, 2021 (March 31, 2021)
- A Proclamation on Transgender Day of Visibility, 2021 (March 31, 2021)
- A Proclamation on César Chávez Day, 2021 (March 31, 2021)
- A Proclamation on Greek Independence Day: A National Day of Celebration of Greek and American Democracy, 2021 (March 24, 2021)
- A Proclamation on National Equal Pay Day, 2021 (March 24, 2021)
- A Proclamation on Education and Sharing Day, USA, 2021 (March 23, 2021)
- A Proclamation on Education and Sharing Day, USA, 2021 (March 23, 2021)
- A Proclamation Honoring the Victims of the Tragedy in Boulder, Colorado (March 23, 2021)
- A Proclamation on National Agriculture Day, 2021 (March 22, 2021)
- A Proclamation on National Poison Prevention Week, 2021 (March 19, 2021)
- A Proclamation on Honoring the Victims of the Tragedy in the Atlanta Metropolitan Area (March 18, 2021)
- A Proclamation on National Consumer Protection Week, 2021 (March 1, 2021)
- A Proclamation on Women's History Month, 2021 (March 1, 2021)
- A Proclamation on American Red Cross Month, 2021 (March 1, 2021)

- A Proclamation on National Colorectal Cancer Awareness Month, 2021 (March 1, 2021)
- A Proclamation on Read Across America Day, 2021 (March 1, 2021)
- A Proclamation on Irish-American Heritage Month, 2021 (March 1, 2021)

February 2021

- A Proclamation on Revoking Proclamation 10014 (February 24, 2021)
- A Proclamation on Remembering the 500,000 Americans Lost to COVID-19 (February 22, 2021)
- A Proclamation on National Teen Dating Violence Awareness and Prevention Month, 2021 (February 3, 2021)
- A Proclamation on National Black History Month, 2021 (February 3, 2021)
- A Proclamation on American Heart Month, 2021 (February 3, 2021)
- A Proclamation on Adjusting Imports of Aluminum Into the United States (February 1, 2021)

January 2021

- Proclamation on the Suspension of Entry as Immigrants and Non-Immigrants of Certain Additional Persons Who Pose a Risk of Transmitting Coronavirus Disease (January 25, 2021)
- Proclamation on the Termination Of Emergency With Respect To The Southern Border Of The United States And Redirection Of Funds Diverted To Border Wall Construction (January 20, 2021)
- Proclamation on Ending Discriminatory Bans on Entry to The United States (January 20, 2021)
- A National Day of Unity (January 20, 2021)

Notices issued by Biden

June 2021

- Notice on the Continuation of the National Emergency with Respect to the Actions and Policies of Certain Members of the Government of Belarus and other Persons to Undermine Democratic Processes or Institutions of Belarus (June 8, 2021)
- Notice on the Continuation of the National Emergency with Respect to the Western Balkans (June 8, 2021)

May 2021

- Notice on the Continuation of the National Emergency with Respect to Securing the Information and Communications Technology and Services Supply Chain (May 11, 2021)
- Notice on the Continuation of the National Emergency with Respect to Yemen (May 11, 2021)
- Notice on the Continuation of the National Emergency with Respect to the Stabilization of Iraq (May 6, 2021)
- Notice on the Continuation of the National Emergency with Respect to the Central African Republic (May 6, 2021)
- Notice on the Continuation of the National Emergency with Respect to the Actions of the Government of Syria (May 6, 2021)

April 2021

- Notice on the Continuation of the National Emergency with Respect to Somalia (April 1, 2021)

March 2021

- Notice on the Continuation of the National Emergency with Respect to South Sudan (March 29, 2021)
- Notice on the Continuation of the National Emergency with Respect to Significant Malicious Cyber-Enabled Activities (March 29, 2021)
- Notice on the Continuation of the National Emergency with Respect to Iran (March 5, 2021)
- Notice on the Continuation of the National Emergency with Respect to Zimbabwe (March 3, 2021)
- Notice on the Continuation of the National Emergency with Respect to Ukraine (March 3, 2021)
- Notice on the Continuation of the National Emergency with Respect to Venezuela (March 3, 2021)

February 2021

- Notice on the Continuation of the National Emergency with Respect to Cuba and of the Emergency Authority Relating to the Regulation of the Anchorage and Movement of Vessels (February 24, 2021)
- Notice on the Continuation of the National Emergency Concerning the Coronavirus Disease 2019 (COVID-19) Pandemic (February 24, 2021)
- Notice on the Continuation of the National Emergency with Respect to Libya (February 11, 2021)

The Fall of the Great American Empire ...

The tipping point, of the ten dominos that fall, to reach the breaking point and burst the giant $600 trillion derivative bubble. The breaking point is estimated to occur by 2024 when the stock market also declines 25% to 20,000 DOW, the Fed discount rate to member banks is increased from 2.5% to 5.0% increasing prime interest rate cost of capital to 10% and American inflation continues to spiral out of control to 25% resulting in small business failures and big business mergers.

The $600 trillion derivative bubble bursts at that time creating worldwide panic as the dollar is replaced by the Chinese Yuan and Japanese Yen with the South Asian Sea consortium moving to control American Enterprise and the world market for microchips, electric automobiles, lithium batteries, pharmaceuticals, production of copper, manganese and rare earth, Covid-19 variant's vaccine production, the World Health Organization, the World Trade Organization, the World Bank and the UN.

The only way to stop this crash of momentous proportions is to break the current Uni-party political gridlock by electing swing vote positions in the Senate of shards and House of cards and a President who understands worldwide enterprise, humanism and peaceful coexistence for establishing a government of the people, by the people for the people to win the battle over woke values and Marxist ideologies that are taking over our institutions. Then marry monetary capital and human capital into a third party. The American Enterprise Party.

Exhibit B

The Ongoing Demise of American Liquidity (Facts Surrounding the 2007-8 Great Depression)

401k plan investments and home values hit the skids in 2007 and 2008 to the tune of $30 trillion in value lost due to the Federal Reserve's raising the Fed rate to member banks and investment houses bringing subprime interest rates up twice previous Greenspan levels causing the 2007-8 version of 1929's Great Depression. See Article Four for impact.

545 individuals directing 330 million followers—democracy have been lost to connections, power, money, and intellectual control financed by the Federal Reserve banking system.

Definitions and data extracted from the Federal Reserve website; historical data demonstrates the manipulations that the Fed does with the monetary system to gambling taxpayer money to control and at times destroy the economy.

Fed funds rate, prime rate, Libor rate, MTA, COFI, CMT indices dictate liquidity in the national and international money markets. The CMT indices are the weekly or monthly average yields on U.S. Treasury securities adjusted to constant maturities. Yields on treasury securities at "constant maturity" are interpolated by the U.S. Treasury from the daily yield curve, which is based on the closing market bid yields on actively traded treasury securities in the over-the-counter market.

The CMT indices are volatile and move with the market. They reflect the state of the economy and respond quickly to economic changes. These indices react more quickly than the COF index or the 12 MTA index

Twelve-Month Treasury Average (12 MTA):

The monthly treasury average is a relatively new ARM index. This index is the twelve-month average of the monthly average yields of U.S. Treasury securities adjusted to a constant maturity of one year. It is calculated by averaging the previous twelve-monthly values of the one-year CMT. Because this index is an annual average, it is steadier than the one-year CMT index.

The MTA index generally fluctuates slightly more than the Eleventh District COFI, although its movements track each other very closely, used with the popular pay option ARM program.

Eleventh District Cost of Funds Index (COFI):

Pronounced *coffee* or called *Eleventh District*, this index reflects the weighted-average interest rate paid by Eleventh Federal Home Loan Bank District savings institutions for savings and checking accounts, advances from the FHLB, and other sources of funds.

The Eleventh District represents the savings institutions (savings and loan associations and savings banks) headquartered in Arizona, California, and Nevada. Since the largest part of the cost of funds Index is interest paid on savings accounts, this index lags market interest rates in both uptrend and downtrend movements. As a result, ARMs tied to this index rise (and fall) more slowly than rates in general, which is good for you if rates are rising, but not good for you if rates are falling.

Federal Funds Rate:

The federal funds rate is the cost of borrowing immediately available funds, primarily for just one day. The effective rate is the weighted average of the reported rates at which different amounts of the day's trading through New York brokers occurs.

London Interbank Offered Rate: One Month LIBOR:

Pronounced *lie-bore*, London Interbank Offering Rate (LIBOR) is an average of the interest rate on dollar-denominated deposits, also known as Eurodollars, traded between banks in London. The Eurodollar market is a major component of the international financial market. London is the center of the Euro market in terms of volume.

The LIBOR is an international index that follows the world economic condition. The LIBOR rate quoted in the *Wall Street Journal* is an average of rate quotes from five major banks: Bank of America, Barclays, Bank of Tokyo, Deutsche Bank, and Swiss Bank. It allows international investors to match their cost of lending to their cost of funds. The LIBOR compares most closely to the one-year CMT index and is more open to quick and wide fluctuations than the COFI rate. It is the European version of our Central Bank system's Fed funds rate. LIBOR is used by both Fannie Mae and Freddie Mac as a standardized adjustable-rate loan index.

London Inter-Bank Offered Rate: Six-Month LIBOR:

London Inter-Bank Offering Rate (LIBOR) is an average of the interest rate on dollar-denominated deposits, also known as Eurodollars, traded between banks in London. The Eurodollar market is a major component of the international financial market. London is the center of the Euro market in terms of volume.

The LIBOR is an international index that follows the world economic condition. It allows international investors to match their cost of lending to their cost of funds. The LIBOR compares most closely to the one-year CMT index and is more open to quick and wide fluctuations than the COFI rate.

Prime Rate

The prime rate is the interest rate charged by banks for short-term loans to their most creditworthy customers whose credit standing is so high that little risk to the lender is involved. In the past, only a small percentage of customers qualified for the prime rate, which tends to be the lowest going interest rate and thus serves as a basis for other, higher risk loans.

Today, the loans use prime plus a margin or prime minus a margin for every borrower. Prime rate has lost its prestige as a true "prime" or premier index. Some may think that if everybody is eligible, it is no longer "Prime." It is humorously thought that the industry doesn't want to hurt borrowers' "self-esteem" by offering anything but prime.

In reality, the prime rate, is a durable and practical index that is easy to follow and the industry standardization is for the benefit of borrowers and investors who purchase the loans from banks. The rate is almost always the same at the major banks. Adjustments to the prime rate are made by banks at the same time, although the prime rate does not adjust on any regular basis.

Typically, when the Federal Reserve adjusts the Federal funds rate and discount rate, the prime rate adjusts the same day or within a few days at most. The prime rate is not a very volatile index; however, it generally rises quickly (increases bank profits) and declines very slowly (maintains banks' profits). It is often the index for home equity lines of credit.

Source Federal Reserve Exchange Rate Tables

Month	2007	2006	2005	2004	2003
January	5.25	4.50	2.25	1.00	1.24
February	5.25	4.50	2.50	1.01	1.26
March	5.25	4.75	2.75	1.00	1.25
April	5.25	4.75	2.75	1.00	1.26
May	5.25	5.00	3.00	1.00	1.26
June	5.25	5.25	3.25	1.03	1.22
July	5.25	5.25	3.25	1.26	1.01
August	5.25	5.25	3.50	1.50	1.03
September	4.75	5.25	3.75	1.75	1.01
October	4.50	5.25	3.75	1.75	1.01
November	4.50	5.25	4.00	2.00	1.00
December	4.25	5.25	4.25	2.25	0.98
Month	2002	2001	2000	1999	1998
January	1.73	5.98	5.45	4.63	5.56
February	1.74	5.49	5.73	4.76	5.51
March	1.73	5.31	5.85	4.81	5.49
April	1.75	4.80	6.02	4.74	5.45
May	1.75	4.21	6.27	4.74	5.49
June	1.75	3.97	6.53	4.76	5.56
July	1.73	3.77	6.54	4.99	5.54
August	1.74	3.65	6.50	5.07	5.55
September	1.75	3.07	6.52	5.22	5.51
October	1.75	2.49	6.51	5.20	5.07
November	1.34	2.09	6.51	5.42	4.83
December	1.24	1.82	6.40	5.30	4.68

The retirement of Alan Greenspan ignited the Depression of 2007-8 but did not cause it ... his replacement Professor Ben "Helicopter" or "Printing Press" Bernanke floats in on a sinking ship called the Bush Administration with Treasury Secretary Henry (Hank) Paulson as its Captain Quigg and falls into the "we have to control inflation using the interest rates as our ammunition" and burst the economic bubble! Rather than letting the air out slowly in the housing and energy markets, thorough slow progression of the interest spreads he lets the Fed go crazy with the flagrant increases in the discount rates thereby bursting the consumer's total balloon by making subprime mortgage payments too high and did not fix anything but his own academic ego and his desire to prove that his book "Essays on the Great Depression" could fix a depression that he caused.

In Alan Greenspan's book "The Age of Turbulence: Adventures in a New World" he realistically analyzes the capabilities of the Presidents he worked for and found Regan and Clinton adept at managing the economy and Bush, sr., and Bush, jr., and Carter inept. Mr. Greenspan should be commended for his steady hand on the interest rudder versus such luminaries as Paul A. Volker (an economic advisor to President Obama in 2009) the interest hiking king for President Carter and Arthur Burns the Bear Market queen for Nixon.

Reprinted From The Prudent Investor:

I am an INDEPENDENT Certified Financial Analyst who worked as a financial journalist for 15+ years and now evaluate global market trends. Analyzing financial and political news permanently I want to share my insight with those who understand that we are in an era of global redistribution of wealth. The US-European centric approach does not work anymore. Five billion people in the developing countries now demand their fair share of the world's resources.

Greenspan's retirement could take longer than 257 days,

Next Thursday is thickly underlined on my agenda, as I had wanted to blog about Fed chairman **Alan Greenspan's** last 250 days in office. *This story* in Wednesday's Washington Post has given it priority a week earlier. According to the speculations in the Washington Post, based on anonymous sources in the administration, President Bush could take a little longer than expected until he names the future Fed chairman. A short extension might be attractive to Greenspan because if he remains at the helm until May 11, he would become the longest-serving Fed chairman ever, exceeding the 18 years, nine months and 29 days served by **William McChesney Martin Jr.**, from 1951 to 1970. Greenspan's personal pride set aside; the hard part will be left to his successor. Since 1970 every incoming new chairman immediately encountered a crisis to master within the first few months in office.

Greenspan, who climbed on the top chair on August 11, 1987, had to iron out the crash of '87, when stocks plunged 22 percent on October 19. He succeeded by keeping the liquidity tap wide open. Although only one of several conference calls of the FOMC after the crash remains *on record* on the Fed's website, it is still very interesting to read the *staff statements* and the *transcript* of the following meeting on November 3, 1987. Some FOMC members were then obviously concerned about the dollar's weakness and discussed whether they had an opportunity "to flip" the trend. Greenspan himself advocated the idea to let the markets go their course.

To quote Greenspan in this past context, "I think we have to remember what the issue of the dollar is. It is not that it is falling per se, but that whatever it is doing creates a judgment in the market that it will continue to do that. There are really two ways to look at this and that is really, I think, what divides the economic fraternity at this stage. If somehow, somebody could wave a wand and move the exchange rate down sharply to a point where the expectation of future change was zero, then the yield spreads between intermediate or long-term issues in dollars and those denominated in the other currencies would dramatically come together: and we would get the type of stability that we would like.

The problem, unfortunately, is that the other potential is that a sharply (falling) dollar merely will be extrapolated, as Sam Cross has implied. Here, we don't know, largely because we don't know where the bottom is. Obviously, the lower we are the closer the bottom is, by definition. Exchange rates tend to be non-negative, though sometimes you wonder. Judging from the way the markets have been behaving the last several weeks, I think the probabilities that a free fall is about to happen or could happen have diminished. Unfortunately, the trouble is that even if the probabilities have diminished, the consequences of that event are extremely dangerous. Even if we get to the point where we are all fully, unequivocally convinced that there are no secondary reaction problems in the exchange rate, I think we had better keep up our guard."

Pe newbies always faced a crisis very soon,

Greenspan was so far only the latest in a row of Fed chairmen haunted by some sort of crisis soon after entering office. **Arthur F. Burns**, chairman from February 1, 1970, climbed the top chair only to oversee the beginning of the **1970's bear market**, the **closing of the gold window** and the first **oil shock 1973**. When he stepped down on August 6, 1979, his successor **Paul A. Volcker** had to fight **double digit inflation** with the highest Fed Funds rates ever seen and conspired with President Carter to mismanage that economic downturn through his tightening only became an on-and-off recession from 1979 to 1982 with GDP never declining more than a quarter in a row. *(For a good book on this look into my profile.)*

With this past and the current uncertain economic outlook hampered by an administration that does not seriously think about fighting the triple deficits, as described in *this post*, it is understandable that every reasonable person will think twice about stepping into Alan Greenspan's oversized shoes.

Mark Thoma says ask the right questions:

Is the Administration somehow rewarding Greenspan for supporting tax cuts? I doubt it. Instead, the possible delay more likely reflects the challenges of finding a suitable replacement. Academic? Industrialist? Financier? Or academic turned industrialist? Moreover, is there pressure in the Administration to appoint simply on the basis on politics, rather than on the best person for the job? This is my greatest fear. The economy can survive a John Snow as Secretary of Treasury. The same is not true for the Fed Chair.

It should also be added that Greenspan never, ever, talked himself into purgatory. His **unsurpassed art of calm and logic rhetoric** under the immense pressure from policymakers and the spotlight of live TV cameras transmitting his every word and movement onto trading floors worldwide never faded for a second. **No man has done more to sedate markets when they needed it most.** This unique capability makes it even harder for his successor; whoever it will be. Greenspan gained so much credibility by steering the markets through the longest economic expansion in a time of war and peace because he kept markets from panicking in the aftermath of October '87.

Any delay could wreak havoc on the markets,

Finding a successor should therefore follow the established schedule. **Keeping Greenspan in office past his scheduled retirement could be seen as a signal that the policymakers in the White House have difficulties making up their mind about who would be best suited to step into Greenspan's shoes.** Any delay in this single most important announcement of the administration regarding the economy could wreak havoc on the markets.

Greenspan sees himself leaving his post on schedule, one can take from his latest public statement, ". . . members of the 2005 graduating class. I have more in common with you graduates than people might think. After all, before long, after my term at the Federal Reserve comes to an end, I too will be looking for a job," he said at the Wharton School on May 15. The countdown marks 257 days to go today.

This in itself could pose a problem for the markets. As it is entrenched in human nature not to take blame for one's own actions, Greenspan could be tempted to act to dovish in the face of accelerating inflation. He certainly would earn a bigger wreath of laurels when the economy is still on a sound path on the day he retires, thanks to a then still accommodative policy of the Fed. Let's hope his care for the markets will stand above any idea of self-importance even the greatest persons in history have fallen victim to too often.

Referring to Mark Thoma's *blog post,*

The shortlist of possible names is in my opinion already one name shorter: **Ben "Helicopter" or "Printing Press" Bernanke** has obviously quoted himself out of the musical chairs game. Markets will not trust a chairman that would rely on the money printing press to throw more paper on every problem that could show up in the future.

Postscript by Author: Mark Thoma's worst fears came to roost with Professor Ben Bernanke being selected by President George W. Bush to replace Allan Greenspan in 2005 ... thus picking Helicopter Printing Press Bernanke as his new Federal Reserve Chairman .. and the printing presses began to spit out billions of dollars of currency to save America banks from our floundering war economy and banking system. Incoming President Barak Obama, street attorney, inherited the collapse of the investment banking, auto and housing industries overnight. The rest is history that has been hidden from home owners and retirement plans as a speed bump in our Wall Street mortgage brokers handling of fraudulent subprime mortgage tranches. Read between the lines ... it was the very incompetence that Greenspan feared as he relinquished the reins to a Harvard professor, an incompetent Treasury Secretary and two Presidents.

Results: the 2007-8 Great Depression labeled recession by those that caused it. Go to Netflix and view the "The Big Short" and "Too Big to Fail" that chronicled the disaster as a Wall Street fraud but failed to demonstrate how it was, more importantly, the classic blunder as that committed by the Carter and Fed Chairman Paul Voelker administration in 1979 ... using a 23% prime rate causing the demise of the Saving and Loan Thrift Bank industry. And the irony of President Obama's response in 2009 to the Bernanke blunder, with stimulus money as directed by his economic advisor ... oh yeah, the same Keynesian, Paul Volker.

Exhibit C

Downsizing of Federal Government Using An Enterprise Model

Problem: redundancy with State agencies and excessive employees and waste in a bureaucracy with no form of accountability or outcome measurement of successful use of taxpayer money. 22 million individuals are employed by the inter related bureaucracies causing redundancy in, cost, mission and outcome with a payroll, benefits and guaranteed pensions amounts to $2 trillion Federal, State and Local annual payroll and unfunded pensions. Certain agencies lend themselves to privatized solutions. The most important being health, education and welfare

Enterprise Model for Downsizing Government:

Example: Department of Health and Human Services (renamed Quality of Life Incorporated)
Current payroll per year (all in 2012 values) (67,000 employees $78 billion dollar payroll, $800 billion budget)

1. (32,375 employees down from 67,000)	$42 billion
2. Pension debt converted to IRA's	-0-
3. Total fixed overhead	$42 billion
4. Benefits Paid Out	
a. Medicare	$480 billion
b. Social Security	$725 billion
5. Variable costs	$1,205 billion
6. Amortized Unfunded entitlement benefits	$250 billion
7. Total Annual Costs	$1,492 billion
8. Medicare and social security revenues	$76 billion

9. Deficit $726 billion
10. Equity Capital Infusion equity assessment $900 billion
11. Net Worth of Health and Human Services $174 billion

Stock ownership in the Enterprise Model would be held by those assessed 5% of their net worth to capitalize the private Enterprise Model ... the return on that investment would be at least the rate paid on Treasury instruments. Downsizing the number of employees and related salary costs would be based on accountability models and pensions withheld from the employees' salary. Services would be charged to private sector. Medicaid would be funded at the State level using the Enterprise Model.

Other Federal Agencies that could be operated by the private sector more efficiently and profitably: Commerce, Housing and Urban Affairs, Corps of Engineers, NASA, Interior, Transportation, EPA, Post Offices: structured as corporations not institutions with shareholders, Boards, accountability, tax funding based on net worth. . while paying their investors a rate of return equal or in excess of the Treasury securities are paying.

Bringing the existing government institutions into an Enterprise mode may seem impossible but it is not as farfetched as assuming the Government can repay $158 trillion dollars in debt when the annual revenues are $3.3 trillion, and the deficit is continuing to grow at the rate of $1.2 trillion* per year and the debt service approaching $1 trillion per year. The treasury, justice, labor, defense, state, GSA, SSA, IRS, Senate, Congress, Supreme Court must all stay in the public sector as the infra-structure for the Better Good and civil administration. An example of privatizing government is Sandy Springs, GA https://www.sandyspringsga.gov/city-history that had the same problem with public agencies, having transparency after the waste happens, then covers it up as political drama. When the real problem is government is using cash basis budgeting and accounting understating their liabilities and overstating their surpluses. Go to www.pearlcity.com and review how they cut cost by 50% and improved results 100% using the enterprise Model versus the traditional institutional model.

YOUR VOTE COUNTS

Exhibit D

Government Commits Fraud and Abuse

Any proposed Medicare cuts are fraudulent and abusing to patients and providers. First of all, Medicare isn't an entitlement. It's each American's savings trust fund account for later use when needed. The Government agencies (who are immune from accountability lawsuits for enforcement tactics) continue to accuse the private sector of fraud and abuse and have contracted with private consulting firms to dig up audit claims for Medicare overpayment that the auditors may deem to be abuse of the Medicare reimbursement system and fraud towards the beneficiaries.

When these auditors ask for claims to review, they threaten the providers with denials first, recovery of past Medicare payments made and take a no prisoner's approach. For this, the auditors are paid 25% of the dollars recovered even though the providers have 5 stages of appeal rights. Also, fraud in this vein does not require intent on the part of the provider be proven, only the opinion of the RAC auditors is needed to trigger a fraud charge, potential jail time and a possible 5-year exclusion from practicing in a Medicare provider business.

Secondly, the Medicare trust funds are not the Government's money . . . it belongs to the beneficiaries who have paid in the money. Thirdly, the Government has been depriving the elderly their Medicare benefits using denial of payment and the RAC (Recovery Audit Contractor) audit Gestapo tactics to suppress Medicare coverage for beneficiaries. This is while the Medicare trust fund money was loaned to the General Fund for fighting the Iraq and Afghanistan wars to the tune of $700 billion dollars. All that is left in the fund are US Treasury Bills while Congress claims entitlements to Medicare are our biggest problem from a budgetary standpoint. Wrong! Big Government fraud is our biggest problem.

Without Government involvement, the Medicare program has a surplus and takes in 40% more than it pays out for health care claims. Even with the paying agent CMS (Centers of Medicare and Medicaid Services) depriving the elderly their benefits using fear inducing conformity tactics against the providers, Medicare pays its bills timely if they meet stringent interpretive guidelines. While Medicaid goes farther into the Obama Care hole. Since 1975 when HEW, the Federal Department of Health Education and Welfare, started denying Medicare claims as not being medically necessary or not improving the patients' functioning, some 30 million seniors over 65 years of age have been deprived of their full entitled 100 day per spell of illness skilled nursing benefit due to the imposition of a little-known rule that allowed the Government to review claims and retrospectively take money back.

This started the suppression of Medicare Part A and B benefits for the elderly to the tune of $600 billion dollars since 1975 to the present and the elderly's right to be restored *to their highest level of functioning* and discharged back to the community.

As the denials rose to almost 50% of the submitted claims in the 1980' and 90's the providers started to cut back on the provided days of Medicare Part A skilled care and as a result more patients were having their long-term care paid by Medicaid that by law is not to be billed until the Medicare benefits are exhausted . . . then, to make things worse, the Government changed the retrospective review and recovery to prospective denial of payment even though the provider in good faith had provided the care and paid for medications, therapy treatments, medical supplies and medical equipment . . . this further cut back on the amount of days the providers were willing to risk to the whims of the government claims reviewers, who were just looking at documents, weren't medical professionals so medical necessity had not been reviewed by a qualified physician.

This is fraud at its worst as the Government literally ignored the patient's need and the provider's loss under the guise the claims were not medically necessary or did not improve the patients' condition. The truth was the bureaucrats did not want to pay and exceed the inadequate budget constraints.

To support this allegation of fraud and abuse by the Federal Government there are two Federal court cases which convicted them of this fact for which they have ignored and continued to flaunt:
Fox v Bowen, Connecticut 1986 "Fox vs. Bowen

In 1986, a Connecticut Federal Judge in a lawsuit (Fox vs. Bowen) determined HCFA (now CMS) had violated Medicare beneficiaries entitled constitutional rights to skilled nursing services and ordered HCFA to revise the Skilled Nursing Manual to clarify the requirements for coverage under Medicare Part A. The court ordered them to reopen 14,000 cases and pay for the skilled care. The court also ordered HCFA to look for a "reason to pay" instead of a "reason not to pay." The court's purpose was to ensure Medicare claims are approved when the requirements for skilled care (licensed nursing, licensed therapists and licensed social workers) are met.

5th District Transmittal 262:
> As a result of Fox vs. Bowen, HCFA took action in 1987 by issuing Transmittal 262, but never sent this information to the providers. It was only sent to the Fiscal Intermediaries who offered no education or training on the transmittal or the court-ordered process, nor have they placed the order in practice during the past 26 years. As a result, the 100-day stay was cut down to an average length of stay (ALOS) of 22 days and during the 1990's began to rise to an ALOS of 34 days. With the initiation of the RAC audits, the purge is starting again to deprive the patients of their rightful Medicare entitled health care benefit in skilled nursing facilities.

Jimmo v Sibelius, Vermont 2012:

One of the tactics which has been used by CMS was to deny Medicare Part A skilled claims if the skilled patient "reached their prior level of functioning". This was subjective, as at what point do you look for their prior level of functioning, but more importantly, as stated by the court ruling, "neither the Medicare statute nor the implementing regulations refer to or suggest an improvement standard." The Federal Court again has ordered CMS to reissue its interpretive guidelines, its manuals, its operating policies and pay retroactively only back to January 2011 based on claims filed and denied. This of course will not pay for the $600 billion fraud committed over the years due to the misapplication and misinterpretation of the Medicare laws and regulations on the Medicare beneficiaries. This also does not touch the amount of the fraud the government has caused due to most providers not even submitting claims in fear of denial and possible fraud allegations.

The true amount of potentially applicable underpayments by the government (CMS) cannot be proven because of Medicare claims not being filed due to fear inducing conformity tactics conducted by the government. The government cannot be sued unless a Medicare claim has been submitted and denied. Effectively, the Government knowingly underpaid and denied Medicare claims, but also never will pay the unfiled Medicare claims just mentioned above. Medicare beneficiaries should be vehemently upset due to not receiving their rightful Medicare entitlements! Additional government settlements will not be paid unless there is a class action of providers who have had Medicare beneficiaries denied claims, who also join the class action law suit join together, this governmental fraud is going to continue.

The bottom-line effect of this fraudulent application of the Medicare program, by the Federal Government, the elderly has been deprived of much needed skilled nursing benefits. Over the last fifty years this fraudulent interpretation has resulted in over a trillion dollars loss of much needed resources for the nursing homes to provide the quality needed to restore millions back to home rather than keeping them on State Medicaid coverage. See more details in my book Health Care for All (How to Fix Nursing Homes and Prevent Pandemics), Page Tuner Media 2021.

Exhibit E

Definitions for Health Care ACRONYMS used throughout the three volumes of The American Enterprise Party

(Complexities of the Government Health Care System of Rules and Regulations)

AI = artificial intelligence (digital algorithms) computer process management systems

ACA = Affordable Care Act (aka, Obama Care)

AARP = American Association of Retired People (trade association)

AMA = American Medical Association (physicians trade association)

AHA = American Hospital Association (trade association)

APA = American Pharmaceutical Association (trade association)

ACO = Accountable Care Organizations (health care agency)

ATD = Antitrust division of the Justice department

ADL = Activities of Daily Living (those activities related to elderly living in long term care)

CDC = Centers of Disease Control (regulatory agency)

CMS = Centers of Medicare and Medicaid Services (regulatory agency)

CPA = Certified Public Accountant

CEO = Chief Executive Officer

COPD = Congestive Pulmonary Disease

CHF = Congestive Heart Failure

CVA = Cardio Vascular Accident

CFO = Chief Financial Officer

CHIP = Childers Health Insurance Payment

CNA = Certified Nursing Assistant

CQI = Continuing Quality Indicator

CMA = Certified Medication Aide

DRGS = Diagnostic Resource Group (Medicare Reimbursement for Hospital)

DON = Director of Nursing

ER = Emergency Room

EKG = Electrocardiogram

FDA = Federal Drug Agency (regulatory agency)

FI = Fiscal Intermediary (insurance companies managing Medicare Part A, B, C and D for the government) (regulatory agency)

FOCUS = Functional Outcome Utilization Score a management progress evaluation

GNP = Gross National Product

GDP = Gross Domestic Product

GAO = Government Accounting Office (regulatory agency)

HHS = Health and Human Services (regulatory agency)

HMO = Health Maintenance Organization

HEW = Health Education and Welfare (regulatory agency)

ISO = International Organization for Standardization

ICD = International Classifications of Diseases (codes ICD-10 latest version)

JC H = Joint Commission for Hospital (regulatory agency)

LPN = Licensed Practical Nurse

LTC = Long Term Care organizations

MDS = Minimum Data Set an assessment instrument for long term care admissions

QUIP = Quality Incentive Payment

OPT = Outpatient Patient Therapies

OASIS – Home Care Medicare reimbursement

PPO = Preferred Physician Organization (insurance contractor with Medicare reimbursement)

PPS = Perspective Payment System for Medicare reimbursement for all health care facilities

PIE = Problem Intervention Evaluation criteria and equation for documenting skilled nursing services

Part A = Medicare payment for Hospital and Skilled Nursing services

Part B = Medicare payment for Physicians services

Part C = Medicare Advertisement payment for A and B services bundled payment

Part D = Medicare and Medicaid payment for prescription drugs

RUGS = Resource Utilization Groups by Body Systems (Medicare reimbursement for Skilled Nursing Facilities)

RVUS = Relative Value Units (Medicare reimbursement for physicians)

RN = Registered Nurse (licensed and registered nurse)

QQ = Quality Quantified Care Evaluation for scoring maximum health care regulations

SNF = Skilled Nursing Facilities (licensed nursing homes)

SHIF = Self Health Insurance Fund a new way to fund health care and internalize self-health

VA = Veterans Administration

REIMBURSEMENT: Title Nineteen of the Social Security Act of 1938 is the governing law for Medicare and Medicaid and the Affordable Care Act regulations that governs Medicare, Medicaid and Obama Care resulting in the following rules and regulations:

Payment to Providers: Medicare, Medicaid, Obama Care, Advantage Medicare HMO's, PPO's, Managed Medicaid, private health insurance pay providers on diagnosis codes and procedure codes without regard to episode, treatment complexity, prescription medications or outcome. Rates are set by zip code, risk pools, population groups. All are averaged rates based on algorithms (per diems or per procedure) not on cures or improvement. It is a bureaucratic mess and the flow of $4.2 trillion dollars to providers does not focus on treating problems or pursuit of cures or prevention. Only pays for approved 77,000 patient diagnosis codes, 10,000 CPT therapy procedure codes and 394 (categories I, II, III) of physician CPT encounter codes.

"Obamacare (ACA the Act) is fully implemented January 1st, even though the regulations haven't been written yet. And Brian, we've got 13,000 pages of regulations that they've already written. If we stacked it up here, it would be seven feet tall."

— Rep. Richard Hudson (R-N.C.), speaking on "Fox and Friends," May 13, 2013

"Implementation has also become a bureaucratic nightmare, with some 159 new government agencies, boards and programs busily enforcing the roughly 20,000 pages of rules and regulations already associated with this law."

— Sen. Mitch McConnell (R-Ky.), on the third anniversary of the law's passage, March 22, 2013

"Medicare is Governed by an estimated 130000 pages of laws and regulations; many Medicare providers are spending as much time navigating their way through [the Health Care Financing Administration's] complicated regulatory process as they are on patient care."

Medicaid is governed by State run buy 5 State Departments of Public Health (Regulations are estimated to be 13,000 pages per State and the New and Increased Pass-Through Payments in Medicaid Managed Care Delivery Systems (in total about 650,000 pages of redundant rules and regulations supporting Managed Medicaid and Medicare Advantage programs (called the dual eligibility program). Author's note: Managed Care has nothing to do with care it is Managed Cost of Care using input codes not outcome service codes. Each State also has their rules and regulations regarding delivery of services under the auspice of the Department of Survey and Appeals that has another 250,000 pages of redundant enforcement rules and civil money penalties for violations. Nursing home regulations taking up most of the enforcement activities.

On January 17, 2017, CMS released a final rule that finalizes changes, consistent with the CMCS Informational Bulletin (CIB) The Use of New or Increased Pass-Through Payments in Medicaid Managed Care Delivery Systems (PDF, 87.89 KB), published on July 29, 2016. The final rule addresses the pass-through payment transition periods and the maximum number of pass-through payments permitted annually during the transition periods under Medicaid managed care contracts and rate certifications. The final rule prevents increases in pass-through payments and the addition of new pass-through payments beyond those in place when the pass-through payment transition periods were established in the final Medicaid managed care regulations effective July 5, 2016.

2016 Medicaid and CHIP Managed Care Final Rule

On April 25, 2016, the Centers for Medicare & Medicaid Services (CMS) put on display at the Federal Register the Medicaid and CHIP

Managed Care Final Rule, which aligns key rules with those of other health insurance coverage programs, modernizes how states purchase managed care for beneficiaries, and strengthens the consumer experience and key consumer protections. This final rule is the first major update to Medicaid and the Children's Health Insurance Program (CHIP) managed care regulations in more than a decade. See the related blog co-authored by the CMS Administrator and the Centers for Medicaid and CHIP Services (CMCS) Director, Medicaid Moving Forward. For questions regarding Manage Care,

email ManagedCareRule@cms.hhs.gov.

Author's commentary: Jerry Rhoads a CPA consultant, has specialized for 60 years on deciphering managed health care for public health, Medicare and Medicaid services. Finding that it's truly not managed care but managed cost wealth care. At its best the Federal and State Governments spend $4.2 trillion per year for prescription drugs and treatment of input diagnosis and procedure codes with no plan of treatment or specified outcome nor cure. At its worse it is not prepared to prevent another Pandemic nor any of the diagnosis and procedure codes because payment (reimbursement) doesn't require a measurable outcome.

Our medical professionals aren't to blame since the Government dictates the standards of practice by the way they pay. Reimbursement, as it is called, infers a payback for the cots expended services accomplishing the content of the billing. If that is for an input code that's what the provider will provide ... it needs to be an output code on what was accomplished called accountability for payment ... not diagnosis or procedure codes when the patients need prevention, or cure, or preservation of health.

To accomplish this my approach was, as a consultant to Federal and State Government, always told by the lawmakers "it's not feasible. It has to be administratively simple and budget neutral". In other words, it is better to waste money than to confuse the administrators and screwup the budget since it issues based politics "to go along to get along". That allows a panic problem to become a Pandemic caused by mismanagement by quack scientists who work for the bureaucracy, supposedly directing our Public Health towards outcomes and away from diseases, not towards grant money and lying about it. For this I now rest my case to privatizing health care for the individual and collective good. Then the Enterprise Health Care Model for pursuing outcomes to justify provider incomes creates budgets that are based on performance not politics.

In this Volume Two, Article Five of the health care reorganization plan are the methods that should be used to get positive outcomes for provider incomes. Everyone can benefit for knowing what they don't know and stand up for prevention of health problems, preserving health and only paying for those principles. That's accountability for the providers to strive for ... the benefit is for their practice, the cost and the patients' health they get paid for to serve. It puts standards of practice and benefits centered care where it has to be to avoid the waste that is bankrupting Medicare and Medicaid, then blaming the providers and patients for that result.

Exhibit F

Words and Elections Have Consequences

Exhibit F for eliciting your opinion for what is a problem versus just an issue to be tabled and call for reform, a classic political stall tactic so the voters forget how that problem was squelched or perverted into a law with regulations that take away our freedoms. "Being politically correct is to go along to get along", Sam Rayburn.

"What is the difference between a cynic and an agent of change . . . the cynic creates the problem then calls it an unresolvable issue and the agent of change defines the problem and imposes a solution."
–Winston Churchill

In my world a problem you have to attack with vigorous solutions, an issue is an argument that only ends in an emotional deferment awaiting the crash dummies to prove it is a problem. Jerry Rhoads, author this is why The American Enterprise Party must become the swing vote to break ties and prevent gridlock of the two-party system at every level as a solution for our ineffective issue debating "go along to get along" Congress and Presidency. Then we can "get along to go along" after our problems.

Is it a political woke Issue or a social Problem?

My definition of issue is a "no worries" discussion not taking responsibility for or making a commitment to, pursuing an argument while a problem is a plan to pursue a solution. The biggest abusers are the mind control freaks in politics, social media and news reporting. This slight twist in reflection freezes creative thought and tables every problem for compromise or calling for reform of thought thus deferring and avoiding constructive positive thought.

My biggest problem is listening to everyone, including my family, calling a problem an issue. What's the difference anyway? Well look at the definition of a problem (a life changing incident that needs to be avoided or solved by change with facts and resolution) and Issue (a disagreement between two entities, human or otherwise, that disagree on an argument affecting both parties and not requiring facts or a solution).

In politics, since that's where such propaganda starts, the art of compromise is the justification for calling problems issues and reforms as the goal is to go along to get along. As Sam Rayburn taught LBJ … if you want to get anywhere "your way go along to get along". In other words, fake the problem into an issue that doesn't require an action unless you decide it's a problem for your solution.

Aha, so that's what's happening in our country with a gridlocked no consensus Congress, a frustrated society and woke being the word of the day to further corrupt rational thought, so the followers are following followers into subservient conclusions. Following is my test of your preferences as designating it as a problem or an issue. Mine are based on our gridlocked no consensus political system that isn't interested in solving problems just passing laws that continue to erode our freedoms and cause social wars, financial jeopardy and conflict despite your political party preference:

Another problem with our verbal vernacular normalizing certain words in the English language to mean something that a noun used as a verb would cause a new interpretation of its vulgar use … example use of f***king in multiple sentences replacing a noun with a verb or adjective to make it vulgar in any circumstance since vulgarity is the percussor to violence in our culture of excesses (AKA Roman gladiators and insurrection in 45BC) … others are issue instead of problem, is it politically correct or incorrect replacing the need for problem solving, no worries replacing "to hell with it":

	(P) A Problem	(I) An Issue
Open borders and qualified immigrants	P	
Defund or expand the Police budgets and authority	P	
Crime in cities across America	P	
Climate change and global warming		I
Money-tics controlling elections	P	
Government $19 trillion payroll and pension debt	P	
Pornographic Sex on TV and social media	P	
Vulgarity and shootings in our schools	P	
Divorce and destruction of the nuclear family	P	
Guns and gangs destroying our society	P	
Drugs, violence and crime in our cities	P	
Elimination of prayer in schools	P	
Two-party gridlocked policies and woke politics	P	
Federal and State bloated budgets, cooking the books	P	
Taxing enterprising and risk-taking Americans in 46 different categories	P	
Inflation and stagnation of a deflating dollar	P	
Weak Dollar in the World... China's fiat currency	P	
Chinese worldwide trade warfare	P	
Culture of Violence, Vulgarity and Excesses	P	
Disinformation and fake media exploiting our social media outlets	P	
Freedom of speech attacked and character assassination	P	
Supreme Court packing using term limits	P	

Redistricting and gerrymandering of voting pools	P
Removal of the Electoral College	P
Voting irregularity with harvesting of illegal voters	P
American's health and welfare costs with negative outcomes	P
Racism Woke-ism as a presumed culture	P
Educational curriculum:	P
(1619 project and Critical Race Theories: Slavery is not a result of racism, but the reason for freedom and opportunity in our culture)	I
Systemic racism from both sides of the color scale	I
Jim Crow red lining versus John Crow and blue lining	I
Standing not kneeling for the national anthem, love our USA or leave it	I
Respecting not burning our flag by being a patriot or leave our nation	P
Mail-in voting irregularities enforced and recounts required	P
Illegals allowed to vote by using rank voting for election fraud	P
School closings and in-home learning decided by Teachers' Unions	P
Chinese Wuhan lab release of Covid-19	P
Dr. Fauci's continued handling of the Pandemic he may have caused	P
President Biden and Hunter Biden's illegal activities using the power of privilege	P
White supremacy does it exist	I
Term limits necessary for new ideas	I

Capitalism is monetary capital that must share	I
Socialism is human capital that must learn to earn for a skill to bill	I
Humanism (Money and People working and sharing together)	I
Political party affiliation based on results	I
Respect for your religion	I
What's your favorite color	I
You're a terrible parent	I
Your kids are unruly	I
Your husband is running around and cheating	I
I don't like your hair	I
I don't like your dress	I
Climate change will kill us all	I
Sanctions on China, Russia, etc. must be used before the fact and act	I
Boycott of Olympics and ignore the UN and our peers	I

My point is we as the enterprising Americans who pay all the bills for the wealthy individuals and corporations are being lied to by using the word issue to pursue an argument even though we know it's a problem pursuing a solution. If you feel this way stand up for a real third party that represents you, as the swing vote to break ties and prevent gridlock of the two-party system at every level of Congress and legislatures across America, to unlock the binary two-party gridlock for the betterment of all Americans by solving our problems ... personal or otherwise ... not pursuing analysis by paralysis with a committee or commission or reform task force to avoid pursuing solutions.

Now we are being brain washed to say "no worries" rather than "no problems" leaving every disagreement as an issue with no responsibility or commitment to solve the problem and hope it is soon forgotten. This results in broken homes, divorces and gangs as the pseudo security blanket.

Obviously, words have consequences: for every word in the dictionary there are negative and positive consequences that impact our personal self-image depending on our choice of words. For most, if not all of us, issue means problem but it's not socially or politically correct, to say so. Somehow, our woke society now thinks like politicians ... better to be appeasing, pleasing and compromising to be popular, than negative and required to propose a solution if you call it a problem. This brings negativity to you and has infected our children, teens and young adults to avoid problem solving and change by calling everything an issue. Believing that the government should decide our fate and become a totalitarian State. "If you lead with money, you won't solve anything" Senator Dirksen.

For example, the magnificent mile versus life in the ghetto is an issue for the Mayor of Chicago (also LA, NY, Baltimore, Philadelphia, Dallas, Atlanta, Minneapolis, Milwaukee, Seattle, Portland, Indianapolis, Phoenix, San Francisco, Cincinnati, Cleveland, Detroit, Albuquerque, Boston, D.C., Pittsburgh, Omaha, Des Moines, Kansas City, St. louis, Little Rock, New Orleans, etc.) and an unresolvable problem for the poor that live and die early there. Add another 2 to 3 million immigrants converging on sanctuary cities and we have another Pandemic of overpopulation, homelessness, drug users, vagrants, tent cities, crime and welfare cases. In the process our leaders have created a third world country inside of America the Beautiful.

Who's right who's wrong. Both are right if we call it a problem or problematic, that must have a solution or both are wrong if we call it an issue. In real life the wrong choices are being made and inactions confirm that nothing will change as Marxist Socialism makes bedfellows with BLM, ANTFI, Poor Boys, KKK, Nazi and woke racists who are using George Floyd as their battle cry. Putting a knee on America's future.

My point is, our Politician's, social media and Teachers have indoctrinated us with propaganda spread by fake news, to take the easy way out and call everything negative an issue. Just "go along to get along". As result, the crime and gang infested hoods, boil over onto the Magnificent Mile then suburbia, breaking and entering to just take it for reparation. Until society changes and slums are eradicated with rehabbed buildings and affordable housing, we will continue to have inhumanity. It must be a priority to have dynamic local small businesses supporting restored families, stable lifestyles and Charter schools in the hoods and rural communities. With the goals to stop gang banging, shop lifting, carjacking, black on black crime, drug dealing, prostitution, teen pregnancy and high school dropout rate. So, improved SAT scores for pursuing opportunity for a higher degree with a career or technical skill to break out of ghetto poverty and fix the problem permanently.

Neither the right (red) or left (Blue) Mayors and Governors are right when problem solving is deferred with inaction until it becomes a glaring George Floyd problem beyond their control. Exacerbated by BLM demanding they defund the police and elect no cash bail prosecutors. Why not turn problem makers into problem solvers by teaching that we all need a "skill to bill and need to learn to earn" so we can share as a team in the profit of our work. Capitalists joining with socialists in an enterprise party solving problems and exposing issues. As a gridlocked society supports protests turning into riots and attacking police as the problem. All it takes is teamwork and profits to share in the rewards:

Talent	**W**ith	**P**lans
Effort	**O**pportunity	**R**eward
Aptitude	**R**isk & reward	**O**ur
Money	**K**ills Poverty	**F**uture
		Investments
		To share wealth's
		Surplus

See Article Thirteen of the reorganization plan, of the American Enterprise Party Platform, that proposes to develop analytics to hold leadership in our States and Cities accountable for specific performance data criteria and reporting to accomplish all of these objectives.

Then the goal is to take the risk and reward actions to solve problems before they become revolutions and Pandemics (panic attacks) where we follow fear as the solution. (Example: quack science followed by closing the schools, bending the curve, social distancing, masks, ventilators, endless testing, contact tracing, shut down of nonessential businesses, for no avail until we learn how to fix our own immunity and community). So, we can fight individually to win the war by not dying too early from poor lifestyles in our cities, rural communities and the ghetto slums. Where poverty, poor housing, hate crimes, prostitution, drug dealing, overdoes and inferior schools are the negative lifestyles. This societal infection must be turned into a powerhouse of enterprising American workers, stable families, entrepreneurs, politicians, millionaires, teachers, supply line manufacturers, athletes and diverse citizens for the rest of the world to follow and/or migrate to through our port of call, controlled borders.

When Does Nonsense Defy Common Sense?

There is an old Iowa farmer adage, "you can't make sense out of nonsense", and a Malcolm Gladwell's statement in his book "Blink" ... "it is more likely the blink of the eye intuition will, in an instant, recognize a fraud if you're an expert in that field".

When nonsense, defies good ole Iowa common sense my mind says fraud. Mindless examples such as, protests are peaceful, crime is down, woke is good, and schools are closed because we have to bend the Fauci quack curve ... more:

1) This $5 trillion piece of legislation is paid for. Fact: Increased taxes will be for 10 years for money spent in the next three years. Fact: common sense intuition says this is a fraud

2) B.B.B., Build back bigger is better and will solve inflation, and improve the economy. Fact: common sense intuition says this is a fraud

3) We got all of those that "wanted" to get out of Afghanistan, out safely. Fact: common sense intuition says this is a fraud

4) Open borders are not a crisis, until we have solved the root cause, of why it exists. Fact: common sense intuition says this is a fraud

5) Climate change, and white supremacy, are our nation's most pressing problems. Fact: common sense intuition says this is a fraud

6) Swing vote, Joe Manchin, is the most important Senator. Fellow Democrats say he's a turncoat manipulator. Fact: common sense intuition says this is a fraud

7) Taxpayers are paying for all this, Build Back Better transformational nonsense ... Fact: when there is no surplus, only new debt and deficit spending, under both the Republicans and Democrats.

8) The books and budgets are balanced, by taxing the rich ... in fact the books are cooked by not recording accrued obligations, hiding past deficits, and future bankruptcy.

9) The reversal of TRUMP policies will build America back better, regardless of the debt limit, and inflation being transitory. Fact: common sense intuition says this is a fraud.

10) The two million illegal immigrants, with no skills and job prospects, will not increase the cost of government welfare one cent. Fact: common sense intuition says this is a fraud

These are only ten of twenty or thirty, I could think up from scratch. Others are A.O.C. and the squad are liberals, pulling America into

Marxism and Communism, for the greater good. Biden and Harris will run again. Trump will be our next President. Russia and China aren't : using Hunter Biden, to get to his father, who is selling the power of privilege and influence peddling. Hunter Biden is an accomplish artist, extraordinarily untalented. Dr. Fauci, is a hero, and above reproach for his behavior in the past. The CDC and FDA and WHO and Institute of Health, are all believable, when it comes to science, Pandemics and problem solving. Fact: common sense intuition says this is a fraud

There will never be an effective third party. Fact: common sense intuition says this is a necessity.

Okay, that's a few more. I'm sure you as a voter can think of your own nonsense, everything anymore is political. If you're Red you're dead in the water. If you're Blue you're bleeding and the independents are lost ... where nonsense Trumps common sense, when you turn on CNN, Fox News, MSNBC, ESPN, the Disney Channel, Face Book, Instagram, Tik Tok, etc. .. All utilize fake news, and denial of freedom of speech, when it fits their identity, and narrative. That is the definition, of the most used word in the English and Spanish vernacular ... "woke" ... second, it's an "issue" not a problem.

So, why should I be any different, as an opinionated podcaster, attempting to promote a third political party. First, I'm from Iowa, secondly, I'm a conservative CPA, and finally I'm the founder CEO of the American Enterprise Party, to stop using nonsense, as a synonym for common sense. Those who claim to be an intellectual pundit, harvesting their opinion for harvesting votes, for one of the two ineffective political parties, fails the smell test for common sense results, and positive outcomes.

Nor, can you be a scrutinizing practitioner, of common sense, as you sit by and let the nonsense take the lead, into the chaos of tyranny, lies for votes, slanted TV political ads, use of millions and billions to get elected, then claim to be an independent, when in fact it comes to using common sense, in deficit spending, and debt. If you fall for nonsense, you will fall for anything.

CHICKEN LITTLE'S THREAT
A fairy tale of ill begotten fate

It was a day that Chicken Little had seen
A falling sky
And the wind was mean
Howling out its final reply

The stage was bare
Looking up I saw the curtain come down
The sun had set on it there
And the crowd was nowhere to be found

For the shore was no longer wet
The day was done
And the Kingdom had come
Fe fi fo fum the night had won

I looked up and the sky was dark
The air was still wiping out the sun
By the wings of that meadow lark
Over a greenhouse deferring a Kingdom done

Chicken Little words I heard
Were being carried from the beaks of a bird
Flying high flying low
Flying around what we already know
For the climate we enjoyed with faith
Had done it all
The system was said to be fail-safe
But the meltdown proved no one can prevent the fall

It took just one hurricane moving
Scanning the skies clean
To set the radar into its mode behooving
What Chicken Little had seen

The falling sky with metal birds that fly
Due to the slipping of a thumb
On the trigger of that A-bomb's outrigger
Holocaust had come

But oh so much bigger
That held the earth's heat estopped
Suffocating mankind before it could be stopped
Leaving behind the controls heat is dropped

Into its fatal freezing pattern
Circling to kill even the rings of Saturn
Moving oh relentlessly on
I looked up to see the destruction of the dawn

And then it was
The flash blotted the sun
As judgement day does
Chicken Little's threat didn't come

As I looked up
The curtain came down
The silence was there after the sound
And the seasons for faith were found

While Chicken Little's threat didn't abound
As the world's end faced another round
Mother Nature begat El Nino' and La Nina'
So, the jet stream and trade winds redeema'
Mankind

(Moral of this parable ...
Our climate and temperature
Is a function of
Mother Nature's embrace
Within Father Time's space
And Chicken Littles' red face)

The final word for this Volume is "wake up America". B.B.B. and M.A.G.A. are marketing programs that never result in reality ... Biden ignores the swamp and Trump never exposed it the way, I'm doing in my books, blogs and podcasts. It's the primary reason, Build Back Bigger and Make America Great, are failures. A swing vote will take on the nonsense in the USA Congress, and in each State legislature, for our collective future.

Unfortunately, the art of common sense is uncommon, and the business of its application is unknown to the American voter. Those topics are presented, and matched with solutions in my recently released Trilogy the American Enterprise Party, Volume One, why do we need an effective third party? Volume Two, how can that happen? and Volume Three, who will do it? Fact: 200 million Enterprising Americans.

The underlying fact: capitalism (monetary capital) and socialism (human capital) are bedfellows, in every one of our American enterprises. Not, arch enemies for competing with the other isms. When all, any of us want, is Americanism with Humanism, that's in stark contrast to Marxism and Communism. It's the best of times and the better of times. The Tale of three political parties. Where the swing vote brings the extreme right and left towards the middle for bipartisan constitutional job and law making that is fiscally and physically secure.

PEACE IS THE REASON

Peace is the reason not religion
Reason minus religion = resolution

This is not an issue
It is the reason we have problems
We do not collectively address

An issue is a disagreement
A problem is not a disagreement
It is in need of a solution

An issue does not demand a solution
It suggests compromise
A problem to be solved demands
Peaceful resolution

Yes this is infallible logic
That talks more to intellect
Than pushing the issue to the political correct

Only to be tabled

Our lives go far beyond the politics of religion
We must deal with differences of course
But religion is not one we will ever agree upon

That's not a problem it is truly an issue
That should be tabled

So we can effectively and collectively
Deal with worldly problems of
Race relations
Nuclear weapons

Peaceful coexistence
Poverty
Aging
Physical disease
Mental disease
Ignorance
Population growth
Environment
World peace

Obviously these are not issues
They are priorities
Not for Politicians
But for those of religion
To come together peacefully

And let the Politicians
Warlords
Military
And Dissidents
Bluster about issues

While we the people
Resolve to
Agree that religion is not the reason
Peace is the reason

Reason minus religion and race = resolution
Peaceful coexistence minus revolution = resolution
Of PROBLEMS

That is the only truth we can't ignore
Or we lose the human rights war

STAND UP

It is said "Stand for something
Or you will fall for anything"

Stand up and be heard
But make sure before you retort
That you put substance in your word
Don't throw yourself upon the mercy of the court

Where they shall show you no mercy
If your point is merely to criticize
Downsize and or abort
What it's already the political resort

The world is in need of leaders
To direct its progress
Not just to satisfy the ire of the history readers
With the least amount of stress

So if you intend to stand up and shout
Above the mingling crowd
And your mind is prepared for the bout
Make sure your voice is loud

It takes courage to face a crowd
That can cast a stone

As you stand up proud
You'll feel as if you're all alone

Stand up don't fall as a shallow prince
But if you're willing to take on the bigger task
The rewards are many due to the suspense
And your answers must be to the questions asked

By not deceiving the clamoring crowd
Be accepted for what you know as truth
Don't present what you haven't vowed
Because seeing the vision is hard despite blue tooth

The American Enterprise Party
Shouting your voice is loud
Standing on your pulpit
You're said to be endowed
Not falling for something counterfeit

Standing on principle and substance
Your foundation is strong
And you'll only get the chance once
To fight for right over wrong

When you have established a following
Then the standing for something
Is a note you will have to sing
With every message you bring

That the American Enterprise Party cause
As the Swing Vote to break ties and prevent gridlock
of the two-party system at every level
divides the left and right wings for saving
The Great American Enterprise

But must not fall out of favor because
Of feeling we, the swing vote, know everything
When all humans have been given life for free but love of life
Has to be earned and shared in good faith for a higher purpose.
Jerry L. Rhoads, founder and CEO of the American enterprise Party

AUTHOR'S BIO

Jerry L. Rhoads, the author has extensive experience in all facets of health care. He was a consultant with Arthur Andersen & Co. that implemented Medicare and Medicaid in hospitals, clinics, nursing homes and long-term care campuses. He was licensed as a Nursing Home Administrator in multiple states and has managed urban, suburban and rural health care facilities. He is a CPA and a graduate of Simpson College, in Indianola, Iowa with a Bachelor of Science and Bachelor's in Business Administration. Simpson College is noted for being the only college that would admit George Washington Carver. The first black man to be admitted to an American college. Where he studied art and piano (1890-1891) and matriculated to Iowa State Agricultural College in Ames, Iowa in 1892. "At Simpson the kind of people there made me believe I was a human being". G.W. Carver.

Mr. Rhoads, his wife and son owned two skilled nursing facilities in Iowa and one in Arkansas. He has invented, with the help of his son, Artificial Intelligence (AI) software for managing the restorative processes for the elderly so they can be returned to the community. The author has also been consultant to State and Federal Government agencies for devising payment methods for health care providers and served on numerous committees developing legislation for long term care and testified before legislative committees as an expert witness. He was a licensed health care administrator in multiple states. The health care nursing home expert for the Illinois CPA Society, the American Institute of CPA's and The Illinois Nursing Home Association, and The American Nursing Home Association. Mr. Rhoads was also an adjunct professor at Triton Community College, in Riverside, Illinois teaching health care administration and application of government regulations in nursing homes.

The author has worked for Arthur Andersen & Co., a large public accounting firm, been a partner in two CPA firms and has owned and successfully run his own CPA businesses for 37 years. During that time, he started a CPA firm specializing in health care and added management consulting and software development to the services offered principally to Nursing homes and small hospitals. Over the years his expertise in Medicare and Medicaid led him to representing long term care Association members in proposed legislation and quality improvement methods for the operators of those small businesses.

He has written extensively and presented seminars and national workshops in 22 different states. He has six books published on the subject that he terms Self-Health books, proposing that the solution to funding America's declining health and escalating cost is to have everyone be responsible for making their own health and welfare decisions. By using funds set aside for them in investment withholding accounts they can make their own decisions in preserving their health while preventing chronic diseases that currently rage nationwide. Of course, without a better method than Obama or Biden Care, funding the health care benefits for 77 million baby boomers will result in rationing their benefits to younger populations and therefore, the elderly will not receive their entitled Medicare benefits they've paid for.

Jerry, 82 and Shari 81, his wife of 62 years now lives in Chicago, Illinois after being displaced to Iowa from 2009 to 2015 reversing their culture shock back to Iowa and Arkansas to run their three skilled nursing homes (small businesses) with their son. In their 70's they started a new business of restoring the elderly and disabled back to their homes… a new version of nursing home care termed Restorative Care. After seven years of fighting with the regulators over how their All-American Care restorative model positively changed the environment and quality of life for their patients, they sold them, and they were turned back into warehouses by corporate chain operators.

They have four grown children, twelve grandchildren and five great grandsons and four great granddaughters so far. Jerry and Shari believe that middle America is and has been by far the greatest place to live after having consulted with nursing homes in 22 different states dealing with the most regulated business of all time . . . nursing homes. It is their mission, through this book and his other health care books, to change the punitive and negative disincentives that exist in the Federal and State survey process to a reinforcement approach that allows the small businesses to direct their own version of quality of life not just bureaucratic, arbitrary and capricious interpretations of the quality of care.

This will require that the payment methods also be changed to performance-based reimbursement **(Article Five Health Care for All, Save Medicare)** using add-on QUIP programs and quality incentives utilized by the state of Illinois in the 1980's that Jerry helped design and implement. For complete coverage of this proposal refer to Jerry's book "Health Care of All" (How to Fix Nursing Homes and Prevent Pandemics) published by Page Turner Press, 2021.

LIST OF SOURCES:

- Google Search engine.
- Wikipedia search engine.
- Orlando Sentinel 2011 article by Charles Reese "Who is the gang of 545 vs. 330,000,000 People (100 Senators, 435 Congressmen, 9 Supreme Court Justices and 1 President)."
- Affordable Care Act of 2012 (Obama Care).
- Medicare regulations.
- George Orwell books ("1984" and "Animal Farm").
- Adam Smith book "Wealth of Nations."
- Aldous Huxley book" A Brave New World."
- US Constitution citations.
- Epoch Times valuable news reporting worldwide (fact rating 10)
- Dennis Prager quote.
- Jerry Rhoads podcast "American Enterprise Manifesto" 2020-21.
- Jerry Rhoads poems, books and articles.
- Margaret Thatcher quotes.
- Ronald Regan quotes.
- John Lennon lyrics.
- www.usdebtclock.org
- www.americanenterprisepoliticalparty.org
- Lee Drutman article for the National Constitution Center "Breaking the Two-Party Doom Loop: The Case for Multiparty Democracy in America."
- Linda Killian, book "The Swing Vote", St. Martin's Press, 2011.
- China's Economic Council long and short-term plans.
- Center of Disease Control quote 2020.
- Federal Disease Administration.

- New York Times quote 2020.
- Governor Cuomo quotes..
- "American Enterprise Manifesto" book published by Xlibris 2012, author Jerry Rhoads.
- "Health Care for All" book published by Page Turner Press 2021 author Jerry Rhoads.
- USA government budgetary information and statistics.
- Marianne Williamson, author of book "The Healing of America"
- John Streusel quotes 148.
- Karl Marx German Philosopher and author of "Communist Manifesto", 1843.
- Be Stein quotes.
- President Biden's Executive Orders, 2021 149.

OTHER TITLES AUTHORED BY JERRY RHOADS (Available in bookstores and on Amazon.com):

- Health Care for All (How to Fix Nursing Homes and Prevent Pandemics) (a self=health book).
- How to Stay Married Forever After (12 vows/habits to live by: forever after) (a self=health book).
- Lifestyles (Of the Healthy, Happy and Prosperous) (a self=health book).
- Never Too Old to Live (a self=health book.
- America in the Red Zone (a self=health book).
- Restore Elder Pride (a self=health book).
- Remedy Eldercide (a self=health book).
- The Monopsony Game (an economic analysis).
- Failing Government Taketh Away (a political analysis) .
- American Enterprise Manifesto (a third political party proposal).
- Basic Accounting and Budgeting for Long Term Care Facilities.

- Americana 1984 2084 2184 (a novel remembering George Orwell).
- Mancology (the science of managing human value).
- Cost Accounting for Long term care facilities.
- The Eighth Wonder of the World (first Wonders poetry book).
- The Ninth Wonder of the World (second Wonders poetry book).
- The Tenth Wonder of the world (third Wonders poetry book)..
- The Eleventh Wonder of the world (fourth Wonders poetry book).
- The Twelfth Wonder of the World (fifth and final of the Wonder series).
- The American Enterprise Trilogy
  - Volume One "The Third-Party Swing Vote". Why Do It?
  - Volume Two "Drain the Swamp". How to Do It?
  - Volume Three "Restore American Patriotism and Work Ethic". Who Will Do It?

JERRY L. RHOADS, CPA, GOVERNMENTAL CONSULTANT

My expertise is in the following business models:

CPA firms, Software developer, Management consulting in long term care, Nursing Home Management, Skilled Nursing Home ownership, Published Author in genres of health care, costing long term care, poetry, novelist, Self-Health, Self-Help, a political third party.
Companies: All-American Care, J.L. Rhoads & Co., CPA firm, Rhoads HealthCare Consulting, Management and ownership, Word Data Processing, software developer, Rhoads Limited Partnership, a tax shelter partnership, MBO Management By Objectives, Cost Report Consulting, ROSE Rhoads Offers System Excellence Profession Group, ROSE Systems, Inc., Rhoads Offers Systems Excellence, MRT Maximum Reimbursement Technology, ROSE Systems implementation.

Founder and CEO of the www.AmericanEnterprisePoliticalParty.org, a third political party, representing a swing vote in America can politics. Supported by Mr. Rhoads' American Enterprise Party Trilogy. Volume one why a Swing Vote for Humanism. Volume two Enterprise Manifesto, how to Keep America Great. Volume three, Restore the patriotic, and ethical world ethic.

You can find him via Spotify as a podcaster, The American Enterprise Swing Vote Party, his blogs with the same link, www.jerryrhoadsauthor.com, www.allamericancaae.com. www.lifestylesforaging.com presenting a memoir with his wife Shari of 65 years, jerry.l.rhoads@gmail.com.
BOOK TITLES AUTHORED BY JERRY RHOADS (Available in book stores, www.jerryrhoadsauthor.com, www.jerryrhoadsbooks.com and on Amazon.com):

Health Care for All (How to Fix Nursing Homes, and Prevent Pandemics)\(a self-health book).
How to Stay Married Forever After (12 vows/habits to live b,: forever after)(a self-health book).
Life Styles (Of the Healthy, Happy, and Prosperous) (a self-health book).
Never Too Old to Live (a self-health book).
America in the Red Zone (a self-health book).
Restore Elder Pride (a self-health book).
Remedy Eldercide (a self-health book).
The Monopsony Game (an economic analysis).
Failing Government Taketh Away (a political analysis) .
American Enterprise Manifesto (a third political party proposal).
Basic Accounting and Budgeting for Long Term Care Facilities.
Americana 2184 (a novel revisiting George Orwell's 1984).
Human Cology (the science of managing human value).
Cost Accounting for Long term care facilities.
The Eighth Wonder of the World (our amazing human eternal mind).
The Ninth Wonder of the World (our amazing human eternal brain).
The Tenth Wonder of the world (our amazing human eternal soul)..
The Eleventh Wonder of the World (our amazing human eternal heart).
The Twelfth Wonder of the world (our amazing human eternal spirit).
Coming soon:
The Thirteenth Wonder of the world (our amazing journey thereafter).

   JERRY RHOADS PUBLISHING 2024

www.ingramcontent.com/pod-product-compliance
Ingram Content Group UK Ltd.
Pitfield, Milton Keynes, MK11 3LW, UK
UKHW061223180426
11947UKWH00027B/1999